A Knight

AT THE Movies

Medieval History on Film

JOHN ABERTH

ROUTLEDGE   NEW YORK & LONDON

Published in 2003 by
Routledge
29 West 35th Street
New York, NY 10001
www.routledge-ny.com

Published in Great Britain by
Routledge
11 New Fetter Lane
London EC4P 4EE
www.routledge.co.uk

Routledge is an imprint of the Taylor & Francis Group.

Printed in the United States of America on acid-free paper.

10 9 8 7 6 5 4 3 2 1

Library of Congress Cataloguing-in-Publication Data.

Aberth, John.
A knight at the movies : medieval history on film / by John Aberth
     p. cm.
Includes bibliographical references and index.
     ISBN 0–415–93885–6 (hardback : alk. paper) — ISBN 0–415–93886–4
(pbk. : alk. paper)
     1. Middle Ages in motion pictures. I. Title.
       PN1995.9.M52A24 2003
       791. 43'658 — dc21   2003001027

A Knight
AT THE Movies

CONTENTS

PROLOGUE

There is a scene about a third of the way into the film, *Monty Python and the Holy Grail* (1975), in which "a famous historian" appears on the screen to comment on the action thus far. Suddenly, from out of nowhere, rides a sword-wielding knight who cuts down the historian in midsentence. Monty Python's historically irreverent antics now can proceed without further interruption . . . that is, until the long arm of the law catches up with the troupe just as the film is about to climax with the storming of Castle Arggh! No doubt there are many more filmmakers who wish that they could do the same to the historians and critics who dissect their creations.

Unfortunately, when it comes to portraying the Middle Ages, that period of European history roughly between 500 and 1500 A.D., far too many targets present themselves. Who can resist ridiculing *The Black Knight* (1954), a film in which sixth-century Arthurian warriors gallop across the plain while in the distance can be distinctly seen twentieth-century telephone poles? Or how about *The Black Shield of Falworth* (1954), in which Tony Curtis, summoning up his best medieval Bronx accent, utters the immortal line, "Yonda is the castle of my fodda"?

To be fair, the Middle Ages is perhaps one of the most difficult eras of history for modern audiences, as well as their cinematic entertainers, to imagine. On a superficial level, we are served up stories of knights in shining armor rescuing damsels in distress, or very contradictory images of barbaric cruelty and superstitious ignorance. Of course, neither extreme can hardly begin to communicate the experience of what it was like to live during the Middle Ages. To penetrate the medieval mentality, one must engage, at least in part, a whole different set of assumptions and way of looking at the world than our own. This was a time when the West was dominated by the Catholic Church and its religious ethos, when society was divided into rigid hierarchies of knight, priest, and peasant, and when men and women, even in towns, lived in a very intimate relationship with their natural surroundings and with each other in their communities. Yet medieval people were also human beings, just like us: they lived and died, loved and suffered, worked and played. They are our ancestors, but also strangers to our modern culture, with its fast-paced technology and increasingly multicultural, global outlook.

Despite this, some movies about the Middle Ages, such as Carl Theodor Dreyer's *The Passion of Joan of Arc* (1928) or Ingmar Bergman's *The Seventh Seal* (1957), must rank among the best and most thought-provoking films in cinematic history. They have achieved this by reveling in the differences between those times and our own and by drawing us into another world in order to better understand and appreciate those differences. All this takes a high degree of imagination and empathy with the past, while at the same time suggesting parallels with the present.

Obviously, movies, even if they are based on real historical events, must be evaluated differently than scholarly books. Rather than trying to educate us as to what really happened, the main goal of cinema is to entertain. It cannot hope, and does not aspire, to achieve the accuracy and comprehensiveness of historical works. Except for some experimental, avantgarde films, a creative narrative cannot allow alternative points of view, cite sources, or utilize a critical methodology. If screenwriters and directors attempted to be ruthlessly historical, their products undoubtedly would be commercial, not to mention artistic, failures.

Nevertheless, movies have taken their place in historians' classrooms, and for some time now have been discussed or reviewed in the pages of the profession's most distinguished journals. There is some unease about this. A fellow medievalist, David Herlihy, has argued that films should not be an integral part of historians' teaching or scholarly scrutiny. Herlihy's main objection is that movies create a make-believe world where viewers are required to suspend their critical judgment and accept the illusion that they are eyewitnesses to past events occurring in the present. The suspension of rational thought that cinema's magic requires, Herlihy argues, is not conducive to the historian's task.

It is taken as a given in this book that cinema neither can nor ought to take the place of historical scholarship. But it would be foolhardy of historians to neglect this medium altogether. For, like it or not, many people, including our students, get their history from such popular sources.

Indeed, the common currency of recognition that films provide can be put to the historian's use in a way that I think Herlihy has overlooked. "Medievalism" is generally defined as the study of the many ways in which modern society and its popular culture interacts with, interprets, and both influences and is influenced by the actual history of the Middle Ages. As such, medievalism can be viewed as a subset of historiography, the science of determining how history is "written," by historians and others. Movies provide an exciting and engaging method of illustrating this complex process to students in the classroom and to the public at large. In making a film, the filmmaker, sometimes with the historian acting as consultant, invariably reflects the current mode of how society wishes to remember its ancestors. Used in this way, film provides historians with a powerful tool for demonstrating the connections to be made between the medieval and the modern.

What is more, it is a little unfair to bring the creative arts to the bar, as Herlihy does, of the "high court of historical criticism." An historian more sympathetic to film, Robert Rosenstone, has pointed out that cinema, unlike written history, depends on fiction and invention in order to tell a linear narrative that audiences can follow up on the screen. Therefore, movies occupy a world apart from the historical, and if historians trespass on that realm, they should acknowledge the different rules of the game. This does not mean that films and their makers should be held unaccountable, but that their possibilities, as well as their limitations, be recognized. Herlihy was gracious enough to admit that films have the advantage in bringing the past to life through their vivid visual textures. Images on the screen can collectively create an atmosphere or mood that captures the spirit of the times. But there is yet another consideration to be made in the cinematic medium's favor that Herlihy may have missed. Movies, freed from the necessity of proof, can dare to speculate on past imponderables that scholarly conventions would not abide. Did Joan of Arc want to die? Did medieval couples, fettered by arranged marriages, ever marry for love? What did it feel like to face the onslaught of the Black Death? Was Richard the Lionheart gay? These are perhaps more mundane questions than scholars are used to asking, but nevertheless, people interested in history want them answered.

Clearly, by the very act of writing this book, I have declared myself in favor of historians soiling their hands with the movies. I believe that the two realms, although they should be kept separate, can make substantial contributions to each other. Cinema may never stand in for history, but it can spark audiences' interest in and enthusiasm for it, as is true in my own case and that of many of my students. In the classroom, films can promote discussions and pose, if not answer, burning questions. In private, they can make us think long and hard about our lives in comparison with those of our predecessors. In return, historians and their study of history can increase the enjoyment and appreciation by audiences for the historical films they see. If Hollywood will listen, historians' advice can make for more thoughtful, entertaining, and even lucrative productions.

This book, therefore, approaches cinema from a strictly historical point of view. It rarely attempts to delve into the intricacies of film theory. I also avoid those films that are largely literary, such as the "Plantagenet" variety that tell the history of England's medieval kings on the basis of Shakespeare's plays. Instead, as an historical critic of the cinema, I try to do more than simply pass judgment on whether a particular film is historically accurate or not. Each chapter begins by giving a general background on the historical issues of the genre being discussed. I lay particular stress on how both medieval and modern chroniclers of the past have viewed the historical events or characters being portrayed, insofar as this can be gleaned from their writings. These sources are important, for they serve as the foundation of our knowledge, be it scholarly or popular, of that distant time. One must also remember that even primary sources and history books can embellish, exaggerate, and, on occasion, fictionalize historical personalities and events, no less than the movies, in order to suit the author's special purpose, or simply to entertain. Nevertheless, such sources, especially the ones written around the time the events were actually taking place, are valuable for the revealing window they provide onto the medieval mind.

I then move on to discuss a selection of movies that illustrate, or at least impinge upon, the historical issues that have been identified. By no means do I attempt to include in my discussion every movie made about that genre. My criterion has been to select films that have something special or unique to say about the Middle Ages and that I have seen personally and can therefore comment on authoritatively. Some of these movies have been Hollywood box office blockbusters; others made by small, independent, or foreign production companies that received little notice by moviegoers or the press. Most of them, in my opinion, made a good-faith artistic effort to portray the Middle Ages. But even a completely bad or boring film can have its lessons for how the medieval past is colored and distorted by our modern lens.

When a film has got its history wrong, I try to identify not only *what* is inaccurate, but *why*. Usually, films are inaccurate for a reason (aside from the possibility of annoying historians). Indeed, the film historian, Pierre Sorlin, cynically observes that "films tell us all we need to know about the policies and opinions of their makers, and no more." Most often, historical fidelity is sacrificed in order to pursue an artistic agenda, or "plot," that the filmmakers have in mind. Sometimes, filmmakers pursue a political agenda that fits in with the mood in the country at large. And on occasion, there is an even more sinister motive at work behind the film. In nearly every case, filmmakers have altered history in order to make their movies, or so they believe, more meaningful and appealing to their audience. Therefore, even though the history may be wrong, the way it is presented in the film reflects, to at least some extent, the way in which modern audiences, filmmakers, and sometimes even historians wish to remember their past.

As we will see, there are many ways in which a film can be historically inaccurate. It can juggle or compress historical time, change the outcome of historical events, and change the actions, motivations, and even personalities of historical characters. Such indignities committed against history may be forgiven, however, if the overall vision of the film remains true to the spirit of the Middle Ages. In other words, does the movie capture some of the essence of the medieval outlook? Does it convey what it was like to live in those times? Does it make you leave the theater with the feeling that you have just experienced an utterly different, but strangely familiar, world? This is the basic criterion I use to judge whether a movie has successfully portrayed the Middle Ages.

Except for films that I feel mangle with malicious intent their medieval subject (and some such movies are discussed in the pages that follow), I try to be even-handed in my evaluation of each filmmaker's creative efforts. The main purpose of this book is not just to give an historical "thumbs up" or "thumbs down" on each film. Rather, it is also to illustrate the complex relationship between modern and medieval history, for how we choose to remember the past reveals much about how we live in the present. Therefore, each film has something of its own to say, if not about the truth of what happened long ago, then at least about why we choose not to tell the truth. In the process, we can learn much not only about our medieval ancestors, but also about ourselves. I believe that this is an important lesson for students, history and film buffs, and movie audiences in general because, as I've already indicated, the re-telling of history on film is not always harmless. Usually, however, a medieval film is made because the filmmaker has a genuine interest in the Middle Ages, and the goal of this book is to discover what that interest is, how it informs the film, and how it fits into both a modern and medieval context. As an historian who has dabbled in the creative arts himself, I can readily appreciate the rigors of the creative process. When reviewing these works, I have aimed for both the astuteness of the critic and the generosity of the fan. Hopefully, I will fare better than the "famous historian" of Monty Python.

CHAPTER ONE

The Holy Grail of Hollywood

King Arthur Films

The Background

King Arthur is perhaps *the* most famous historical figure to emerge from the Middle Ages. This is rather strange, for he is also, with the possible exception of Robin Hood, the one historical figure about whom we know the least in terms of cold, hard facts. Nevertheless, King Arthur is recognized and beloved throughout the Western world. More movies have been made about him than about any other medieval character. Indeed, one recent compilation has identified no less than 262 films, TV shows, and cartoons with an Arthurian theme, beginning in 1904 with the Edison Film Company's silent version of Wagner's opera, *Parsifal*, down to *Star Wars: The Phantom Menace*, the first prequel to the *Star Wars* science fiction trilogy, released in 2000. And this is but the tip of an iceberg of modern Arthuriana that encompasses nearly every other possible medium in the creative arts: novels, short stories, plays, poetry, opera, ballet, choral and orchestral works, musicals, popular music, paintings and illustrations, sculpture, stained glass, tapestries, photographs, comic books, postage stamps and coins, jewelry and silverware, and a variety of trinkets, collectibles, and souvenirs. King Arthur has enlisted the talents of some of the most famous writers and artists of the nineteenth and twentieth centuries: novelists such as Mark Twain and T.H. White; poets such as Alfred Lord Tennyson, Edwin Arlington Robinson, and T.S. Eliot; composers such as Richard Wagner, Alan Jay Lerner and Frederick Lowe, and Richard Rodgers and Lorenz Hart; painters such as the pre-Raphelites, Dante Gabriel Rossetti and Edward Burne-Jones, and illustrators such as

1

Gustave Doré and Aubrey Beardsley. Many of these men's productions later became the basis for films. Truly, the modern cult of King Arthur can be said to be an industry all unto itself.

But before one can unmask the modern Arthur, as portrayed on film, it is essential to come to know the medieval one. Almost from the very beginning, there were, in fact, two Arthurs: one being the King Arthur of history, if such a man existed; the other, the King Arthur of legend. King Arthur's myth making had indeed begun by the high Middle Ages, and this was made possible by the fact that so little was known about the real Arthur who was already several centuries old. Because of his obscurity, the King Arthur of history gave way to the King Arthur of legend, who was a far more influential and attractive figure to those who wished to pass on his memory. The King Arthur of history became an ideal blank slate on which succeeding ages could write their own versions of his legend that suited their particular tastes and ideological needs.

There are various and competing theories as to who the real King Arthur was. According to Geoffrey Ashe, he is to be identified with Riothamus, a high king of the Britons who had secured enough peace against marauding Saxons and Picts to lead a large army over to Gaul, corresponding to modern-day France, where he may have ended his life in the late 460s. Other Arthurian detectives, the team of Graham Phillips and Martin Keatman (who also claim to have revealed the real Robin Hood), declare that Owain Ddantgwyn, a Welsh chieftain of the Votadini tribe who ruled at the end of the fifth century, was the real King Arthur. It is not necessary to go into the long and detailed arguments made for each claimant, as neither is conclusive. In fact, most professional historians regard the search for the historical Arthur as a pointless exercise, preferring to instead explore the political and cultural context of his later legend. Although it seems likely that there existed a British leader who assumed responsibility for resistance against invaders after the fall of the Roman Empire, there simply is not enough historical evidence to identify beyond doubt who exactly Arthur was.

What evidence we do have is scanty and scattered in time. The earliest reference to an "Arthur" dates to around 829–830 A.D. in a work called the *Historia Brittonum*, or *History of the Britons*, attributed to a Welsh monk called Nennius. It should be noted that this is three centuries or more after the real King Arthur supposedly lived. Already, Arthur is a largely legendary figure who is capable of superhuman feats of biblical proportions, apparently modeled on the Old Testament champion of the Israelites, Joshua. Arthur is described as the victor of no less than twelve battles against the Saxons, the last being his greatest victory at Mount Badon, thought to have taken place around 500 A.D., "in which 960 men fell in one day from one charge by Arthur." Except for Badon, hardly any of the battle sites can be verified as having an independent historical existence outside of Nennius' text. The author is, above all, concerned to portray the Britons as a united, favored people of the Lord, in order to contest the unflattering image of them in earlier, pro–Anglo-Saxon histories, such as by Bede the Venerable. Arthur also serves to justify the reign of King Merfyn of Gwynedd in Wales (c. 825–844), whose new dynasty needed an historical precedent, which the author, perhaps a court historian, was only too happy to provide.

By the time we arrive at the next major tale of King Arthur's exploits, his myth making is in full swing. The first so-called "biography" of Arthur was written c. 1135–1138 by the Breton bishop of St. Asaph, Geoffrey of Monmouth, and was incorporated into his *Historia Regum Britanniae*, or *History of the Kings of Britain*. This is an important work, for it lays the foundation for the full-blown King Arthur of legend. The main outlines of that legend are almost all here: the begetting of Arthur through the adulterous passion of Uther Pendragon for Ygerna (later Igraine), wife of Gorlois, duke of Cornwall; the wizard Merlin, whose magic enables Uther to assume the form of Gorlois in order to seduce Ygerna at Castle Tintagel; the enchanted sword Caliburn (later Excalibur), with which Arthur defeats his Saxon enemies; the magnificent court at Caerleon-upon-Usk (later Camelot); the bloody yet victorious campaign against Lucius, emperor of Rome; the betrayal of Arthur by his nephew, Mordred, and by his wife, Queen Guinevere; the final battle in which Arthur defeats Mordred but himself is mortally wounded; and his departure to the Isle of Avalon to be healed, holding out the promise—albeit never explicitly stated—that he will return. Despite the title of his work, Geoffrey of Monmouth was not writing a history at all, although he borrowed much of his material from older sources. Instead, he was composing what was to become known as "the matter of Britain," an account that placed the island at the center of world events, thereby glorifying both Geoffrey's Celtic ancestors and his new Norman masters, whose legitimacy as rulers of lands on both sides of the Channel could only be helped by the precedent of a British ruler campaigning on the Continent. Geoffrey's Arthur also provided a model of a strong monarch, loyally supported by his nation's political community, which no doubt proved attractive during the long civil war that marred the reign of the weak King Stephen (1135–1154).

One of the remarkable things about the King Arthur legend is that what started out as an exclusively British phenomenon exerted such great appeal across the Channel as well. This went against the grain of most cultural contacts between the Continent and the island nation. However, the French "romances" about King Arthur's court, as these were developed during the twelfth and thirteenth centuries by such authors as Chrétien de Troyes, Robert de Boron, and the anonymous Vulgate Cycle, shifted the focus, naturally enough, from the person of Arthur to that of the French knight, Sir Lancelot. Elements of French pride can be detected in the fact that Lancelot is made out to be the best knight at King Arthur's court, in both arts of love and war. He defeats all challengers to single combat and captures the heart of the most desirable lady, Arthur's queen, Guinevere. It is the Arthurian romances, in fact, that are largely responsible for linking together the martial ideal of chivalry—loosely defined as the code by which a medieval knight was expected to conduct himself in battle—with the ideal of courtly love, which described rules of courtesy and devotion by which a knight would prove himself worthy of the love of his lady. But perhaps the most important contribution the French romances made to the King Arthur legend was their introduction of the Grail Quest. This firmly tied King Arthur to Christianity, as the Grail was taken to refer to the cup used by Jesus Christ at the Last Supper, and the Round Table as the successor to the table used by Christ and his disciples. Yet the paradox is that Lancelot, though he be the "perfect" knight, cannot fulfill the Quest because of his adulterous affair with Guinevere, which ultimately leads to the destruction of Camelot and the death of Arthur.

The tragedy of Lancelot, Guinevere, and Arthur must have had particular relevance to audiences of the late twelfth century, for it probably reminded them of real incidents of treason and betrayal. In 1173–1174, King Henry II of England faced a revolt led by his queen, Eleanor of Aquitaine, and his three eldest sons, Henry, Richard, and Geoffrey. Although Henry II was able to quell the revolt, it poisoned his relations with his family and led to a 15-year imprisonment of his wife. Both Henry and Eleanor were patrons of Arthurian literature. Their court historian, Robert Wace, translated into Anglo-Norman French Geoffrey of Monmouth's history and presented the *Roman de Brut* to Eleanor in 1155. Eleanor's eldest daughter by her first marriage, to King Louis VII of France, was Marie, countess of Champagne, to whom Chrétien de Troyes dedicated his third Arthurian romance, *Lancelot.*

The legend that was forged out of the dim history of King Arthur quickly began to insinuate itself into the historical acts of England's later medieval kings. Thus began a complex symbiosis between history and the legend surrounding King Arthur. The real Arthur of history was not as important as the political and propagandistic uses that could be made of his legend in order to create an historical image of a ruler as the true heir to Arthur's legendary qualities. Already this process was well under way by the close of the twelfth century, not long after the first Arthurian romances had been written. According to the Welsh chronicler, Giraldus

Cambrensis, Henry II instituted a search for Arthur's "grave" at Glastonbury Abbey in Sussex, perhaps in order to quell Celtic unrest that had coalesced around rumors of the coming of another "Arthur." Yet it was not until after Henry's death that in 1190–1191, an excavation uncovered the bones of a large man and a woman under a lead cross whose Latin inscription allegedly read, "Here in the Isle of Avalon lies buried the renowned King Arthur, with Guinevere, his second wife." Probably a pious fraud to bring renown and benefactions to the abbey, which had just suffered a devastating fire in 1184, the "discovery" of Arthur's grave nonetheless was taken seriously enough that nearly a century later, in 1278, King Edward I and his queen, Eleanor of Castile, presided over the translation of what were believed to be the bones of Arthur and Guinevere to the abbey's high altar, where a black marble tomb was installed.

It was Edward's grandson, Edward III, who was perhaps the most skillful and enthusiastic in exploiting Arthur's legacy. In 1344, Edward III staged his own Arthurian event with a public announcement at Windsor Castle that "when the opportunity should be favorable to him, he would set up a round table, in the same manner and condition in which Lord Arthur, formerly king of England, left it." Although Edward's round table never was realized, it probably was the inspiration for his order of chivalry, the Order of the Garter, that survives to the present day. When he died in 1377, Edward was compared favorably to King Arthur by the chronicler, Jean Froissart: "His like had not been seen since the days of King Arthur, who once had also been king of England, which in his time was called Great Britain." However, in death Edward was not entirely successful in controlling Arthurian propaganda. The alliterative *Morte Arthure*, a poem composed toward the end of the fourteenth century, seems to criticize Edward's warlike policies by portraying Arthur as a bloodthirsty and ambitious tyrant, whose war against the Roman Emperor Lucius only brought misery on both sides of the Channel, just as many in the author's own time wanted a respite from the Hundred Years War between England and France.

Ironically, it was during the latter half of the fifteenth century, when England was ruled by a weak king and political chaos reigned during the Wars of the Roses, that there was born what many consider to be the greatest and most powerful expression of the medieval Arthur legend. This was *Le Morte D'Arthur* by the raffish Warwickshire knight, Sir Thomas Malory of Newbold Revel. Malory did not so much author this work as translate, edit, condense, and collect a variety of French and English legends about Arthur and his round table knights and present them as one, relatively unified whole. The great value of Malory's work is the way in which it encapsulates almost the entire preexisting Arthurian tradition. *Le Morte D'Arthur* is, therefore, a kind of grand summation of medieval Arthuriana from both sides of the Channel.

Malory's twofold status as an active player in the rough-and-tumble politics of late fifteenth-century England and as the author of a work that seems to embody the very soul of medieval chivalry presents something of a conundrum to King Arthur scholars. It is an inescapable fact that Malory wrote *Le Morte D'Arthur* while in prison: At the end of *The Tale of King Arthur*, corresponding to the first four books in Caxton's printed edition, Malory calls himself a "knyght presoner," while at the very end of the entire opus, he requests his readers to pray for his "good delyveraunce" and informs us that "this book was ended the ninth yere of the reyne of King Edward IV [March 4, 1469–March 3, 1470]." Malory was in prison almost continuously from July 1451 until July 1460 and then again from at least July 1468 until October 1470. He died five months later in March 1471. During his first term of imprisonment, Malory was charged with a variety of crimes, including rape, theft, extortion, and attempted murder. His guilt or innocence, however, was never proved, as his case never came to trial. Malory's second term of imprisonment is even more mysterious, as there is no record of him even being charged with a crime, let alone tried. Indeed, the only reason we know that he was in prison at this time is that he tells us so in *Le Morte D'Arthur*.

All of this is hard to reconcile with the same man who extols the virtues of "prouesse," "curtosye," "worshyp," and "honoure" as demonstrated by the "noble actes of chyvalrye" of the roundtable knights. Malory's hypocrisy is nowhere more apparent than at the end of Book 3 in the *Tale of King Arthur*, when the king charges his knights to "allwayes to do ladyes, damesels, and jantilwomen and wydowes socour: strengthe hem in hir ryghtes, and never to enforce them uppon payne of dethe." This from an author who was accused of forcing himself sexually upon a woman, Joan Smith of Coventry, twice, in May and August of 1450. There are any number of possible explanations for the paradox. Joan may in reality have willingly eloped with Malory, especially since it was her husband who brought the charge under a new law that classified even consensual elopement as rape. Alternatively, Malory may not have regarded Joan as a "jantilwoman" worthy of protection. A third possibility is that Malory, feeling the pangs of conscience in his old age, wished to admonish others from doing what he himself could not keep his hands from. In the end, we simply will never know how this obviously complex man married his high-flown rhetoric to his unsavory reputation.

It is clear that from the very beginning, *Le Morte D'Arthur* struck a popular chord among English-speaking readers. There were good reasons for this. Malory's Arthurian saga was the first of its kind to be printed: In 1485 the London printer, William Caxton, was "enprysed to enprynte a book of the noble hystoryes of the sayd kynge Arthur and of certeyn of his knyghtes, after a copye unto me delyverd, whyche copye syr Thomas Malorye dyd take oute of certeyn bookes of Frensshe and reduced it into Englysshe." The book subsequently went through five more printings in the next 150 years, and very few of the early editions survive despite their large print runs, suggesting that they were widely accessible and heavily read. As Caxton's preface indicates, Malory was also the first to make the French romances about Arthur available to the English public, particularly the Vulgate Cycle, containing tales of Lancelot and the Quest of the Holy Grail.

But, above all, Malory and Caxton published *Le Morte D'Arthur* with excellent timing, when the Arthur legend would have resonated with the political and social turmoil so many Englishmen had been experiencing since 1455 during their civil war known as the Wars of the Roses. It seems clear that both Malory and Caxton were well aware of this. Toward the end of the last tale, that of the "Morte Arthur" itself, Malory as narrator addresses his readers with a lament that links events in the story with those of his own times:

> Lo, ye all Englysshemen, se ye nat what a myschyff here was? For he that was the moste kynge and nobelyst knyght of the worlde, and moste loved the felyshyp of noble knyghtes, and by hym they all were upholdyn, and yet myght nat thes Englyshemen holde them contente with hym. Lo thus was the olde custome and usayges of thys londe, and men say that we of thys londe have nat yet loste that custom. Alas! Thys ys a greate defaughte of us Englysshemen, for there may no thynge us please no terme.

This lecture comes just before the final battle between Arthur and Mordred, when "muche people drew unto sir Mordred and seyde they wold abyde wyth hym for bettir and for wars." Perhaps Malory is scolding his fellow countrymen for likewise dividing the realm into two armed camps, one siding with the Lancastrian party (the Red Rose) as the rightful claimants to the throne, the other with the Yorkist side (the White Rose).

Undoubtedly, *Le Morte D'Arthur* also appealed to a wistful nostalgia many of its readers must have felt for an earlier, more innocent time, when there was a more clarified sense of right and wrong. Such yearnings may be said to be universal, but fifteenth-century Englishmen had particular cause to look back longingly to the not-too-distant past, when many of them, including Malory himself, would have witnessed the rise and fall of a northern French empire founded by their warrior king, Henry V, who died in 1422 at the untimely age of 36. Caxton, with the marketing savvy of a publisher, seems to have picked up on both the nostalgic and contemporary potential of Malory's work. In his preface, he writes that he is printing *Le Morte D'Arthur*:

> to the entent that noble men may see and lerne the noble actes of chyvalrye, the jentyl and vertuous dedes that somme knyghtes used in tho dayes, by whyche they came to honour, and how they that were vycious were punysshed and ofte put to shame and rebuke; humbly bysechyng al noble lordes and ladyes wyth al other estates, of what estate or degree they been of, that shal see and rede in this sayd bok and werke, that they take the good and honest actes in their remembraunce, and to folowe the same.

Like good historians, Malory and Caxton want their readers to not only remember the past, but learn from it and apply its lessons to their present situation.

It is hard to say which side Malory was on in the Wars of the Roses, or to be more specific as to how he intended *Le Morte D'Arthur* to reflect his political context. Like that of so many others during this era of "bastard feudalism," Malory's politics were a muddle. He seems to have had an unlucky knack for backing the losing side at different stages of the war. His first term of imprisonment during the 1450s was perhaps largely due to his Yorkist sympathies, whereas the second from 1468 to 1470 was probably in retaliation for his switch to the Lancastrian cause. If there is any consistency in Malory's political career, it is to be found in his loyalty to his local lord, Richard Neville, earl of Warwick, who played a pivotal role in the war as "kingmaker" and who likewise changed sides, although not with the same exact timing as Malory.

Since Malory was a committed Lancastrian at the time he was finishing *Le Morte D'Arthur*, it is possible that he identified Arthur with the Lancastrian king, Henry VI. Henry was known for his religious piety, and indeed after his death in 1471, he was pictured on a church rood screen in Norfolk as a saint. He was also generous, compassionate, and devoted to education reform, as evidenced by his foundations of King's College, Cambridge, and Eton public school. Unusually for a royal, he was also a prude, remaining a virgin until his marriage to Margaret of Anjou in 1445 at the age of 24. Allegedly dominated by his new wife, Henry, who was not a warrior king (this role was coopted by Margaret), perhaps reminded his subjects of the cuckolded side to King Arthur's character. He may also have reminded readers of the Fisher King, called in *Le Morte D'Arthur* the Maimed King Pellam or Pelles, who is wounded by Sir Balin with the "dolerouse stroke" of a magic spear and whose kingdom is straightaway turned into a wasteland, which can only be healed by Sir Galahad's achieving of the grail. In August 1453, Henry VI went insane and was to remain so for at least the next year and a half, precipitating the protectorate of the duke of York and the start of the Wars of the Roses. On the other hand, there were probably plenty of people who were prepared to compare the York champion, Edward IV, with Arthur. Edward was handsome, well dressed, a courageous leader of men on the battlefield, and, perhaps best of all, descended through the Mortimer line from Welsh kings. His life paralleled Arthur's in some ways, for against great odds, he returned from exile in 1471 to defeat Neville and the Lancastrians and reclaim his crown. Although lacking the literary genius of a Chaucer or a Shakespeare, Malory was astute enough to let his sources speak for themselves and not align them too closely with his political preferences, which might alienate potential readers.

What made Malory's work so influential is that it found great favor not only with his contemporaries but with posterity as well. *Le Morte D'Arthur* ends with the promise of the *Rex quondam rexque futurus* (translated by T.H. White as "the once and future king"), or in other words, "that kynge Arthur ys nat dede, but . . . shall com agayne." This holds great appeal for any society in any age seeking redemption from domestic strife and upheaval. It was Malory's version of the legend that was to provide nearly universal inspiration for modern interpretations of King Arthur, whether on paper, canvas, musical instrumentation, or on film.

The Movies

Films about King Arthur tend to be either very good or very bad. The reason for this may be that, since so little is known about the real King Arthur of the fifth or sixth centuries, and with the long history of inventing legends about him, filmmakers have given free rein to their own imaginations about Arthur, bringing with that creativity both the rewards and risks it inspires. Rarely do films tackle the King Arthur of history. Instead, the medieval setting of these movies is almost always indebted to his legend, which usually can be traced back to Sir Thomas Malory's *Le Morte D'Arthur* of the fifteenth century. Therefore, the atmosphere of most Arthurian films belongs to the later Middle Ages rather than to Arthur's own historical time period.

There is one film, however (and it is the only one to my knowledge), that makes a brave effort to capture the actual history of King Arthur, as such a man may have existed at the dawn of the Middle Ages: *King Arthur: The Young Warlord* (1975), directed by the team of Sidney Hayers, Patrick Jackson, and Patrick Sasdy and starring Oliver Tobias as Arthur.

Originally a 24-episode British television series entitled *Arthur of the Britons* (1972–1973), the condensed film version was released in video format only, rather than in theaters. At times disjointed in its storyline because of its episodic character, *King Arthur: The Young Warlord* nevertheless dispenses with Arthur's legend and gives us a credible history of the man. During the brief introduction narrated by Arthur himself, we are served up "the simple facts" of British history "in the time of the sixth century." The island, we are told, "had no one name, no single leader" but after having been abandoned by the Romans was being contested by various tribes, including the Saxons, Angles, Jutes, Picts, and, of course, the Celts, led by Arthur. Significantly, Arthur is here portrayed as simply a local leader trying to end the "plunder, chaos, and bloodshed [that] were a common part of life in these insular communities." He debunks his own legend by telling us that "fierce skirmishes of my youth would grow into major battles in later years. Tales of my exploits would also grow, well beyond the truth of them." This sets a documentary-like tone from the very beginning of the film in which much of Arthur's legend is grounded in a plausible reconstruction of his historical life.

An excellent example of the film's method comes in the very first episode, when Arthur stages his own death in order to lure chieftains of other Celtic tribes into an alliance against the Saxons. Arthur's "funeral" is followed by Arthur himself walking in on the other leaders, who are flabbergasted to discover that Arthur is not dead after all and that they have walked into a trap. In this way, the legend of Arthur's death and promised return from the Isle of Avalon is explained as a political maneuver to unite the contentious Celts against their common enemy, the Saxons. This is quickly followed by the debunking of another legend, the sword in the stone. Arthur challenges his fellow chieftains to pull a sword out from under a large rock: he who does so will become the acknowledged leader of all the Celts. After each man tries and fails, Arthur, in order to persuade them that victory over the Saxons must be a joint effort, gets everyone to lend a hand to the rock and push, allowing Arthur to draw out the sword. Thus, what was in Malory's version an elaborate ritual — Arthur's pulling of Excalibur out of an anvil on top of a stone — designed to demonstrate Arthur's divine right to rule, is here transformed into a lesson in cooperation and mutual dependence.

This distinctly unromantic presentation of Arthur is continued in a later episode that shows Arthur's wooing of Princess Rowena, daughter of Yorath the Jute. Instead of wedding Rowena and making her his queen, Arthur prefers to play the field, for although "moved by many affairs of the heart . . . none brought me to a proposal of marriage. There would be time for that later." Eventually, however, he must fight for Rowena's love with

Mark of Cornwall, to whom she is betrothed. The Rowena character seems derived from Geoffrey of Monmouth's *Historia Regum Britanniae* (*History of the Kings of Britain*), where she is the daughter of Hengist the Saxon and a pagan witch who becomes the wife of Vortigern rather than of Arthur. The film also seems indebted to Geoffrey for the character of Ambrose, a Celtic chieftain who, in the first episode, is shown urging his men to march in the manner of Roman legions and who worships the ancient sun god, Mithras. On the other hand, *The Book of Sir Tristram* from *Le Morte D'Arthur* seems to be the inspiration for Arthur's rival, Mark. As played by Brian Blessed, he comes across as Sir Thomas Malory's blustering and jealous buffoon.

The film ends with Arthur waging peace rather than war with his Saxon enemy, Cerdic. The truce ends abruptly through the accidental slaying of a Saxon by a Celtic knife thrower. Throughout *King Arthur: The Young Warlord*, the legendary image of Arthur as a heroic warrior king ruled by destiny is constantly downplayed. The film comes as close as we probably will ever get to the King Arthur of history. But it is not the Arthur that most audiences have learned to expect or come to see.

One aspect of Arthur's history that is not addressed in *King Arthur: The Young Warlord* is Christianity and its conflict with the pagan religions it eventually displaced. This is ostensibly the subject of our next Arthurian film, *The Black Knight* (1954), directed by Tay Garnett and starring Anthony Bushell as King Arthur and Alan Ladd as the movie's main character, John, the Black Knight. Like *King Arthur: The Young Warlord*, *The Black Knight* does not owe its storyline to any legend about Arthur. This does not mean, however, that it tries to be historically accurate. As a reviewer noted in the *Monthly Film Bulletin* for October 1954, "The film is gleefully disrespectful of history and tradition." In fact, *The Black Knight's* history is a complete mess. Its characters are culled from widely separated time periods during the early Middle Ages: Arthur from the late fifth or early sixth centuries; "Sarracens," or Muslims, who invaded Europe from North Africa during the early eighth century, but who got no further than Poitiers in southern France, let alone as far north as Britain; and Viking marauders, who landed in southern and eastern England for the first time toward the end of the eighth century. Cramming all these historical figures into one time setting is like putting soldiers from the American Revolution, the Civil War, and World War II into one battle.

The only historical aspect of the film remotely plausible is the plot line of Arthur and the Black Knight as the champions of Christianity against pagan forces within the realm. The earliest source on Arthur, Nennius's *Historia Brittonum* (*History of the Britons*), describes him at his eighth battle at Castle Guinnion as wearing "the image of the Holy Virgin Mary on his shoulders; on that day the pagans turned in flight and were slaughtered in great numbers through the grace of Our Lord Jesus Christ and of his Holy Mother, the Virgin Mary." According to the Anglo-Saxon historian, Bede the Venerable, Christianity came to Britain as early as 156 A.D. under King Lucius. But the island did not become fully converted until the mission of St. Augustine of Canterbury in 597. Even then, Augustine and his fellow missionaries were advised by Pope Gregory the Great that pagan temples and even animal sacrifices "should not be destroyed, but . . . that they should be transferred to the service of the true God." Contrast this tolerant approach with a scene in *The Black Knight* that purports to explain how the magnificent megaliths of Stonehenge became a ruin. After he executes the pagan high priest of the "sun god" (actually, Stonehenge is thought to have been used for astronomical calculations), Arthur orders his knights to "destroy this evil place. Scatter these stones and let them lie as witness in years to come of heaven's wroth against the evil practiced here." Evidently, Christians who actually confronted paganism in the so-called "Dark Ages" were more enlightened than their twentieth-century imitators.

As noted above, *The Black Knight* prefers to invent its own plots rather than borrow these from Arthurian legend. There is no mention here of the Grail, Lancelot and Guinevere, Merlin and Excalibur, or Mordred and Avalon. Nevertheless, the film is indebted to Malory for the names of several of its main characters. For anyone familiar with *Le Morte D'Arthur*, the film becomes even more bizarre when one realizes that its characters take on almost polar opposite identities to those they possess in the original. Palamides (played by the horror film star, Peter Cushing) is the movie's villain and the inveterate archenemy of Christianity, which in turn is embodied in the character of John, the Black Knight. In Malory's world, however, Sir Palomides, although also a Saracen, converts to Christianity by the end of *The Book of Sir Tristram* and becomes a model of piety to the other knights as they begin their Quest of the Holy Grail. Even more astonishing is the transformation of Lady Linet, in the film a sweet, good-natured, adoring young thing played by Patricia Medina, but in *Le Morte D'Arthur* is a shrewish, sharp-tongued creature who incessantly mocks and scolds her champion, Sir Gareth, for having been a "kychyn knave" at Camelot. The film's choice of black for its hero's colors is also extremely odd, for in Malory's *Tale of Sir Gareth*, the "knyght of the Blak Laundis" is actually slain by Sir Gareth, who, as a humble kitchen boy working his way up to knighthood, most closely resembles John, whom we see at the beginning of the film working at his forge as a common blacksmith. The oddity of a Black Knight for a hero is only amplified by the fact that in the same year, 1954, another Arthurian film was released, *Prince Valiant* (based on the comic strip by Hal Foster), which had its villain, Sir Brack, assume an identity as the Black Knight.

The Black Knight is a bad film made only worse by its poor production values. It is impossible to take an Arthurian film seriously when it shows medieval knights riding off into a distance that includes ye olde telephone poles, or when jousters fall off their horses *before* they are struck with a lance. (During the filming of these outdoor action scenes, all shot at various castle locations in Spain, Garnett was perhaps distracted by the fact that he was also on his honeymoon.) Added to these visual embarrassments is the sound of Alan Ladd, a popular American film star, attempting to pronounce Anglo-Saxon words such as "boon" (meaning a favor or blessing) while English actors all around him pronounce them effortlessly. A columnist for *Time* magazine parodied Ladd's accent brilliantly in a merciless review of November 8, 1954: "Nay, more, nor kann this knight e'en parler ye Englysshe langue, bot muttereth mayhappe in Frensshe, as, 'Yagottalissena me. Englans gonnabeen vaded.'" Fortunately, this was Ladd's only foray into the Middle Ages, a casting against type for an actor more at home in modern crime thrillers and Westerns. Yet he was by no means the only 1950s screen cowboy to be brought down by a stray experiment in a medieval film. Two years later, John Wayne (who obviously had not consulted Ladd about the wisdom of his venture) did an equally, if not more, disastrous turn as Genghis Khan, the thirteenth-century Mongol leader, in *The Conqueror* (1956). Both performances are so awkward it seems that the actors themselves realize they are in the wrong picture. The only reason *The Black Knight* and *The Conqueror* are noted by film buffs is that they have the dubious distinction of making most lists of the worst films ever made, films that are so bad they are (unintentionally) funny.

Even so, *The Black Knight* is worth noting in a work on film and history because, with few exceptions (such as Sergei Eisenstein's *Alexander Nevsky*, to be discussed in Chapter 3), it is perhaps the most politically driven film ever set in the Middle Ages. As the Arthurian scholar, Alan Lupack, has pointed out, *The Black Knight* needs to be viewed in the context of the "red scare" that swept America during the early 1950s. Americans' paranoia concerning its Cold War Communist rival, the former Soviet Union, and concerning real or imagined Communist subversives "in our midst" suffuses and informs the entire film. Indeed, once one realizes that *The Black Knight* has an ulterior motive besides simply bad entertainment, it begins to make perfect sense.

The year of the film's release, 1954, marked a watershed in the "witch hunts" against suspected Communist spies and traitors, led by Senator Joseph McCarthy of Wisconsin. By that time, more than six million people, including 350 movie stars and crew members working in Hollywood studios, had been subpoenaed and questioned by McCarthy and his House Committee on Un-American Activities. Those who refused to cooperate and confess to having had Communist sympathies or to name names of fellow suspected Communists were blacklisted or imprisoned. Despite the sheer improbability of such a large conspiracy, an air of reality accompanied all the hysteria due to the fact that America was involved in a war with a Communist enemy—North Korea, backed by China and Russia—and by the fact that a married couple with two young sons, Julius and Ethel Rosenberg, were put to death by electric chair in 1953 for passing atomic secrets to the Soviets. Given such pressure, it is easy to see how Tay Garnett and his screen writer, Alec Coppel, would have wished to give a medieval melodrama such as *The Black Knight* a highly "patriotic" gloss.

Yet the irony is that by the time the film was playing in the theaters, McCarthyism was on the wane. The previous year, 1953, removed two bugbears that had supplied ammunition to the Red baiters: Joseph Stalin, leader of the Soviet Union, who died in March, and the Korean War, which came to an end in July. At the same time, McCarthy began to overreach himself. Decrying "21 years of treason" in the U.S. government, he took on the Department of the Army, and by implication President Dwight Eisenhower himself, claiming that there were spies in the Signal Corps. Barely a month after *The Black Knight* was released, McCarthy was publicly condemned by the U.S. Senate on December 2, 1954, for having "acted contrary to senatorial ethics and tended to bring the Senate into dishonor and disrepute." Never has a film dated so quickly.

The Black Knight's pro-American, anti-Communist agenda can be discerned from the very start of the film, when it also shows itself "disrespectful" to Arthurian tradition. The film opens with John laboriously hammering a sword on an anvil, rather than drawing it magically out of one, so as to emphasize the American values of hard work over the whims of inheritance. Next we see Linet, who, instead of cursing John for his low birth, lovingly tells him that just because she's an earl's daughter "doesn't make me any better than you are. A birthright's an accident, nothing more." Sir Ontzlake, a very minor character in *The Tale of King Arthur* from Malory's masterwork, becomes a crucial character in the film, since he, too, embodies the American dream of rags to riches, or, as the director, Tay Garnett, expressed it in his memoirs, "one of those boot-black-to-President things." Ontzlake serves as John's mentor throughout the film, an example of how "knighthood is a flower to be plucked," since he, also, "was not always a knight. . . . Some are born to knighthood; I was not. There comes a time in every man's life when he must fight for what he wants most. I did just that." Such egalitarian sentiments would have horrified medieval men like Malory, who assumed that everyone had an immutable status in society—whether it be knight, priest, or peasant—and for whom the rags-to-riches story of Sir Gareth is possible only because Gareth, unbeknownst to others, is nobly born in the first place.

Later Ontzlake (played by André Morell) serves yet another role in the film: as a kind of CIA/FBI recruiting officer for John. In order to convince John to spy on Arthur's covert enemies at Camelot, Ontzlake spouts something that very nearly could have been taken right out of the mouth of McCarthy: "There is treason all about us and it must be stamped out before all of us—you, I, and King Arthur himself—are overwhelmed." John is then instructed by Ontzlake to undertake a top secret mission—of which Arthur will deny all knowledge should he be captured: to infiltrate King Mark's castle at Tintagel with the help of a mole, an "old woodcutter whose loyalty is to Arthur." More is at stake here than the gay court life at Camelot. John is also the last hope of Christianity, which is made manifest in a scene where the abbot of the new monastery blesses him as "a good Christian" just before the abbey is attacked by Palamides's Saracens disguised as Vikings.

As a Cold Warrior in medieval garb, John faces two kinds of enemies, one from without and another from within, that correspond to those perceived during the red scare. The Saracens—Sir Palamides and his sidekick, Bernard—are clearly the suspicious foreigners and inveterate "infidel" enemies of Christianity. But, at the same time, they function as enemies from within, for Palamides is also a knight of King Arthur's Round Table. The threat from traitors inside the realm is further underlined by the fact that Palamides is in league with King Mark, another trusted member of Arthur's court and, what is more, a native. Mark is a pagan who, like Palamides, is out to destroy not only Camelot but Christianity as well. He fears that the new religion will make the English "people united beyond belief," acting as a kind of loyalty oath demanded of all Arthur's subjects, himself included. Mark therefore represents the "Godless Red" who appears in so many anti-Communist films of the late 1940s and early 1950s. In addition, *The Black Knight* follows a familiar pattern set by other Cold War films in "tainting" its villain with homosexuality. When not wearing his outlandish "red" armor, Palamides wears outlandish makeup and jewelry.

Both sides prove willing to use subterfuge and skullduggery to achieve their ends. Palamides and his cronies dress up as Vikings when making their raids, and Mark pretends to be a "baptized Christian king . . . to deceive Arthur." Meanwhile, John assumes an alternate identity as the Black Knight in order to "go undercover," to borrow espionage parlance. The difference, of course, is in their morals. As in other Cold War films, the villains in *The Black Knight* remorselessly condone the most heinous crimes, including murder, rape, and backstabbing of each other, while the hero refuses to stoop to such means even against his enemies. The most violent

John becomes is when he punches out Bernard and performs on Palamides a back-flip maneuver that could have been scripted by the World Wrestling Federation.

If *The Black Knight* was out of date already by the end of 1954, it will seem positively reactionary to most audiences today who become aware of its politics. Judging by the spreading popularity of pagan wedding ceremonies and Wiccan groups on American college campuses, many young people would empathize more with King Mark and his high priest rather than with the prudish Arthur, Ontzlake, or John. Indeed, the most recent reincarnation of the Arthur legend, the television miniseries, *The Mists of Avalon* (2001), based on the novel by Marion Zimmer Bradley, privileges the druidic cult of the "goddess" as equal to Christianity in status and power in Celtic Britain. McCarthyism is so discredited nowadays that any film that identifies with its ideology risks derision. It is significant that Garnett, when reminiscing in 1973, preferred to explain the film as an allegory of the American Dream rather than of the Cold War, which he does not mention at all. *The Black Knight* is an object lesson in the dangers of tying an historical film too closely to a modern cultural climate or mood. While granting the film relevance to its immediate audience, its political subtext renders it obsolete to posterity.

It is a curious fact, therefore, that later Arthurian films have nonetheless continued to imitate *The Black Knight*'s premise, along with its mediocrity. Will Hollywood never learn? In 1963, a film called *Siege of the Saxons* duplicated, at times scene for scene, the basic plot line of *The Black Knight*. The most recent reincarnation of what has been dubbed "The American Middle Ages of Democratic Possibility" is *First Knight* (1995), directed by Jerry Zucker and starring Sean Connery as King Arthur. Like John, the hero of the film is a self-proclaimed "common man" who rescues his lady and the kingdom from the forces of evil. This humble hero is none other than Lancelot, played with cocky swagger by Richard Gere, another actor who, like Ladd, is more at home in modern settings. *First Knight* demonstrates that it is just as willing as *The Black Knight* to disregard original source material while borrowing its characters' names. As Zucker confided to Louis Parks of *The Houston Chronicle*:

> I was worried about deviating from "The Legend," but there is no one legend. When we were working on this script, someone gave me a book that had hundreds of deviations of the legend in it. They're all different. Aficionados may be upset, but I'm making a movie for mainstream audiences.

But even mainstream audiences cannot help but pick up on *First Knight*'s embarrassingly outlandish costumes and props, which include "shoulder shields," hand-held crossbows, and outfits that seem straight out of *Star Trek*. In this respect, Zucker seems bent on supassing Garnett.

The difference is that, while following *The Black Knight* in casting aside all history and legend in telling its own version of the Arthur story, *First Knight* has nothing substantial—political or otherwise—to put in place of the void that can make Arthur's world relevant to ours. The best Arthurian scholars can come up with is to say that *First Knight* is an allegory of a 1990s-style conflicted male—Gere's Lancelot—seeking masculine identity and fulfillment from an older role model—Connery's Arthur—when besieged by a strong female type—Julia Ormond's Guinevere. But in order for a film to have a coherent message, it must at least know what the context of that message is. *First Knight* takes place in an almost complete historical vacuum: It may as well be set in another dimension as in sixth-century Britain. Indeed, so dismissive is the director of history that he is rumored to have blurted out to a reviewer that he didn't give a "fuck" about the Middle Ages. With a contemptuous attitude such as this, no wonder *First Knight* carries no conviction.

Aside from Garnett's second stab at the Arthurian genre, *A Connecticut Yankee in King Arthur's Court* (1949), based on Mark Twain's 1889 novel of the same title, the only musical film version about King Arthur is *Camelot* (1967), directed by Joshua Logan and starring Richard Harris as Arthur. This is based on the Lerner and Loewe musical that debuted on Broadway in 1960. The play, in turn, was derived from *The Once and Future King*, a four-volume novel completed in 1958 by T.H. White, who, like Twain, was indebted to Malory's *Le Morte D'Arthur* for inspiration. *Camelot* is similar to *Connecticut Yankee* in that it aspires to be a lighthearted romantic comedy, at least through its first half. It then follows the stage play in abruptly turning to a dark and somber mood with the budding love affair between Lancelot and Guinevere (played in the film by Franco Nero and Vanessa Redgrave) that will presage the downfall of Camelot. Some criticized the film's casting of its lead roles with Harris and Redgrave, who had to follow the act of Richard Burton and Julie Andrews on Broadway.

Since, like the *Connecticut Yankee* films, *Camelot* trivializes its literary source, it doesn't have much of anything interesting to say about either the history or legend of King Arthur. Yet *Camelot*, both in its stage play and movie versions, is unique in that its presentation of medieval history exerted a powerful influence upon its contemporary modern context. This is rather the reverse of how film and history relationships usually work. As exemplified by *The Black Knight*, most often it is modern preoccupations that color, to one degree or another, our perceptions of the Middle Ages.

The Lerner and Loewe musical on which the film is based appeared a mere three weeks after the election of one of the youngest, most handsome, and most romantic presidents in U.S. history, and one whose first lady was more than a match for him in all these qualities. When John F. Kennedy was assassinated on November 22, 1963, his tragically curtailed presidency seemed ripe for an Arthurian makeover. It was the president's widow, Jacqueline Bouvier, who began Kennedy's apotheosis into Arthur shortly after his death, when she confessed to the journalist, Theodore White:

> At night, before we'd go to sleep, Jack liked to play some records; and the song he loved most came at the very end of this record. The lines he loved to hear were: "Don't let it be forgot, that once there was a spot, for one brief shining moment that was known as Camelot."

Lerner and Loewe's mythical Camelot and its "one brief shining moment" was quickly taken up by Kennedy historians as a symbol to sum up the president's legacy. The "Camelot School," as scholars sympathetic to Kennedy came to be known, included Theodore Sorensen, Kennedy's long-time aide and speechwriter, and Arthur Schlesinger, Jr., a Harvard academic whom Kennedy had recruited to be among the "best and the brightest" serving as advisers to the president. Their experiences in the White House lent authority to their hagiographies of Kennedy as a modern-day Arthur figure. Kennedy himself at least partly collaborated in his Arthurian image making. He invited composers Lerner and Loewe to the White House to play songs from the musical for a private audience. His mother, Rose Kennedy, recalls in her memoirs published in 1974 that her son as a boy loved to read A.M. Hadfield's *King Arthur and the Round Table*.

Yet Kennedy's "Camelot," much like the musical itself, was more about style than substance, more illusion than reality. It took more than a decade before historians began to objectively reassess the Kennedy presidency, to uncover the rampant philandering, crippling disease, hair-trigger brinkmanship, covert operations, and ghostwriting that underlay all the glamor and glitz. Strangely enough, despite these subsequent exposés, the Camelot image of Kennedy retains a powerful hold on America's popular imagination. As noted with *King Arthur: The Young Warlord*, it's as if the public prefers the fairy-tale legend of Arthur/Kennedy to the inconvenient facts of history.

It should not be imagined that such an appropriation of the Arthur legend by a modern politician is entirely harmless. Adolf Hitler, after all, was enamored of Wagner's operas, *Lohengrin* and *Tristan und Isolde*, whose Arthurian themes no doubt contributed in the Führer's mind to an heroic conception of himself and his country's destiny. Kennedy's Arthurian associations, although surely not as sinister as Hitler's, nevertheless are disturbing to those who demand a strict adherence to the original conception

Lancelot (Franco Nero) brings Sir Dinadan back to life as King Arthur and Guinevere (Richard Harris and Vanessa Redgrave) and their court look on in *Camelot*.

in the U.S. constitution of a true republic. Largely due to its skillful manipulation of the Camelot image, the Kennedy family was treated like royalty by popular news magazines during the commemoration of the twentieth anniversary of JFK's death: *Newsweek* called the assassination a "regicide" of "the young prince," while the *New Republic* christened the Kennedys "our first and only truly royal family." This comes dangerously close to establishing a de facto dynasty, an expectation that a Kennedy has a right to rule, which JFK's political heirs, his younger brothers Robert and Ted, were able to use to their advantage. To preserve the Camelot image, JFK's widow and other family members were not adverse to resorting to censorship and secrecy, to the point that one of Kennedy's biographers, William Manchester, compared his "persecution" by them to "a kind of American *Nach und Nebel Erlass* [a Hitler decree]."

By 1967, when the movie version of *Camelot* came out, America was beginning to question its involvement in Vietnam and experience an imperial hesitancy that is perhaps echoed in Arthur's song of self-doubt, "What went wrong?" sung at the opening of the film. The country was ready for the return of the "once and future king," for another Kennedy presidency. That this was no idle fantasy of the Camelot School was demonstrated in March 1968, when a "fan" from Evanston, Illinois, one of 5000 urging Senator Robert Kennedy of New York to run for the Democratic nomination for president against the incumbent, Lyndon Johnson, invoked the Arthurian metaphor that had been cultivated by his elder brother: "Please reconvene the round table. We want Camelot again." *Camelot* therefore captured not only the disillusionment, but also perhaps the hopes of its audience that it would see the rise of another Arthur-like politician to redeem the turmoil that had set in since Kennedy's assassination. Indeed, if there is any political message to be read in the movie, its timing would suggest not so much an homage to JFK as an appeal, similar to that of the Evanston fan, to his brother and putative successor. In the event, LBJ announced that he would not seek a second term, while RFK did decide to run. The dream of an Arthurian resurrection in Bobby Kennedy, however, was cruelly blasted on June 5, 1968, when he was gunned down at the Ambassador Hotel in Los Angeles after winning the California primary. His death, coming two months after the assassination of yet another charismatic and inspiring public figure, Martin Luther King, Jr., seemed to mark a turning point in the history of the 1960s. With no more Arthurs to unite and lead them, Americans embarked on the bitterly self-destructive denouement to that decade.

Just as *King Arthur: The Young Warlord* is the one film that attempts to grapple with the Arthur of history, so *Excalibur* (1981), directed by John Boorman and starring Nigel Terry as Arthur, represents Hollywood's best effort to capture visually the Arthur of legend, as this has come down to us in Malory's *Le Morte D'Arthur*. Yet Boorman's film was not the first to openly proclaim that it was bringing Malory's epic to the silver screen. In 1953, the MGM spectacular, *Knights of the Round Table*, with an all-star cast of Mel Ferrer as Arthur, Robert Taylor as Lancelot, and Ava Gardner as Guinevere, announced in its opening credits that it was "based" on *Le Morte D'Arthur*. (Boorman's closing credits say instead that his film is "adapted from" the book.) A souvenir booklet that was issued along with the film further claimed that MGM researchers had stuck "close to the facts," whatever these might be, in Malory's "studious work." Despite this declaration of documentary-like intent towards the legend, *Knights of the Round Table* is a typical Hollywood melodrama that focuses, almost to the exclusion of all else, on the "love angle"—the doomed triangle between Arthur, Lancelot, and Guinevere. *Excalibur*, although giving full play to the romance between Lancelot and Guinevere and its betrayal of Arthur, nonetheless engages Malory on a more comprehensive and deeper level.

Uryens' army besieges King Leodagrance's castle in *Excalibur*. On the extreme right, a knight smokes a very anachronistic cigarette.

Some have criticized *Excalibur* for its historical faux pas of portraying Arthur's sixth-century knights in full suits of improbable plate armor, which never seem to come off, even when the knights are making graphic love to their damsels. But this is to confuse the intent of the film — which is to serve us up the legend, not the history, of King Arthur. Gaudily armor-plated knights are entirely in keeping with how Malory's fifteenth-century audience would have conceived of his characters — the past reenacted in contemporary garb. Boorman himself says as much in a couple of interviews about the film. He tells Harlan Kennedy in *American Film*, for example: "I think of the story, the history, as a myth. The film has to do with mythical truth, not historical truth. . . . So the first trap to avoid is to start worrying about when or whether Arthur existed." To Philip Strick of *Sight and Sound*, Boorman pontificates: "Listen carefully to the echoes of myth. It has much more to tell us than the petty lies and insignificant truths of recorded history."

This is not to say, however, that *Excalibur* is, by any means, a perfect rendition of Arthur's legend. Despite the lush cinematography, the film, like *The Black Knight*, occasionally slips into anachronism. What are we to make, for example, of the knight assaulting King Leodagrance's castle, who tosses away his cigarette just as he is about to scale the walls? More seriously, Arthurian scholars have pointed out the many omissions Boorman has made from Malory's original material: *The Tale of the Noble King Arthur that was Emperor*, *The Tale of Sir Gareth*, and *The Book of Sir Tristram*, for instance, are wholly left out. Moreover, in what remains, characters and events are often conflated and altered almost beyond recognition: The female banes of Arthur and Merlin—Morgause, Nenyve, and Morgan le Fay—whom we read of in *Le Morte D'Arthur*, become one figure, Morgana, in Boorman's film; Arthur's sword, Excalibur, which Malory introduces out of the blue as the sword in the stone, acquires a history in the film as the sword of Arthur's father, Uther Pendragon; Lancelot and Guinevere, whom Malory has caught out in their adultery by Agravain and Mordred, are instead challenged by Sir Gawain in *Excalibur*, while Arthur's brother/son, Mordred (cousin/son in *Le Morte D'Arthur*), isn't even born yet. Even so, these changes can be justified by the necessity to pare down the more than a thousand pages of Malory's printed text and fit them into a just under 2 ½ hour-long movie. What is more, Malory's own work provides a precedent for just such an endeavor, since he himself did an enormous amount of editing and condensing of the legend when he "dyd take oute of certeyn bookes of Frensshe and reduced it into Englysshe." So Boorman is perfectly correct when he explains to Harlan Kennedy that he is following a long tradition in creating almost anew his own version of the legend. He apparently instructed his actors, "that they are not re-enacting a legend. They are creating it, and so they themselves don't know what's going to happen—it's unfolding."

Still, there is one major alteration that Boorman makes to Malory's legend that I believe is a mistake, because it drains the film of the religious element that is essential to the medieval character of the original. The change comes at the point where the film portrays the Quest of the Holy Grail, corresponding to Malory's *Tale of the Sankgreal* that he allegedly adapted from the French Vulgate Cycle. Boorman transfers the focus of the Quest from Galahad, Lancelot's son who is omitted entirely from the film, to Perceval, and he conflates Arthur with the Fisher King, or the Maimed King Pellam, for whom the Grail will bring healing, both to himself and to his wasted kingdom. Again, these changes can be justified for the sake of clarity in a film that is attempting to distill the unwieldy bulk of Arthur's legend. But what of confusing Arthur with Christ? As the Arthurian scholar, Norris Lacy, observes in his discussion of the film, this seems to happen in the scene where Perceval has his second vision of the Grail at the Castle of Carbonek. A portentous voice offscreen asks Perceval:

Arthur: What is the secret of the Grail? Whom does it serve?
Perceval: You, my lord.
Arthur: Who am I?
Perceval: You are my lord and king. . . . You're Arthur.
Arthur: Have you found the secret that I have lost?
Perceval: Yes: You and the land are one.

A vision of Arthur in shrouded armor fades in and out of this scene, which ends with Perceval finally grasping the Grail cup and urging it to the lips of a wasted Arthur.

The audience is surely thinking in the back of its mind that this is the cup used by Jesus Christ at the Last Supper. Yet nowhere is this stated in the film. (Perceval calls it the "chalice," but does not elaborate.) Indeed, the inference that Boorman leads us to draw is that Arthur is his own savior: He needs no one else—human or divine—to heal himself, except Perceval as a kind of introspective sounding board.

The scene is emblematic of the religious emasculation that takes place throughout the movie. A few references to Christianity occur here and there in *Excalibur*: the magnificent wedding scene between Arthur and Guinevere, presided over by a priest, with the Turin shroud behind the altar and the booming echoes of Kyrie eleison ("Lord have mercy") in the background, or Merlin's lament to Morgana during the ceremony: "The days of our kind are numbered. The one God comes to drive out the many gods. The spirits of wood and stream go silent. It's the way of things, yes. It's a time for men and their ways." Yet even during this overtly Christian sequence, the focus is on the pagan necromancer, Merlin, who, as played by Nicol Williamson, seems to be the real star of the film, stealing nearly every scene he is in. This is no accident, for the Merlin character is given a much greater role here than either in *Le Morte D'Arthur* or in other Arthurian films. (Boorman's original title for the movie, *Merlin Lives*, had to be abandoned for reasons of copyright conflict.) In Malory's version, Merlin is disposed of fairly early, well before the end of the first tale, *The Tale of King Arthur*, when he is trapped under a "grete stone" in Cornwall by the Lady of the Lake, Nenyve. In *Excalibur*, by contrast, Merlin is allowed to survive well beyond the midpoint of the movie, and even then is resurrected in time for Arthur's last battle, with Mordred. At times it almost seems as if Boorman is making up for the bad rap paganism receives in *The Black Knight*, by thrusting Merlin's magic center stage.

Unlike his other changes that clarify the story-line, Boorman's de-Christianization of the Grail legend only leads to confusion. How can Arthur be both king of England and Christ, even in a symbolic sense? Although many kings' and saints' lives during the Middle Ages provided parallels with Christ's, their persons would never have taken the place of Christ in medieval minds. To do so would have been tantamount to thinking heresy, to raising mortal men to a status rivaling God's. Perhaps Boorman could claim that he is simply following Malory in reducing the religious significance of the Grail Quest in order to cater to the more secular tastes of his audience. (Actually, Boorman says he was inspired by Jessie Weston's pagan reinterpretation of the Grail symbol in Weston's 1920 book, *From Ritual to Romance*.) But the man who argued most vehemently that Malory trivialized the Christian message of the Grail—Eugene Vinaver, in his introduction to a three-volume, 1947 edition of the Winchester manuscript of *Le Morte D'Arthur*—has since withdrawn his case. Unlike some earlier mentions of the Grail by twelfth-century authors such as Chrétien de Troyes, Malory is, in fact, careful to explain the religious meaning of the cup and its connection to Jesus Christ. Moreover, the Grail's appearance marks a transformation of Malory's chivalric ideal from one of earthly values to more transcendental origins, and it is wrapped up in the final message of redemption that plays a large part in the powerful appeal of his work. The religious symbolism of the Grail, at least, must be retained in any film about Arthur that aspires to be medieval. But it may well be that Boorman intends his film to be timeless.

Our last Arthurian film is, in my opinion, the best interpretation of both the history and the legend of King Arthur. This happens to be the satiric sendup, *Monty Python and the Holy Grail* (1975), directed by Terry Gilliam and Terry Jones and starring the rest of the Monty Python troupe—Graham Chapman, John Cleese, Eric Idle, and Michael Palin—as assorted Arthurian characters. Monty Python's comedy, which is reminiscent of Twain's own irreverence in *A Connecticut Yankee*, works on several levels. For one, Monty Python parodies various legends about King Arthur, including some references that are obscure. The film bucks tradition in that it chooses to focus on Arthur's Quest for the Holy Grail rather than on the romantic triangle of Arthur, Lancelot, and Guinevere, the last never appearing as a character at all. Fairly typical of the Python approach is the scene where Arthur and his knights receive their Quest from a cantankerous God—portrayed as one of Monty Python's signature cartoons: immediately the portentousness of the Quest is undermined by angels' trumpets being blown out their asses.

The legendary characters of each of Arthur's knights are then subjected to similar treatment as they individually pursue the Quest. Sir Galahad, deceived by a "Grail-shaped beacon," arrives at Castle Anthrax, where his renowned chastity is sorely tested by "eight score young blondes and brunettes, all between 16 and 19½." The invincible Sir Lancelot, believing he is rescuing a damsel in distress who may lead him to the Grail, butchers all the guards and eight wedding guests at Swamp Castle, where he finds only an effeminate bridegroom named Herbert with a penchant for maudlin singing. The Merlin-like enchanter who leads Arthur and his knights to the "Cave of Caer Banough," guarded by a killer rabbit, is an overacting "mangy Scotch git" named Tim. Audiences may be puzzled as to why a Trojan Rabbit shows up at the siege of the Frenchmen's Castle, yet this is no mere bit of Monty Python silliness. It is in fact a reference to a Welsh legend, repeated in the histories of Nennius and of Geoffrey of Monmouth, according to which Britain was founded by Brutus, a refugee of the Trojan Wars. The "Bridge of Death" scene, where a bridgekeeper tells Arthur and his knights that each one "must answer me these questions three, ere the other side he see," seems inspired by an old Welsh poem that has Arthur name all his companions to a gatekeeper, Glewlwyd Mighty-Grasp, before he can enter a fortress.

Monty Python and the Holy Grail also parodies film technique. The famous opening scene, where the sound of a horse's galloping hooves is juxtaposed with the visual image of Arthur and his squire, Patsy, banging together "two empty halves of cocoanuts," is a comic twist on sound fidelity. Lancelot's endlessly replayed attack on Swamp Castle makes a mockery of film editing, normally done to achieve continuity of time and space. Arthur's ridiculously bloody fight with the Black Knight—hacking him to pieces with Excalibur until his dauntless opponent is left with no arms or legs—seems a reference to a French Arthurian film that came out the previous year, *Lancelot du Lac*, whose opening sequence features a close-up shot of a sword severing a knight's head and slicing through a helmet. *Lancelot du Lac*, which is greatly admired by some film scholars for its cinematic technique, may strike other, especially English-speaking audiences, as pretentious; there is thus a rivalry between French and English tellings of the Arthur legend—traceable not only in film but as far back as the literature of the Middle Ages—that also comes in for Monty Python's wicked satire. At one point, Arthur and his Round Table knights find themselves besieging a castle in England manned by a "strange [French] person" who taunts them mercilessly in an "outrageous accent" and who informs them that, rather than join their Quest for the Holy Grail, "he's already got one . . . it's very nice." When Galahad asks the Frenchman, "What are you doing in England?" the Frenchman indignantly replies, "Mind your own business!" But Frenchmen contesting "English types" for control over transmission of Arthur's legend is not so unusual as the bafflement of this scene's characters would suggest.

Finally, *Monty Python and the Holy Grail* makes some very perceptive commentary on historians' efforts to recover the history of King Arthur, and of the Middle Ages in general. One scene where this occurs is the so-called

King Arthur and his knights, Sir Lancelot, Sir Bedevere, and Sir Galahad (Graham Chapman, John Cleese, Terry Jones, and Michael Palin) attempt a parley with the "strange person" inside the French Castle in *Monty Python and the Holy Grail*. John Cleese doubles in the scene as the French knight who taunts King Arthur.

"Marxist" sketch, where Arthur, "riding" in among what appear to be typical medieval peasants, accosts an "old woman," who, it turns out, is a 37-year-old man and member of an "anarcho-syndicist commune." Dennis proceeds to spout some extremely anachronistic Communist doctrine, such as telling Arthur that he became king "by hanging on to our dated imperialist dogma, which perpetuates the economic and social differences in our society," or that "supreme executive power derives from a mandate from the masses, not some farcical aquatic ceremony," such as the delivery of Excalibur to Arthur by the Lady of the Lake. Eventually, an exasperated Arthur attempts to silence Dennis by "repressing" him, which merely confirms Dennis's convictions about "the violence inherent in the system." The joke is that some medieval historians, such as R.H. Hilton, C.H. Brenner, and Guy Bois, really do apply Marxist theory to the Middle Ages, particularly to the English Peasants' Revolt of 1381, which seems to lend itself to a class-based interpretation. Monty Python is only carrying to extremes the misguided attempts of Marxist scholars to impose their thoroughly modern historical models on the medieval past, where Dennis's obnoxiously combative jargon would sound just as foreign as in a medieval film.

But by far my favorite sketch is the "famous historian" scene, which is the only one that can claim a unifying presence throughout the film. An Oxbridge-looking don in natty tweeds and bow tie, identified as "a famous historian" in white letters at the bottom of the screen, abruptly intrudes his unwanted presence into the film right after Arthur's dismal failure to penetrate the French Castle from inside a Trojan Rabbit. The famous historian proceeds to give a pompous exposition on the previous scene and on what will happen next:

> Defeat at the Castle seems to have utterly disheartened King Arthur. The ferocity of the French taunting took him completely by surprise, and Arthur became convinced that a new strategy was required if the Quest for the Holy Grail were to be brought to a successful conclusion. Arthur, having consulted his closest knights, decided that they should separate and search for the Grail individually. Now this is what they did . . .

We then hear the familiar sound of a horse's hoofbeats off camera, but lo! instead of a knight banging cocoanuts together, we get a real knight riding by on a real horse, who fatally slashes the famous historian in the neck with his sword as he utters a suitable warlike grunt. As David Day notes in his essay, "Monty Python and the Medieval Other," there thus commences a struggle between the troupe's efforts to re-create the Middle Ages and the modern world's officious determination to barge in on their overrealistic reenactment. Academic historians may impose their modern interpretations on medieval reality, as seems to have happened in the "Marxist" episode, but here the real Middle Ages takes its revenge on presumptuous historians, cutting them down in midsentence. Nonetheless, the famous historian has served his purpose: to provide a transition to the next scene, but not before his wife cries out in alarm and runs up to stand desolate over her husband's body. For now the chase is on: Arthur's first encounter with the Knights Who Say "Nee" is followed by the famous historian's wife consulting with policemen at the crime scene. Later, after Arthur has used the "Holy Hand-Grenade of Antioch" to destroy the killer rabbit before the Cave of Caer Banough, a detective and two policemen follow the explosion's trail from the shrubbery that was used to appease the Knights Who Say "Nee." Lancelot is then frisked down against a squad car after crossing the Bridge of Death, and the whole film is put rudely to an end by a policeman's hand covering the camera lens as Arthur is led away into a paddy wagon with a blanket over his head. This abrupt ending comes as a greater disappointment for the fact that it interrupts a rousing battle scene, just as Arthur and his army—portrayed here with impressive realism, despite the leaders "riding" in without horses—are about to storm Castle Arggh! where the taunting French knights still hold the Grail. Yet the anticlimactic finale is appropriate, for there can be no other ending to any modern attempt—be it cinematic or scholarly—to bring to light the entire historical truth of the Middle Ages. Our quest for the King Arthur of history, Monty Python suggests, is a Quest for a Holy Grail that lies eternally beyond our grasp.

CHAPTER TWO

Lights! Camera! Pillage!
Viking Films

The Background

The Vikings in Europe of the 8th and 9th century were dedicated to a pagan god of war, Odin. Cramped by the confines of their barren, ice-bound north-lands, they exploited their skill as shipbuilders to spread a reign of terror then unequalled in violence and brutality in all the records of history. . . .

Thus intones the booming, doubt-me-if-you-dare voice of Orson Welles, who too neatly sums up Viking history for his audience in the narrative overture to *The Vikings* (1958), perhaps the most popular English-language film on the subject. Such an image of the "northmen" was not out of line with the scholarship then current. The leading English authority on the Vikings, T.D. Kendrick, had written in 1930:

As buccaneers, thieves, and murderers, the Northmen horrified all western Christendom, startled even the Greek Empire, and more than once shocked the Muslim people of the Caliphate. In this respect they were no worse than other robbers and pillagers of history, either before their day or long after it, yet it is an idle and dishonest task to attempt to defend them against the charge of plundering and massacre. . . . History also knows them as blood-thirsty and abominable barbarians, enemies of society capable of infamous, indefensible outrages of arson and slaughter.

The charge of obstreperous violence leveled against Scandinavians' forbears can ultimately be traced back to contemporary complaints about Viking behavior. Year after year, Dark Age annalists in England, Ireland, and France record yet another ferocious Viking attack. "From the fury of the northmen, O Lord, deliver us," seems to have been a popular prayer of the times. Simeon of Durham, writing in the twelfth century but basing himself on earlier sources, describes one of the first Viking assaults on Britain in 793: "In the same year, of a truth, the pagans from the northern region came with a naval armament to Britain, like stinging hornets, and overran the country in all directions, like fierce wolves, plundering, tearing, and killing not only sheep and oxen, but priests and Levites, and choirs of monks and nuns." Alcuin of York, teacher of Charlemagne, after describing how in that year "the pagans desecrated the sanctuaries of God, and poured out the blood of saints around the altar" at the monastery of Lindisfarne on the northeast coast, expresses his shock in a letter back home to King Ethelred of Northumbria: "Lo! It is nearly 350 years that we and our fathers have inhabited this most lovely land, and never before has such a terror appeared in Britain as we have now suffered from a pagan race, nor was it thought possible that such an inroad from the sea could be made." Similar incredulity was expressed by Paschasius Radbertus, reflecting on a Viking attack on Paris in 845 or 856:

> Who among us would ever have believed or even imagined that in so short a time we would be overwhelmed with such fearful misfortunes? Today we tremble as we think of these pirates arrayed in raiding bands in the very vicinity of Paris and burning churches along the sides of the Seine. . . . Who could have thought that a kingdom so vigorous would be so humiliated and defiled by such a base and filthy race?

Ermentarius of Noirmoutier continues the dreary tale during the 860s, adding a host of French towns besides Paris to the list of victims of the Vikings: "The number of ships grows; the endless stream of Vikings never ceases to increase. Everywhere the Christians are victims of massacres, burnings, plunderings: The Vikings conquer all in their path, and no one resists them." In 884, the annalist of St. Vaast also bemoaned the unstoppable progress of the northmen, who "continue to kill and take Christian people captive; without ceasing they destroy churches and dwellings and burn towns. Along all the roads one sees bodies of the clergy and laity, of nobles and others, of women, children, and infants. There is no road on which the bodies of slain Christians are not strewn." Finally, the anonymous twelfth-century Irish chronicle, *The War of the Irish with the Foreigners*, claims that "all the Ghaedhil [Irish] suffered in common, both men and women, laity and clergy, old and young, noble and ignoble, of hardship, and of injury, and of oppression, in every house, from these valiant, wrathful, foreign, purely pagan people."

That so many medieval sources cite the Vikings as merciless marauders lent an air of authenticity to this popular portrayal of them in *The Vikings*. Yet a sea change has occurred in Viking-era scholarship since 1958 and is continuing down to the present day. It started just two years after the film came out with the work of the Danish scholar, Johannes Brøndsted, and was followed up in the ensuing decades with other revisionist histories by Gwyn Jones, P.G. Foote and D.M. Wilson, Else Roesdahl, F. Donald Logan, and, above all, P.H. Sawyer. The cumulative effect of all their efforts is a more rounded and complex image of the Vikings that places as much emphasis on their peaceful, yet no less impressive, activities as traders, shipbuilders, settlers, and explorers, as it does on their inescapable deeds as conquerors and pirates. So it is nowadays that any film or book that attempts to peddle the old story of berserk-eyed heathen raiders arriving in their dragon ships risks running the gauntlet of critical derision.

Such an overhaul of the Viking image was long overdue, for the testimony of the mostly monastic writers during the Middle Ages was uniformly one sided. Churchmen were understandably upset that Vikings were plundering their monasteries and, on rarer occasions, killing their monks, but their tone of righteous indignation needs to be tempered somewhat with other perspectives. The *Anglo-Saxon Chronicle*, commissioned by King Alfred of Wessex and possibly compiled by a layman for a secular audience, barely mentions any Viking assaults on monasteries after 835. This does not mean that monasteries were not attacked, but that from the chronicler's perspective, it was the survival of the royal house of Wessex, not the survival of religious life on the island, that was mainly at stake. We should also keep in mind that native English, Irish, and Frankish kings looted and warred against each other just as much as did the Vikings. A northern version of the chronicle that was incorporated into Simeon of Durham's *History*, for example, takes a noticeably different attitude toward the Vikings than its southern variant, seeing them as sometime allies—supported even by the archbishops of York—against threats to Northumbrian independence from the rising power of Wessex. Reading the rather alarmist wailings of monastic chroniclers may, paradoxically, give an exaggerated impression of the Vikings as all-powerful instruments of divine vengeance. Yet we know from other sources, such as the *Anglo-Saxon Chronicle*, that the Vikings were not always so invincible, nor their enemies so helpless. In addition, the more "legitimate" activities of the Vikings, such as their trading or settling efforts, which we know to have occurred from archeological and other evidence, are not dwelled upon, naturally enough, by their hostile monastic observers. Of course, one can go too far with this revisionism. The historian Donald Logan seems to provide an almost Nietzchean view of the Vikings vis-à-vis their foes when he writes:

> The dynamic and vital forces in Europe are not to be found in a decaying civilization but rather in the exuberant, at times destructive, young warrior seamen who sailed out of the fjords of the northern European peninsulas and whose legacy can be traced in line through Normandy, Sicily, the Crusades, and an Anglo-Norman state whose laws have come to form the basis of legal systems in North America and elsewhere.

To view the Vikings through only one lens, therefore, is to easily and fatally misunderstand them.

Consequently, we begin this background history of the Vikings with a brief overview of what we know about their society itself, in its own context, before venturing into the controversial waters of their infamous raids. The Viking period extends roughly from the end of the eighth century through to at least the middle of the eleventh. The origin and meaning of the term, "Viking," is disputed: It could be derived from the Norse word *vík* for creek or inlet, indicating a people who hid in such places for purposes of plunder. Alternatively, the term could have referred to the *Vík* or *Víken*, the land on either side of the Oslo Fjord in Norway, where the first Vikings who raided England are thought to have come from. In any case, Viking is used by scholars to refer to the society and culture that produced raiders and pirates who harried Europe and beyond from the sea; they were the inhabitants of what are today called the Scandinavian countries of Denmark, Norway, and Sweden.

Like almost every other European medieval society, the Vikings organized themselves according to a hierarchical social structure in which one's status was based on land ownership. They also relied, as elsewhere, upon a ruling elite of kings and chieftains as well as on an elaborate system of laws in order to maintain public order. Their houses conformed to the European pattern of timber frames and wattle-and-daub construction built around a central hearth, and their clothes were also similar: stitched leather for shoes and woven woolen garments fashioned into dresses for women and tunics and trousers for men. Perhaps Vikings bathed and combed their hair more often than other Europeans, although the chronicler who records this, John of Wallingford, says it was done by their men "in order the more easily to overcome the chastity of women and procure the daughters of noblemen as their mistresses." By Muslim standards of cleanliness, however, Ibn Fadlan found Vikings to be "the filthiest of Allah's creatures," not washing after performing any of their bodily functions. As in most European armies, Viking warriors wielded shield, sword, spear, axe, or bow; wore, for those who could afford it, chain mail and helm; and built earthenwork defensive fortifications or battered these down with siege engines. Much like Anglo-Saxon or Germanic warrior cultures, the Vikings placed a high value on courage and loyalty in battle and on generosity in sharing out booty. Their tactics, straightforward and direct, were no doubt also adopted by their enemies; in the words of Foote and Wilson, these consisted "largely of bashing hell out of the opposing side."

But the Vikings differed from their fellow Europeans in several important respects. The most obvious and significant difference, of course, was that they were pagan. They worshiped a pantheon of gods and goddesses, chief among them: Odin, the fickle god of war; Thor, the more trustworthy god of the natural elements; and Frey, the god of fertility. Worshipers held feasts in honor of their gods in their chieftains' halls or at home, and also sacrificed to them at special outdoor sites such as groves, hillsides, or springs. Apparently, both humans and animals could be offered in sacrifice. Slain warriors were conducted by female Valkyries to Valhalla, Odin's hall in Asgard, while other dead were destined for Hel, a dreary underworld, or to continue dwelling in their original graves. The gods created the universe, including Asgard, the home of the gods, and Midgard, the world of men, out of the dead body of the giant, Ymir. Yet even the gods were themselves created out of the primeval chaos or great void, known as Ginnungagap, when the giants mated with creatures in human form that had been licked into being by the great cow, Audhumbla. The Viking gods are therefore not eternal and all powerful, as is the Christian God. At the same time, there are clear parallels between Viking mythology and Christianity. In order to gain wisdom, Odin hangs himself for nine days and nights on Yggdrasill, the World Tree, an act that bears striking similarities to the passion of Christ. Just as in the Christian Last Judgment, the Viking Apocalypse, Ragnarok, is a time of chaos, rampant death and destruction, and seemingly unchecked evil. The gods are destroyed along with the world they created, but out of the chaos rises a new order that includes Baldr the Good, Odin's beautiful son, who is resurrected from the dead in Hel. It is entirely possible that later Viking Age religion imbibed much of Christian belief, especially since most of our knowledge about Viking myths comes from sagas and poems written down by Christian Scandinavians during the thirteenth century.

One important difference between Viking paganism and Christianity is that Viking dead were accompanied in their burials or cremations by grave goods, which at their most sumptuous could include whole ships and wagons as well as sacrificed slaves and animals, to help speed the deceased on their journey to the other world. Christians may have abhorred and out-lawed this practice, but it has proved a great boon to modern archeologists. Above all, one must remember that Viking religion, unlike Christianity, was neither exclusive nor evangelical. A good example of the Scandinavians' pragmatic approach to faith is the story of the conversion of Iceland, as told by Ari Thorgilsson in his *Islendingabók* (*History of Iceland*). It was a heathen lawgiver, Thorgeir, who decided that his countrymen should be baptized on the grounds that, for the sake of internal peace and good relations with Norway, the country should have one faith, and, after all, Christianity seemed a "reasonable religion." Even so, an easygoing accommodation was reached, in which outlawed pagan practices, such as worship of the old gods, eating horsemeat, and even infanticide, could still go on if conducted behind closed doors. Thor hammers have been found alongside Christian crosses in late Viking Age graves, and the pantheism of Viking theology did not preclude worship of Jesus Christ. Many Viking leaders accepted bap-tism in the new religion in order to settle down in new lands with no appar-ent pangs to their religious conscience. Denmark and Norway became fully converted shortly before and after 1000 A.D., with Sweden following a more gradual suit during the rest of the eleventh century.

Alongside paganism came slavery which, by contrast, had died out in the Christian West by the tenth century. Slavery in the Viking world had a religious justification. The god Ríg, or Heimdall, was said to have begot-ten the first slave, known as Thrall, on Ai and Edda, the poor great-grand-father and great-grandmother of the human race. Vikings' contemptuous attitude towards slaves is illustrated by their description of Thrall. In the poem, *Rígsthula* (*Ríg's Saga*), he is described thus:

> rough were his hands
> with wrinkled skin,
> with knuckles knotty
> and fingers thick;
> his face was ugly,
> his back was humpy,
> his heels were long.

He and his children—Noisy, Byreboy, Roughneck, Horsefly, Lazybone, Beanpole, Fatty—are good only for manual labor of the worst kind, such as dunging fields, digging peat, carrying firewood, herding pigs, and the like. Slaves were commonly regarded as cowardly and stupid; to call a free-man a slave or to die at a slave's hands was the worst insult and shame. With some minor exceptions, Scandinavian law accorded slaves no legal rights. They could be killed with impunity by their masters, could own no property, and could not participate in marriages, business transactions, public assemblies, judicial proceedings, or armed expeditions. A slave was the property, pure and simple, of his owner. It should be borne in mind, however, that slavery at this time was a part of other, non-Christian societies, most notably the Muslim-held territories of southern Russia and central Asia, the Middle East, North Africa, Spain, and the Sudan, with some of whom the Vikings seem to have carried on a brisk trade in slaves. Viking slaves at least had the opportunity to move up the social ladder, as concubines or trusted servants of great men, or to win their freedom by gift, purchase, or the performance of some heroic deed. This was not unknown. A Danish slave expressed his gratitude toward his former master in 1050 by erecting a rune stone that reads: "Toke the Smith raised this stone in memory of Thorgisl Gudmundarson, who gave him gold and liberty."

Another group who occupied an inferior position in Viking society were women. They are at last receiving their historical due, becoming the object of studies devoted entirely to them, such as that by Judith Jesch, who has extracted much information about their lives from archeological finds, runic inscriptions, and Scandinavian literature. In law, women occupied a position similar to that of slaves in that they were legally represented by another, either their father or husband. Generally speaking, Viking women had little to no political or economic power. They could inherit no land (unless there were no brothers as heirs), bring no case at law, and sit at no assembly, or Thing. With the exception of inheritance rights, the same was more or less true of women's status in the rest of Europe. On the other hand, Viking sagas certainly portray their women as assertive Germanic females goading their men on to war. In addition, Viking women may have had more leeway than elsewhere with regard to social mores and household management. Since many men were away for long periods on raids, control and supervision of estates would have necessarily been left to their wives, which, according to Foote and Wilson, may have fostered in them some "initiative and independence." Appreciation of just such a role is indicated on a Swedish rune stone raised by Holmgaut in memory of his wife, Odindis:

A better housewife
will never come
to Hassmyra
to run the farm.

Arabic authors noted the greater sexual freedom enjoyed by Viking women compared to the customs of their own society, although it is possible that any Western woman would have been found more wanton. Al-Tartushi, visiting Hedeby in Denmark around 970, recorded that "their women have the right to declare themselves divorced; they part with their husbands whenever they like." Another Muslim observer of the Vikings, al-Ghazal, wrote of being told by a Viking queen: "Our women stay with our husbands according to their choice. The woman stays with him as long as she wishes, and parts from him if she no longer desires him." This is in contrast to contemporary Christian efforts to make marriages inviolable. Al-Tartushi also noted that infanticide, by throwing unwanted children into the sea, was practiced and allowed.

The last great difference between Viking society and the rest of the West was in their shipbuilding and seamanship. Here, the Vikings excelled in every way. Indeed, their famous raids would not have been possible without these superior skills. Survivals of burial ships at Oseberg and Gokstad in Norway from the ninth century and of five ships dredged from the Roskilde Fjord at Skuldelev in Denmark from the eleventh century have allowed us to gain a good picture of the manner of construction and use of Viking ships. These were built using planks, or "strakes," split radially from oak tree trunks so as to preserve the strength of the grain of wood. The ships were then "clinker built," as the planks were attached first to the keel and then to each other with iron rivets and the hull strengthened by frames and cross beams lashed with spruce roots for flexibility. The result was a fast, lightweight, and pliable ship that drew as little as 90 centimeters, or 3 feet, of water, allowing it to navigate down all but the shallowest rivers, and able to attain speeds of 10 knots or more on the open seas. A replica of the Gokstad ship was made in 1893 and sailed across the Atlantic by Magnus Andersen, who gained thereby a great appreciation for the seaworthiness of Viking vessels. He noted that the gunwale was so elastic it could twist out of true by as much as 6 inches, and that the rudder, mounted on the side rather than on the stern, proved to be a most efficient steering device. Viking ships were powered by oar as well as sail and included, in addition to the well-known longship or knarr that plied the ocean waves, more bulky cargo vessels designed for local traffic. As Orson Welles observes, "the compass was unknown" to the Vikings as a navigational device; instead "they could steer only by the sun or the stars," although it is not true that "they never sailed out of sight of land." In truth, the Vikings also used other navigational techniques, such as sailing from memory and making keen observations of landmarks and the presence of birds and whales.

We come now to the most controversial aspect of the Viking era: their raids. Most of the speculation in this regard has centered on their motive. What could have possessed the northmen to burst so suddenly and rudely on the "civilized" world of the late eighth and early ninth centuries? We have already encountered the explanation according to *The Vikings*, that the northmen were "cramped by the confines of their barren, ice-bound northlands," or in other words, their population outgrew available land in Scandinavia. While this may have been true of western Norway, whose region is highly mountainous and therefore unsuitable for arable agriculture, there is no evidence that it was so for the rest of the Viking world. Moreover, the previous estimate of the numbers of northmen who first arrived on Western shores in their longships has been scaled down from thousands to hundreds. The first Viking raiders wanted loot, not land, since they didn't stay to colonize their conquests until later. Nor is it credible any longer that the Vikings, as is suggested by another film, *Alfred the Great* (1969), were out to "paganize" Britain and Europe, or destroy Christianity and reintroduce pagan beliefs. Such may be suggested by the string of monasteries that were the victim of Viking raids, but the outright killing of monks, as opposed to ransoming them, seems to have been rare. The example cited by most scholars of a Christian martyr created by militant paganism, the monk beaten to death at the monastery of St. Bertin in France in 860, was in reality the result of provocation of his captors until the desired end, that "his name be entered on the commemoration lists of his brother-monks," was gained.

The scholar who has given the most thought and spilled the most ink on this subject, Peter Sawyer, is convinced that the Viking raids had their origin in "the commercial expansion in north-west Europe that had begun over a century before the first reported raids." Scandinavians had been very much a part of this expansion, trading their highly coveted furs, for example, for European manufactured goods and silver. These commercial contacts between the North and the West, according to Sawyer, led to the raids in three ways: (1) Scandinavians adopted the use of the sail from the West, which greatly improved the mobility of their ships; (2) they began to learn about the fabulous wealth and the political divisions within Britain and Europe that made this wealth ripe for the taking; and (3) the increased trading activity in the Baltic close at hand provided tempting opportunities for Viking pirates. They then may have been encouraged to look for other targets further to the West in the North Sea, especially when Danish kings began establishing their hegemony and protection at home during the ninth century. In addition to the commercial explanation, with its ramifications of piracy and political expansion in Denmark, Johannes Brøndsted has pointed to the colonizing efforts of the Vikings, with the goal of conquering land rather than acquiring wealth. However, this motive cannot be said to have come into its own until the end of the ninth century, and was not fully successful in England until the early eleventh century.

The Vikings first attacked the mainland of Europe in 799 at the island monastery of St. Philibert in Noirmoutier on the west coast of modern-day France near the entrance of the Loire River. In 810, a Danish party, perhaps with the consent of King Godfred of Denmark, raided Frisia along the north coast of what is now the Netherlands. In line with Sawyer's argument, this region had numerous trading links with Scandinavia, especially the town of Hedeby in Denmark, which was nearby, and was known for its production of silver that supplied all of Europe. The attack on Frisia occurred during the last years of the reign of Charlemagne, who is said to have cried when he spied the Viking ships off the coast of his realm. Nevertheless, defensive measures undertaken by Charlemagne and by his son, Louis the Pious, seem to have been effective, for raids on the Frankish empire did not pick up until the 830s and 840s, when Louis' sons, Lothar, Louis the German, and Charles the Bald, began a succession dispute which the Vikings exploited to their advantage. Indeed, Lothar invited Danish Vikings in as a political move against his rivals. Raiding continued, mostly it seems from Denmark, throughout the rest of the century, reaching another high in the 880s when the West Frankish kingdom was disputed after the death in 877 of Charles the Bald. Viking attacks on Europe eventually died down during the tenth century, but not before a permanent Viking enclave was created at Rouen in Normandy around 911 under a Norwegian or Danish chieftain, Rollo.

The Vikings were not just a European but a worldwide phenomenon. To the east, Scandinavians, mostly from Sweden, invaded Russia and the Ukraine, where they were called the Rus (from *Ruotsi*, the Finnish term for Sweden) and established their capital at Kiev. To the west, the Vikings, mainly Norwegians, occupied the Shetland, Orkney, and Hebrides islands off the northern coast of Scotland, as well as the Isle of Man; they also established a kingdom based at Dublin in Ireland and colonized Iceland, Greenland, and, for a brief period, Newfoundland in North America (known as Vinland). In addition, Vikings wintering in France raided further south against Islamic cities in Spain and North Africa and, penetrating further into the Mediterranean, reached Italy.

But the main focus, both of Viking scholars and Viking films, is on their activities in England. There is good reason for this: Viking raids upon England were among the most numerous, most intense, most enduring, and best chronicled of all. They started in 793, with an attack upon the northern monastery of Lindisfarne and, at around the same time, a raid on Portland on the southern coast, both recorded in the *Anglo-Saxon Chronicle*. Although these first raiders are thought to have been Norwegians, from 835 Danish Viking armies arrived and, throughout the rest of the century, established a swath of territory stretching from Northumbria in the north through the middle kingdom of Mercia and on down to East Anglia in the southeast. This Danish-held region became known, naturally enough, as the Danelaw. A center of native resistance to the Vikings, however, emerged in the southwest in the kingdom of the West Saxons, or Wessex, under its greatest ruler, Alfred, and his successors beginning in the late ninth century and continuing into the tenth. By the reign of Ethelred, nick-named, somewhat unjustly, as "Unready," between 978 and 1016, the Vikings were back with a vengeance. Ethelred's policy of attempting to buy off the Vikings with tribute, known as Danegeld, sometimes reaching as high as £48,000 (1012) or £72,000 (1016) in a single payment, only con-vinced the Danes that England was wealthy enough to be worth conquer-ing. Consequently, England became a Viking kingdom, first under King Sven Forkbeard of Denmark in 1013 and then under his son, Cnut, from 1016 until 1035. Thereafter, England was ruled again by the house of Wessex until new and more lasting conquerors arrived in 1066, who were descended from the Viking settlers in Normandy.

Since one of our Viking films, *Alfred the Great*, deals as much with Alfred as with the Vikings, a little more needs to be said about this hero of the English resistance. As with the Vikings, Alfred and his legacy have been considerably reassessed by historians in recent years. Alfred, who reigned as king of Wessex from 871 until 899, faced the largest-scale Viking invasions of the island before Sven's conquest, and he is often cred-ited with single handedly saving Anglo-Saxon culture. The dean of Anglo-Saxon studies, Sir Frank Stenton, wrote of Alfred in 1943:

> His early victories had saved the elements of English culture and learning from utter obliteration, and the relations which he maintained with Ethelred of Mercia had given a new unity of command to the forces available for their defence. He had created at least a rudimentary organization for the protec-tion of his people, and had made the greatest of English towns an outpost against the national enemy. On any estimate, he was the most effective ruler who had appeared in western Europe since the death of Charlemagne.

The basis for this reputation is largely Alfred's victory over the Danes, led by their king, Guthrum, at Edington in 878. Alfred's triumph at Edington is all the more remarkable for the fact that just four months earlier, around the Twelfth Night of Christmas in January, Alfred was forced to flee from his enemy into the wild "fen fastnesses" of Athelney. Edington became a symbolic turning point in the history of Anglo-Saxon resistance to Danish domination, much like Marathon had been for the Greeks against the Persians in 490 B.C. Nevertheless, Alfred was forced to fight off a second, perhaps even larger, Danish army during the 890s.

Indeed, Edington tends to obscure the many other achievements for which Alfred is justly famous among Anglo-Saxon historians. These include major internal reforms that Alfred inaugurated after 878—a new navy, a rotating fyrd, or army, and fortified burghs or towns—as well as the issuance of a new legal code and his scholarship, consisting of translations and prefaces to no less than three works of late Antiquity—St. Gregory's *Pastoral Care*, Boethius' *Consolation of Philosophy*, and St. Augustine's *Soliloquies*—and patronage of several other texts, including the *Anglo-Saxon Chronicle*. Clearly, Alfred was "great" for more than just fighting off the Danes, but his exploits vis-à-vis the Vikings are necessarily the focus of this chapter.

The problem, of course, is that the sources for Alfred's life, like those for the Vikings, are one-sided, this time uniformly favorable. Aside from the *Anglo-Saxon Chronicle*, composed possibly under Alfred's supervision, there is a biography of the king that is traditionally attributed to a tutor and close friend of Alfred's, the Welsh cleric and later bishop of Sherborne in Dorset, Asser. Asser's *Life of King Alfred* is problematic, for although its author claims to have composed it during Alfred's lifetime—his forty-fifth year in 893—it nevertheless reads more like the life of a saint than of a warrior king who resisted the Danes. Particularly suspicious are Asser's claims that his hero's piety went to extreme, ascetical lengths and that Alfred suffered from unnamed, mysterious illnesses that he allegedly had requested from God in order to cure his "carnal desire." The leading modern authority on Alfred, the historian Alfred Smyth, is convinced that Asser's *Life* is in fact a late tenth- or early eleventh-century forgery composed by a monk of Ramsey Abbey, Byrhtferth, and modeled on Einhard's *Life of Charlemagne* and Odo of Cluny's *Life of Count Gerald of Aurillac*. Moreover, both Asser's *Life* and the *Anglo-Saxon Chronicle* seem constrained at all times to put the best spin on events that could legitimately be construed as reversals in Alfred's war with the Danes.

The best window we have onto what Alfred was really like are his own writings. Unlike Asser's portrait of a "neurotic invalid" who longs to spend all his time in study and prayer and who ruled "almost unwillingly," Alfred reveals himself to be a man convinced of his divine right to rule, who coveted wealth (apparently for the sake of being a generous gift giver), and who placed a high value on lordship and loyalty. In short, he was the typical Anglo-Saxon/Germanic warrior king. As noted before, this cultural outlook, at least in political terms, was not so different from that of the Vikings.

Despite the anxiety Alfred evinces for his earthly reputation, his recent biographers, such as Alfred Smyth, have made inroads into his legacy as an Anglo-Saxon war leader who was more than a match for the Vikings.

The celebrated victory at Edington, for instance, has been reduced by Smyth to a mere "skirmish between Alfred's massed army and a Danish foraging party from Chippenham." Alfred's real achievement, according to this biographer, came during the unglamorous aftermath of the battle, when Alfred managed to persuade Guthrum to convert to Christianity and observe a twelve-year peace that gave Alfred the breathing room he needed to strengthen his country's defenses in anticipation of the next Danish attack. Smyth, however, discounts recent revisionist scholarship on the Vikings, which he claims peddles a whitewashed version of them as "long-haired tourists of the Early Middle Ages, who were given a bad press by narrow-minded monkish chroniclers who enjoyed a monopoly on reporting." Instead, Smyth is inclined to take contemporary descriptions of Viking ferocity at face value, which was all the more threatening in Alfred's day because it was bent on the complete conquest of the island. What is more, Smyth is at pains to portray Alfred's Viking enemy as ideologically opposed and virulently hostile to Christianity, which makes Alfred's achievement in bringing Guthrum to baptism appear all the greater. This seems to be supported by Alfred's famous statement from his preface to St. Gregory's *Pastoral Care*, that he "recollected how before everything was ransacked and burned, the churches throughout England stood filled with treasures and books." Yet nowhere does Alfred say that these churches were targeted because they were religious centers; their present misfortune may owe simply to the fact that they were filled with "treasures." Even the so-called Asser concludes that the present decline in monastic observance could be due just as much to a reduced religious fervor among his people as to "the depredations of foreign enemies whose attacks by land and sea are very frequent and savage." If the Vikings were the scourge of God—the instruments of His retribution let loose on a sinful people—as many Christians viewed them, this does not mean that the Vikings themselves were viewed as anti-Christian, any more than other disasters of supposedly divine origin, such as plague or famine, would have been.

The *Anglo-Saxon Chronicle*'s silence on the matter of Viking assaults on monasteries may be discounted as pro-Alfred propaganda, but, by the same token, one can also take this silence as evidence of Alfred's political, rather than religious, perception of the Viking threat. If Alfred and his contemporaries viewed their war with the Danes as primarily one between Christians and heathens, why would the *Chronicle* not highlight, rather than suppress, Viking outrages on martyred monks and nuns? Ironically, the chronicle of one monastery that lay in the Vikings' path, Abingdon in Berkshire, portrays Alfred himself as their spoiler—not the Vikings—because the king alienated some of their land, probably in order to help pay off the Danegeld he offered to the enemy in 871 and 876. Guthrum's all-important conversion to Christianity in the aftermath of Edington may have happened just as easily because the Dane had no ideological reason not to convert, as through Alfred's influence. That the Vikings were destructive there is no doubt. But among all their victims—whether these be pagan, Christian, or Muslim—their goals seem to have been material, not religious.

The Movies

Hollywood's best attempt to portray the Viking age is United Artists' *The Vikings* (1958), directed by Richard Fleischer and starring Ernest Borgnine as the Viking king, Ragnar; Kirk Douglas as his spoiled son, Einar; Tony Curtis as an English slave, Eric; and Janet Leigh (who was Curtis' wife at the time) as the Welsh princess, Morgana. *The Vikings* presents a "Hagar the Horrible" kind of stereotype of Viking bravado and brutality, yet this is perhaps to be expected in a film that appeared before the revisionist history on the Vikings that began in the 1960s. Even so, the film's indelible images and music remain deeply etched in our popular culture. Replicas of Kirk Douglas' black leather jerkin studded with silver stars that he wore in the film's battle scenes are currently offered by specialty costumers to medieval reenactors. The musical phrase that one hears in almost every scene of the film, composed by Mario Nascimbene, has become the theme music of Ricola cough-drop ads.

The storyline of the film, adapted from Edison Marshall's 1952 novel, *The Viking*, may be pure fiction, but certain plot elements and characters are based on reality, or at least on the version of it according to medieval Viking sagas. Borgnine's character of Ragnar is based on a legendary Viking named Ragnar Lothbrok, his surname signifying "hairy breeches." According to the twelfth-century *Ragnar Lothbrok's Saga*, he died in a snake pit at York at the hands of King Aella of Northumbria, where his magical hairy breeches that had protected him from harm in battle could not help him. His last words are alleged to have been: "The piglings would be grunting if they knew the plight of the bear!"—a mixed metaphor that foretold the revenge his sons would exact for his death. This is perhaps more of a mouthful than is practical for a film; screenwriter Calder Willingham simply has Borgnine yell "Odin!" before he gleefully jumps into the pit with his sword. The film also changed the snakes into wolves, which still presented logistical problems for the producer, Jerry Bresler, who had to substitute black-painted Alsatians for real wolves that had proved to be a little too realistic. The legendary figure of Ragnar Lothbrok may or may not correspond to a real Ragnar, who we know from an account written by a monk of St. Germain-des-Prés to have raided Paris in 845. He was paid off with 7,000 pounds of gold and silver by the king of the West Franks, Charles the Bald, and apparently died of the plague back in Denmark.

The existence of King Aella is also attested by historical sources. The *Anglo-Saxon Chronicle* notes tersely that in 867 the people of Northumbria "had deposed their king, Osbert, and taken a king with no hereditary right, Aella." (In the film, Osbert is changed to Edwin and is slain in the opening scene by Ragnar.) Later that year, the two kings were reconciled in order to face a new Viking attack on York, which the Vikings took after "an immense slaughter was made of the Northumbrians . . . and both kings were killed." The anonymous *Historia Regum*, or *History of the Kings of England*, calls Aella a "tyrant," whereas Simeon of Durham in his *History* says that the death of both kings was in retribution for their alienation of lands from the church of St. Cuthbert. Aella, as played by Frank Thring, suitably becomes the bad guy of the film. The scene where he cuts off the left hand of Eric in retaliation for handing a sword to his unbeknownst father, Ragnar, just before he jumps into the wolf pit, realistically conveys the bloody savagery of which both sides—Viking and English—were perfectly capable. The point is driven home with some pathos in an earlier scene when Ragnar, upon hearing of the wolf pit practice from his English ally, Egbert, comments, "You see, the English are civilized," little realizing that in a short while it will be used upon himself.

As in the film, the real Ragnar's death was avenged by his sons, including Ivar the Boneless (perhaps a reference to his double jointedness). According to Scandinavian lore dating to the eleventh and twelfth centuries, Aella was killed by Ivar in 867 in particularly gruesome fashion. This was the "blood eagle," referring either to the act of carving an eagle form on Aella's back, or that the victim's ribs were hacked away from the spine and his lungs ripped out and spread in the shape of wings on either side. Allegedly, the latter torture was done while the victim was still alive and was considered a sacrifice to Odin in return for victory. Douglas' Einar, although having the satisfaction of killing Aella, doesn't survive the film, in contrast to Ivar, who, according to Irish annals, went on to be styled "king of the northmen of all Ireland and Britain" and died in 873. An Eric does appear later in history as a Norwegian king of York in 947 or 948; he was nicknamed "Bloodaxe" and, as the sobriquet implies, he died violently in 954 at Stainmore in Northumbria after an uneasy reign. The figure of Morgana in the film seems to be derived from Arthurian legend.

The portrayal of Viking life and culture in the film is similarly a mixed bag. On the one hand, reconstructions of Viking ships, attire, weapons, housing, and the like are extremely well done. The film was financed by Kirk Douglas' own production company at the princely sum (for those days) of $4 million. This allowed for the building of a 30-acre Viking village on location in Norway and three full-size replicas of Viking longships, manned by 200 actual Scandinavian oarsmen, members of the rowing clubs of Norway and Denmark. The scene shown about a third of the way into the film of a majestic dragon-headed longship sailing down an even more majestic fjord is superbly evocative. According to a souvenir booklet that accompanied the film, the cast, including Douglas, Curtis, Leigh, and Borgnine, toured a museum of Viking artifacts in order to acquaint themselves with realistic props. The depiction of what went on historically behind all the costuming, on the other hand, is not so convincing.

The film casts one of its major stars, Tony Curtis, as a Viking slave who has a secret identity as the illegitimate son of Ragnar and the Northumbrian queen, Enid. (Even though the slave is the main character and narrator in Marshall's novel, Curtis must share center stage with Douglas.) Certainly Britain was a major source of slaves during the Viking period, but even more came from the Slavic region along the Baltic Sea, where the word "slave" originated (from Slav, designating the natives of Slavonia). Curtis, in the role of Eric, is appropriately sentenced to death for turning on his master, Einar, and he is likewise believably redeemed, and apparently freed, for an act of courage in handing his sword to the condemned Ragnar in defiance of the wishes of Aella. Otherwise, we see next to nothing of what Eric's life as a slave was like, except for a brief scene showing him unloading a booty-laden ship under the wrathful eye of Einar. Nor would we guess from this film that Scandinavians themselves were enslaved, sometimes voluntarily in order to pay off a debt. However, the casting of a black actor, Edric Connor, as Eric's mute companion, Sandpiper, does make the point that slavery during the early Middle Ages was an equal opportunity oppression, not based on race. On a minor note, technically, if not morally, Einar was perfectly justified in attempting to take Eric's hawk from him, for which he paid with the loss of his left eye; in Viking law, slaves could own nothing.

More scandalous, in light of both recent scholarship and women's liberation, is *The Vikings'* portrayal of women. In a famous scene, a yellow-haired Viking wench (played by Almut Berg) who is called in the credits as simply "Pigtails," is forced to stand trial for adultery by crouching with her head through a hole in a wooden "testing board" on which her three thick braids are nailed, while her husband attempts to cut them off from across the room with a throwing axe. The trial contains the typical logic of the ordeal. As explained by Ragnar to Egbert, who listens with an air of civilized condescension, it goes like this:

Egbert: This is rather an interesting game.
Ragnar: It's not a game. It's Odin's test for unfaithful wives.

Egbert: Is she an unfaithful wife?

Ragnar: Ask Einar.

Einar: Her husband says she is.

Egbert: Which is he?

Einar: He's throwing the axes.

Egbert: But, um, if she's innocent?

Ragnar: Her husband will succeed. The braids will be cut.

Egbert: Supposing he misses the braids and hits her?

Ragnar: Well, then she's guilty.

Egbert: Oh I see. What happens if he misses both the girl and the braids?

Ragnar: Three misses and we drown him!

In this case, Pigtails really is guilty of adultery, for we see her in an earlier scene trysting with Einar just before the arrival of Ragnar's ship. Fortunately, her lover saves both her and her husband by assuming the last throw and cutting her braids. The gulf between men and women in *The Vikings* is emphasized by the fact that male onlookers laugh uproariously at this spectacle while their female servers look on warily as Pigtail's life hangs literally on an axe edge.

It is true that Viking justice used the ordeal, but scholars believe that this practice was actually introduced from the Christian West, where the ordeal by red-hot iron or the ordeal by water was well known in Germanic societies as a test of God's judgment on the accused. Legend has it that Poppo, a Christian priest, convinced the king of Denmark, Harald Bluetooth, to convert in circa 960 by putting his hand without harm into an iron glove heated white hot. For women, the most common ordeal was *ketiltak*, literally "kettle taking," in which she had to pluck a stone from the bottom of a vat of boiling water. More usually, the accused attempted to clear himself from the charge by swearing an oath and convincing a number of others, known as "oath helpers" or compurgators, to swear that his word was good. The ordeal was only used as a last resort. It is hard to believe that the independent-minded women of the Viking age would have allowed themselves to be subjected to such a humiliating experience as that portrayed in the film. Aside from this scene, all we see of Viking women is that they serve beer in drinking horns dipped in large vats, or that they are the objects of Einar's boorish lust.

Even the famed battle sequences leave a little to be desired. Viking ships attacked in line after having been tied together; this severely restricted maneuverability but increased stability, allowing the warriors to fight as if on land, and made flight difficult. Despite having three replicas at their disposal, the filmmakers opted to show no more than a one-on-one

Einar (Kirk Douglas) battles his half-brother, Eric (Tony Curtis), atop Aella's castle in
The Vikings. The scene was shot at Fort La Lotte on the coast of Brittany in France.

naval battle between a Viking ship and its clunkier Anglo-Saxon rival
(which looks remarkably like a sixteenth-century galleon). The climactic
siege of Aella's castle (filmed at Fort La Lotte on the Brittany coast) does-
n't show the Vikings building their own fortified camp, which they invariably did when they conducted more than a hit-and-run raid, just in case
they were forced to retreat. Understandably, the film cuts right to the
chase of the attack. But throwing axes at an upraised drawbridge? Real
Vikings surely had more sophisticated siege techniques than that.

Most puzzling of all, however, is *The Vikings'* treatment of religion. On
one level, the film adopts a sympathetic approach and seems to take pagan
beliefs at their face value. This is demonstrated in the long scene intercut
with Pigtail's trial, in which Eric is sentenced to be thrown into the slop
pool and drowned as punishment for setting his hawk upon Einar's face.
Are the filmmakers trying to make a subtle point that the status of women
and slaves was intertwined? Perhaps. The most powerful woman in the
film, the sage Kitala (played by Eileen Way), tries to save Eric and champions his cause. Although the existence of the equivalent of priests or medicine men in the Viking religion is not known, the sagas and other sources
do present women as seers or as sometimes fulfilling a religious function.

A Muslim observer of Viking customs, Ibn Fadlan, witnessed a female "Angel of Death" presiding over the funeral ceremony of a Russian Viking chieftain. Kitala obviously commands respect in this male-dominated society, for after drawing everyone's attention by shaking her iron rings, she peremptorily tells Ragnar: "You can't kill the slave." She then casts her runes and announces solemnly: "The curse of Odin waits on him who kills the slave." Ragnar defies her by sentencing Eric to die anyway, but Kitala has the last laugh, as she calls on Odin to "send a wind and turn the tide." The wind does eventually come, but the skeptical Christian, Egbert, tells Kitala that "they were only flying clouds." In reply, Kitala gazes ecstatically heavenward and says: "You're blind. They were Odin's daughters [Valkyries]. I heard the singing of their battle swords as they rode across the sky." And indeed we get on the soundtrack a lot of scale-climbing, high-soprano singing, accompanied by violins and windy special effects, so that even Egbert looks convinced. From the film's perspective, the power of the pagan god is real. Another respectful treatment of Viking religious customs comes at the end of the film, when Einar is cremated in his Viking ship complete with his weapons and gear all around him, to the tune of Nascimbene's theme music played to a rousing crescendo. From a Christian point of view, such a burial was a prime example of "heathenism" and would have been outlawed.

On the other hand, the triumph of paganism in the film is not what it seems. Odin is the only Norse god, out of a pantheon of many, who is worshiped in the film, except for a fleeting reference to Thor by Kitala: "If Odin willed that Eric should die, Thor's hammer would sound his death knell." Even though Thor, the god of thunder who wields a mighty hammer, Mjollnir, is here mentioned, he still is given second place to Odin and made an instrument of his will. Odin is portrayed as the chief god of the Vikings. From what we know of surviving evidence, this is not true. It is Thor who should be given pride of place, judging from the numerous place names and artifacts dedicated to him that can be traced. Amulets in the shape of Thor's hammer are most often found from the late Viking age in juxtaposition to the Christian cross. Place-name evidence points to Odin being virtually unknown in Norway, and while there was an official cult to Odin in Denmark, in Sweden, it was Frey, the god of fertility as symbolized by his giant phallus, who seemed most popular.

A real Viking viewing the film would laugh out loud at Kitala's and Eric's invocation of Odin to send a wind, for that was not Odin's department. According to Adam of Bremen, an eleventh-century Christian observer of Viking religion, it was Thor, the "mightiest" of the gods, who "presides over the air and governs the thunder and lightnings, the winds and rains, fair weather and crops." Even the Christian convert, Helgi inn

Magri, is recorded by the Icelandic *Landnámabók* (*Book of Settlements*) to have prayed to Thor when his ship was tossed by storms at sea. The man who places his trust in Odin in such a situation, on the other hand, is inevitably disappointed, as happened to Egil Skalla-Grímsson, who rebuked the god in his poem, *Sonatorrek*, for allowing his son to drown. Thor was the reliable Norse god, "the protector of mankind" prayed to by most of Viking society, especially by the yeomen or peasant farmers for whom Thor's good graces were so important to their livelihood. Odin, by contrast, was the god of warrior aristocrats who could afford weapons and armor. He was most untrustworthy, often changing sides in a battle; he could even change his gender, something that was looked upon with great suspicion by Vikings.

So why does Odin tyrannize the film? It's possible that Eric invokes Odin in order to (unconsciously) reveal his true aristocratic origins, proving that he is a true son of Ragnar, who also calls upon Odin in his capacity as Viking chief. But I think the real motive behind the Odin obsession is that it allows the filmmakers to elide the difference between Christianity and Viking paganism. *The Vikings*, after all, may simply be following medieval precedent in this regard. The thirteenth-century sagas from which much of our information about Viking mythology comes down to us were written by Christian authors anxious to draw parallels between the new religion and the old and to make Odin out to be the chief Norse god. That the same intent is at work in *The Vikings* is made clear in the following exchange between Eric and Morgana on their escape voyage back to Britain:

> Morgana: Do you know which of all the oceans is the widest?
> Eric: The Poisoned Sea.
> Morgana: No. The ocean between a Christian and a heathen.
> Eric: Our hands can reach across it as easily as that . . .
> Morgana: But that's just a joining of the flesh.
> Eric: What else is missing?
> Morgana: The joining of our souls.
> Eric: If our hands are touching, our souls must be touching.

Odin is allowed to have power in the film only because he prefigures and can be identified with the Christian God who is to come. But this does little justice to Viking religion as it may have existed in its own right without the prejudice of Christianity.

Our next Viking film devotes its celluloid to one of the few enemies of the Vikings to successfully resist them, Alfred, king of Wessex (871–899). Not surprisingly, the film is called *Alfred the Great* (1969), directed by Clive Donner and starring David Hemmings as Alfred and Michael York as his

Danish archenemy, Guthrum. A recent biographer of Alfred, Richard Abels, calls the film "dreadful," and indeed, *Alfred the Great* is filled with many flaws. One is the characterization of Alfred himself, who from the opening scene of the film is shown to be a man who must be dragged out of a monastery in order to lead the Wessex army in the stead of his elder brother, King Ethelred, and fight the Danes. An astonishing invention of the film is that Alfred, sporting a tonsure, is about to take vows as a priest before the royal messenger, Athelstan, turns up to talk him out of this "foolery." When next we see Alfred, he lingers over his prayers as his army waits impatiently for him to lead them against the Danish enemy, who is preparing to attack at Ashdown. Later that same year, in 871, Alfred must be tricked by his council, or witan, into succeeding to the throne upon the death of his brother; he indignantly berates his council for getting "me to renounce the priesthood and be a warrior king." All this is preposterous. If Alfred had really been like this, it is hard to imagine him ever becoming king. There were two sons of Ethelred who, although minors at the time of Alfred's accession, it is certain would gladly have relieved him of his burden when they came of age.

The film's pacifistic interpretation of Alfred, while carried beyond credulity, is not entirely made up. It is in fact based on a biography of Alfred attributed to a contemporary, Asser, bishop of Sherborne, who is portrayed in the film as Alfred's bosom companion. In his biography, Asser says that Alfred took the reigns of government "almost unwillingly" and "kept by him day and night" a prayer book which he took "around with him everywhere for the sake of prayer, and was inseparable from it." Yet Asser also claims that it was Ethelred, not Alfred, who arrived late for the battle at Ashdown because he "was still in his tent at prayer, hearing mass and declaring firmly that he would not leave that place alive before the priest had finished mass, and that he would not forsake divine service for that of men." Perhaps for simplicity sake, the film transfers such sentiments to Alfred. Asser's statements, however, must be used with caution, for the work that is attributed to him actually seems to have been written by another author who lived a century or more after Alfred's reign. The true Alfred, as far as this can be judged from his own writings, was a man who, although greatly valuing learning and religion, did not shirk from war or his God-given right to rule. Most likely, he would have welcomed his witan's machinations to make him king, not shunned them. In his preface to his translation of St. Gregory's *Pastoral Care*, Alfred holds up as models the kings of "happy times . . . who had authority over this people, obeyed God and his messengers; and how they not only maintained their peace, morality and authority at home but also extended their territory outside; and how they succeeded both in warfare and in wisdom." Yet the film's

portrait of Alfred as a would-be monk who'd rather pray than fight fits in
perfectly with the counterculture in America and Britain during the 1960s;
when the film came out in 1969, disillusionment and protest over the U.S.
war with Vietnam was at its height.

What of the film's portrayal of the Vikings? This, too, is a mess. About
halfway through the film, Guthrum harangues his Viking brethren:

> We are the sons of Odin. And we shall take this land, its slaves, its riches, all
> will be ours. So let the Saxons sleep. They sleep in fear because they have
> deserted the gods we know. They say they have a new god, a god of peace
> and charity. Will such a god defend them? They are afraid of life, afraid of
> death, but most of all, they're afraid the gods they've turned from will now
> destroy them. Let us feed their fears.

Almost immediately the film cuts to the Danish army gleefully pillaging a
Saxon nunnery. Significantly, Guthrum strides up to the altar, takes down
the big gold cross, and spits on it before throwing it into the pile of other
religious plate collected as booty. His companion, Ivar the Boneless, drinks
some of the holy water before spewing it out and smashing the vessel. The
nuns are either raped on the spot or carried away to become slaves.

In a later scene, Alfred and Guthrum, in the midst of negotiations over
Danegeld, indulge in a lengthy debate on the merits of their respective religions during a game of chess:

> Alfred: My God is life eternal. Your gods are dead.
> Guthrum: Not dead. They speak in thunder and in battle, in
>   birth-cry and from the loins of lovers. Here are my gods. They
>   were your gods of old. Men say all Saxon kings are sons of
>   Odin.
> Alfred: They lie.
> Guthrum: He's a cruel god, lusting for power and knowledge. He
>   was hanged upon a tree to prove himself and to find wisdom.
> Alfred: He found nothing. Your gods teach nothing. They have
>   no wisdom.
> Guthrum: They have wisdom. The wisdom of the blood.
> Alfred: Of blood. There is no wisdom there, only pain and
>   hunger and lust. Christ conquers passion so that life and wis-
>   dom can begin.
> Guthrum: You have passion?
> Alfred: Yes, else we are animals.
> Guthrum: And would you be master of all passion? . . . Now I
>   see it. You are Odin's son!

All this clearly establishes that, from the film's point of view, the Vikings were extremely hostile to Christianity. The invaders represent the forces of crude barbarism trying to stamp out the light of Christian civilization.

The one good thing about these scenes is that Guthrum does point to a common culture that the Vikings and the Anglo-Saxons shared, if not in terms of religion, then of the Germanic warrior ethos. As Guthrum indicates, pre-Christian Germanic religion, which was described by the Roman historian, Tacitus, in the first century A.D., was similar to that of the later Vikings. But in truth, if late Scandinavian lore can be trusted, Viking paganism and Christianity also shared similar beliefs. Although Guthrum may boast that he is "Odin's son," he doesn't seem to know his father very well. For surely a Viking warrior who worshiped Odin would know that he, no less than the crucified Christ, hung himself on the world tree "to find wisdom." Perhaps the movie wants us to believe that Guthrum can only understand Christianity through transference of Odin to Christ. But if so, it would be very odd for a pagan devotee sparring with a Christian rival to denigrate (by implication) his own god as "cruel." The whole anti-Christian premise to the film's understanding of Viking religion falls apart at this point.

The film does imply, on the other hand, that Danes and Anglo-Saxons shared a military culture, and there is sound historical basis for this. After all, the best expression of warrior ethos in the Anglo-Saxon language, the eighth-century poem, *Beowulf*, is all about characters and events that take place in Denmark and Sweden. Yet this message is drowned out in the film by the religious confrontation. As mentioned in the background section, no perception of such a conflict is recorded by the chroniclers on either side, English or Viking. If the Vikings attacked monasteries, they seem to have done so not because they were religious centers but because they contained loot and potential hostages (unless the monks proved willing to martyr themselves). Although such attacks characterize the early Viking raids, such as the sacking of Lindisfarne in 793, not a single monastery is mentioned in the *Anglo-Saxon Chronicle* as suffering from the Danes during Alfred's reign. We cannot even be sure that the Vikings raped, since this is hardly mentioned either in contemporary sources. One of the most detailed accounts of Viking attacks, the *Annals* of St. Bertin in France, mentions only two cases of rape—one of nuns—but both committed by native Christians, not Vikings. The Danish invaders of England also proved willing to convert to Christianity when it suited them, as Guthrum did in 878, three weeks after his defeat to Alfred at Edington.

Then why, against all the available historical evidence, does *Alfred the Great* push this portrayal of the Vikings as inveterate enemies of Christianity? Part of the answer may be that the film is relying on outdated

David Hemmings and Prunella Ransome rehearse their lines on location in Galway, Ireland, as they prepare for a love scene between Alfred and Ealhswith in *Alfred the Great*. Both actors must contend with inaccurate headpieces.

perceptions of the Vikings as purely monastic spoilers, created, naturally enough, by monastic authors writing in the midst of such attacks. But there is another agenda at work here. From the moment the Vikings burst onto the screen and arrive off the shores of Wessex, they display a remarkable synchronization, whether it be rowing oars or brandishing spears and marching into battle. Similarly, their equipment, in evident contrast to that of the Anglo-Saxons, is rigidly uniform. These are, in fact, Viking versions of the Nazis, coming to spread their pagan ideology, just as Hitler seemed to be spreading fascism in the 1940s. This Nazified portrayal of the Vikings in the film was undoubtedly derived from Sir Frank Stenton, who published his history, *Anglo-Saxon England*, in 1943 in the depths of World War II. The parallels between Alfred facing the Viking onslaught and modern-day Britain facing the Blitz were too good to be missed.

Whereas *The Vikings* focuses exclusively on the cult of Odin, the Danes in *Alfred the Great* seem obsessed by the fertility god, Frey. Historically, this would more likely make them Swedes, not Danes, but no matter. Late in the film, Guthrum is shown presiding over a sacrificial ritual where the blood of oxen, sheep, and Saxon prisoners flows in abundance as an offering to Frey. As Guthrum explains to a horrified Ealhswith: "They make a sacrifice in blood to the gods so that the seed is fertile: nine creatures of each kind as slaughter!" This is lifted from Adam of Bremen's account of a major sacrifice to Frey, Odin, and Thor held every nine years at the pagan sanctuary of Uppsala in Sweden:

> The sacrifice is of this nature: Of every living thing that is male, they offer nine heads, with the blood of which it is customary to placate gods of this sort. The bodies they hang in the sacred grove that adjoins the temple. Now this grove is so sacred in the eyes of the heathen that each and every tree in it is believed divine because of the death or putrefaction of the victims. Even dogs and horses hang there with men, and a Christian told me that he has seen 72 bodies suspended promiscuously.

Of course, these are the words of a Christian designed to play up the repulsiveness of such barbaric practices in "civilized" eyes. In *Alfred the Great*, the worship of Frey seems to give the Vikings an excuse to rape everything in sight. Indeed, rape seems to be the only sexual activity on offer in the Dark Ages, for even Alfred is shown raping his queen on their wedding night. According to Asser, this would have been impossible, since Alfred came down with a "severe illness" on that momentous occasion.

Aside from misrepresenting Alfred and Guthrum, the secondary characters of the film are not served well either. We know very little about Alfred's wife, Ealhswith, daughter of King Burgred of Mercia. She and Alfred married in 868 and went on to sire five children—two sons and three daughters—not counting births that did not survive, within the next 18 years. The film brings Alfred's wedding to Ealhswith forward to 871, after the battle of Ashdown, and takes the even greater liberty of inventing an episode where a pregnant Eahlswith becomes Guthrum's hostage—and subsequent lover—for four years between 874 and 878! It is scarcely credible that a king would barter his queen in such a fashion. Asser says of her that "she was a notable woman, who remained for many years after the death of her husband a chaste widow." She died in 902, three years after Alfred.

Ivar the Boneless (the same historical figure who serves as the basis for the character of Einar in *The Vikings*) is introduced by Guthrum in the film as "my warrior chief . . . called the Boneless because his mother made him with gristle instead of bone." He is portrayed as Guthrum's half-mad berserker sycophant, when in fact he was a Viking king in his own right and never seems to have associated with the other conqueror. Alfred's West Saxon nobles are shown in the film to have been alienated by Alfred's high-handed attempts to introduce a rotating fyrd, or army. When they arrive at Alfred's rallying point at Egbert's Stone, they claim that they have come to kill him rather than fight at Edington. Alfred staves off this catastrophe by promising to "make a book of laws that every man can read." In actual fact, Alfred inaugurated his military reforms only after his victory at Edington, while his law code was not drawn up until a decade had passed after 878. According to Asser, Alfred had no difficulties calling upon the levies of Somerset, Wiltshire, and Hampshire to meet him at Egbert's Stone in May of 878, just two months after he had set up camp in the marshes of Athelney.

The one saving grace of *Alfred the Great* is the realism of the battle scenes. These are by no means perfect. Alfred's victory at Ashdown is presented in isolation, so that we have no inkling that it was in fact followed by three successive Saxon defeats—at Basing, Meretun, and Wilton—before the close of the year 871. It is highly unlikely that the common people, including women and monks, fought alongside Alfred's picked warriors at Edington, as is shown in the film. Guthrum was not present at Ashdown, nor Ivar at Edington, since the latter was dead by 873. At Ashdown, the West Saxons did split their forces, as is shown in the film, but Ethelred fought in the battle alongside his brother instead of lying lamely in his tent; it was his late and unexpected arrival on the field that apparently saved the day. The reenactment of the battle of Edington, nevertheless, does a very good job of demonstrating one of the standard battle tactics of the day: the tightly packed, wedge-shaped formation which the Vikings called *svínfylkja*, or the "swine array." This tactic is shown being used to achieve a defensive victory by Alfred's warriors, but it was also obviously known to the Danes. According to the film, Alfred got the idea to use the *svínfylkja* from a manuscript of an ancient Greek text depicting the "Spartan phalanx." This may well be true, but it is more likely that it was simply a well-known tactic. The "Spartan phalanx" portrayed in *Alfred the Great* may actually have been inspired by another film: In 1962, *The Three Hundred Spartans* dramatized in a very similar fashion the Spartan stand at Thermopylae in 480 B.C. Another debt to a Greek source may be the film's portrayal of Ivar whipping his Viking soldiers into battle: The ancient Greek historian, Herodotus, reports that at Thermopylae, the Persian army of Xerxes was goaded into battle by "captains with whips in their hands [who] flogged on every man of them, pressing them ever forward."

Even though Alfred's modern-day historian, Richard Abels, dismisses the film as "dreadful," its depiction of Edington follows closely his explanation of how battles were fought in Alfred's time:

> Given the weapons at their disposal, it is not surprising that battles between West Saxon and Viking armies were in large measure pushing and thrusting matches, not unlike the hoplite warfare of Classical Greece. The standard battle formation was the "shield-wall" in which the warriors closed rank in preparation for rushing or receiving the enemy's attack.

The film ends with Guthrum, despite his earlier pagan fanaticism, declaring to Alfred, "I bow to your god." (He was baptized three weeks later at Aller.) Guthrum's ready willingness to accept Christianity undercuts the whole premise of the rest of the film, that Alfred's war with the Danes was a war of one religion against another.

As with King Arthur films, it is left to a comedy to produce some of the most intelligent commentary on the Vikings. Once again, members of the Monty Python troupe use their eclectic brand of satire to undermine popular notions about their subject. *Erik the Viking* (1989) combines the talents of Terry Jones (serving as both actor and director) and of his fellow troupe member, John Cleese, with those of another British comedian, Tim McInnerny (from the *Black Adder* series). They are joined by the American comic actors, Tim Robbins as Erik, and Mickey Rooney as his grandfather.

From the first scene of the film, it is made clear that this will not be your standard portrayal of rough-and-ready Viking marauders. In an opening shot reminiscent of that of *The Vikings*, we see houses burning and Viking warriors rampaging through a village, accompanied by the cries of both the Vikings and their victims. Our expectations of Viking-style rape and slaughter are quickly denied, however, when Erik, dressed in full Viking garb, enters a peasant hovel to assault a comely lass named Helga. He tries desperately to perform the wicked deed, but can't seem to undress himself. Finally, his putative victim takes pity on him and engages him in conversation:

> Helga: Have you done this sort of thing before?
> Erik: Me? Of course. I've been looting and pillaging up and
>   down the coast.
> Helga: Looting and pillaging, eh?
> Erik: Yes.
> Helga: What about the raping?
> Erik: Shut up!
> Helga: Well, it's obvious you haven't raped anyone in your life!
> Erik: Shh!

Helga: Do you like women?

Erik: What? Of course I like women! I love 'em.

Helga: You don't love me.

Erik: Well, no, I don't. Mind you, I'm not saying I couldn't get to like you. As a matter of fact, I actually prefer that there's some sort of mutual feeling between two people.

Helga: What? Rape?

Erik: Well no! Obviously then it wouldn't be rape, then, would it?

Helga: Get it over with!

Erik: I don't suppose that you . . . no, no.

Helga: What?

Erik: I don't suppose that, um, you . . . you do like me, at all?

Helga: What do you expect? You come in here, burn my village, kill my family, and try to rape me! . . . You don't like it, do you?

Erik: Well, I just think it's a little bit crude, that's all.

Helga: What about all the killing and looting? That's just as crude, isn't it?

Erik: Well, you have to do them!

Helga: Why? Why do you have to go around killing and looting all the time?

Erik: To pay for the next expedition, of course.

Helga: But that's a circular argument. If the only reason for the expedition is the killing and looting and the only reason for the killing and looting is to pay for the next expedition, they cancel each other out!

Erik, the "vulnerable" Viking, doesn't believe in the image that his contemporaries, Hollywood, or historians have imposed on him. He embodies the revisionism on Viking history that had been taking place for three decades before the film came out.

The point is underlined in the next scene, which is again a complete knockoff of the original episode in *The Vikings*. A blonde-haired woman stands in a Viking hall with her long braids nailed out on a wooden board, while drunk Vikings try to cut them with axes. The axes go everywhere but at their target, smashing pottery and one even burying itself in the back of a hapless Viking. Meanwhile, a Ragnar-like Mickey Rooney squints at the spectacle and cackles gleefully. This time, however, the women stick up for themselves: An old matron demands that they "let her go!" and a Viking maiden picks up a smoking brazier and clobbers Sven with it. The scene ends in a full-scale Viking brawl.

The rest of the film is devoted to Erik trying to reach Asgard, the home of the gods, in order to bring back to life Helga, whom he accidentally killed in the opening scene, and to bring the age of Ragnarok to an end. *Erik the Viking* gives the fullest treatment to Viking religion and beliefs of any English-language film. Not only do we get an explanation of Ragnarok, the Viking version of the Christian Apocalypse when "brother would turn against brother, and men would fight each other until the world was finally destroyed," we are also introduced to several figures from Viking mythology who are far less known than Odin, Thor, or Frey. These include Fenrir the Wolf, the monster who has "swallowed the sun so that a great winter settles on the world"; Loki, the clever trickster who delights in causing trouble, persuading Ketil Blacksmith to sabotage Erik's expedition, since the end of Ragnarok will be bad for business; and Freyja, sister of Frey and mistress of the feminine arts and of wizardry, who tells Erik that to reach Asgard he must sail to Hy-Brasil "far out in the midst of the Western Ocean," where he will find the Horn of Resounding that will waken the gods. While the presentation of these characters has been adapted to the film's plot, their identity is essentially the same as that in the original myths.

When, toward the end of the film, we finally meet the main gods, such as Odin and Thor, we are in for a surprise. Although the hall of Valhalla where they live is very grand and imposing, the gods themselves are small children. By casting the Viking gods in this manner, Terry Jones conveys their capricious quality, particularly of Odin. We also get the message that their power is limited, which is demonstrated in Viking mythology by the fact that during the time of Ragnarok, the gods who do battle with the giants will be defeated. Here's how Odin responds to Erik's plea that he do something about the world's plight:

Erik: You have to help us.
Odin: We don't have to help anybody.
Erik: Fenrir the Wolf covers the sun, men fight and kill each
    other all the time.
Odin: Why should we care?
Erik: Because you're the gods!
Odin: So?
Erik: So bring the age of Ragnarok to an end and stop all this
    fighting and bloodshed.
Odin: Erik the Viking, the things you seek are not in our power.
    We don't make men love each other or hate each other.
Erik: But you're the gods!

This is very much in line with how Vikings viewed Odin, as a god whose oath was not to be trusted. Like many ancient deities of Greece and Rome, Odin is indifferent to men's travails. This was not true, however, of Thor, who wielded his hammer to protect both the gods and men from the World Serpent and other giants that symbolized the forces of chaos. But in the film, Thor is just another snotty, godlike brat.

Christianity's rivalry with Viking paganism is also given its due in *Erik the Viking*. Harald, the Christian missionary, is accepted into the community of Ravensfjord, even to the point of acquiring his own Viking concubine. But in sixteen years he has "not made a single convert in all that time," except for Thorbjorn Vigilsson's wife, who became a Buddhist. Every time he tries to convert someone, he is told to "go away" or comes up against an unyielding Viking faith on which he was "just checking." The Vikings tolerate his missionary efforts, perhaps because these have no effect on them. On the other hand, Harald refuses to entertain any of the Viking beliefs, even when presented with the physical evidence of Valhalla in Asgard. His response is to myopically declare, "There's nothing there," when everyone else (including the audience) can see it perfectly well. Ironically, it is this unbelief that allows Harald to save the Vikings from their own religion, since only he can go in and out of Asgard at will and thus blow the third note on the Horn of Resounding before his companions fall into the pit of Hel. The film suggests a complex relationship between Viking paganism and Christianity: Although medieval Christians, such as Adam of Bremen, approached Viking "heathenism" with a closed mind, they nonetheless did their rival religion a service by preserving a memory of its very existence.

There are other nice comic touches to be appreciated by Viking connoisseurs. In addition to showing how Viking ships were built, the film also imagines what occurred at a Viking sendoff when the ship was launched. Thorfinn is told by his anxious mother: "If you have to kill somebody, kill them, don't stop to think about it." Erik's mother brings him his father's "favorite pillow" so that he can rest his head on the long voyage. Sven the Berserker (played by Tim McInnerny) is lectured to by his dad on what he already knows, that he "must only let the red rage take hold of you in the thick of battle"; thereupon he instantly goes berserk, with everyone looking on and telling him it's "dangerous." In his farewell speech, Erik seeks to comfort loved ones left behind by enumerating all the evils they will face straight out of Viking lore: "You see, even if the hordes of Muspell tear us limb from limb, or the fire giants burn each and every one of us to a cinder, even if we are swallowed by the dragon of the North Sea, or fall off the edge of the world, don't cry." Before they set sail, the Vikings, egged on by Snorri the Miserable, quarrel over their seating arrangements. We also get a portrait of bad Vikings, led by Halfdan the Black (played by

John Cleese), who doles out cruel punishments—beheading, garrotting, flaying alive—with bureaucratic boredom. (The real Halfdan the Black, a 9th-century king of Norway, was himself cut in four so that each part of his kingdom could have a piece of him after his death.) Halfdan's ship is rowed by slaves who are whipped by a Japanese slavemaster whose insults must be subtitled. The only place where the film drags is the episode on Hy-Brasil, the island containing the Horn of Resounding where no blood can be shed, much to the Vikings' confusion. Terry Jones' turn as King Arnulf, in complete denial when his island sinks beneath the ocean, is a strange and irrelevant performance.

So what is the future of Viking films? It would seem that after *Erik the Viking*, the old story of Viking pillagers and rapists is dead. Yet what else will please a crowd coming to see a Viking film? A similar dilemma seemed to be facing "sword and sandal" flicks set in Ancient Rome, until along came *Gladiator* in 2000 that won the Oscar for best picture that year. Viking films had their heyday in the 1950s and 1960s, when the overexposure of the genre was made all too clear by cheap schlock movies such as Roger Corman's *The Viking Women and the Sea Serpent* (1957). This was followed in short order by a string of Italian productions that were the Viking equivalent of "spaghetti Westerns": *The Last of the Vikings* (1960), *Erik the Conqueror* (1961), *Invasion of the Normans* (1962), *Vengeance of the Vikings* (1964), and *Knives of the Avenger* (1965).

A year before *Gladiator*, Hollywood likewise tried to revive the Viking genre with a film called *The 13th Warrior* (1999), based on Michael Crichton's 1976 novel, *The Eaters of the Dead*. It stars Antonio Banderas as "Ahmad ibn Fahdlan," an Arab ambassador sent to accompany 12 Vikings back to an unnamed part of Scandinavia where the villages are being attacked by crazed warriors dressed in bear-shirts, the "Wendols," who feast on their victims once they kill them. The plot—which is an adaptation of the *Beowulf* legend, with a dash of primitive cannibals from the Neolithic epic, *Quest for Fire*, thrown in—cleverly allows the filmmakers to serve us up all the sword swinging and gore gushing that we've come to expect in a Viking film without all the historical baggage that makes such scenes seem outdated.

Banderas' character is actually based on a real historical figure, Ibn Fadlan, who served as secretary on a diplomatic mission in 921–922 from the 'Abbasid caliphate at Baghdad to the Bulgars on the Upper Volga River in present-day Russia. In his *Risala*, or personal account of his journey, Fadlan describes the Rus—the Swedish Vikings and their descendants who settled in the area. Although Fadlan clearly admires the Vikings as "perfect physical specimens," describing them as "tall as date palms, blond and ruddy," his account is best known for its graphic depiction of a shockingly brutal Viking funeral. According to Fadlan, the ceremony, held for "one of their outstanding men," lasted for ten days and included excessive bouts of drinking, promiscuous rape, and finally the sacrifice of both animals and a female slave. Fadlan does not pass judgment on the Vikings he observes, but given Islamic proscriptions against alcohol, sexual licentiousness, and infanticide, one can imagine that he was horrified.

In its early scenes, the movie does a good job of giving us a picture of what Viking society was like according to Fadlan's account, including the famous funeral sequence. (A nice touch of realism is that the Vikings speak their own language unsubtitled until Fadlan learns it, whereupon the dialogue changes over into English.) But the rest of the film contents itself with being a straightforward action adventure, with little to no historical content. Not even its innovation of pairing an Arab with the Vikings is particularly impressive, for it was not the first film to do so. In 1963 *The Long Ships* was released by Warwick Films, the same company that made *The Black Knight* (see Chapter 1). Rolfe (played by Richard Widmark) is pressed into the service of El Mansuh, a Moorish leader (played by Sidney Poitier), in order to capture the "Golden Bell" of St. James. In real life, al-Mansor, otherwise known as Ibn Abi Amir, was ruler of Córdoba in southern Spain from 976 to 1002. In 997 he raided Santiago de Compostela in the northwest of the peninsula, where he removed the iron bells from the church of St. James before demolishing the building and carrying the bells back to Córdoba on the shoulders of his Christian captives. The film is based on a sliver of Frans Bengtsson's popular 1941 novel, *Röde Orm* (better known by its English title, *The Longships*), and proved to be such an embarrassment that it was disowned even by its stars. Yet the film does make the point that the Vikings did reach the Mediterranean (they raided Seville in 844) and that Vikings were generally bested by the Moors on land but that the Scandinavians were far superior on the sea.

Perhaps the solution to be found for Viking films is to change audiences' expectations of typical Viking activity. Hollywood could start by making more movies that allow Vikings to do something besides rape, pillage, and plunder—such as go on voyages of discovery or convert to Christianity. An effort was made in this regard in 1978 with the release of *The Norseman*, starring and produced by Lee Majors of *Bionic Man* fame. Although it purports to be about Vikings sailing to America, *The Norseman* is really a rehashed Pochahantas story. Thorvald Helge, played by Majors, stands in for Captain Hastings, who must rescue his father from his Indian captors with the help of a female native, disappointingly *not* played by Majors' former wife, Farrah Fawcett. A Viking by the name of Leif Eriksson, otherwise known as "Leif the Lucky," was reported by the sagas to have sailed circa 1000 A.D. far to the west to a land the Vikings called

"Vinland," probably the northern coast of Newfoundland. It is here, at L'Anse aux Meadows, that archeologists have found traces of temporary Viking dwellings. *The Norseman* claims in its opening credits that its story "is based on fact"; although I have not personally seen the film, the critic Kevin Harty reports that "any connections between this Viking film . . . and the travels of Leif Erickson . . . is coincidental."

More recently, it has been left to Scandinavian filmmakers to take up the task of expanding the Vikings' exploits on screen. An Icelandic film, *The White Viking* (1991), directed by Hrafn Gunnlaugsson, is perhaps the only movie in the Viking genre to seriously tackle the subject of the pagans' conversion to Christianity. The film is set during the reign of St. Olaf Haraldsson, king of Norway from 1015 to 1030, who ruthlessly imposed the new religion on his subjects in Norway and Iceland. Another Scandinavian production, *Prima Veras Saga om Olav den Hellige* (*Prima Vera's Saga of the Viking Saint Olav*), made in 1983 by the Norwegian comedy troupe, Prima Vera, provides a more humorous—some might say blasphemous—take on its holy subject.

Two films by the Danish director, Gabriel Axel—*The Red Mantle* (1967) and *The Prince of Jutland*, or *Royal Deceit* (1994)—are faithful adaptations of the *Gesta Danorum* (*Deeds of the Danes*), a history of Denmark during the Viking age written in around 1200 by a Danish cleric, Saxo Grammaticus. Although the *Gesta Danorum* was used by Shakespeare as his inspiration for *Hamlet* (in Grammaticus' version, the story has a happy ending), scholars are more suspicious as to how reliable it is as a source of Viking history. The author, whose name means "Grammatical Saxon" and who wrote in Latin according to a classical style, seems to have been more enamored of the history and culture of Ancient Rome than of his immediate ancestors.

Unfortunately, these Scandinavian productions are not widely available on film or video in the United States. (I have not been able to view any of them except for *The Prince of Jutland*.) To gain access to the English-speaking market, the films would have to be remade by Hollywood in a translated format intelligible to American audiences who, by and large, possess next to no knowledge of Danish or Norwegian history. Even so, the future of Viking films may well lie in the movies made by the Vikings' direct descendants.

CHAPTER THREE

God (and the Studio) Wills It!
Crusade Films

The Background

The *Oxford English Dictionary* defines a crusade as "an aggressive movement or enterprise against some public evil." By this definition, a crusade can be undertaken in the name of almost any cause and for the sake of almost any objective. One can have a crusade for adult literacy, for example, or a crusade to save the environment. Yet modern calls for crusade still carry loaded connotations of medieval holy war. When al-Qaida terrorists attacked the World Trade Center and the Pentagon on September 11, 2001, U.S. President George W. Bush characterized America's forthcoming response as a "crusade"; he soon regretted using the word. Nonetheless, three months later *National Review* magazine decided to grace its cover with an illustration of President Bush decked out in a medieval crusader's costume. Obviously, crusades continue to make news.

In the Middle Ages, crusade had a quite specific meaning. The term "crusade" dates to the twelfth or thirteenth century and comes from *cruce signati*, Latin for "signed with the cross." This signifies that those who went on this armed pilgrimage between 1095 and 1291 (and beyond) believed themselves to be following in the footsteps of Jesus Christ. Their goal was Jerusalem, the place where Christ was crucified, buried, and rose again on the third day, a site commemorated by the Church of the Holy Sepulcher (sepulcher means tomb). For medieval Christians, it was intolerable that this most holy place should be in the hands of the Muslim "infidel," who had conquered Jerusalem in 638 A.D. under Caliph 'Umar. By the early eighth century, the Umayyad caliphs held sway from Spain in the west to India in the east, encompassing North Africa and the present-day Middle East. Of course, the Christians' claim to Jerusalem conveniently ignored the fact that the city was also sacred to two other religions. It had served as the ancient capital of the Hebrew kingdom of Israel during the tenth century B.C., when the Temple housed the Ark of the Covenant, said to contain the stone tablets of the Ten Commandments that Moses had brought down from Mt. Sinai. (The only remnants of the Temple is the present-day Jewish prayer site, the Wailing Wall.) For Islam, Jerusalem is the third most holy city, after Mecca and Medina, where the Prophet Muhammad ascended into the heavens from a site enshrined in the mosque known as the Dome of the Rock.

The medieval crusades can be said to have officially begun on November 27, 1095. It was on that date that Pope Urban II delivered his famous sermon calling for a crusade to the East to an assembled crowd of clergy and laity in a field outside the town of Clermont in south-central France. The First Crusade that resulted from that sermon was to be the only one to successfully capture Jerusalem by force. It is puzzling why Hollywood has never made a movie about it. The Austrian bodybuilder-turned-actor, Arnold Schwarzenegger, was rumored to be planning one of his signature action films on the subject, but if so, the project never made it to the screen. This was probably for the best, since Arnold's accent would have betrayed him as one of the German crusaders who in May of 1096 took a rather circuitous route to the East, by marching north along the Rhine river in order to massacre Jewish communities there. (Admittedly, some other German crusaders were legitimate, such as those who accompanied Godfrey of Bouillon, duke of Lower Lorraine, who was to become the first crusader king of Jerusalem.) Yet it was the First Crusade that launched a movement, and therefore its history is essential to an understanding of any crusade film.

There are five contemporary accounts of Urban's sermon at Clermont, along with several letters the pope wrote on the subject shortly afterward. Three chroniclers of Urban's famous speech — Robert the Monk, Guibert of Nogent, and Fulcher of Chartres — are thought to have been actually present at Clermont to hear it. Together, all these sources give us a pretty clear idea of the message the pope was trying to convey to his audience on that fateful day in November 1095.

The pretext for Urban's crusade was to bring succor to Eastern Orthodox Christians in the Greek Empire of Byzantium, with its capital at Constantinople. Such a message is prominent in the sermon as reported by Robert the Monk and Fulcher of Chartres and also in Urban's letter to the Flemings of December 1095, just days after he delivered his crusading call. A new Muslim power had arisen in the East — the Seljuq Turks — who had advanced from their homeland on the central Asian steppes to inflict a crushing defeat on the Greeks at the battle of Manzikert in eastern Anatolia in 1071. From the beginning of his pontificate in 1088, Urban had been exchanging diplomatic correspondence with Constantinople concerning the possibility of reunifying the Catholic and Orthodox churches, which had split only three decades earlier in 1054. Urban's decision to give a sermon at Clermont in 1095 seems to have been precipitated by a formal appeal he had received earlier that year from the Byzantine emperor, Alexius Comnenus. Although the Greek request for military aid against the Turks is portrayed by Urban as being for defensive purposes, Alexius may, in fact, have wished to go on the offensive after learning of the recent disintegration of Turkish leadership in Syria. There was ample precedent for Urban's action: In 1074, his predecessor, Pope Gregory VII, proposed leading an army of 50,000 "knights of St. Peter [*militia Sancti Petri*]" to the East in order to make good the disaster at Manzikert.

But whereas Gregory had narrowly conceived of a Christian army led and loyal only to the pope, Urban considerably broadened the appeal of fighting for the Church by identifying his cause with Christ's, not just the papacy's. As Fulcher of Chartres has Urban say in his sermon: "Now, let those, who until recently existed as plunderers, be soldiers of Christ [*milites Christi*]; now, let those, who formerly contended against brothers and relatives, rightly fight barbarians; now, let those, who recently were hired for a few pieces of silver, win their eternal reward." Urban's crusade was the culmination of centuries of effort by the Church to develop a theology of just war and to control Christian violence. In the fifth century, St. Augustine had expounded the concept that Christians, despite the peaceful injunctions of Christ in the Gospels, were allowed to shed blood and wage war, but only under three conditions: (1) if the war was declared by a "legitimate authority"; (2) if it was fought for a "just cause"; and (3) if the Christian army went to war with the "right intention." The last condition was most important, for it was this that made the Christian act of war a charitable deed and a fulfillment of Christ's command to "love thy neighbor." By calling for a holy war against the infidel, Urban could legitimately claim that only a crusade fulfilled all three conditions of Augustine's just war. Moreover, since the late tenth and early eleventh centuries, the Church had been attempting to curb the scale and scope of Christian violence against fellow Christians in the Peace and Truce of God movements, with rather limited success. This was coupled with a growing reform movement to improve the quality and religious fervor of monasteries, the priesthood, and the papacy itself. The enthusiastic response to Urban's sermon greatly increased the prestige and authority of the papacy—especially vis-à-vis the Holy Roman emperors of Germany—a development that perhaps Urban did not foresee. But the crusade also proved to be a far better solution to the problem of endemic Christian violence, by redirecting Europeans' martial energies away to a new target in a new land.

Finally, Urban married the concept of just war to the institution of penitential pilgrimage to Jerusalem. Normally, pilgrimages were undertaken as an unarmed act of penance: in the case of the arduous journey to Jerusalem, to atone for a particularly grave sin, such as murder. Jerusalem had been a destination for Christian pilgrims since the fourth century; from the seventh century onward, however, they had to cope with the city being in the hands of a hostile religion. Usually this did not present a problem, since even devout Muslims—including the recently converted Seljuq Turks, who had conquered Jerusalem in 1071—did not want to discourage the lucrative tourist income that pilgrims brought. On occasion, anti-Christian pogroms did occur: In 1009–1010, the Church of the Holy Sepulcher was razed on the orders of the Fatimid caliph, al-Hakim, and in 1064–1065, a group of between 7,000 to 12,000 German pilgrims were allegedly molested in Palestine by Muslim bandits. But the lurid descriptions of tortures and desecrations that adorn the accounts of Robert the Monk and Baldric of Dol are surely exaggerated. In any case, by 1097–1098, Jerusalem had once again changed hands, from the Sunni Turks back to the Shi'ite Fatimid caliphs of Cairo. According to Muslim sources, Jerusalem's new masters, far from wishing to antagonize Christians, were more interested in making common cause with them against their coreligionist rivals in Syria.

By appealing for a Christian liberation of Jerusalem—especially prominent in the accounts of Guibert of Nogent and Baldric of Dol and in his letter of September 1096 to the Bolognese—Urban astutely played upon the spiritual yearnings of Europe's laity, especially the military aristocracy. Here was a chance for Christian knights to fulfill their holy vows by doing what they do best: fighting. The goal of freeing Jerusalem from its Muslim "defilers" had tremendous emotional power, particularly when crusade preachers pitched their appeal in militaristic terms that most warriors could understand: the blood feud. Christ became the victim of a vendetta being waged by a rival religious family, whose outrages had to be avenged. As one crusade preacher put it: "If an outsider were to strike any of your kin down would you not avenge your blood relative? How much more ought you to avenge your God, your Father, your Brother, whom you see banished from his estates, crucified; whom you hear calling, desolate and begging for aid." In addition, Urban, according to the second-hand accounts of his sermon, held out the promise of the "glorious reward of martyrdom" and the "remission of sins" to those who went on his crusade, as opposed to their "eternal death and sure damnation" if they stayed and fought each other. Urban, although not an innovative thinker, had nonetheless achieved a grand summation of religious ideals that proved irresistible to his listeners.

Best estimates indicate that approximately 136,000 people "took up the cross," or made a vow to go on crusade, in response to Urban's appeal. A third of this number probably never left for Palestine. Of those remaining, half went on a "first wave" of departure for the Holy Land in the spring of 1096. Commonly known as the "People's Crusade," this first crusading army was enthusiastic but largely undisciplined and untrained for serious warfare. It was annihilated the following autumn outside of Nicaea by the Turkish forces of Kilij Arslan, sultan of Rum in modern-day Turkey. One thing the People's Crusade did accomplish was to lull the Turks into underestimating the "second wave," or "Lord's Crusade," which comprised at least 43,000 crusaders, at the core of which was a force of about 7,000 professional warriors or knights, most of them from France. This second army, on the whole well led and organized, left Europe piecemeal in the late summer and autumn of 1096. Among the highlights of its exploits were the capture of Nicaea in June 1097, the seizure of Antioch in June 1098, and, of course, the final triumph at Jerusalem on July 15, 1099.

The motives of these first crusaders have been much debated over the years. An older generation of scholars, led by Sir Steven Runciman, author of a three-volume *History of the Crusades* that appeared in the 1950s, believed that mercenary motives were just as influential, if not more so, as religious idealism. Taking their cue from Robert the Monk's report of Urban telling his audience at Clermont that "this land which you inhabit . . . is too narrow for your large population . . . and it furnishes scarcely food enough for its cultivators," these historians have assumed a land-grab mentality among disinherited noble second sons and a peasantry impoverished by bad harvests and Viking attacks. This view has now been effectively challenged and debunked, most notably by Jonathan Riley-Smith, Giles Constable and Marcos Bull who have conducted much research into the charters recording financial transactions made by the first crusaders in preparation for their departure. These reveal that a considerable sum of money was required in order to make the long trek to the East—not the sort of adventure likely to appeal to landless knights. Moreover, most crusaders were not happy-go-lucky travelers, since the fortunes of entire families were wrapped up in their enterprise. Should they not come back, patrimonial estates, usually mortgaged to local monasteries, would be put in jeopardy. And the agricultural depression that occurred in the years leading up to the crusade, by lowering land values, would have made such a journey even more expensive, and correspondingly less attractive, to those who could afford to go. The fact of the matter is that, with the exception of a few adventurers such as Bohemund of Taranto, the most able military commander of the First Crusade who made himself prince of Antioch, the vast majority of the first crusaders returned home after they had fulfilled their vow by conquering Jerusalem. Indeed, many crusaders, including Count Stephen of Blois, were homeward bound even before 1099: Desertions were rife, for example, during the long, debilitating siege of Antioch between October 1097 and June 1098. Despite the immigrant fantasy—common to all ages and partly derived from the Book of Revelation—that Jerusalem was a land "flowing with milk and honey," most crusaders did not stay to make their fortunes in the East. For the remainder of its existence, in fact, the crusader states of Outremer suffered from a chronic shortage of manpower. Only genuine religious conviction can explain such heavy material investment with so little expectation of return.

Religious enthusiasm was also largely responsible for the unique perseverence and military success of the First Crusade. This was demonstrated at the battle to defend Antioch on June 28, 1098, when the crusaders, for the most part wasted by starvation and disease, were nevertheless able to defeat a numerically superior Muslim force led by Kirbogha, ruler of Mosul in present-day Iraq. Key to this victory, apparently, was the discovery of the Holy Lance, the spear used by the Roman centurion Longinus to pierce the side of the Crucified Christ, in the church of St. Peter in Antioch by a poor Provençal knight, Peter Bartholomew. The papal legate, Bishop Adhemar of Le Puy, is pictured in a thirteenth-century illumination as bearing the Lance before the army into battle, even though he is reported by Fulcher of Chartres to have been skeptical about the relic. (A second Holy Lance resided in Constantinople, where Adhemar stayed in the spring of 1097.) Another crusader, Radulph of Caen, was equally suspicious of the Lance's authenticity, as was the Muslim chronicler, Ibn al-Athir. Even so, the morale-boosting powers of the Lance for a demoralized Christian army seems to have been real enough.

A second incident illustrative of the first crusaders' religious motivation came at the siege of Jerusalem in July 1099. A priest by the name of Peter Desiderius prophesied on July 6 that if the crusaders held a procession around the walls of Jerusalem, the city would fall in nine days. Despite the jeering and spitting of the Muslim defenders, the procession was duly held on July 8, and the walls were subsequently breached on July 15. Religious fanaticism also had its downside: Both Fulcher of Chartres and the anonymous *Gesta Francorum* (*Deeds of the Franks*) report that when the city was taken, a massacre ensued of its inhabitants—including men, women, and children—to the point that the victors' feet were stained up to the ankles with their victims' blood. Afterward, according to Fulcher of Chartres, the bodies of dead Muslims were picked apart or cremated by the Christians in order to "pick out besants [gold coins] from their intestines, which they had swallowed down their horrible gullets while alive." Meanwhile, the clergy and rest of the laity went in procession to the Holy Sepulcher to give thanks for the victory.

Later crusades were never to match the idealism and religious motivation behind the First Crusade. By the thirteenth century, a crusade was well on its way to its more modern, diluted definition. Two crusades at either end of that century—the Fourth Crusade of 1202–1204 and the Sicilian Vespers of 1282–1285—proved that crusading could now be directed against almost any target, even fellow Christians, and for almost purely political purposes.

It is instructive to contrast the Christian point of view on the First Crusade's success with the Muslim perspective. Islamic chroniclers of the First Crusade include Ibn al-Qalanisi and al-'Azimi, both of whom were contemporaries of the events, and Ibn al-Athir, who wrote nearly a century after the Christian conquest. None of these authors mention the religious inspiration behind the Christians' sudden and unexpected invasion of their land, nor the central place that Jerusalem held in crusader ideology. Instead, they all place the blame for the Muslim defeat squarely on their own shoulders; little to no credit is accorded to the Christians for their victories. Of decisive importance to the Muslims was the death in 1092 of Malikshah, the Seljuq Turkish sultan of Iraq and Persia, leaving behind a fragmented leadership in the Muslim Near East and Syria. Equally disastrous was the religious schism between the Sunni Turks based at Baghdad and the Fatimid Isma'ili Shi'ite caliphs centered at Cairo in Egypt. (This schism had its origins in a succession dispute in the seventh century as to who was the true religious and political heir of Muhammad.) Both these developments prevented the Muslims from presenting a united front against the crusaders in Palestine. This was especially evident at Antioch, where the army of Kirbogha melted away in disaffection and disarray, and at Jerusalem, which had been wrested away from the Turks by the Fatimid Shi'ites only a year before the crusaders arrived. Ibn al-Athir even reports a rumor that the Fatimids "sent messages to the Franks inviting them to go out to Syria to conquer it so that they [the Franks] would be between them [the Fatimids] and the Muslims [the Turks]." How much the crusaders knew beforehand of Muslim disunity is open to speculation, but even if the Fatimid vizier, al-Afdal, had hopes of making common cause with the Christians, he seems to have sorely misjudged their inflexible resolve to regain Jerusalem.

Both Ibn al-Athir and al-'Azimi are particularly astute in taking a broad, global view of the crusading movement, linking the Christian Reconquest of Spain with the First Crusade's drive to the East. Their assessment in this regard was unquestionably correct: Pope Urban, after preaching his crusade in 1095, urged Spaniards to stay at home and fight the Moors there, since "it is no virtue to rescue Christians from Muslims in one place, only to expose them to the tyranny and oppression of the Muslims in another." He even offered the same indulgence, "forgiveness of sins," to those who died in the Spanish Reconquest as to those who went to Jerusalem. Just like the Muslim commentators, Urban, according to Riley-Smith, "made little distinction between the East and Spain."

If the First Crusade was the most important of the crusading movements, then the Third Crusade of 1189–1192 was perhaps the most romantic. It has proved irresistibly attractive to Hollywood and other film studios because of its cast of two towering characters: the king of England, Richard the Lionheart, and the sultan of Syria and Egypt, Saladin (in Arabic, Salah al-Din, meaning "upholder of the law"—his birth name was Joseph). Although the Third Crusade had other participants, such as Frederick Barbarossa, Holy Roman emperor of the Germans, and Philip Augustus, king of France, it is these two who stand out and dominate the screen in any film portrayal.

Saladin has not been accorded any less chivalry and romance by the West simply because he was a Muslim. Kaiser Wilhelm II of Germany, in a state visit in 1898 to Saladin's tomb in Damascus, eulogized him as "a knight without fear or blame, who often had to teach his opponents the right way to practice chivalry." Even contemporary Christians, otherwise unreservedly hostile toward their Muslim foe, acknowledged Saladin's personal qualities of generosity and humanity. At his death in 1193, one observer, 'Abd al-Latif, remarked, "I have seen no other ruler for whose death the people mourned, for he was loved by good and bad, Muslim and unbeliever alike." In the *Ordene de Chevalerie* (*Order of Chivalry*), an anonymous northern French poem composed by 1250, Saladin is accorded the honor of being inducted into the Christian order of knighthood by his captive, Hugh of Tiberias.

For Christians, therefore, Saladin was primarily a figure of chivalry. Although an infidel Muslim, he shared many of their values that we have already seen in Arthurian romance: honor, courtesy, prowess, and the like. He was the acceptable Muslim, an enemy who, while occasionally demonized by Christian sources, was one that the West felt comfortable losing to once in a while. This does not mean that Muslims themselves did not appreciate Saladin's chivalrous qualities. His most famous act of mercy— rescuing a Christian girl from a Muslim slave market and returning her to her mother—is told by his Arab biographer, Baha al-Din. But for Muslims, Saladin is much more than just a kind ruler: He is the champion of jihad, the Islamic version of holy war, who expelled the unclean Christian presence from Muslim territory. Above all, he is the liberator of Jerusalem, Islam's third most holy city.

Nonetheless, Saladin was not immune from criticism, not even from his fellow Muslims, and throughout his career, he had to contend with the formidable reputation, especially in terms of religious policy, wielded by his predecessor, Nur al-Din, sultan of Syria from 1154–1174. For many Muslims, including Ibn al-Athir, it was Nur al-Din, not Saladin, who was the ideal *mujahid*, or jihad fighter. Not even Saladin's admirers can hide the fact that he came to the jihad cause of liberating Jerusalem late in his career. During the 1170s and early 1180s, it can fairly be said that Saladin battled rival Muslim princes rather than Christian crusaders and proved willing to even ally himself with the infidel in order to consolidate his power base. The cult of Saladin as a countercrusade hero for the Muslim world did not really begin until he was rediscovered by Arab scholars in the late nineteenth century.

The Third Crusade actually began in 1187, when news reached the West that Saladin had reconquered Jerusalem in September of that year, after having defeated a large Christian army at the Horns of Hattin the previous July. The return of Jerusalem to Muslim hands, along with the Islamic holy sites of the Dome of the Rock and the Aqsa Mosque, was much celebrated in Muslim accounts and was presented by Saladin's apologists as definitive proof of his commitment to jihad and the culmination of his career as a *mujahid*. According to his biographers, Saladin timed his ceremonial entry into Jerusalem on October 2 to coincide with the anniversary of the prophet's Night Journey into Heaven, and he immediately set about cleansing the city's mosques of all traces of the Frankish occupation. On the Christian side, the fall of Jerusalem less than a century after its conquest was much lamented and provoked a highly emotional appeal from Pope Gregory VIII for a new crusade.

The resulting expedition, which saw the participation of three European kings and thousands of English, French, and German crusaders, did achieve some successes. Acre was retaken for the Christians on July 12, 1191, and Richard was able to win a narrow victory over Saladin at Arsuf in September, which allowed him to refortify Jaffa on the coast opposite Jerusalem. Twice Richard came within twelve miles of Jerusalem—to the heights of Beit Nuba overlooking the city—in January and June 1192, but he was not to achieve this ultimate goal. On September 2 of that year he and Saladin concluded a truce that was to last nearly four years and provided Christians with free passage to Jerusalem and to the Church of the Holy Sepulcher. Richard, who was apparently ill and anxious to return home to defend his English and French possessions from his own brother, John, and from his French rival, Philip Augustus, left the

Holy Land on October 9, 1192 without exercising his visiting rights to Christ's city. He was kidnaped and held for ransom on his way home by Duke Leopold of Austria and Emperor Henry VI of Germany in violation of the protection afforded crusaders. Saladin died less than a year later on March 4, 1193.

Compared to those available for the First Crusade, Muslim sources on the Third Crusade are voluminous, allowing for a more even-handed picture of events when balanced with the Christian accounts typically used by Western crusade historians. The Christian source most often used to recount Richard's exploits on the Third Crusade is the *Itinerarium Regis Ricardi* (*Itinerary of King Richard*), written down in the thirteenth century but probably incorporating earlier, eyewitness accounts. This can now be balanced by several Arabic sources available in English translation. These include *The Perfect History* of Ibn al-Athir and two detailed biographies of Saladin by men who were close to him and undoubtedly witnessed some of the events they describe: Baha al-Din, Saladin's *qadi*, or army judge, and Imad al-Din, the sultan's private secretary. Of the latter two, Baha al-Din and his *Sultanly Anecdotes* is infinitely preferable by reason of his greater reliability and readability, as compared to the excessive flattery, overblown rhetoric, and impossible syntax of Imad al-Din.

Two incidents will serve to illustrate the vastly different approaches of the Christian and Muslim sources to the personalities and events of the Third Crusade. On August 20, 1191, Richard ordered the execution of his Muslim hostages who had been handed over to him when he had taken Acre on July 12. The massacre took place on the plain just outside the city walls in full view of Saladin's army still encamped nearby. From the Christian perspective, as represented in the *Itinerarium*, this killing of prisoners, even though it went against the normal protocol of warfare, was justified by the fact that the Muslims violated the terms of an agreement that had been negotiated when Saladin's garrison at Acre had surrendered the city. Of crucial importance to the Christians was Saladin's failure to return the relic of the True Cross, which he had captured at Hattin. Saladin's indifference to the fate of his men, rather than Richard's severity, is blamed for the massacre. According to the *Itinerarium*, Richard decided on this act only after consulting "a council of the greater men among the people," and after having determined "that Saladin had hardened his heart and cared no longer about ransoming the hostages."

From the Muslim point of view, on the other hand, Richard's massacre was nothing short of murder. While admitting "that Saladin delayed in carrying out the terms of the treaty" after the surrender of Acre, Baha al-Din nevertheless asserts that it was Richard, not Saladin, who broke his word. According to the Muslim chronicler, Richard had promised that even if their ransom was not paid, the prisoners would be kept alive as his slaves. For Baha al-Din, it was the ransom money—200,000 dinars—not the True Cross, that Richard was after. Indeed, Baha al-Din claims that Richard did receive both his money and the 600 Christian prisoners that had been part of the agreement, but that he killed the Muslim hostages anyway. (The *Itinerarium* mentions that no less than 2,500 Christians were to be returned.) Richard's actions are explained by Baha al-Din as a ruthless tactic of war: either "as a reprisal for their own prisoners killed before then by the Muslims," or because, before marching south, the king of England "did not want to leave behind him in the city a large number of enemy soldiers." Christian and Muslim sources even disagree on the numbers killed and the manner of their killing. The *Itinerarium* says that 2,700 were beheaded by executioners who "rushed up and quickly carried out the order," but that "the greater and more noble" of the hostages were spared for possible ransom or prisoner exchange. Baha al-Din, by contrast, cites "more than 3,000 men" led to slaughter in chains and killed "in cold blood, with sword and lance." It should be noted that when Muslims exacted retaliatory executions, they, too, exempted "well-known persons and strong men who could be put to work."

The other disputed incident is the truce signed between Richard and Saladin on September 2, 1192, but which had been in the negotiation stage since October 1191, one month after Arsuf. Both sources—the *Itinerarium* and Baha al-Din's *Sultanly Anecdotes*—agree that the two principals, Richard and Saladin, never met but instead used go-betweens: on the Muslim side, Saladin's brother, al-'Adil, and on the Christian, the son of Humphrey of Tibnine, an erstwhile claimant to the kingdom of Jerusalem through his former wife, Isabella, second daughter of King Amalric and presently remarried to Conrad of Montferrat. The two sources also agree on the final terms of the treaty: that the Christians were to hold the coast between Tyre and Jaffa, that Ascalon was to be dismantled, and that both Christians and Muslims were to have free passage throughout Palestine, including Jerusalem. But the motives and personalities responsible for these events are portrayed very differently. Richard is presented by the *Itinerarium* as unwaveringly devoted to the conquest of Jerusalem:

> [Richard's] legates informed Saladin in the hearing of many of his satraps
> that Richard had in fact sought this truce for a three year period so that he
> could go back to visit his country and so that, when he had augmented his
> money and his men, he could return and wrest the whole territory of
> Jerusalem from Saladin's grasp if, indeed, Saladin were to even consider
> putting up resistance. To this Saladin replied through the appointed messen-
> gers that, with his holy law and God almighty as his witnesses, he thought

King Richard so pleasant, upright, magnanimous, and excellent that, if the
land were to be lost in his time, he would rather have it taken into Richard's
mighty power than to have it go into the hands of any other prince whom he
had ever seen.

The infidel sultan's compliment—extremely gracious considering the arrogance of the original message—was to contribute in no small degree to
Richard's later fame as a warrior king and to the movies' romanticized relationship imagined between them.

Baha al-Din, however, supplies the more detailed and revealing narrative of this interchange. No less than in the Christian source, Richard is
portrayed here as inflexible with regard to Jerusalem. In a missive written
to Saladin, Richard is reported as declaring: "Jerusalem is for us an object
of worship that we could not give up even if there were only one of us left."
He also insists upon the return of the True Cross, which somewhat con-
tradicts the earlier account of Richard's greedy handling of the ransom for
the hostages of Acre. Rather than humbly admiring Richard's forcefulness
of character, Saladin, according to Baha al-Din's version, is able to give as
good as he gets. He is made to be the champion of Muslims' religious
claims on Jerusalem:

> Jerusalem is ours as much as yours; indeed it is even more sacred to us than
> it is to you, for it is the place from which our Prophet [Muhammad] accom-
> plished his nocturnal journey and the place where our community will
> gather [on the day of Judgment]. Do not imagine that we can renounce it or
> vacillate on this point.

If sent to the Christian delegation, this message must have provided them
with an illuminating education on Islamic beliefs. Saladin also reportedly
reminded his enemies that Muslims were the original occupiers of
Palestine before the crusaders arrived and implied that the True Cross
could not be handed back, as it had been destroyed on religious grounds.

Baha al-Din is at pains to present Saladin as extremely reluctant to
agree to Richard's truce and doing so only at the urging of his council and
the army. A similar picture is painted by Imad al-Din, who adds that
Saladin's subjects were tired of fighting and concerned about the long-term
economic decline that might set in should the war go on for too long. These
hard-line attitudes attributed to Saladin are most unconvincing. Although
we should not rule out the possibility that Saladin experienced a genuine
religious conversion and had an eye toward his jihad legacy, he seems on
the whole to have been a pragmatist and a realist, if also a poor spendthrift,
in most of his policies. Both Baha al-Din and Imad al-Din were extremely

anxious to rehabilitate Saladin's reputation as the supreme *mujahid*. According to Baha al-Din, "for love of the Holy War . . . he left his family and his sons, his homeland, his house and all his estates." In this case, at least, propaganda seems to have trumped Baha al-Din's normally more sober judgment.

When treating of King Richard, on the other hand, Baha al-Din reveals a grudging admiration that faintly echoes Saladin's encomium in the *Itinerarium*. Richard is admired chiefly for his military abilities: He is a man "of great courage and spirit" who "showed a burning passion for war" and whose arrival in the Holy Land "put fear into the hearts of the Muslims." Yet during the truce negotiations, the English king is portrayed as being true to his word in all his dealings with al-'Adil and as taking the initiative in bringing a much-needed peace to a bleeding and war-torn land. Again and again, Saladin is "impressed" by Richard's equitable proposals and chivalrous messages of "friendship and affection." It should be borne in mind, though, that at this same time, Saladin was entertaining rival proposals from Conrad of Montferrat, who promised military support even against fellow Christians in exchange for a vassal state based at Tyre. Perhaps Richard felt the need to compete with this rival, until Conrad was struck down on April 28, 1192 by the Assassins, a breakaway Shi'ite sect headquartered at Alamut in northwestern Iran. (Some say Richard put the Assassins up to the murder, others, Saladin.) Despite all this, Baha al-Din's flattery toward Richard seems sincere.

Finally, it is Baha al-Din who serves up the surprising twist in the tortured history of this diplomatic wrangling. According to him, Saladin's brother, al-'Adil, proposed to Richard that he marry the king's sister, Joan, widow of King William II of Sicily. While a medieval marriage between a Christian and a Muslim may seem preposterous, the union did make a certain amount of strategic sense: The two would each bring with them a "dowry" of Palestinian territory controlled by either side, thus neatly resolving through dynastic marriage the thorny ideological and historical differences between the crusaders and the Muslims. Saladin even seems to have endorsed the idea, giving his assent three times to the "formula of consent" addressed to him by his advisor, Baha al-Din. Richard also seems to have been willing, but we are given no indication as to what the feelings of the lady were on the matter. Significantly, Baha al-Din qualifies these extraordinary negotiations by remarking that Saladin regarded the whole thing as "a trick and a practical joke," whereas Richard employed the out of claiming that consent to the marriage was not forthcoming from his holy father, Pope Celestine III. Improbable as the entire affair seems, it rings true. Although the marriage proposal goes unmentioned by the *Itinerarium* and Imad al-Din, it is unlikely that Baha al-Din would have invented it altogether. After all, he was writing under the patronage of the very man who allegedly had made the proposal: al-'Adil, Saladin's brother and successor to his Ayyubid empire.

Crusades in the Baltic states and Spain do not have the glamor and prestige of the main ones to Palestine, and they often receive short shrift in crusade textbooks. Therefore, it is their great good fortune to be the subjects of by far the most well-known and highly regarded films of the crusade genre: *Alexander Nevsky* (1938) and *El Cid* (1961). It is important to familiarize oneself with the history behind each of these films; although both are justly celebrated as classics of the movie-making art, they nonetheless horribly distort, for modern propaganda purposes, the history they are meant to represent.

Crusading in the Baltic region and in Russia experienced its heyday during the thirteenth century. Yet its origins go back a century earlier, when St. Bernard of Clairvaux preached a crusade in 1147 against the pagan Wends in eastern Germany. Although professing a mission to convert the heathen, the crusade against the Wends was carried out with ruthless severity. "We utterly forbid," Bernard wrote to the crusaders, "that for any reason whatsoever a truce should be made with these peoples [the Wends] . . . until such a time as, by God's help, they shall be either converted or wiped out." As in the Spanish theater, indulgences equivalent to those promised to crusaders journeying to Jerusalem were offered to those fighting in the Baltic. Led by Henry the Lion, duke of Saxony, the crusade ended in a military stalemate, with the Wends agreeing to convert to Christianity and ally themselves with the Germans.

The military order that was to oversee further crusading ventures in Prussia and beyond was the Knights of the Order of the Hospital of the Blessed Virgin Mary of the German House of Jerusalem—better known simply as the Teutonic Knights—which was founded during the Third Crusade. As their full name implies, the Teutonic Knights were created as a field hospital by German merchants during the siege of Acre in 1190 and dedicated to the Virgin Mary. Eventually they were to receive their own rule, modeled on that of the older military order of the Knights Templar, as well as their own hierarchy headed by a Grand Master, or *Hochmeister*, and their own distinctive dress, a black cross on a white mantle, which was to be adopted by the modern German military as their "iron cross" symbol. Under perhaps their greatest master, Hermann of Salza, who had close ties with the German emperor, Frederick II, the Teutonic Knights were invited in 1225 to conquer the province of Culmerland (modern-day Chelmno) in northern Poland by its duke, Konrad of Masovia, who had been suffering from raids across the River Vistula from the heathen Prussians. This grant was confirmed in the following year by the Golden Bull of Rimini, by which Pope Honorius III made Salza the imperial prince of Culmerland, thus giving the Teutonic Knights authority to establish their own independent state. It seems that, initially at least, Salza regarded the Prussian Crusade as merely a training ground for his Knights before sending them over to the main action in Palestine. Their success in this "sport" of fighting Prussians was, however, to eclipse any of their exploits in the Holy Land.

During the 1230s, the Knights expanded eastwards into Prussia and Livonia (modern-day Latvia and Estonia) and at the same time absorbed two other military orders in the region, the Order of Dobrin and the Sword-Brothers. Campaigns of conquest were followed up by colonizing efforts that involved building castles using forced Prussian labor, bringing in German burghers to stimulate trade, and employing Dominican friars to convert the pagans. By 1240, the Teutonic Knights were ready to expand even further eastwards, into northern Russia. Although they were Christian, the Russians adhered to the Orthodox faith instead of the Catholic, at a time when antagonism between the two Churches was still high as a result of the West's conquest of the Greek Orthodox capital at Constantinople during the Fourth Crusade in 1204. The Knights captured the Russian town of Pskov in 1240 but were defeated at Lake Peipus (present-day Lake Chudskoye) in the Battle on the Ice on April 5, 1242. Tradition has it that the Knights' heavy chain-mail armor caused them to sink through the melting spring ice on the lake and drown, thus succumbing to their own military superiority. The hero of the hour on the Russian side was the prince of Novgorod, Alexander Yaroslavich, who had acquired the sobriquet "Nevsky" after his victory over the Swedes at the Battle of the Neva River in 1240. Our main source for these events is the hagiographical *Tale of the Life and Courage of the Pious and Great Prince Alexander*, written some forty years later by an author, perhaps Metropolitan Kirill of the Orthodox Church, who was anxious to portray Nevsky as the Church's champion against the hated Catholics. A useful corrective is to look at local chronicles, especially those for Novgorod where there were divided loyalties towards Nevsky, and relevant chronicles from the western point of view. These reveal that the Battle on the Ice may not have been the decisive turning point that Nevsky's *Life* makes out, but simply a frontier skirmish in which the Teutonic Knights suffered maybe a score of casualties, not the hundreds boasted of by the Russian sources. In any case, the main threat to Russia from the West at this stage seems to have been the heathen Lithuanians, not the Germans.

By 1237 the Russians had a far more formidable enemy to worry about who came this time from the East—the Mongols. Through to the end of 1240, the Mongols undertook a campaign of conquest that swept nearly

the whole of Russia, except for Novgorod. In 1241, the Mongols invaded
Poland and Hungary and appeared before the gates of Vienna. All of western Europe was now dangerously exposed to the seemingly unstoppable
Mongol horde. This, at least, was the perception throughout the 1240s in
Rome, where Pope Innocent IV gave the Teutonic Knights a free hand to
fight all enemies on the northeastern frontier, even granting them the
power to dispense indulgences in their own name to all who joined their
crusade. Little did the pope know that the year after it defeated two
Christian armies in April 1241, the Mongol tide was on the wane as the
result of the death of its leader, the khan of khans, Ogedai, son and successor to the great conqueror, Temujin, or Genghis Khan.

In the meantime, Alexander Nevsky became a puppet of the Khanate
of the Golden Horde. With Mongol help he defeated and forced into exile
his rivals to the throne—his own brothers Andrei and Yaroslav, who
favored a stance of resistance to the invaders—and assumed the title of
grand prince of Vladimir in 1252. For the rest of his eleven-year reign,
until his death in 1263 (probably by natural causes instead of poison, as
tradition holds), Nevsky pursued a policy of active collaboration with his
Mongol master. This strategy of appeasement, some would call abasement,
of an implacable foe did not go unopposed. In 1255 Nevsky faced a revolt
against his rule in Novgorod that pitted most of the population, including
the "common people" allied with the merchants and the "lesser boyars,"
againt the "greater boyars" who were still loyal to the prince. Then in 1257
and again in 1262, popular uprisings erupted in Novgorod and the
province of Suzdalia, respectively, as a result of the Mongols' harsh taxa-
tion and military recruitment efforts, all of which Nevsky loyally supported. Far from siding with his own people, Nevsky traveled to the court
of the Golden Horde to answer for these rebellions. A leading historian of
medieval Russia, John Fennell, concludes that Nevsky's appeasement did
not necessarily spare his country from Mongol interference and that, in the
long term, his policies "spelled the end of effective Russian resistance to the
Golden Horde for many years to come."

During the rest of the thirteenth century, the Teutonic Knights were
forced to suppress a series of Prussian revolts before consolidating their
gains there by 1283. They then turned their attention south, against Poland
and Lithuania, leaving the crusade against Russia to the Norwegians and
the Swedes. Throughout the fourteenth and early fifteenth centuries, the
Teutonic Knights and their friends conducted yearly campaigns, known as
reisen, against the pagan Lithuanians. This ended only when the Catholic
Poles made a dynastic marriage with the Lithuanians in 1386 that was followed by a crushing defeat of the Teutonic Knights at Tannenberg, or
Grunwald, on July 15, 1410, by a combined Polish and Lithuanian army.

This time, the Knights' bane was a converted Lithuanian duke, Jogaila, who by marriage to the Polish queen, Jadwiga, had ascended the Polish throne as King Wladyslaw II. By defeating Poland's implacable foe and rival to the West, Wladyslaw, despite his foreign origins, entered the pantheon of Polish heros and consolidated the fledgling Polish kingdom.

The Christian Reconquest of Spain from the Moors is dominated by the figure of Rodrigo Díaz de Vivar, better known to posterity as El Cid: Ironically, the term came from the Arabic, *sayyid*, an honorific title meaning "lord" or "master" that was reserved for descendants of the Prophet Muhammad. We don't know if Rodrigo was actually addressed as "mio Cid," or "my lord," during his lifetime; the first mention of it is in an anonymous Latin poem composed in 1147 at the earliest, nearly half a century after the Cid's death. There is a form of address that does seem to be contemporary with Rodrigo Díaz: *campeador*, the Romance version of the Latin, *campi doctor*, or literally, "teacher of the field," an archaic term that was used in the later Roman Empire to signify a regimental drill instructor. By Rodrigo's time, *campeador* probably had a meaning more akin to "conqueror," an honorific title intended to celebrate his early military exploits as recounted in another Latin poem, the *Carmen Campi Doctoris* (*Song of the Campeador*), composed circa 1083, at the cusp of the Cid's odyssey as a soldier-in-exile.

Unquestionably, it is anachronistic to talk of the historical Cid as a crusader. The vast majority of his career predates the advent of the crusading movement. Rodrigo's most famous exploit—and the one on which his putative reputation as a crusader is based—is the conquest of Valencia, an important port city on Spain's eastern coast along the Mediterranean. This took place on June 15, 1094, nearly a year and a half before Pope Urban II delivered his sermon at Clermont calling for the First Crusade. According to tradition, Rodrigo died peacefully at Valencia on July 10, 1099, a week before Jerusalem was to fall to the soldiers of Godfrey of Bouillon. Although Spain, no less than Jerusalem, was in Urban's mind when he ignited the crusading spark, it is hard to believe that Rodrigo Díaz was ever motivated by such feelings, even after the fact.

The bare outlines of the Cid's career, in so far as these are agreed upon by historians, can briefly be told. He was born between 1043 and 1047 into an aristocratic family from Vivar, six miles from Burgos, the capital of the Christian kingdom of Castile. Raised in the household of the Castilian *infante*, or prince, Sancho, Rodrigo subsequently served his lord in a military capacity when he ascended the throne as Sancho II in 1065. In 1072 Sancho annexed the neighboring kingdom of León after sending its king and his own brother, Alfonso VI, into exile at the Muslim court of al-Ma'mun in Toledo. Though most of the chronicles hint at treachery when

Sancho was assassinated outside Zamora in October of that year, Rodrigo readily transferred his loyalty, with no apparent qualms, to Alfonso when he assumed a reunited kingship of León and Castile in November 1072. An indication of Rodrigo's favor at Alfonso's court is that the king arranged the Cid's marriage to a royal relative, Jimena, daughter of an Asturian nobleman, in 1075–1076.

Nevertheless, Alfonso exiled Rodrigo twice—in 1081 and 1089—and on the latter occasion even went so far as to imprison the Cid's wife and children for a short time. On the first occasion, Alfonso seems to have been more than justified in punishing his vassal, who had undertaken an unauthorized raid into the lands of the king's Muslim tributary, al-Qadir of Toledo. The second rupture seems to have resulted from a breakdown in communication between the two sides when Rodrigo failed to keep a rendevous with Alfonso at the castle of Aledo in the southeast of the peninsula. A third misunderstanding occurred in 1091 and was caused by Rodrigo's violation of camp protocol when he pitched his tent before the king's outside the Muslim city of Granada. In all this, Rodrigo can fairly be said to have been as much to blame for his own misfortunes as the king's judgment.

Yet the fact of the matter is that the king's exile was a blessing in disguise for Rodrigo and was to open the door of opportunity to make his fortune. During his first period of exile, from 1081 to 1086, his military services were retained by three successive Muslim rulers of Zaragoza in northeastern Spain: al-Muqtadir until 1082, his son al-Mu'tamin until 1085, and his son al-Musta'in until 1086. Among the Cid's accomplishments at this time were the defeats in pitched battle of Ramón Berenguer I, count of Barcelona, in 1082, and of Sancho Ramírez, king of Aragon, in 1084. Both adversaries were allies of al-Mu'tamin's rival and brother, Mundhir al-Hayib. Undoubtedly, his victories secured for Rodrigo the generous gratitude of his patron, al-Mu'tamin, in addition to whatever plunder he had garnered on his own account during the abundant raiding that accompanied these campaigns.

The year 1086 represents a turning point, not only in the history of the Cid's relationship with Alfonso, but also in the fate of al-Andalus, that part of Spain (mostly in the south) occupied by the Moors. For on October 23, 1086 at the battle of Sagrajas, also known as Zalaca, in east-central Spain, Alfonso and the Christian Reconquest suffered its first major defeat, to a rising Muslim power based in Morocco in North Africa: the Almoravids. (The name was a Romance corruption of the Arabic al-Murabitun, or "the people of the ribat.") A fundamentalist sect of Islam, the Almoravids waged perpetual jihad from their Moroccan base camp at Marrakech. Eventually, through the military genius of Yusuf ibn Tashufin, a cousin of one of the founder's disciples, they established an empire that extended over the entire Sahara region in North Africa. Although they had been invited into Spain by the taifa kings of al-Andalus, particularly by al-Mu'tamid of Seville, the Almoravids were looked upon by their coreligionists across the Straits of Gibraltar as rather fanatical and backward. Nonetheless, Spain's Muslim rulers for some time had been strafing under the heavy tribute payments demanded by Alfonso and feared his growing power to the south. In the words of al-Mu'tamid, it would be better for them, so they believed, to be "a camel-driver in Morocco than a pig-herder in Castile."

Although the check to Alfonso's advance at Sagrajas was serious enough to bring about a reconciliation between him and the Cid, the Almoravids did not follow up their victory. For a rabidly militant conqueror, Yusuf was extremely cautious. He retreated back to Morocco immediately after Sagrajas, probably in order to settle a succession crisis upon the death of his cousin, Abu Bakr. Thereafter, as a result of further urging from al-Mu'tamid, he returned to Spain in March 1089 without achieving very much, and came back a third time in June 1090. While he was unable to dislodge Christian-held Toledo and Valencia, Yusuf did undertake a sweeping takeover of al-Andalus, deposing in short order the Moorish rulers of Granada, Málaga, Córdoba, and Seville. This was not an unwelcome development among the Muslim citizens of these cities. One of the emirs deposed, 'Abd Allah of Granada, frankly admitted that his and others' subjects approached the Almoravid leader "in droves to lay their complaints against their rulers." Chief among their protests was that they were being taxed beyond what was authorized in the Koran. The Almoravid conquest of al-Andalus could thus be said to have enjoyed at least some popular support.

Meanwhile, the Cid took Valencia in 1094 after a siege that lasted nearly a year and after two failed rapprochements with Alfonso. The Cid conquered Valencia as very much his own man: A charter that survives from 1098, by which Rodrigo endowed the new cathedral church of Valencia, styles him as "prince" of the city but makes absolutely no mention of his former liege lord, King Alfonso. Moreover, during his long career as a soldier of fortune, the Cid fought *against* Alfonso: once on behalf of his Muslim employer, al-Musta'in of Zaragoza, when the king laid siege to the city in the summer of 1086, and a second time on his own behalf as protector of Valencia, when Rodrigo invaded the Rioja region of Castile in order to draw off Alfonso and his army, who were making their own attempt to take the city in 1092.

Nevertheless, Rodrigo's rule in Valencia benefitted Alfonso indirectly (and perhaps unintentionally) by helping to distract the Almoravid threat to Christian Spain. The Cid defeated no less than two Almoravid armies, one at the battle of Cuarte in 1094, when the Almoravids tried to retake Valencia, and another at Bairén along the coast south of Valencia in 1097. In both instances, the Almoravids were led by Yusuf's nephew, Muhammad, not by the great leader himself. These victories proved, however, that the once-invincible Almoravids could be defeated in open battle using the heavy cavalry charges and the outflanking maneuvers that the Cid employed. They also took the pressure off Alfonso's defense of his conquests at Toledo and in Portugal to the west. That the Cid's rule in Valencia was not unpalatable to Alfonso is indicated by the fact that the king attempted to lead a relief army to Valencia, apparently in response to Rodrigo's appeal for help, when the Almoravids besieged the city in 1094. After the Cid's death in July 1099, his widow, Jimena, held on in Valencia until the spring of 1102, when she evacuated the city accompanied by an escort provided by Alfonso. Both the Cid and his wife were buried in the Benedictine monastery of Cardeña, near Burgos, in Rodrigo's homeland of Castile.

The main source of our knowledge about all these events in the Cid's career is an anonymous Latin prose work called the *Historia Roderici* (*History of Rodrigo*). Like the *Carmen Campi Doctoris*, the *Historia Roderici* calls its hero the *campeador*, but never the Cid. Scholars have debated when the *Historia* was written, estimates ranging from 1110, just eleven years after the Cid's death, to 1150. Richard Fletcher, editor of a new English translation of the *Historia*, argues for an early date. His reasoning, which seems convincing, rests largely on paleographical grounds—that the manuscript bears traces of an older Visigothic script that was rare after 1125—and on the fact that the author seems clueless about important landmarks in the Reconquest during the early decades of the twelfth century, such as the fall of Zaragoza in 1118. Added to this is the author's impressive knowledge of events during the Cid's exile and as prince of Valencia—all told comprising 66 out of 77 chapters, the vast majority of the work. He also is privy to an extraordinary amount of detailed information—including documents and letters issued by the Cid and roll calls giving the numbers and names of hostages taken in battle. This suggests that he had access to a "Cidian archive" available for a brief time after the Cid's death; he also may have benefitted from eyewitness testimony of those who had fought on the Cid's campaigns.

The picture of the Cid that emerges from the *Historia Roderici* is of a great warrior who, although devout, has no qualms about fighting on the side of Moors against fellow Christians. The author actually boasts of Rodrigo's favor at the court of al-Mu'tamin of Zaragoza: The Muslim emir is described as being "very fond of Rodrigo," more so even than of his own son, and as having entrusted his *taifa* to Rodrigo's care, "relying upon his counsel in all things." Rodrigo, in turn, served his Muslim master "faithfully and guarded and protected his kingdom and land." Among the chapters describing Rodrigo's rule of Valencia, King Alfonso is mentioned only once, in chapter 70, as a potential ally of the citizens of Murviedro *against* Rodrigo. Toward Yusuf and the Almoravids, the author is implacably hostile. Indeed, he never calls the Almoravids by their proper name, but instead refers to them as the "Moabites" and "Ishmaelites," terms borrowed from the Old Testament that denoted the enemies of Israel. He also seems to share with Muslim authors the view that the Almoravids were culturally inferior, since he calls them "barbarians."

Nowhere does the Cid's basic character as a mercenary, freelance soldier come across so strongly as in Chapter 50, significantly, the only place where the author is critical of his subject. The chapter describes Rodrigo's raiding of the Rioja region of Castile (where the author perhaps came from) in 1092. As already mentioned, this was done in order to distract Alfonso's attention from a conquest of Valencia, toward which Rodrigo himself had an eye. In a rare show of emotion, the author condemns Rodrigo's actions on this occasion as "savage," "merciless," "irreligious," and "impious." His plunder, while enormous, "was saddening even to tears" and seems to have been kept for Rodrigo alone, instead of being distributed to his followers. The remainder of the work, however, makes a concerted effort to rehabilitate Rodrigo's reputation as an admirable military leader who honored his agreements, even when betrayed by his enemies, and who fulfilled his duties as a good Christian by establishing churches in the Muslim cities he conquered. This indicates that, even at this early date, some debate existed as to how to remember the Cid after his death.

A useful corrective to the Cid's laudatory treatment in the *Historia Roderici* are contemporary narratives by Muslim chroniclers, such as Ibn Bassam and Ibn 'Alqama. The latter's history, "An Eloquent Account of the Great Calamity," although available only second hand, is still valuable as the work of a native of Valencia at the time of the Cid's conquest. While admiring his military prowess—Ibn Bassam calls him "a miracle among the great miracles of God"—the Muslim authors nonetheless depict the Cid as a ruthless, even cruel, man. Ibn 'Alqama calls the Cid a "ravening wolf" who "with his immense power attacks us every day, raiding us and carrying off our goods each day with his cavalry." These hit-and-run raids on the city's suburbs were designed to starve Valencia into submission, and once in possession, Rodrigo threatened to put the entire Muslim population to the sword if the Almoravids attacked. Violating his promise not to oppress his Muslim subjects—in particular, not to tax them beyond what was authorized by the Koran—the Cid governed Valencia harshly. According to Ibn 'Alqama, he hired Jewish tax collectors and officials to make sure that each Muslim "contributed something to the treasure-chests of the master of Valencia. If he failed to do this, he was killed or tortured." Rebellions and emigrations of the city's Muslim inhabitants continued well after the Cid's conquest of 1094.

Ibn Bassam tells an even more horrific tale of Rodrigo's treatment of Ibn Jahhaf, the former *qaði* (judge) and vizier of the city who had surrendered its keys to the *campeaðor*. In order to discover the whereabouts of the hidden treasure of al-Qadir, the murdered ruler of Valencia who had been his tributary, the Cid ordered that Ibn Jahhaf be tortured. The unfortunate Muslim was then executed, on the grounds that he had been responsible for al-Qadir's death, in an especially brutal fashion. According to Ibn Bassam:

> A hole was dug for the *qaði*, who was put in it up to his waist. The ground was leveled out round him, and he was encircled by fire. When it got near him, and lit up his face, he said, "In the name of God, the Compassionate, the Merciful," and pulled it [the burning material] towards his body and was burnt to death, may God have mercy on him!"

Apparently, Rodrigo intended to do the same to Ibn Jahhaf's wife and children, but relented only at the last minute through the intervention of both Christians and Muslims. Perhaps it was incidents such as these that impelled the author of the *Historia*—who is remarkably reticent about his hero's administration of Valencia—to eulogize the Cid in an attempt to favorably contest his memory.

Rodrigo's metamorphosis into a legend owes to an epic poem composed in old Castilian Spanish, the *Poema ðe Mio Cið* (*Poem of My Cið*). Its date is equally contested as that of the *Historia*. The doyen of Cidian studies, Ramón Menéndez Pidal, who published a definitive edition of the *Poema* in 1908–1911 and a biography of the Cid in 1929, believed that the poem gave an authentic account of its subject since, although not written down until much later, it could have drawn on oral traditions that were contemporary with the hero. Such an argument is impossible to prove and has by now been thoroughly discredited. A recent scholar of the poem, Colin Smith, favors a date of composition of 1207, more than a century after the Cid's death. His conclusion is based largely on an obvious point, that at the end of the sole surviving manuscript copy of the poem, an inscription informs us that it was written "in the month of May" in the year 1207 by an anonymous abbot, whom Smith believes to have been the actual author, rather than a mere copyist. Others have advanced additional reasons for dating the poem after 1200, including evidence pointing to linguistic usage peculiar to the early thirteenth century and to an epic structure inspired by the French *chanson* tradition, which did not emerge until the late twelfth century.

So what is the *Poema*'s legendary image of the Cid? Richard Fletcher, whose recent biography of Rodrigo has effectively replaced that of Pidal, see three agendas at work in the poem. First, the *Poema* is at pains to emphasize Rodrigo's Castilian origins; second, the poem portrays the Cid as "uncompromisingly Christian," who fought only against the Moors, never alongside them; and third, and most important, the poem presents the Cid as unwaveringly loyal to his Christian lord and king, Alfonso, despite the fact that the latter treats him unjustly and ungenerously. As José Fradejas Lebrero noted in his monograph, *El Cid*, from 1962, and as both Fletcher and Smith reiterate, such a picture is more in tune with the times of King Alfonso VIII, who ruled Castile from 1158 to 1214, than of Alfonso VI. It was during the thirteenth century that crusading ideology in Spain reached its maturity. Fletcher further observes that the *Poema*'s role model of the Cid would have had great appeal to those who were dismayed by the factional strife and infighting that went on in Alfonso VIII's kingdom; this at the very moment when Christians were facing a new, militantly fanatical Muslim enemy, the Almohads, who had succeeded to the Almoravid empire in North Africa. The situation was considered particularly serious after Alfonso's defeat to the Almohad caliph, Ya'qub, at Alarcos in 1195. It was not until 1212, when Pope Innocent III proclaimed a new crusade in Spain that attracted some Frenchmen to the cause, that the Christians regained the initiative with a crushing victory over the Almohads at Las Navas de Tolosa. By the middle of the century, the Christians, led by St. Ferdinand III of a reunited crown of Castile and León, reconquered as far south as Córdoba and Seville. This was to be the furthest extent of the Reconquest until Granada fell to Isabella of Castile and her Aragonese husband, Ferdinand, in 1492.

All this is not to say that similarities don't exist between the *Poema* and the far more reliable *Historia Roderici*. Both portray the Cid as practically obsessed with money, in the form of raiding loot and ransoms, in order to be a good lord to his soldiers and attract still more men to his war band. The *Poema* also follows the *Historia*'s lead in stressing the Cid's Christian virtues. But even though the prosaic *Historia* undoubtedly influenced the making of the epic poem, the two diverge in significant ways. In the *Historia*, the Cid is a Christian, but not a crusader: His inveterate enemy may be the "barbarian" invaders, the Almoravids, but not the native Moors. Most of its action is set far from Castile, to the east in Zaragoza and Valencia, where Rodrigo did indeed spend most of his time as a mercenary free agent. And the *Historia* seems not in the least concerned to make the Cid loyal to Alfonso, which in the poem could just as well be Alfonso VIII as Alfonso VI. For the *Poema*, the Cid is Spain's King Arthur, a man whose legend is far more important than his historical identity. This proved no less true of the Cid's cinematic biography, for which the poem was to be a most crucial source.

The Movies

Hollywood's first serious stab at a crusade film came in 1935 with Paramount's *The Crusades*, directed by Cecil B. DeMille, who was to go on to *Ten Commandments* fame. This was by no means the first film made on a crusading theme. In 1911, the Edison studio produced *The Crusader*, a romantic piece of fluff that had little to do with any historical crusade, and whose plot of two lovers separated by the event was very similar to other crusade films being made at around the same time by the Gaumont and Cines studios, in France and Italy respectively. Nor was this the first movie on a medieval subject that DeMille directed. In 1917 he made *Joan the Woman*, a propaganda appeal for America to enter World War I (see Chapter 6). *The Crusades*, which DeMille believed was "one of the best pictures I have ever made," is an early exemplar of the director's epic blockbuster style: It employed a cast of thousands and some of the biggest names then in Hollywood, including Henry Wilcoxon as Richard the Lionheart, Loretta Young as his wife, Berengaria, and Ian Keith as Saladin. No less than in *Joan the Woman*, *The Crusades* carries a political subtext, but, as we will see, one that is diametrically opposed to that of DeMille's earlier film.

As he explains in his autobiography, DeMille intended *The Crusades* to be a "telescoping" of "several crusades extending over two centuries." For dramatic purposes, the film mainly concerns itself with events of the Third Crusade of 1189–1192, which squared off the two dominant personalities of Richard, king of England, and Saladin, sultan of Syria and Egypt. Yet elements of other crusades are worked into the film, mainly in the form of the wandering hermit preacher, Peter (played by C. Aubrey Smith). For DeMille, Smith's character "was meant to embody Peter the Hermit, Bernard of Clairvaux, and all the zealous preachers who stirred Europe to arise and take the cross." The real Peter the Hermit was a fanatical preacher from Amiens in northern France who led the first wave of the First Crusade—often called the People's Crusade—to ignominious defeat outside Nicaea in October 1096, after having committed atrocities against Jews and others along the way. Naturally, these unsavory aspects of Peter's career are conveniently ignored in the film, which portrays him as a saintly man who inspires crusading enthusiasm wherever he goes.

DeMille, according to his autobiography, had as one of his objectives in *The Crusades* "to bring out that the Saracens were not barbarians, but a highly cultivated people, and their great leader, Saladin, as perfect and gentle a knight as any in Christendom." Certainly, the opening of the movie has a strange way of going about this. One of the first images we see is of Saracens pulling down a giant crucifix on top of the Church of the Holy Sepulcher in Jerusalem, while others gleefully cast Christian icons, holy books, and the wood of the True Cross into a raging bonfire. Next we cut to a scene showing captive Christians being led away in chains as slaves, followed by a bevy of Christian women being sold at a Muslim slave auction. The beauty of the "tall and slender" Christian captives (one of them an actress who was to go on to greater fame, Ann Sheridan) contrasts with the lecherous old Arab men who ogle and jeer as they make their bids.

All this seems virtually lifted from Robert the Monk's account of Pope Urban's sermon calling for the First Crusade. Harold Lamb, who wrote the screenplay and music for the film, was himself an historian of the crusades and surely had in mind that part of Urban's speech where he says:

> From the confines of Jerusalem and the city of Constantinople a horrible tale has gone forth and very frequently has been brought to our ears, namely that a race from the kingdom of the Persians [i.e., the Seljuq Turks] . . . has invaded the lands of these Christians and has depopulated them by the sword, pillage and fire; it has led away a part of the captives into its own country, and a part it has destroyed by cruel tortures; it has either entirely destroyed the churches of God or appropriated them for the rites of its own religion.

Needless to say, this is pure propaganda on the Christian side, a product of the religious fervor whipped up by the First Crusade movement.

By contrast, even Christian sources admit that when Saladin conquered Jerusalem in October 1187, he allowed a large proportion of its Christian population to ransom themselves and leave the city with all their possessions. According to Ibn al-Athir and Imad al-Din, even the poor who were unable to pay their ransoms were freed for a lump sum of 30,000 dinars. Muslim chroniclers further claim that it was in fact the Christian defenders who threatened to tear down holy places, namely the Dome of the Rock and the Aqsa mosque sacred to the Islamic religion, if Saladin would not come to terms with them. According to al-Athir, the only cross torn down was that on top of the Dome of the Rock, whereas the Christian patriarch was permitted to leave the city with all his treasures from the Holy Sepulcher. Imad al-Din says that even though some advised Saladin to demolish the Christian church, most of his councillors urged him to preserve it, on the grounds that such a policy was rooted in Muslim tradition dating all the way back to when Caliph 'Umar took the city in 638.

Both of the main characters of the film, Richard and Saladin, undergo dramatic transformations that are entirely unconvincing. At the beginning, Richard is a gruff, cynical, warlike man who only takes his crusading vow in order to get out of marriage to the Princess Alice of France (played by DeMille's daughter, Katherine). By the end, he has turned into a humble, penitent, mild-mannered true believer who makes peace with Saladin so that unarmed Christian pilgrims can visit Christ's tomb, even though this means that he must break his vow to Berengaria, "to go to Jerusalem with my sword." Richard has become the sacrificial agent of peace, not war. The historical reality, as we know from the *Itinerarium Regis Ricardi* (*Itinerary of King Richard*), is that the English king vowed to continue the war against Saladin after the truce expired until Jerusalem was back in Christian hands. Saladin's admiring reply is retained by the film — "By Allah, I wish you might had been my brother, not my foe!" — but not the historical context in which it makes sense. Curiously, the film at this point also has Saladin give a true assessment of Richard's original character — "You wear the cross . . . but you have no faith in that cross" — even though Richard has already undergone his transformation. The scene ends, not as we might historically expect, with Richard manfully defiant, but with the complete humiliation of his warmongering policies: After breaking his sword over his knee, he walks out of Saladin's tent, head down and dejected.

The film's portrayal of Saladin is even more problematic. We first see him immediately after the slave market scene mentioned earlier, where his arrival is heralded by a procession of his slaves beating upon huge drums. When confronted by Peter the Hermit, Saladin acknowledges that it is he who is behind all the atrocities we have just been witnessing:

> Go, hermit. Carry your thunder across the sea. Tell your Christian kings what you have seen: your women sold as slaves, your knights trampled under our horses, your gospels cast into the flames, the power of your cross broken, forever!

This is the image of Saladin according to the hostile Christian sources. The *Itinerarium*, for instance, calls Saladin a "pimp, king of the brothels" and a "greedy tyrant."

When next we meet Saladin, toward the middle of the movie, he is suddenly changed into a refined and cultivated figure, irresistible to the ladies. The scene is set in a tent pitched before Acre where gather all the crusade leaders, including Richard, Philip of France, and Frederick Barbarossa of Germany, whose appearance here is historically impossible, as he had drowned a year before in an Armenian river on his way to Palestine. In comes Saladin, announced by the ever-present drums and decked out in his outlandish, crescent-adorned armor, in order to issue his ultimatum to the Christians. Berengaria looks on admiringly and remarks, "They told me he had horns like the devil. I think he's magnificent!" Richard, still in the character of a vulgar oaf, makes the faux pas of offering his Muslim rival alcoholic refreshment, the consumption of which is proscribed by the Koran. (Even so, the real Saladin in his youth did apparently drink wine.) Then follows an episode straight out of Sir Walter Scott's 1825 novel, *The Talisman*. Richard tries to impress the sultan by cleaving an iron mace in two with his long broadsword, while Saladin replies by slicing through a delicate piece of silk with his scimitar. The whole scene contrasts the boorish demeanor of Richard with the gracious deportment of Saladin.

In the latter half of the film, Saladin becomes the chivalrous and magnanimous leader depicted by his Arab biographers. He rescues Berengaria, wounded by an arrow, and nurses her back to health, falling in love with her in the process. He foils an attempt by Conrad of Montferrat, in league with Richard's brother, Prince John, to assassinate "the Lion King" (a title now forever marred by Disney). And he generously offers Richard "terms your sword could never win," after which he releases Berengaria to rejoin her husband. Most of these plot elements are, with slight changes, again indebted to Scott's *Talisman*. Although farfetched, they're not entirely made up. Saladin's biographers, Baha al-Din and Imad al-Din, both testify that Conrad did attempt to betray the crusaders, but ironically it was he who became the victim of the Assassins' dagger. A Muslim–Christian marriage was on the negotiating table in 1191–1192, but the proposed alliance would have been between Saladin's brother, al-Adil, and Richard's widowed sister, Queen Joan of Sicily. Yet the film's Saladin is entirely at odds with what his biographers have to say on two important points. First, the historical Saladin was not indisposed to entertain the treacherous proposals of Conrad of Montferrat. Second, he was most reluctant to make a truce with the crusaders, which would mean suspending jihad, and did so only at the urging of others. There seem to be two Saladins in *The Crusades*: One is the universal hero of chivalry; the other is the infidel foe of Christianity. The gap between them is simply too wide to be bridged in a two-hour movie.

Finally, there is Loretta Young's portrayal of Berengaria. She is made to be the mouthpiece of the film's peace-loving agenda. Although it is not true that she utters the ignoble line — "You've just got to save Christianity, Richard. You gotta!" — she is given the most turgid dialogue in the movie. At first, she attempts to sacrifice her own life in order to end the divisive feuding between Richard and Philip outside Acre. A Muslim archer on the

Loretta Young as Berengaria in the harem tent of Saladin, played by Ian Keith, from *The Crusades*. Both are just about to learn that King Richard is on his way to reclaim his wife from the amorous sultan.

city walls, mistaking her for a crusader, is only too happy to oblige, but her plans go awry owing to the solicitous medical attention of Saladin. At this point, Berengaria becomes a female arbiter for peace, a role that was expected of queens during the Middle Ages. Most audiences who view the film nowadays find humor, rather than pathos, in Loretta Young's rather too-eager assent to Saladin's demand that she "open your arms to my love" in return for thwarting Conrad's assassination attempt on Richard. When the king brusquely bursts into Saladin's tent in order to retrieve his wife, he finds her dressed as a Muslim houri in the sultan's harem. Berengaria, acting as a kind of medieval League of Nations, then lectures her two lovers on why peace is needed in the world right now, not war:

> Berengaria: Oh Richard, you must believe. I've never loved any-
> one but you. I love you now. Don't make me suffer more. If
> only we could put an end to pain. If only we could have peace.
> If you fight on, thousands and thousands more will die.
> Richard, you mustn't.

Richard: You know how to yield to a conqueror. You think to
teach me?

Berengaria: We've been blind. We were proud, dearest, when we
took the cross. And in our pride we fought to conquer
Jerusalem. We tried to ride through blood to the holy place of
God. But now, now we suffer.

Saladin: The holy city of Allah!

Berengaria: Oh what if we call him Allah or God, shall men fight
because they travel different roads to him? There's only one
God. His cross is burned deep into our hearts. It's here, and
we must carry it with us wherever we go. Oh don't you see,
Richard, there's only one way. Peace. Make peace between
Christian and Saracen.

Richard: You ask me to lay down my sword?

Berengaria: If you love me.

Whereas DeMille's earlier medieval heroine, Joan of Arc, was
intended to incite Americans to go to war in 1917, here, in 1935,
Berengaria goads them to make peace. Indeed, the word "peace" is mentioned on no less than eleven occasions in this scene. The times had
changed. Americans had retreated into isolationism after the incredible
carnage of the First World War, and both they and Europeans wanted to
avoid at all costs another worldwide conflict, where millions upon millions—not just "thousands upon thousands"—of men could now die. The
year of the film's release, 1935, marked the passage of the first of four neutrality laws by the U.S. Congress. Clearly, DeMille had taken the measure
of the public's new mood and changed his tune accordingly. (He was to do
so again in 1956 with *The Ten Commandments*, into which film scholars have
read a Cold War subtext.) One only wonders what the film may have
looked like if it was made just half a decade later.

An intriguing alternative to Hollywood's muddled attempts to portray
the clash of Christian and Muslim cultures during the twelfth century is a
crusade film that came out of the Egyptian film industry, by far the largest
in the Arab world. The movie is *Saladin* (1963), which was Lotus Films'
answer to a DeMille-style, blockbuster production. It starred the Arab
matinee idol, Ahmed Mazhar, as Saladin and was directed by Youssef
Chahine. Unfortunately, most English-speaking audiences will never see it,
as the film (with English subtitles) is only available in the United States
through specialty Arab language distributors.

The basic plot of *Saladin* is almost a mirror image of that of the earlier
Hollywood film, but from the Arab point of view. Like *The Crusades*,
Saladin starts off by showing a brutal atrocity that is designed to provoke

sympathy for the heroes of the film and righteous indignation at the bad guys. Except that this time, the vile deed is perpetrated by a Christian against defenseless Muslims. The villain is Reynald of Châtillon, lord of Transjordan. In Muslim sources, he is known as Arnat of al-Karak, after the strongest castle in the region, Karak-in-Moab, which lies on the southeastern side of the Dead Sea overlooking the caravan route between Damascus and Egypt/Arabia. In the film, Reynald conspires—much against the advice of the old king of Jerusalem—to attack an unarmed Muslim pilgrim caravan in the Hijaz, which is in present-day Saudi Arabia along the Red Sea. Rather than film the massacre as a conventional action sequence, Chahine violates almost every editing protocol imaginable. But Chahine knows what he is doing: He utilizes what is known in film textbooks as discontinuity editing—including graphic, rhythmic, spatial, and temporal discontinuities, as well as the nondiegetic insert—in order to heighten the violent shock of Reynald's attack. The Russian master of discontinuity editing, Sergei Eisenstein, (who called his technique "montage") seems to serve as the muse behind Chahine's efforts here; no doubt the Egyptian director was well aware of Eisenstein's classic contribution of 1938 to the crusading genre, *Alexander Nevsky* (of which more later).

To fully appreciate Chahine's unconventional—to say the least—film style, let us consider each of the discontinuities mentioned above as they occur in this remarkable two minute sequence. It begins, ironically enough, with a conventional transition in film editing, the dissolve: In this instance, continuity is emphasized by a graphic match between the candelabra from the previous scene and the pilgrims kneeling in prayer. Graphic discontinuity, in which two shots of different composition are juxtaposed together, occur throughout this sequence as images of a crusader plundering the caravan or his horse's trampling hooves are interspersed with shots of male and female pilgrims and their clothing lying bloodied in the sand. Whereas Hollywood often uses graphic discontinuities in crosscutting or shot/reverse shot editing techniques to advance the storyline, no such orderly progression takes place here. Toward the end of the sequence, Chahine presents graphic discontinuities at their most basic level, alternating shots of white and red drapery in order to symbolize that the pilgrims' purity has been violated. At this point, Chahine also introduces rhythmic discontinuity, whereby the tempo of the scene dramatically changes. The length of time of each shot is drastically shortened to a second or less, greatly increasing the pace of the film. Spatial and temporal discontinuities occur when Chahine violates conventions of film space and timing from frame to frame. For example, Chahine places his camera in the center of a circle and films horse's hooves and bloodied pilgrim clothing whirling by on a disorientating 360-degree axis. The shots are presented in no particular order, so that we have no idea as to the duration of time over which the attack takes place. Moreover, some shots, such as of a crusader's exulting face or a pilgrim's anguished one, are repeated, violating the rules of frequency by which each image is supposed to be shown only once in the course of the film. In a nondiegetic insert, a crusader sword with blood running slowly down it suddenly appears to symbolize the crusaders' inhuman brutality. In the background are the almost omnipresent bloodied pilgrim clothing, whirling by at a dizzying rate, much faster than that at which the blood flows down the sword. (The limitations of Egyptian production design are given away by the thick matte line around the sword.)

Although this has been a rather technical digression into film theory, it is essential in order to understand the overall agenda at work behind the film. It is quite clear that Chahine is trying to marry his film technique to his message. In portraying an atrocity committed by the West against the Arab world, he deliberately rejects classical Western film conventions in favor of an alternative method—one that owes much to the Soviet montage style. This adds subtle political overtones to the film, especially when viewed in the context of Egypt's role on the world stage around the time of the film's release.

In historical terms, Reynald of Châtillon, while not cutting a conspicuous figure in Western crusade annals, nonetheless caught the belligerent attention of Muslims, and particularly of Saladin. The Arab chronicler, Ibn al-Athir, calls him "a violent and most dangerous enemy of Islam" and reports that Saladin twice vowed to "kill him with his own hand." Reynald's first goad to Saladin's ire occurred in 1182–1183, when he launched a naval squadron into the Red Sea and the Hijaz region that raided within a day's march of Mecca. This aggressive act threatened Islam at it very heart, the birthplace of the religion's founder, Muhammad, and was widely denounced in the Arab world. (It also played upon Muslims' aversion to the sea and naval warfare.) The affront could not go unanswered by Saladin, and he unsuccessfully besieged Reynald's capital at Karak-in-Moab in 1183–1184. In 1186–1187, Reynald committed his second provocation, an attack upon a Muslim caravan (probably composed of merchants, not pilgrims) as it passed near his territory on its way from Cairo to Damascus. This was in violation of a truce then in force between the two sides. In the meantime, Saladin had succumbed to a serious illness, which his biographer, Imad al-Din, takes as a turning point whereby Saladin transformed himself into a true *mujahid* committed to the cause of liberating Jerusalem. But the sultan's resolve was equally stiffened by Reynald's audacious acts, which Saladin seems to have regarded as beyond the pale of the ordinary state of hostilities in Palestine. When Reynald refused to make restitution, Saladin used the caravan incident as his own excuse to disregard the truce and engage the Christians at Hattin in early July 1187.

Saladin telescopes Reynald's two atrocities into one by relocating the second provocation in the Hijaz and depicting it as against unarmed Muslim pilgrims, presumably on their way to Mecca. In the process, the film exaggerates Reynald's villainy and amplifies Muslim feelings of indignation at his deeds. While Reynald did defy the king of Jerusalem in carrying out the caravan attack, as the film shows, the caravan was also, according to Ibn al-Athir, not defenseless but accompanied by "a large armed escort." That Reynald considered his attacks to be legitimate acts of war is indicated by his reply to Saladin's indictment for his "crimes" after his capture at Hattin. The whole exchange is reported by Saladin's secretary, Imad al-Din, who was probably present at the scene:

> When the Prince [Reynald] was brought before him he [Saladin] made him sit beside the King [Guy of Jerusalem], and reproached him for his treachery and paraded his wickedness before him. "How often have you made a vow and broken your oath; how many obligations have you failed to honor, how many treaties made and unmade, and agreements reached and repudiated!" The interpreter passed on this reply from him: "This is how kings have always behaved; I have only followed the path of custom."

Naturally, the film is interested in presenting only the Arab point of view and the one most flattering to its hero.

Saladin devotes considerably more screen time than its Western alter ego, *The Crusades*, in giving us the background behind the Third Crusade movement. The battle at the Horns of Hattin on July 4, 1187, while not even mentioned in DeMille's epic, here receives its own elaborate set piece. This is certainly justified, as Saladin's victory there over a Christian army largely composed of garrison troops from their cities allowed him to subsequently capture most of these, including Acre and Jerusalem. Since the sources give only sketchy details about the course of the battle itself, these must be supplied by the film. Chahine's *Saladin* anticipates both Kenneth Branagh's *Henry V* (1989) and Mel Gibson's *Braveheart* (1995) by having the enemy impale itself on wooden stakes set obliquely into the ground and concealed until the last moment of grisly impact. As for the rest, the Hattin battle sequence dishes out such tidbits as are provided by the Arab sources: We get a speech from Saladin to his men before the battle; the cutting off of water to the crusaders; the lighting of fires by the Arabs in order to intensify the Crusaders' thirst; the hail of arrows from the Muslim archers, which Ibn al-Athir says were "like thick swarms of locusts"; and the last stand made by King Guy on the Horns with the Wood of the True

Cross. The film's emphasis on the divisions within the Christian camp, with the king of Jerusalem urging avoidance of battle and Reynald impetuously boasting of victory, also owe much to Ibn al-Athir. In reality, the debate was played out between Reynald and Count Raymond III of Tripoli, whose arguments the film puts instead into the mouth of the king of Jerusalem. According to al-Athir, the debate was ended when Reynald goaded his rival to attack: "You have tried hard to make us afraid of the Muslims. Clearly you take their side and your sympathies are with them, otherwise you would not have spoken in this way. As for the size of their army, a large load of fuel will be good for the fires of hell." At any rate, Muslim sympathies were clearly with Raymond, for Saladin's nephew, Taqi al-Din, allowed him to escape from the battle.

When next we see Reynald and the king of Jerusalem in the film, they are being held prisoner in Saladin's palace awaiting his pleasure. In walks the victorious sultan, hailed by his court as the "liberator of Jerusalem" (in striking contrast to *The Crusades*, where Saladin is addressed by Peter the Hermit as "conqueror"). Saladin then proclaims an edict of "equality for all Muslims and Christians," as well as generous ransom terms and right of pilgrimage to the Holy Sepulcher for the Christian captives. Thus the film elides Saladin's victory at Hattin not only with his reconquest of Jerusalem three months later, but also with the terms of the truce he made with Richard at the conclusion of the Third Crusade in five years' time. Saladin's two-week siege of Jerusalem that culminated in his triumphal entry into the city on October 2, 1187, is omitted entirely, which is remarkable in light of the fact that so much space and rhetoric is devoted to the event in the Arab accounts.

The highlight of this scene is Saladin's treatment of his obnoxious prisoner, Reynald. All three chroniclers—Ibn al-Athir, Baha al-Din, and Imad al-Din—state that when iced water was brought to King Guy of Jerusalem to quench his thirst, he passed the cup to Reynald, at which Saladin immediately stated his intention not to honor the Muslim tradition of hospitality that safeguarded a guest from harm. Thereafter, the sultan with his own hand, as he had promised, cut off Reynald's head in front of the king, who immediately began to fear for his own life before Saladin quickly reassured him. (Imad al-Din deviates from this collective version slightly by adding that Saladin left Reynald alone for a while "to roast himself at the fire of his fear" and then struck him on the shoulder with his sword, leaving the actual beheading to his attendants.) The film, while remaining fairly faithful to the iced-water incident—Reynald grabs the water for himself instead of waiting to be handed it—departs significantly from the sources when it comes to Reynald's execution. Rather than kill him outright, as his advisers urge him to do, Saladin orders that Reynald be given a sword so that they might fight a duel as honor demands. Reynald is duly killed, but only after a long sword fight, in the course of which Reynald acquires the advantage of a second weapon, an axe (perhaps offset by the comical appearance of his little red boots!). Saladin's renowned chivalry is thus made to extend even to his most hated adversary, a piece of cinematic hyperbole that surpasses anything imagined by Saladin's fawning biographers.

The film goes on to portray the major events of the Third Crusade, including the siege of Acre, the battle of Arsuf, and the Christian occupation of Ascalon. Once again, anecdotes from the Arab sources find their way into the film. Ibn al-Athir reports that during the siege of Acre, a man from Damascus invented an inflammable device that burned down three of the Franks' siege towers, so that those crusaders who had before mocked the defenders' missiles were now burned alive. Another Muslim hero of the siege, according to Baha al-Din, was the brave swimmer, Isa, who carried messages and money from Saladin to the defenders inside Acre until one day his dead body washed ashore, bearing his last mission. Both characters and their exploits appear in the film, but in greatly modified form in order to fit the plot. The Damascene's fire is used, not at Acre, but to thwart the crusaders' siege of Jerusalem, a siege that in fact never took place. (Richard decided not to risk the siege, as his supply lines were overextended and his forces too small to garrison the city.) Isa does swim to Acre, not to succor its defenders, as the city is already in Christian hands, but to bring the Damascene and his invention back to Jerusalem. Moreover, Isa, whom the film converts into an Arab Christian fighting on Saladin's side, does not die, since he is vital to the love story subplot of the movie.

Yet another famous incident manipulated by the film is Richard's massacre of 3000 Muslim prisoners from Acre. Baha al-Din is the source here, but he would not recognize the portrayal as his own. The film places the massacre after the battle of Arsuf, when the whole point of the atrocity, according to Baha al-Din, was so that Richard wouldn't be encumbered with prisoners on the march south. Moreover, Richard is spared the indignity of giving the command to his firing squad to shoot: Instead it is Philip Augustus of France who blurts out the order. (Historically, Philip was not present at the massacre, having gone home three weeks earlier on July 31.) Just as the massacre is about to take place, the Frankish prisoners arrive from Saladin's camp. Although this follows Baha al-Din, Christian sources tell another story: that Richard was provoked into the act by Saladin's failure to deliver the ransom money and the prisoners on the appointed date.

The crusaders' siege of Ascalon is likewise historically implausible. Ascalon was a strategic port city on the extreme southern coast of Palestine, within easy striking distance of Egypt. It was therefore one of the three targets—the others being Jaffa and Jerusalem—of Richard's campaign in the south. Richard entered the city on January 20, 1192, after it had been abandoned by Saladin's forces the previous year. The film once again shuffles the timing of the event, placing it before the battle of Arsuf, which historically happened much earlier, on September 7, 1191. Saladin's defence of Ascalon, as this is concocted by the film, seems based on 'Abd al-Latif's famous encomium to Saladin's personal role in refortifying Jerusalem in 1193. According to al-Latif, Saladin supervised in person the building of walls and digging of trenches around the city, and he "even carried stones on his own shoulders, so that all, rich and poor, strong and weak, followed his example." This corresponds to the film's portrayal of Saladin manning the walls of Ascalon in the face of the crusader attack, after a superfluous bit of bravado in which Mazhar vaults onto a horse, only to ride it to the walls just a few yards in front of him! The scene is supremely ironic, considering that the historical Saladin ordered that the walls of Ascalon be dismantled and the city abandoned shortly after the defeat to Richard at Arsuf. It was in fact Richard who was to refortify Ascalon, only to have its walls dismantled yet again by the terms of the truce. At least this scene gives Chahine one more opportunity to parade his esoteric technique, in the form of another nondiegetic insert: the ocean's waves, which symbolize the crusaders "washing over" Ascalon's defenders.

Chahine is obviously anxious to demonstrate that Egyptian filmmaking can be independent of the West and that his screenplay pays homage to Arabic, rather than Christian, sources. Even so, this does not invalidate the fact that *Saladin* owes its principal plot elements to Hollywood, and ultimately, to Sir Walter Scott. As in *The Crusades*, Saladin in Chahine's film must foil a plot against Richard's life, hatched this time by the king's close advisor, Arthur, who is in league with Prince John. (In history, Richard considered setting aside John as his heir in favor of his nephew, Arthur, duke of Brittany.) The scene showing Arthur and John plotting their treachery is also our first introduction to Richard in the film, and it is a little disconcerting to Western eyes to see one of the most celebrated heroes of medieval Europe looking and speaking like an Arab. (No doubt the same has been said by Arab audiences of Hollywood's portrayals of Saladin.) Just for good measure, Conrad of Montferrat is also exposed in the course of the film to be a traitor. This occurs in a rather innovative scene in which Saladin speaks to Richard of the betrayal across a split screen showing the separate courts of the two kings: an allegory of the written proof from the sultan that Richard flourishes in his hand. Still another party to the treachery is the military order of the Knights Templar, who kill Richard's messenger and make it look as if it was Saladin's doing, because "the Templars would stop at nothing to stop anyone from delaying the Holy War." This could have been inspired by *The Talisman*, where the Grand Master of the

Templars conspires with Conrad to kill Richard. On the other hand, it could equally be inspired by the Arab sources, where the Templars are the implacable military and ideological foes of Islam. According to Imad al-Din, after his victory at Hattin, Saladin ordered that 100 prisoners from the Christian military orders be beheaded. While his sufis (Islamic mystics) lined up to volunteer as executioners (some with gruesome results), the sultan sat on a dais and watched, "his face joyful."

There are several scenes where *Saladin* seems almost a mirror image of its Hollywood counterpart. One occurs midway through the film, when Saladin comes alone to meet with the assembled leaders of the Third Crusade. As in DeMille's *The Crusades*, each of the leaders proudly rattles off his name and shouts his defiant answer of "War!" in response to Saladin's ultimatum to withdraw from Arab territory. (Full credit must be given to Chahine for having the historical sense to leave the dead German emperor, Frederick Barbarossa, out of the assembly.) Meanwhile, Saladin and Richard take the measure of each other, but without the mace- and silk-splitting demonstrations from *The Talisman*. Another scene indebted to Scott and Hollywood is the obligatory portrayal of Saladin as a healer: He arrives incognito into the crusader camp in order to cure the English king of a wound received from his would-be assassins. And just like in *The Crusades*, Saladin and Richard hold a final parley that results in peace.

Chahine also borrows a page from DeMille in blending characters and incidents from the First Crusade in with the Third. During the siege of Acre sequence, the city falls not to the military valor of the crusaders but through the treachery of its Muslim governor, who dumps the city's weapons supply into the sea and opens the gates to the Christian army. This is not how Acre was actually taken: Both Arab and Christian sources agree that the city capitulated only after a long, hard siege in which the Christians gradually whittled away at the city's walls and its Muslim defenders put up a stout resistance. Yet the film's portrayal *is* how Antioch surrendered to the army of the First Crusade on July 3, 1098. One of the commanders of Antioch's 400 towers, an armor maker named Firuz, who apparently was from Armenia (a predominantly Christian region to the north of Syria), was persuaded to betray his defensive section to Bohemond, the Italian Norman who was to go on to become the first crusader prince of the city. Getting back to the film, once inside Acre, the crusaders (one of whom, coincidentally, is "Behmond, prince of Antioch") mercilessly slaughter women and children. As it served in DeMille's film, the elision between the First and Third Crusades allows Chahine to manipulate his audience into feelings of moral outrage and indignation toward the "infidel."

The portrayal of women in the film is deceptive. On the surface, *Saladin* pays women the compliment of giving them major roles and even allows them to don armor and lead armies into battle, which we almost never see in historical epics coming out of Hollywood, except, of course, for those depicting the career of Joan of Arc (Chapter 6). But beneath this faux-liberating veneer, the movie is in fact deeply conservative and chauvinistic in its overall treatment of the fair sex. One of the central female characters, Virginia, is played as a stereotypical "scheming bitch" type. Not only is she the wife and later widow of the archvillain, Reynald, she succeeds in subsequently sleeping with, it is none too subtly implied, nearly all the other bad guys in the film: Philip Augustus, Conrad of Montferrat, Arthur, even the treacherous Muslim governor of Acre. She is like a black-widow spider who, after using her lovers for her nefarious ends, quickly abandons them. She is behind every deception and betrayal of both Saladin and Richard. She will stoop to anything and stop at nothing in her lust for power. Her physical beauty hides a roiling cauldron of corruption and immorality. Perhaps worst of all, Saladin refuses to address her as a lady (equivalent to calling her, in colloquial parlance, a "slut"). Virginia's willingness to fight alongside men, in striking contrast to cinema's respectful treatment of Joan of Arc's role in this regard, is therefore not a cause for celebration or admiration. Instead, the film makes it clear that this is a thing grotesque and unnatural, tolerated by the decadent Christians, but hardly to be countenanced within the religiously righteous army of Saladin.

It is hard to say what figure from history Virginia corresponds to, aside from Stephanie, Reynald's obscure widow. Perhaps it is Isabella, second daughter of King Amalric of Jerusalem (1163–1174), who contested the throne with her half-sister, Sibylla, after the death of their brother, the leper-king, Baldwin IV, in 1185. She was married no less than four times; in 1190, she wedded Conrad of Montferrat after her timid first husband, Humphrey of Tibnine, had been set aside in order that she and her new husband could be proclaimed king and queen of Jerusalem in defiance of the claims of the current monarch, Guy of Lusignan, Sibylla's widower. (Isabella and Conrad were supported by Philip Augustus, Guy by Richard.) In the film, Virginia finally gets her just desserts when a burning siege tower outside the walls of Jerusalem crashes down on top of her. She is left to linger on the battlefield, horribly disfigured, until her lover, Arthur, comes along and strangles her as she confesses their plot to kill Richard. (A similar incident occurs between Conrad and the Grand Master of the Templars in *The Talisman*). Such is the fate meted out by the film to an independent-minded woman who dares to act like a man.

Saladin's antifeminist message is accentuated by the contrast it sets up between Virginia and her "sister-in-arms," Louise de Lusignan. (Note that she bears the same surname as Isabella's rival, Guy.) Like Virginia, Louise is a symbol of a degenerate religion and culture that would allow a woman to parade like a man. But in the course of the film, Louise transforms herself into the Arab model of a good woman, but only by setting aside her manly, military lifestyle. When she is first introduced to her future lover, Isa, at a prayer tent set aside for Christian prisoners at Hattin, Louise is a "knight of the Hospitallers," which was theoretically possible, as the Knights of the Hospital of St. John did admit women, but only as "nursing sisters," never as front-line soldiers. Louise also sheds her first tears, which establish her feminine sensibilities, as opposed to the hard and cruel demeanor of Virginia. When next we see her, this time in a dress, Louise has been handed over by Saladin into Isa's custody. He asks her to marry him, but she refuses, saying that she'd rather kill herself than be united to an Arab. Isa generously grants her liberty rather than force the issue, and Louise subsequently decides to "put down my weapons" and assume a more acceptable role as nursemaid. It is while she is nursing Isa, who has been wounded on his swimming mission to Acre, that she discovers that she loves him. When they go off together at the end of the movie, it is understood that Louise will settle down to a proper, conventional life as Isa's faithful and obedient wife.

Saladin's misogyny does have a medieval precedent. Imad al-Din, the sultan's biographer, is probably the inspiration for the film's plot device of Christian female crusaders, for he records that at the siege of Acre: "Among the Franks there were indeed women who rode into battle with cuirasses and helmets, dressed in men's clothes; who rode out into the thick of the fray and acted like brave men although they were but tender women, maintaining that all this was an act of piety, thinking to gain heavenly rewards by it, and making it their way of life." That transvestitism was married to sexual licentiousness in Imad al-Din's mind is indicated by the fact that in this same passage, he announces the arrival of the crusaders' camp followers, "three hundred lovely Frankish women, full of youth and beauty, assembled from beyond the sea and offering themselves for sin," who "glowed with ardor for carnal intercourse." Imad al-Din was clearly not alone among the Arabs in being both fascinated and repelled by the loose reputation of Western women, for he confesses that the whole Arab army was "at a loss to know how such women could perform acts of piety by abandoning all decency and shame [in acting as consorts to the crusaders]." Nonetheless, the seductively alluring presence of Christian women posed a grave threat to Muslim morale, according to Imad al-Din, who laments that "a few foolish Mamluks and ignorant wretches slipped away, under the fierce goad of lust, and followed the people of error."

Inevitably, Imad al-Din give free rein here to his elaborate rhetorical flourishes, indulging in an orgy of sexual innuendo:

They [the Christian women] dedicated as a holy offering what they kept between their thighs. . . . They plied a brisk trade in dissoluteness, adorned the patched-up fissures, poured themselves into the springs of libertinage, shut themselves up in private under the amorous transports of men, offered their wares for enjoyment, invited the shameless into their embrace, mounted breasts on backs, bestowed their wares on the poor, brought their silver anklets up to touch their golden earrings, and were willingly spread out on the carpet of amorous sport. . . . They were the places where tent-pegs are driven in, they invited swords to enter their sheaths, they razed their terrain for planting, they made javelins rise toward shields, excited the plough to plough, gave the birds a place to peck with their beaks, allowed heads to enter their ante-chambers and raced under whoever bestrode them at the spur's blow.

Incredible as it may seem, the author goes on in this vein for many more lines, piling on one pornographic double entendre after another. It is a sad commentary on the state of modern Islam that so little had changed in Muslim attitudes toward women from 1190 to 1963.

But by far the most astonishing invention of *Saladin* is that it allows Richard to visit Jerusalem, twice! The first time, Richard is invited to Jerusalem for Christmas by Saladin, but he is shot by an assassin's poisoned arrow just as he is about to enter the city gates. The second time, when he actually makes it into the city, is to celebrate the final truce agreed upon by the two sides. Such a scenario goes against both history and Hollywood with regard to the Third Crusade. Yet it is essential to the film's emphasis upon the notion that Jerusalem under Arab rule is a city open to both Christian and Muslim alike. Already, after his victory at Hattin, Saladin declares that "pilgrimage to Jerusalem is authorized to all Christians" (which in fact only occurred in 1192). When Isa tries to persuade Louise to stay in an Arab-conquered Jerusalem and be his wife, he tells her: "Jerusalem has always been an Arab land. We shall prove that we can rule it in peace and with respect." (Here the swimmer Isa is conflated with another Isa, Saladin's governor of Jerusalem, also mentioned by Baha al-Din.) After the battle of Arsuf, Saladin personally attends a wounded peasant crusader from Normandy and, when told of the peasant's desire to visit Jerusalem before going back home, reassures him, "You will soon." When making their truce, Saladin tells Richard: "You'll leave this country, but you'll always be welcome back as pilgrims to the holy places." At their final leave taking, Saladin once again assures Richard, "We hope to see you again in Jerusalem," a rather disingenuous statement in light of the excessive trouble the Lionheart had caused to the sultan's dominions.

Like *The Crusades*, *Saladin* promotes peace wherever it can, even while it dishes out crowd-pleasing scenes of gore. In particular, it is at pains to portray the Arabs as a peace-loving people who fight only when attacked by the aggressively warlike Christians of the West. This seems an almost word-for-word illustration of Muhammad's exhortation from the second *sura*, or chapter, from the Koran: "Fight for the cause of God against those who fight against you; but commit not the injustice of attacking them first." For example, in the film, Saladin fights at Hattin only when provoked by the atrocities of Reynald, and he fights Richard only when the English king invades Palestine at the duplicitous urging of Virginia, who has fed him a concocted story that "Christian children are dying of thirst, pilgrims to Jerusalem taken prisoners, places of worship are being destroyed . . . " The message is hammered home as well in the love-story subplot of Isa and Louise. When they first meet, Louise is perplexed to meet a Christian in Arab armor and asks Isa why he fights his "brothers in Christianity." Isa responds, "Those who use the cross as an excuse to invade my land are not brothers." Again, when Isa tries to persuade Louise to stay in Jerusalem, he tells her: "I'm a better Christian than you. I believe that taking what is not mine is an unforgivable sin."

Saladin, of course, is the ultimate mouthpiece of this Arabs-under-assault theme. At his meeting with all the crusade leaders, he conducts the following exchange:

> Philip Augustus: If you want peace, here are our terms . . .
> Saladin: Since when do aggressors impose conditions on the
>   legitimate owners? You started this war; if you want peace
>   truly, leave my country.
> Conrad of Montferrat: Is this a declaration of war?
> Saladin: I hate war. Islam and Christianity condemn bloodshed.
>   Yet we shall fight if necessary to save our land.

A short while later, Saladin indignantly defends himself against Richard's charge that he "persecutes Christians and defiles Christ's grave." While he defiantly tells his adversary that "Jerusalem belongs to the Arabs," in the next breath Saladin points out that "the holy shrines are open to those of all religions." A nice play on words concludes the parley, when Richard tells Saladin that, "My Christian conscience would never rest while the city of olive groves is in Arab hands," to which Saladin replies, "Yet you burn the olive branches with your own hands."

Eventually Richard begins to comprehend the horrors of war as he views the dead on the battlefield of Arsuf, a scene that was perhaps inspired by another rhetorical flight of fancy from Imad al-Din, who enumerates in grisly detail all the mangled body parts left over from the slaughter at Hattin. Yet even after being healed by Saladin, Richard is determined to conquer Jerusalem:

Richard: You're afraid to see me enter Jerusalem.
Saladin: You shall visit it soon.
Richard: Soon I shall be king of Jerusalem.
Saladin: Why you specifically?
Richard: Jerusalem is the birthplace of Christ.
Saladin: Christianity is respected here; you know that. Jerusalem belongs to the Arabs. Stop this bloodshed. That would satisfy God and Christ.

The English king finally comes round only after his failed assault on Jerusalem and upon learning from Louise of Arthur's betrayal. Meanwhile, Saladin, at the urging of his generals, prepares to lead a night-time counterattack so that, "We'll teach them once and for all never to invade our land again." He quickly relents, however, and lays aside his sword when, upon hearing the tolling of Christian bells, he remembers what day it is and leads his men in wishing Isa a "Merry Christmas." There then follows one of the most touching scenes of the film, in which a muezzin's call to prayer gradually gives way to the crescendoing strain of the Latin hymn, *Adeste, fideles* ("Come all ye faithful"). When Richard comes to Saladin's tent to beg for terms, he tells him that, "this war has stopped making sense. . . . On my way here I saw thousands of corpses littering the trail. I could not tell the corpses of the crusaders from those of the Arabs—all are alike." Saladin thanks his rival "for being the Richard I've always imagined" and imposes no conditions on their peace, except that, "We only pledge not to fight any longer." All this is manifestly unhistorical, since according to contemporary sources, Saladin and Richard had been haggling over terms for nearly a year before signing their truce.

Saladin clearly distorts history in order to push an agenda, one that insistently portrays Arabs as peaceful victims of Western aggression and at the same time as capable custodians of the Holy City worthy of the West's trust. Why? Perhaps the film casts an eye toward the future of an independent Palestinian state, with Jerusalem as its capital. But there is a more immediate political context that relates to both the Egyptian origins of the film and the timing of its release in 1963. This was the Suez Crisis of 1956, which pitted Egypt and its dashing young president, Gamal Abdul Nasser, against the combined powers of Britain, France, and Israel. In the film, these three adversaries are symbolized by the colors of the troops arrayed to confront Saladin at the parley: red for Britain, blue for France, and white for Israel. The Suez Crisis was a turning point that made Egypt and Nasser the undisputed champions of Arab nationalism and pan-Arab unity in the face of what was regarded as a century of Western colonialism and imperialism in the region.

Immediate causes of the crisis included an arms deal concluded between Nasser and the Soviet Union, through Czechoslovakia, in 1955, and Nasser's decision to nationalize the Suez Canal, a vital waterway linking the Mediterranean to the Red Sea, in July 1956. Nationalization of the canal became an important symbol of Arab "dignity," of a new willingness to stand up to and defy the West, while the Czech arms deal underlined Egypt's independence by demonstrating that she could realign herself toward a new power bloc (a factor that is reflected in Chahine's montage style that pays homage to the great Soviet director, Eisenstein). In strictly military terms, the Suez Crisis was a complete humiliation for Egypt that was most unlike what we see in the film. In just nine days, from October 29 to November 6, 1956, Israeli forces captured the Sinai Peninsula east of the canal zone, while British and French paratroopers occupied the canal itself. But diplomatically, the result was a complete victory for Nasser: By January 1957, international pressure had forced all three aggressors to disgorge their gains and their troop presence to be replaced by a United Nations Emergency Force (UNEF). In the long term, the crisis led to the terminal decline of British and French influence and presence in the Middle East, and to Nasser's rise as a pan-Arab leader. In February 1958, Egypt and Syria were united under Nasser as head of the United Arab Republic, an event that must have struck echoes of a similar achievement by Saladin, who had made himself master of both Syria and Egypt by 1183.

The analogy was not lost on Nasser: In his speeches he often referred to Saladin as an Arab leader who enabled Egypt and Syria to resist their medieval imperialists, the crusaders, which provided a clear precedent for his own role in a similar capacity. Arab nationalism was a key ingredient of "Nasserism," and we see it reflected again and again in *Saladin*. Perhaps the most blatant reference comes at the beginning of the film, when Saladin, having been informed by one of his commanders, Hossam Eddin, that "the Arabs await you," exclaims: "I can't ignore their call. My dream is to see the Arab nation united under one flag." In the medieval context, Arab nationalism is no less anachronistic than the idea that Richard, a king whose first language was French and who spent most of his reign in his French territories, was leader of an English nation. For his contemporaries, Saladin was above all an Islamic leader, not an Arab one. (Ethnically speaking, Saladin was not an Arab at all, but a Kurd, from what is modern-day northern Iraq.) Equally anachronistic is another component of Nasserism that creeps into the film: Arab socialism. As expressed in Nasser's National Charter of 1962, socialism was to provide for a more equitable and just society, both economically and politically, in Egypt. In the film, Saladin expresses similar sentiments to his brother, al-'Adil, when persuading him to reject the treacherous overtures of Conrad of Montferrat: "We don't fight over a patch of land, but for the triumph of moral and spiritual values." Those values are implied to be of Arabic, rather than Islamic, origin.

Religion indeed plays a small role in the anti-imperialist message of *Saladin*, as it also did in Nasserism. This is in great contrast to current Arab hostility toward the West, which is heavily tied up with Islamic fundamentalism. Nasserism was predominantly a secular ideology that displayed none of the aversion to modernization and technological innovation that we now find in much of the Muslim world. Quite the contrary, modern technology was crucial to Nasser's dream of an independent Egypt, which can be seen in his efforts to obtain Western funding for the Aswan High Dam; failure to obtain this funding led to the nationalization of the canal in order to divert its fees to Egypt's development. Therefore, Egypt's relationship to the West under Nasser was a strangely dualistic one: on the one hand, keeping Europe at arm's length, on the other, playing to a Western audience the reassuring message that the values of its "revolution" were not so different from our own. (Nasserism was actually prefigured by the modernizing efforts of Muhammad Ali in the nineteenth century, under whose successors the Suez Canal was originally built.) During the Suez Crisis, for example, Nasser made it a priority to show that an Egyptian-owned canal respected "freedom of navigation and shipping" and that it could be run just as efficiently and openly as a British-controlled one.

For the film, Jerusalem is Saladin's "canal," his opportunity to prove to the West that as an Arab city, it is just as open and tolerant, indeed more so, than under crusader imperialism. As ever, Isa is a covert spokesman here: He not only lectures Louise on Arabs' right and ability to rule Jerusalem, he educates her on the West's mishandling of the Holy City. Having turned the "holy places into markets," the crusaders, Isa explains, force people to "pay for your blessings," while "the money goes into Europe's coffers" and "anyone who poses a threat to these profits faces fire, water, and death." These same words could very well have been said by Nasser regarding fees formerly paid to the Suez Canal Company. But for Saladin's contemporary biographers, the reconquest of Jerusalem was above all a victory for Islam; any concessions to Western sensibilities were a secondary consideration at best.

Saladin's much-vaunted chivalry also played into the hands of Nasserite propaganda. Egypt's image as a victim of unprovoked aggression was essential to Nasser's triumph in the Suez Crisis and to winning crucial

U.S. support against its erstwhile allies of Britain, France, and Israel. When, in the film, Saladin wishes to justify his rejection of Conrad's treason, he explains to his brother that "the Arabs see that a defeat with honor is better than a dishonorable victory." Although it is hard to imagine any Western audiences seeing this movie in 1963, there is no question that at least some of its dialogue is geared toward foreign observers. For example, when Richard and Saladin conclude their truce, the sultan instructs his Western counterpart: "When you return to your country, tell the peasants and the aged . . . tell the simple people of England and tell all those in Europe that war is not always the solution." Such a harangue is hardly credible in a medieval context; but it echoes what Nasser was telling the world in 1955, when he wrote in an article in *Foreign Affairs*: "War has no place in the constructive policy which we have designed to improve the lot of our people."

The biggest difference between the historical Saladin and the Nasserized version of him as depicted in the film is the role of jihad in the hero's career. According to Saladin's contemporary Muslim biographers, this Islamic concept was of paramount importance to the sultan's motives and drive to reconquer Jerusalem and expel the crusaders. By contrast, both Nasser and the film downplayed religion's role in their ideology, perhaps because of its inflammatory potential. The only lip service the film pays to religion comes at the very end, when Saladin utters a prayer to the heavens giving thanks for having "vanquished the enemy." At the same time, Nasser's secularism allowed him to be, like the historical Saladin, the "acceptable" Muslim in Western eyes: the enemy to whom it was "OK" to lose. Unfortunately, this is no longer possible in the radicalized state of Middle Eastern politics today. The decline of Nasserism was already apparent during its namesake's lifetime; just four years after the film's release, Egypt was to be humiliated a second, and more enduring, time by Israel in the Six-Day War.

This does not mean that the historical figure of Saladin is no longer attractive to some of the Arab world's current religious and political leaders. If anything, Islamic fundamentalism has made Saladin's jihad appear even more relevant today. During the 1980s, when he was fighting a bitter war with Iran, Saddam Hussein commissioned a mural painting that paired a turbaned Saladin on the left with the Iraqi leader (wearing shades) on the right, and medieval warriors on horseback with modern tanks and guns. (The comparison is now supremely ironic, considering that Hussein since then has carried out a genocidal campaign against the Kurds.) A large and elaborate statue of Saladin was erected in 1992 in Damascus, the capital of Syria, in perhaps a flattering comparison to the many statues of President Hafez Asad. And Islamic terrorist groups—such as Hezbollah, Hamas, Islamic Jihad, and Osama bin Laden's al-Qaida network (also known as The World Islamic Front for Crusade against Jews and Crusaders)—all compare their activities to a crusade.

But, as in the West, there are two Saladins for the modern Middle East. One is the *mujahid* who will stop at nothing to rid the Arab world of the hated Western presence. The other is the Muslim leader who, while the enemy of foreign aggression and interference, is content to live at peace with the West and abide by a common sense of humanity, decency, and civilized conduct. Which Saladin will today's Muslim leaders, in the Middle East and around the world, wish to emulate? The answer remains far from clear.

Our next film, *Alexander Nevsky* (1938), directed by Sergei Eisenstein, provides yet another countercrusade perspective, one whose point of view is clearly on the side of the putative victims of Western aggression. With the possible exception of *The Black Knight* (Chapter 1), *Alexander Nevsky* is the most blatantly politicized film ever set in the Middle Ages. Consequently, it has almost nothing to say about the historical Nevsky, whose memory, in any case, is largely mined from an hagiographical legend composed long after his lifetime. Indeed, it was the paucity of information available on the real prince of Novgorod that attracted Eisenstein to his story. When his colleague, Mikhail Romm, point out to him that "Alexander Nevsky is largely a mystery," the famous director replied:

> And that is exactly why it appeals to me. Nobody knows much about him, and so nobody can possibly find fault with me. Whatever I do, the historians and the so-called "consultants" won't be able to argue with me. They all know as well as you and I do the evidence is slim. So I'm in the strongest possible position because everything I do must be right.

But in actual fact, the screenplay for *Alexander Nevsky* (under its original title of *Rus'*) was vetted by a panel of experts, which included some historians, when it was first published in the journal *Znamia* in 1937. Although many of the experts' comments concerned historical accuracy, the main purpose of the vetting process seems to have been to assure Eisenstein's political conformity, which was a sensitive issue at the time. Historians pointed out that archeological excavations proved that medieval Novgorod was dominated by an agricultural economy, not a mercantile one as implied in the screenplay, and that the Teutonic Knights would have preferred to convert their captives rather than simply kill them. To this we can add that the historical Nevsky was a far cry from the people's champion who single-handedly saved Russia at the head of a peasant army. Instead, Novgorod hired princes like Nevsky to defend them with their armies of private retainers, and a much graver threat to Russia's independence than German aggression proved to be Nevsky's obeisance to the Mongols. Although the original screenplay did include a coda that had Nevsky make a fatal visit to the Golden Horde, historians objected that the Mongols would hardly poison their collaborator, even one who, in this account, was acting in Russia's best interests.

In any case, Eisenstein was not at all interested in what he called the "museum approach," or recreating an authentic image of the Middle Ages. Instead, he wanted to make a "contemporary picture" whose historical themes, although set in the distant medieval past, would resonate with modern audiences experiencing their own momentous events. As he stated explicitly in an essay written shortly after the film's release:

> The theme of patriotism and natural defense against the aggressor is the subject that suffuses our film. We have taken a historical episode from the thirteenth century, when the ancestors of today's Fascists, the Teutonic and Livonian knights, waged a systematic struggle to conquer and invade the East in order to subjugate the Slav and other nationalities in precisely the same spirit that Fascist Germany is trying to do today, with the same frenzied slogans and the same fanaticism.

To understand *Alexander Nevsky*, therefore, one must comprehend the political and artistic context of Eisenstein's career in the former Soviet Union.

Like so many Communist agitators of the early twentieth century, Eisenstein came from a prosperous middle class background. The Bolshevik Revolution in Russia of October/November 1917 gave Eisenstein the opportunity to rebel against his bourgeois upbringing and become an artist, in defiance of his father's plans for him to pursue an engineering career. While his father, Mikhail Osipovich, fought for the whites, Sergei Mikhailovich sided with the Red Army during the ensuing Civil War. Right from the start, Eisenstein was assigned the task of disseminating party propaganda to the masses. It was in the course of his early work in the theater that Eisenstein developed his famous theoretical model of the "montage of attractions" that he was to carry over into cinema. Montage, from the French word for "assembly," basically refers to the editing process whereby a series of "attractions" are assembled together; "attraction" was defined by Eisenstein as "any element of it [i.e., a theatrical production or film] that subjects the audience to emotional or psychological influence, verified by experience and mathematically calculated to produce specific emotional shocks in the spectator." In other words, montage provokes in the audience the desired response through the juxtaposition of images, often violent, that generate feelings of tension and friction. This was an aggressive, antagonistic approach designed to assault the viewers' sensory and nervous system: Eisenstein was famously quoted as saying, "It is not a Cine-Eye that we need but a Cine-Fist." At its most extreme, the method could be very violent indeed, as when Eisenstein set off firecrackers underneath the seats of his audience during the theatrical production of *The Wisemen* in 1923. Montage was modeled after the dialectical materialism of Karl Marx, who presupposed class conflict as a theme occurring throughout history, and the violence of the montage method mirrored the violent language of Lenin's manifestos. Another famous theory Eisenstein developed at this time was "typage," in which the actor adopts stereotypical poses and delivers exaggerated gestures, again in order to provoke the desired response from the spectator.

Eisenstein's ideas were part of a broader movement in the emerging Soviet cinema known as Formalism or Constructivism, which advocated an abstract, theoretical approach to filmmaking. In contrast to the "decadent" movies of the West, whose only aim was to entertain, Soviet films were thought to serve a higher, nobler purpose: to reeducate the masses and capture their hearts and minds for the cause of Bolshevism. Eisenstein himself made no secret of the fact that his films were almost wholly political in character. In a 1924 essay on montage, he argued: "A film cannot be a simple presentation or demonstration of events: rather it must be a tendentious selection of, and comparison between, events, free from narrowly plot-related plans and molding the audience in accordance with its purpose." He was even more explicit in 1930, when he wrote: "With us 'art' is not a mere word. We look upon it as only one of many instruments used in the battle fronts of the class struggle and the struggle for socialist construction."

The new Soviet state was not slow to exploit the propagandistic possibilities of the new medium. Films, especially the early silent ones, offered distinct advantages over any other entertainment form. They could be readily understood by all, in an empire whose inhabitants spoke over 100 different languages; they associated the new regime with technology and progress; and they could be easily controlled, since few could afford the expensive equipment required to make and show movies. In 1919, Lenin — who declared that, "Of all the arts, for us cinema is the most important" — nationalized the Soviet movie industry and placed it under the supervision of the People's Commissariat for Enlightenment. By 1922, movies could only be distributed through a state organization, Goskino, renamed two years later as Sovkino. By 1925, the state secret police, the People's Commissariat for Internal Affairs (NKVD), was monitoring the medium through a front organization called the Society of Friends of the Soviet Cinema, headed by the former NKVD director, Felix Dzerzhinsky. Its purpose was to control audiences' viewing of films in order to encourage "the cultural development of the masses of workers and peasants." That Soviet cinema equaled Soviet propaganda was made absolutely clear by the Central Committee of the Communist Party at its conference in March 1928. It was resolved that:

> Cinema, "the most important of all the arts," can and must occupy an important place in the process of cultural revolution as a medium for broad educational work and Communist propaganda, the organization and education of the masses around the slogans and tasks of the Party and their artistic education, wholesome rest and entertainment.
>
> Cinema, like every art, cannot be apolitical. Cinema must be an instrument of the proletariat in its struggle for hegemony, leadership and influence in relation to other classes and "in the hands of the Party it must be the most powerful medium of Communist enlightenment and agitation." [quotations from Lenin]

The silent films made in Russia during the 1920s tended to portray recent events in the Communist Revolution and, in line with Marxist ideology, depicted the clash of world forces between the proletariat and the bourgeoisie. Individual personalities were subordinated to mass movements and events, and stock characters were employed symbolizing "workers" and "oppressors." Eisenstein's most famous films from this period include *Battleship Potemkin* (1926), portraying the abortive 1905 revolution at Odessa, and *October* (1928), meant to commemorate the tenth anniversary of the Bolshevik Revolution. His commitment to a "pure," intellectual cinema, and to Marxist ideology, is demonstrated by the fact that he contemplated making a film, *Capital*, that would contain no plot but would be a cinematic illustration of Marx's last, uncompleted work of the same title. Stalin squashed the idea in 1929.

For the next four years, Eisenstein traveled abroad, ostensibly in order to learn about the new movie technology of sound. In the United States, he met with Hollywood stars such as Mary Pickford, Douglas Fairbanks Sr., and Charlie Chaplin, and with fellow directors D.W. Griffith and Josef von Sternberg. Although he signed a contract with Paramount Studios, none of his proposed projects were considered commercially or financially viable. He was commissioned by the writer, Upton Sinclair, to shoot a film in Mexico, but the end result was suppressed on orders from Stalin.

When Eisenstein returned home in 1932, he came back to a changed Soviet Union. Stalin, having ousted his rival, Leon Trotsky, was in firm control of the Communist Party and the entire Soviet state. The consequences were catastrophic for all categories of the country's citizenry. While Eisenstein had been abroad, the state had embarked on its first Five-

Year Plan for the collectivization of agriculture and the rapid industrialization of the economy. Those who resisted this "modernization" program, derisively labeled by Stalin as "kulaks," were summarily shot or deported to prison labor camps, known as gulags; all told, up to 6.5 million people died as a result of Stalin's "dekulakization." It is estimated that 7 million more died in 1932–1933, mostly in the Ukraine, as a result of forced grain confiscations. The historian Robert Conquest has called this tragedy "perhaps the only case in history of a purely man-made famine." What is more, beginning in 1936, Stalin conducted a purge of his perceived enemies and "saboteurs" in the party and the army, as well as politically suspect historians, scientists, writers, actors, and other members of the academy and cultural establishment. By 1938, the total number of casualties of the "Great Terror" included perhaps 1 million executed outright and as many as 7 to 8 million in the gulags. In the words of the Marxist scholar, Leszek Kolakowski, the dictator had successfully carried out, and would continue to do so until his death in 1953, "probably the most massive warlike operation ever conducted by a state against its own citizens."

Eisenstein and his circle were not immune from the Terror. In 1930, a new cinema agency was created, Soiuzkino, that was to exercise far greater control than hitherto over the Soviet film industry. Soiuzkino was headed by Boris Shumiatsky, an ideological foe of Eisenstein who introduced more party members into the studios in order to monitor the production as well as distribution processes. By 1934, a new theoretical model for Soviet filmmaking had been officially adopted—Socialist Realism—to which all artists were compelled to adhere. Although vaguely expressed by party officials, Socialist Realism was virtually the complete opposite of Formalism: It espoused simple plot lines, straightforward storytelling, and the reclamation of Russia's pre-revolutionary history under its autocratic tsars—a subject that the first Soviet filmmakers had disdained—which now became a stand-in for the new Stalin personality cult. In place of the egalitarianism, internationalism, and collective spirit of the 1920s films were elitism, an inward-looking patriotism—emblematic of Stalin's new policy of "socialism in one country"—and the "great man" principle. As Shumiatsky explained, the films of the 1930s were to be the new opium of the masses: "The victorious class wants to laugh with joy. That is its right and Soviet cinema must provide its audiences with this joyful laughter." In the midst of all the slaughter of these years, one can imagine that few people were laughing.

In 1935, Eisenstein, the lightning rod of the now unfashionable intellectual cinema, was publicly humiliated at a conference of his fellow filmmakers, which was held to commemorate the fifteenth anniversary of Lenin's nationalization of Soviet studios. He received the lowest honor, the

Award of Honored Art Worker, and was menacingly told by one colleague, "Sergei Mikhailovich, if you fail to make a film within twelve months at the latest, I beg you never to make one at all. We will have no need of it, and neither will you." Eisenstein did shortly embark on a new film, *Bezhin Meadow*, but it was abruptly canceled by Shumiatsky in March 1937. Quite possibly under fear of arrest and execution, Eisenstein denounced his own film and repudiated his entire oeuvre in an official confession of his "mistakes" written later that year. Toward the end of his retraction, he clearly signals his new conversion to the party line of Socialist Realism: "There is only one possible subject for my next work: spiritually heroic, following the Party's ideology, treating of war and defense, and popular in style. . . . In preparation for the making of this film, I see the path through which I shall obliterate the last traces of elemental anarchy from my world view and my creative method." The consequences for Eisenstein if he had not performed this humiliating act of self-abasement were demonstrated by the fates of his more defiant colleagues. Vsevolod Meyerhold, Eisenstein's revered mentor and substitute father figure from his theater days, was arrested in June 1939 and subsequently tortured before being shot in February 1940. Ironically, it was the arrest and execution in 1938 of Eisenstein's enemy, Shumiatsky, on trumped-up charges of introducing "savage veteran spies and saboteurs" into the Moscow studios that cleared the path for the making of Eisenstein's next film, *Alexander Nevsky*.

Nevsky amply exudes the principles of Socialist Realism and, above all, the personality cult of Stalin. The opening scene of the film shows the hero standing up to the Mongol hordes—clearly meant to represent the Soviet Union's eastern enemy, Japan—while his fellow Russians all bow to the conquerors. Nevsky strikes a defiant pose and his voice "reverberates like a manifesto" (stage direction from screenplay) when he refuses point blank the Mongol offer to join the Golden Horde: "We have a saying—'Better to die in your own land than to leave it.'" (The historical Nevsky was to do the exact opposite.) After the Mongols leave, Nevsky tells his comrades, "The Mongols can wait, methinks. We face more dangerous foes. Closer at hand are they and fiercer, and will not be paid off . . . The Germans!" The scene ends with Nevsky wading into the waters of Lake Pleshcheyev in order to fetch his fishing nets. This last image seals the identification of Nevsky with Christ; by this means, Eisenstein was able to eliminate Christianity from the film, which would have been problematical to Stalin's censors. But since Nevsky had been canonized in 1547 under another ideological ancestor of Stalin's leadership cult, Tsar Ivan the Terrible (who was to be the subject of Eisenstein's next film), the director could not ignore Nevsky's "saintliness" altogether. His solution was to redefine "saint" as a purely secular icon: draining the concept of its reli-

The climax of the Battle on the Ice from *Alexander Nevsky*, in which the title character challenges the Grand Master of the Teutonic Knights to single combat, as their respective armies look on. Sergei Eisenstein filmed the scene in summer 1938 on a backlot at Mosfilm Studios in Moscow, with sodium silicate standing in for ice.

gious meaning "which the clerics have exploited for ages" and presenting it in terms of "the commanding personality of Alexander Nevsky."

Nevsky, therefore, is portrayed as a monumental, paternal, flawless figure in an exact parallel of Stalin's own apotheosis. Like Saladin in Chahine's film, Nevsky is not allowed to have any romantic ties or to crack any jokes (although an early version of the script did have him married with children). He is too formidable for that. At the same time, however, Stalinist propaganda dictated that Russia's leader be shown to be a "man of the people." He will not fight unless asked to do so, but when he does take up the sword, it is for the manly strategy of attack, not defense. An unmistakable message is driven home—that only a single, dictatorial leader can unite the people in their dire hour of need. When, for example, the citizens of Novgorod clamor for a rival, Domash Tverdislavich (a character lifted from the chronicles), to lead them, he meekly makes way for the greater man, "one whose arm is stronger and whose mind is clearer. One who is feared in this land and far beyond it. There is only one such—Prince

Alexander." The rallying cry of "Summon Alexander!" is dutifully taken up by the younger, more virile men of the city. Domash then becomes one of the emissaries from Novgorod who arrive at Nevsky's hall at Pereyaslavl to beg him to lead a peasant army against the Germans. When they urge him to "Stand for Novgorod," Nevsky, the soul of nationalism, replies, "I will stand up for Rus." Later, Nevsky arrives at his capital to confront the nation's enemies and traitors—the merchants and churchmen who seek to appease the Teutons and sell the Russians into slavery. The merchants are finally brought to heel when they are threatened by Mikula: "Better go willingly you moneyed men, else will the peasants crush your bones for you." This is a chilling line in view of what had been happening to the "kulaks" only a few years before the film's release. Novgorod's citizens then engage in a thinly disguised medieval version of the Five-Year Plan. Spearmakers set themselves a quota of 1,000 spears; shieldmakers, 500 shields; and smiths, 500 axes. The armorer Ignat heroically sacrifices himself by giving away all his arms and armor until he is left with only a short mail shirt that will result in his death on the battlefield. This paralleled real-life heroes of Stalin's industrialization, such as Alexei Stakhanov, the coal miner who spectacularly exceeded his production quotas during the 1930s and lent his name to a new Russian superlative, Stakhanovite.

The film ends with an iconic set-piece of Nevsky as the stern, paternalistic leader of his people. He rides triumphantly into a liberated Pskov on his gleaming white charger with children in his arms, followed by his victorious army and the vanquished enemy. (Stalin is also frequently shown cradling children in his propaganda films.) In the midst of the celebrations, Nevsky commands silence and addresses the crowd from the steps of Pskov Cathedral:

> All noise and shouting and no thought for affairs of state. Had we lost the battle on the ice, never would Rus have forgiven us! That must you remember and pass on to your children. If you forget it—you will be as Judases all, traitors to the Russian land. If trouble comes—all of Rus will I call to arms. If aside you stand, punished will you be. While I live, I shall myself punish you. When I die, my sons will.

Although the last line is delivered with a smile, the words were chillingly realized by Stalin during the dekulakization, Great Famine, and the Great Terror. Eisenstein leaves us in no doubt that Nevsky is meant to double for Stalin. In an essay he wrote for *Izvestiya* in July 1938 just as he was filming the famous Battle on the Ice, he concludes:

> For if the might of our national soul was able to punish the enemy in this way, when the country lay exhausted in the grip of the Tartar [Mongol]

yoke, then nothing will be strong enough to destroy this country which has broken the last chains of its oppression; a country which has become a socialist motherland; a country which is being led to unprecedented victories by the greatest strategist in world history—Stalin.

The last scene of the film is of Nevsky staring grimly from the screen and delivering the famous lines: "Go and tell all in alien lands that Rus lives. Let all come and be our guests. But he who comes to us sword in hand, by the sword shall perish. On that our Russian land will forever take its stand!"

As in *The Black Knight*, there are two kinds of enemies faced by the protagonists of *Alexander Nevsky*: the traitor from within and the unprincipled foe from without. Tverdilo Ivanovich, the mayor of Pskov who betrays the city to the Teutonic knights, and the craven Orthodox monk, Ananias, represent treasonous forces inside Russia. In real life, Anania Feofilaktovich, the *posadnik* or mayor of Novgorod, died a martyr to the cause of popular and principled opposition to Nevsky's pro-Mongol appeasement. But in the film, the traitors' fates, especially that of Tverdilo, are symbolic of the show trials that Stalin staged against accused "Troskyite" agents and so-called German spies and saboteurs. The "confessions" of the most prominent victims put on display in 1936 and 1938—Bukharin, Kamenev, and Zinoviev—were extracted by torture methods that became the basis for George Orwell's nightmarish world of *1984*. When Nevsky at the conclusion of the film commands the people of Pskov to decide a suitable punishment for Tverdilo—who cowers in a jingling horse harness as the film cuts to a haloed image of the slain Ignat, whom Tverdilo had literally stabbed in the back—the crowd obligingly slaughters the traitor. In similar fashion, executions of countless victims of the Great Terror were justified by choreographed street demonstrations demanding the heads of the accused.

Nevsky's fearsome foreign foe, the Teutonic knights, are, of course, fronts for the Nazis. They are portrayed as the inhuman, faceless enemy behind riveted bucket-helms of the commanders and the stormtrooper-like helmets of the foot soldiers. (The latter inspired Darth Vader's costume in George Lucas' *Star Wars* films.) Their disciplined charge at the Battle on the Ice is designed to evoke the Panzer tank divisions of the Wehrmacht. Nowhere is this connection made more explicit than in the famous "Rape of Pskov" scene. The heraldic emblem of an upraised hand atop the helm of one of the knights, Sir Dietlieb, evokes the Nazi "Heil" salute, while the gloves worn by the presiding Roman Catholic bishop are adorned with swastikas (which also grace the miter he later wears into battle). That the Teutons are a cold and merciless conqueror is shown all too clearly when an "iron wall of knights," as instructed by the screenplay, "mows down the unarmed population" at a "motion of the hand" from the Grand Master. Meanwhile, the foot soldiers "snatch the children from the women's arms and fling them onto the fires" just after they are blessed by a black-robed priest. In a reversal of traditional color symbolism, white—the color of the robes of the Order—take on a sinister meaning. (Remember that the "Whites" opposed the Red Army during the Civil War.) The scene climaxes to an emotional pitch when Vasilia's father, Pavsha, is strung up above an angel carved on the cathedral turret as he cries out with his dying breath, "Dead Pskov calls to you, [Alexander] Yaroslavich!"

We know from articles Eisenstein wrote to accompany the film that he intended the "Rape of Pskov" scene to evoke modern atrocities—no less than medieval ones—being committed by the Germans. The terror bombing of Guernica in Spain by Nazi-backed Nationalist forces in April 1937, Hitler's occupation of the Sudetenland in Czechoslovakia in September 1938, and the *Kristallnacht* pogrom against German Jews two months later, all add—in the director's mind—to the contemporary relevance of audience indignation aroused by the disturbing images on the screen. As Eisenstein explained in an essay translated for English readers of *International Literature* in 1939: "When you read the chronicles of the thirteenth century alternately with current newspapers, you lose your sense of the difference in time, because the bloody terror which the conquering Orders of Knighthood sowed is scarcely distinguishable from what is now being perpetrated in Europe." At the same time, communism can be portrayed as "leading the front line against this bloody nightmare, standing for recovery, for the creation of a barrier against it, for the mobilization of resources for the struggle. . . . The struggle for the human ideal of justice, freedom, and national identity." Moreover, the film takes on "not just those themes joined in blood with the struggle waged by the Soviet Union in defense of its integrity and inviolability against constant acts of aggression, but also broader themes, going beyond the frontiers of our country." Mussolini's Italy, for example, also comes in for *Nevsky's* polemical attacks. The Catholic bishop urges on the Teutonic knights to the sack of Pskov by declaring, "One Rome shall rule the earth." In the long, climactic scene depicting the Battle on the Ice, the Germans' "invincible wedge" is defeated by a "pincer movement" that Eisenstein described as a recreation of "Hannibal's manoeuver at Cannae," where the ancient Romans were crushed in 216 B.C. This was a particularly needling dig at Mussolini and his own propaganda, which claimed that his Fascist state was reviving the glory of the Roman Empire. Eisenstein was therefore taking aim at an entire ideology: "We want our film not only to mobilize even those who are in the very thick of the worldwide struggle against Fascism, but to bring spirit, courage, and confidence to those parts of the world where Fascism seems as indestructible as the Order of the [Teutonic] Knights appeared in the thirteenth century." Yet this was necessarily a hypocritical exercise, for, as historians like Alan Bullock have demonstrated, Stalin's murderous socialism was little different from Hitler's fascism.

Eisenstein succeeded in making a contemporary film, indeed so much so that one begins to wonder why it was set in the Middle Ages at all. The real Nevsky was no more conscious of Russian nationalism than was Saladin of Arab nationalism. Moreover, the Nevsky of history can be shown to have collaborated with the Mongols when his political survival was at stake, which does find a parallel in Stalin's own actions around the very time that the film was making its debut. Less than a year after *Alexander Nevsky* was released on December 1, 1938, it was abruptly withdrawn from distribution upon the conclusion of a Non-Aggression Pact between the Nazis and the Soviets signed in August 1939. This inaugurated in Stalin's regime a remarkable collaboration with Germany, as well as a breathtaking reversal of anti-Fascist propaganda, from which Eisenstein was not exempt. In December 1939 he was commissioned to stage Wagner's opera, *Die Walküre*, at the Bolshoi Theater, which he described as part of a new effort "to bring Germanic and Norse epic closer to us." Although the German invasion of Russia in June 1941 made *Alexander Nevsky* relevant again and it was duly rereleased, the film was eventually to fall prey once more to new political events. Its portrayal of Nevsky as a Stalin-like leader of a medieval socialist state became horribly dated once the de-Stalinization of the Soviet Union began under Nikita Khrushchev in the 1960s, and was to be even more irrelevant upon the collapse of the Communist government in 1991. These days, the film is mainly viewed by college students in courses on film-making or on the history of the cinema.

Despite his own renunciation of abstract film theory, Eisenstein did try to incorporate some of his earlier "intellectual illusions" into *Alexander Nevsky*. Typage of characters in order to evoke broader themes beyond their individual identities was worked into the subplot of the rivalry between Vasili Buslai and Gavrilo Oleksich, who were meant to symbolize, respectively, the courage and wisdom inherent in Nevsky's superhuman personality. Throughout the film, but particularly in the Battle on the Ice scene, Eisenstein aimed for what he called "vertical montage." This called for an "organic unity," not juxtaposition, of the film's pictorial elements and its music, as composed by another Soviet émigre who had returned in 1932, Sergei Prokofiev. *Alexander Nevsky*, Eisenstein's first sound film, was supposed to achieve a "wonderful inner synchronization of plastic and musical images," so close that the visuals could be treated as simply another staff on Prokofiev's vertical score.

Nevertheless, *Alexander Nevsky* is a conventional film of the Socialist Realism era. During filming, Eisenstein was surrounded by Stalin's agents, who made sure that he did not stray back into old habits. His "codirector," Dmitri Vasiliev, was a favorite of Stalin's since 1934, when his film, *Chapayev*, was pronounced by the dictator to be "by far, the best film ever made in the Soviet Union." The screenplay for *Nevsky* was cowritten with Pyotr Pavlenko, a KGB agent and Stalinist novelist who was assigned to Eisenstein in 1937 by the party's Politburo. Nikolai Cherkasov, who played the film's title role, was the Leningrad representative in the Supreme Soviet. Despite all these precautions, the film did not escape censorship. There is the famous story told by Eisenstein's colleague, Viktor Shklovsky, of how an entire reel from the original film, showing a brawl between merchants and workmen on the bridge of Novgorod, was omitted from the final cut because the crew neglected to show it to Stalin at a private screening one night while the director was asleep at the editing table. According to his memoirs, Eisenstein had originally scripted a different ending to *Alexander Nevsky*, in which the hero was to be tragically poisoned after making obeisance to the Mongols in order to buy time for their eventual defeat by Dmitri Donskoi in 1380. But the scene was heavily criticized by authorities at the Main Film Directorate (GUK) and in the end, according to Eisenstein, was simply deleted in red pencil by a hand that wrote, "Such a fine prince could not die!" The censor's hand was perhaps Stalin's, who pencilled out name after name of his victims during the Great Terror.

Alexander Nevsky was the only film that Eisenstein had completed in over ten years. It reestablished him as a filmmaker of international stature and rehabilitated him as a loyal artist within the Soviet Union. Honors were heaped upon him: a doctorate from the Academy of Sciences, the Order of Lenin, the Stalin Prize—first class, and, most importantly, the personal approval of Stalin himself. At the film's Moscow premiere on November 23, 1938, the man of steel shook the director's hand, slapped him on the back, and declared, "Sergei Mikhailovich, you are a good Bolshevik after all!" But Stalin's approval came at a price. The new Eisenstein, as embodied by the film and his writings, was said to be "unrecognizable" to his friends. A perceptive reviewer, Franz Hoellering, wrote in 1939 that *Alexander Nevsky* was "not proof of Eisenstein's resurgence but of his suppression." Eisenstein's other film project at this time— which dared to treat of a contemporary event—was pretty disturbing in its subject matter. *Ferghana Canal*, a film begun in the fall of 1939 and then aborted, was to be about the heroic construction of a state project in Uzbekistan, which in reality used punitive slave labor. Alexander Solzhenitsyn, the famous author and survivor of one such gulag, has a prisoner in his novel, *One Day in the Life of Ivan Denisovich*, say of Eisenstein:

"Call him an ass-kisser, obeying a vicious dog's order. Geniuses don't adjust their interpretations to fit the taste of tyrants!" Above all, Eisenstein acknowledged that he had betrayed himself. In a revealing passage from his memoirs, Eisenstein recalls the censored scene of Nevsky's submission to the Mongols that he had originally planned for his film: "In my own personal, too-personal history, I myself too often perpetrated this heroic deed of self-abasement." Although Eisenstein justifies his "abasement" as allowing him to pursue his art, this is the closest that he comes to admitting that he was wrong to make films that glorified Stalin and his brutal regime.

Most puzzling of all, however, is why biographers and film historians refuse to take Eisenstein to task for his fateful decision to return to, and participate in, a Stalinized state. To those who would say that an artist's politics are a separate matter from his creative activities, we know from his own writings that Eisenstein himself did not believe this to be so. Despite this, the academy continues to lionize Eisenstein. Norman Swallow, in a 1976 biography subtitled, *A Documentary Portrait*, calls him "one of the greatest directors in the history of the cinema." David Bordwell, the coauthor of a widely used textbook on film theory and who also published an admiring study of the director in 1993, rationalizes Eisenstein's capitulation to Stalinist dogma during the 1930s and 1940s as "a sustained attempt to lift certain premises of Socialist Realism to the realm of serious aesthetic reflection." Even *Nevsky's* simple narrative structure, which violated Eisenstein's previous ideas on montage, is excused by Bordwell as "an occasion for experimentation" which supposedly "constructs a rich and detailed poetics of film." The same year, 1993, also saw the appearance of a collection of essays that claims to "rediscover" Eisenstein, in which Ian Christie warns in his introduction against "irresponsible allegations" that accuse the director of collaborating with the Stalinist regime, which Christie characterizes as "a rising tide of impatience and recrimination" in the wake of *glasnost*. Most recently, Barry Scherr, writing in an essay collection that "reconsiders" Eisenstein to mark the 1998 centenary of the director's birth, absolves Eisenstein of any complicity in *Alexander Nevsky's* Stalinist agenda. Instead this is due, Scherr claims, to Pavlenko's contributions to the screenplay and censorship of the film. Rather implausibly, Scherr argues that the film focuses not on Nevsky as Stalinist hero but on "a separate homage to the Russian spirit" that remains true to Eisenstein's previous body of work. Specialists in medieval history seem no less enamored of *Alexander Nevsky*. Norman Cantor, for example, includes it as one of the six best films to "invent" the Middle Ages; in particular, he admires Eisenstein's "superb recreation of medieval political iconology."

Yet the bottom line is that *Alexander Nevsky* was part of an effort to justify the liquidation of millions of people, whose only crime was to be perceived as standing in the way of a dictator's iron grip over his country. Acrobatic apologetics for Eisenstein are not only morally reprehensible, they are also hypocritical when viewed in the light of posterity's treatment of another brilliant, but ethically flawed, director of the 1930s: Leni Riefenstahl. Labeled Hitler's "favorite filmmaker," Riefenstahl directed *Triumph of the Will* (1935), which recorded the Nazi party congress at Nuremberg in September 1934, and *Olympia* (1938), about the XI Olympiad at Berlin in 1936. There are numerous parallels between Riefenstahl and Eisenstein. Like her Soviet contemporary, Riefenstahl elevated propaganda into "high art," was widely admired for her camera and editing techniques, was lavished with honors at home but received a less than enthusiastic reception in Hollywood, and, above all, willingly served a ruthless, dictatorial regime at a time when it was asserting a suffocating control over the film industry that effectively curtailed its creative productivity. After completing *Triumph of the Will*, characterized by film scholars as "the most successful propaganda film ever made," Riefenstahl was even invited to work in the Soviet Union. If she had gone, she no doubt would have met Eisenstein, whose film, *Battleship Potemkin*, was cited by the Nazi minister of propaganda, Joseph Goebbels, as one of the few movies he admired. To this day, Riefenstahl is vilified and shunned, and rightly so, for her collaboration with a hateful government and its ideology. But why hasn't the same fate been meted out to the equally compromised legacy of Eisenstein?

There are several reasons for the double standard. Eisenstein's elaborate theoretical ideas about the cinema, articulated in over 150 books and articles, and his former status as a teacher of film theory have undoubtedly seduced many modern academics. Nor can one discount plain chauvinism as working against Riefenstahl, who was unique, both in her times and ours, as a female director in an almost exclusively male profession. But by far the most decisive factor was the fact that Eisenstein was on the winning side of World War II. In this light, *Alexander Nevsky* could be presented as part of the worldwide effort against fascism and Nazi Germany. The United States was keen to demonstrate support for its ally, the Soviet Union, during the war. In 1943, Warner Brothers, with the blessing of the Office of War Information and, apparently, of President Franklin Delano Roosevelt himself, released *Mission to Moscow*, a film purporting to be a documentary account of Joseph Davies' turn as American ambassador to the Soviet Union between 1936 and 1938. Directed by Michael Curtiz of *Casablanca* fame, *Mission to Moscow* is a good example of how wartime sympathy for Stalin could excuse propaganda that rewrote history, particularly of the notorious show trials in Moscow that purged Stalin's rivals in the Communist Party, and of Soviet acts of aggression against Poland and Finland in the wake of the Non-Aggression Pact with Germany. The film was made with the help of Jay Leyda, a former student of Eisenstein's at the State Cinema Institute (VGIK) in Moscow and the English translator of his major works. Even after the war, Hollywood's flirtation with communism, although greatly exaggerated by the McCarthy witchhunts, has continued. In 1981, Warren Beatty directed and starred in *Reds*, which romanticized the career of John Reed, the American Communist who participated in the Bolshevik Revolution and wrote about it in *Ten Days that Shook the World* (the alternative title to Eisenstein's film, *October*). Western historians seem united in condemning the Nazis under Hitler and all those who cooperated with them. But the American Left has yet to come to terms with its toleration of fascism's mirror image: Soviet communism under Lenin and Stalin.

Alexander Nevsky became an influential film for the entire movie industry, but none more so than for the medieval and crusading genres. It proved particularly appealing to non-Western productions, such as Youssef Chahine's *Saladin*. We've already noted that the Egyptian director was perhaps inspired by Eisenstein to experiment with alternative film styles and to portray Saladin as an Arab nationalist and Nasser stand-in. *Nevsky's* theme of a native people rallying to resist an unscrupulous and inhumane invader was likewise imitated by another foreign-language film, *Krzyzacy* (also known by its English title, *Knights of the Teutonic Order*), which was released in 1960 and directed by the "dean of Polish filmmaking," Alexsandr Ford. The parallels between *Krzyzacy* and *Nevsky* are especially strong since in both films, the heros are Slavic and the enemies are German—the Teutonic Knights. Just as *Nevsky* climaxes with the Battle on the Ice, *Krzyzacy* builds (slowly) up to the Battle of Grunwald (also known as Tannenberg) on July 15, 1410. There is even a scene in the Polish film where two knights duel to the death in a swampy marsh, whose footing is highly reminiscent of the treacherous ice floes reproduced by Eisenstein (who, despite filming in summer, achieved the effect using liquid glass and deflatable pontoons). Yet for most of its three hours, *Krzyzacy*, which is based on Henryk Sienkiewicz's 1900 novel of the same name, focuses not on the hero of Grunwald, King Jogaila (also known by his Polish name, Wladyslaw II) of Lithuania-Poland, but on a love triangle—this time a man torn between the love of two women—that formed only a subplot in *Nevsky*. A young Lithuanian nobleman, Zbyszko of Bogdan, impulsively pledges his love to Danusia, the daughter of a Polish lord, Jurand of Spychow. When Jurand protects some Polish grain merchants who have been seized by the Knights, the Teutons retaliate by killing the lord's wife, kidnaping his daughter, and cutting out his right eye, tongue, and right hand. By the time Zbyszko rescues Danusia, she has gone mad from her captivity (the implication is that she has been repeatedly raped), and she soon dies. Zbyszko then transfers his love to his childhood sweetheart, Jagna, the daughter of a neighbor of his beloved uncle, Matthew of Bogdaniec.

Aleksandr Ford was a product of the Socialist Realism school of the Soviet Union, to which he fled after the Nazi invasion of Poland in 1939 (perhaps little realizing that the Russians were helping themselves to his homeland as well). No doubt the violence that the Germans did to his country during the war inspired the portrayal of the Teutonic Knights as the consummate villains in the film. In a memorable scene, when Jurand comes to the Knights' castle on the Polish-Lithuanian border to plead for the return of his daughter, he encounters a nightmarish, apocalyptic landscape like out of a Hieronymus Bosch painting—a wasteland dotted with corpses hanging from their gallows. Jurand's guide informs him that this is the punishment the Knights mete out to anyone—even women and children—who refuse to pay their taxes. Later, when a delegation from King Jogaila arrives at the Grand Master's castle at Malbork (Marienburg), the Poles are given a grisly tour of the Knights' oppressive enslavement of their subjects (in this case Prussians). As the guide explains, "mutineers, heretics, heathens" are all "working for the glory of God," but in reality we see them toiling night and day under the overseer's lash in order to make weapons for the Knights' next war. The following scene portrays the Knights in their great hall indulging in drunken and ostentatious revelry, which belies their status as holy monks. They feast on peacocks (whose feathers they also wear in their helmets), a symbol of their vanity and pride. Impish jesters constantly interrupt the serious discussions between the Teutons and the Poles.

As might be expected in a film that was made when Poland was part of a Communist bloc of East European nations, *Krzyzacy* expresses an anachronistic solidarity among members of the Warsaw Pact. Russian Tartars, for example, are depicted as fighting alongside the Poles and Lithuanians at Grunwald, even though, historically speaking, Lithuania had been locked in a bitter struggle to conquer its eastern neighbor since 1399. (The Czechs are also thrown into the battle for good measure, in the form of Hlava, groom to Zbyszko.) As in *Nevsky*, the film is not adverse to distorting history in order to present the winning side as unadulterated heros. Although the Poles' war with the Knights is accurately portrayed as over the Order's incursions into Lithuania, the Germans were not technically the aggressors at Grunwald. Rather, it was the Polish offensive against Malbork that started the war; but in the film, this act of aggression is turned, incredibly, into a mission of "conciliation" that King Jogaila sends to the Knights for a last ditch attempt to sue for peace. Grunwald also was not the all decisive battle it is portrayed in the film; the Teutonic Knights managed to keep most of their possessions by the peace of Torun of 1411. The victory did, however, seal the union of Poland and Lithuania that had been initiated by Jogaila's marriage to the Polish heiress, Jadwiga, in 1385.

On the surface, therefore, *Krzyzacy* seems to be a typical film in the Socialist Realism school, one that merely imitated the model provided by Eisenstein. But when one digs deeper into the film, it soon becomes apparent that this is Ford's declaration of independence from Socialist Realism and Soviet influences. Instead, the film can be classified as part of the Romantic Nationalism movement in East European cinema, when many filmmakers in the Soviet satellite countries, led by those of Czech nationality, began in the latter half of the 1950s to make films that celebrated the formerly taboo subject of pre-Communist, native national history, when these countries were independent of foreign domination. It should be remembered that in 1956, just four years before the film came out, Poland had changed its Communist regime for one that was more independent of Moscow, while Hungary's uprising on behalf of complete separation was narrowly averted with the help of Red Army tanks. The difference between *Krzyzacy* and its Russian predecessor can be most clearly seen in its superior technical qualities, as well as in its far more realistic costumes and sets. Equally impressive is the way that Ford was able to capture some spectacular nature and animal footage. But what is more intrinsic to the historical quality of the film is that Ford evidently refused to make the political concessions to Soviet ideology that mar *Nevsky*. Polish grain merchants, as victims of the Germans' incursions into their Baltic Sea trade, are accurately portrayed as on the side of resistance—not collaboration—to the Teutonic Knights' oppression. Class distinctions are rigidly maintained, with the nobles and the commoners keeping to themselves, rather than the scarcely credible, comradely commingling in Eisenstein's film. Toward the beginning of *Krzyzacy*, for example, an envoy from the duchess of Masovia announces her imminent arrival at an inn, whereupon the innkeeper shoos away his patrons by telling them, "Get out scum! Too grand company for us!" At the climax of the film at Grunwald, King Jogaila wisely heeds the advice of the grand duke of Lithuania to not mix with the troops, but "survey the battle from a post." In a significant departure from *Nevsky*, the national leader does not personally participate in the battle that saves his homeland, but prefers to direct the action from behind the lines, at one point even halting a premature charge about to be made by the Polish knights. Meanwhile, the Teutonic grand master, Ulrich von Jungingen, rashly ignores the same exhortation to stay aloof from the fighting, with the result that he is ignominiously cut down by common foot soldiers armed with pikes. Nor is the Church demonized: Nobles on both sides pointedly sing the same religious hymns before battle. The wandering German monk Sandorous, whom Zbyszko rescues from a snowstorm on his way to the Masovian court, may be a figure of fun and amusement: He offers to sell indulgences "for eternity, for 500 and 30 years" and an assortment of relics that include the "hoof of the donkey the Holy Family fled on, a feather from Gabriel's wing dropped at the Annunciation, some oil in which the heathens fried St. John, a step from the ladder Jacob dreamed of, and a phial of the wind that blew in Bethlehem." But in the end he is a sympathetic figure, who enables Zbyszko to rescue Danusia by disarming her captors. Perhaps Ford anticipates in his film the widespread support that Lech Walesa and Pope John Paul II were to receive in Poland and around the world during the Solidarity labor movement that eventually resulted in Polish independence during the 1980s.

Unlike Eisenstein, Ford is also not unwilling to invest even the hated German enemy with a touch of humanity. The aging grand master who receives the Polish delegation at Malbork is portrayed as a pious mediator between the two sides, who is inclined to accede to the Poles' demands and, with his dying breath, urges peace upon his fellow Knights. He is a remarkably similar character to the king of Jerusalem who appears three years later in Chahine's film, *Saladin*. (The two films likewise share a striking shot in which the audience assumes the perspective of a knight looking out from his visor, an effect that was reprised 25 years later in the Hollywood film, *Ladyhawke*.) One of the German nobles who fights alongside the Knights, Seigneur de Lorche of Lotharingia, is stabbed in the back for trying to prevent the abduction of Danusia and later bears witness against the Order concerning the crime before King Jogaila. Even the superevil Teutonic commander, de Loewe, who masterminds Danusia's kidnaping and mutilates her father, is allowed some human feeling, as he mourns over the slain body of his favorite knight, Rotbert (albeit this is done with some homosexual overtones and is accompanied by the gruesome trophy of Jurand's severed right hand). When the tables are turned and de Loewe finds himself in Jurand's power, he is set free unharmed in an act of Christ-like forgiveness. Overcome by remorse, the commander upon gaining his liberty almost immediately proceeds to hang himself by his horse's reins. On the whole, *Krzyzacy* is a more historically true and balanced portrayal of Slavic resistance to Teutonic oppression than its more famous Russian counterpart.

Despite the fact that those who had to live under Soviet rule were learning to disown the Stalinist legacy of Socialist Realism, Western filmmakers, ironically, continued their slavish admiration of *Alexander Nevsky*, which retained a powerful influence over their films. Laurence Olivier's 1944 adaptation of Shakespeare's play, *Henry V*, modeled its main battle sequence at Agincourt on Eisenstein's staging of the Battle on the Ice, and, in addition, took a cue from the Soviets in turning medieval history into wartime propaganda. But the English language film that chiefly lays claim to *Nevsky*'s mantle is *El Cid*, which came out in 1961 and, except for an Italian production of 1910, has the distinction of being the only movie to portray Spain's most famous crusading hero. Directed by Anthony Mann, the film stars Charlton Heston in the title role. In remarks made to his filmographer, Jeff Rovin, Heston, who describes himself as "a fan of *Nevsky*," frankly admits that Eisenstein's film provided a key inspiration for *El Cid*: "I admire *Nevsky* and Eisenstein because he did it first; Eisenstein thought it all up! For *El Cid*, we simply drew from his example." And indeed, *El Cid* follows *Nevsky*'s lead in turning the title character into yet another anachronistic national hero, a figure who unites his country several centuries before such a concept as patriotism was born.

El Cid looks and feels like a big, blockbuster epic that was a fairly typical product of the Hollywood studios during the 1950s and early 1960s. Heston, in fact, agreed to do *El Cid* fresh from his Oscar-winning performance in *Ben Hur* (1959), and not long after another epic turn as Moses in *The Ten Commandments* (1956). But although the film was distributed by Allied Artists, *El Cid* was most definitely *not* a Hollywood production. Instead, it was produced by a Spanish company headed by an American expatriate, Samuel Bronston. This brash Texan had fallen in love with Spain and attempted to build a film empire there, based at the former Chamartín Studios just outside Madrid; eventually, Bronston boasted, the success of his company would force the old Hollywood studios to relocate to a "new Hollywood" in Spain. And indeed, *El Cid*'s production values rival anything coming out of Hollywood at this time, even the notoriously excessive *Cleopatra* (1963).

Filming in Spain, especially on a Spanish medieval subject, certainly had its advantages. These included authentic castles and walled cities to serve as exterior sets and plenty of cheap native labor. Filming the Cid's siege of Valencia—the climax of the movie—required only cosmetic changes to the suburbs of Peñiscola, about 124 miles down the coast from the original, in order to recreate a completely realistic medieval walled town. Although the geography was not completely cooperative—2,622 truckloads of sand had to be brought in to make the beach footing safe—the people certainly were. Thousands of them came from miles around to man both the Christian and Moorish armies, augmented by 1,700 troops of the 31st Valencia division of the Spanish army and 500 horsemen from the Municipal Honor Guard of Madrid. About three dozen fishing boats were put out of action in order to double as the Almoravids' invasion fleet—with Bronston's wages more than making up for the lost revenue. As if this wasn't enough, the locals put in 2,880 round-the-clock man-hours to help build eight full-scale replica siege towers, which ended up taking space on the screen without even being used to conduct a mock siege.

Charlton Heston in the title role about to lead the attack against the Almoravids outside the city of Valencia in *El Cid*. The low wall in the immediate foreground was specially built in order to mask modern homes that clash with the medieval fortress on
location at Peñiscola in Spain.

Yet the elaborate staging of the siege of Valencia was merely the tip of
the iceberg of Spain's contributions to *El Cid*. According to a publicity publication, *The Making of El Cid*, that accompanied the release of the film,
Chamartín Studios built, on Bronston's orders, a full-scale replica of the
Romanesque cathedral of Burgos that became, so it was claimed, "one of
the largest, most magnificent exterior sets ever built in Spain, taking 90
days and 70,400 man hours to erect." The entire female population of three
villages near Madrid were employed by a local costume supply company,
Casa Cornejo, in order to churn out 2,000 costumes designed by the film's
art consultants, Veniero Colasanti and John Moore. Thousands of props
were made to order by various Spanish companies: Casa Cornejo provided
3,000 war helmets and hundreds of iron-studded leather jerkins; the
Garrido Brothers of Toledo crafted 7,000 swords, scimitars, and lances;

Anthony Luna, a Madrid prop manufacturer, produced 40,000 arrows, 5,780 shields, 1,253 medieval harnesses, 800 maces and daggers, 650 fake suits of chain mail (woven from hemp and coated with a metal varnish), and 500 saddles.

In a sense, Bronston conceived of the film as a collective effort involving the whole of Spain. As the above figures convey, the sheer scale of the contributions of the nation's industry and manpower to the spectacle were indeed staggering. But there was a price to be paid for Bronston's collaboration with the only Fascist regime to have survived World War II. *Generalísimo* Francisco Franco, the victor of Spain's Civil War between 1936 and 1939 that claimed a million lives, was still in firm control of the country when the film was being made and would continue to rule until his death in 1975. These circumstances ensured that *El Cid* would contain its share of political propaganda whose message, although more subtly expressed than in *Alexander Nevsky*, is just as sinister as that of its ideological rival.

There are actually three agendas at work behind the scenes of *El Cid*. One is medieval in origin, while the other two are modern. The medieval inspiration for Heston's portrayal of the Cid is the epic Spanish poem—the only one to have survived from the Middle Ages—the *Poema de Mio Cid* (*Poem of My Cid*). As previously mentioned in the background section, the *Poema* is thought by its most recent scholars to have been composed sometime after 1200—more than a century after the Cid's death in 1099—when Christian Spain had developed a crusading ethos that simply had not existed during the Cid's own lifetime. Despite the fact that other sources more contemporary with the Cid were available, Heston and the filmmakers decided to base their interpretation of the Cid almost exclusively on the poem. In his autobiography, Heston admits that the *Poema* was written long after the Cid's death ("two centuries" according to him), but that even so, the poem was where "I found the man I was looking for, a man I felt I could play." It does not seem that he consulted other, more reliable medieval accounts of the Cid—especially the *Historia Roderici* (*History of Rodrigo*)—that may have helped him to formulate a more nuanced interpretation of his role. His journal entry for July 28, 1960, for example, expresses his frustration that "for one of the outstanding men of the twelfth century [actually the eleventh], there's damn little contemporary comment."

As noted earlier, the agenda of the *Poema de Mio Cid* is to portray Rodrigo Díaz as supremely loyal to his king, Alfonso VI (1072–1109), in the face of every adversity the monarch could throw his way. This was an especially important message to convey in the context of the turbulent reign of Alfonso VIII (1157–1214), who was the Alfonso that ruled at the time the poem was composed. Inevitably, the *Poema*'s vision of the Cid

helped shape Heston's own conception of his role. As he writes in his autobiography: "Even if we strip away a thousand years of mythic excess, history still gives us a battered, striving man, stubbornly loyal to the king who
exiled him and imprisoned his wife and daughters." This interpretation
comes through most clearly in the film in the scene where the Cid, after
riding triumphantly through the gates of Valencia, accepts the city's crown
at the urging of his allies, but not in the way that they expect:

> I take Valencia in the name of my sovereign lord, Alfonso, king of Castile,
> León, and Asturias, of Sagunto and Almenara, of Castellón and Alcántara,
> king of Christians and Moors. [Holding the crown aloft] Valencia for
> Alfonso, by the grace of God, king of Spain!

In actuality, as the *Historia Roderici* and the Cid's foundation charter for the
cathedral church of Valencia can attest, the Cid took Valencia in the name
of none other than himself. Although loyalty to one's lord was certainly
part of the feudal culture of the eleventh century, loyalty to the monarch of
the sacrificial kind expressed in the poem and in the film is nowhere in evidence among the Cid's actions during his lifetime.

A second, more modern agenda woven into the film's fabric came from
the man who, at the time the movie was being made, was universally
acclaimed to be the leading authority on the Cid and who served as
Heston's historical consultant: Ramón Menéndez Pidal. Access to Pidal's
world-renown expertise was considered to be yet another asset of filming
El Cid in Spain. It was a resource of which Heston, who took pride in
knowing more about his role "than anyone else on the film," readily availed
himself. In the course of a personal interview I conducted with him, Mr.
Heston told me of a visit he paid Pidal in Madrid:

> He [Pidal] was considered the outstanding historian in the world on the
> Cid, and so I wanted a chance to talk to him. He was then in his nineties,
> but he was still quite spry. I drove out to his house, and the door burst open
> and a withered old man said, "Venga!" I thought, "Oh, this is going to be
> fun," but that was his butler. Of course, my own Spanish was not very good,
> but we managed to communicate.

In his autobiography, Heston adds that Pidal looked every inch the academic: "trimmed white beard, clear black eyes, and a blazingly vigorous
mind. . . . I'll never forget the fervor with which he led me through his
subject." Heston left Pidal's house loaded with books which included, no
doubt, Pidal's own masterwork of 1929, *La España del Cid* (*The Cid and His
Spain*). Moreover, Pidal's son, Gonzalo, a professor of literature at Madrid

University, also lent a hand as "literary advisor" throughout the filming. Pidal had good reason to be so hospitable to Heston. "Dr. Pidal," Heston writes, "clearly realized that our film would provide the permanent public impression of the man to whom he had devoted much of his life. He knew the power of film; he wanted to do his best to make sure we got it right." Pidal's vision of the Cid was therefore even more of an influence on the film than the *Poema's*. But this does not mean that it was any more correct.

Much of Pidal's interpretation of the Cid was in fact lifted right out of the *Poema*, which he paraphrases and quotes extensively throughout his biography. This was only natural for a man who first made his academic reputation by writing a linguistic essay on the *Poema* and entering it in a contest sponsored by the Royal Spanish Academy. Pidal was duly awarded the prize in 1895, which led to his being further rewarded with a newly created chair in philology at the University of Madrid in 1899 and election to the Royal Spanish Academy in 1901, all when Pidal was just entering his thirties. A crucial advantage held by the young Pidal at this meteoric stage of his career was his noble family connections: His uncle, the Marqués de Pidal, owned and gave him unlimited access to the only surviving medieval manuscript copy of the *Poema*. It must be emphasized here that Pidal was not an historian by training; rather, he was a philologist, which means that he studied the origins of language. Legend has it that Pidal acquired a new interpretive model for the *Poema* in 1900 while in the company of his student-bride, María Goyri, on their honeymoon, which the couple spent retracing the steps of the Cid's exile from Burgos. (Their first child, Jimena, was named after the Cid's own wife.) On one stop of his honeymoon, Pidal heard a washerwoman sing an Old Castilian ballad dating to the fifteenth century, which convinced him that oral traditions, no less than written chronicles, could keep alive a true and authentic account of historical personalities and events. Even though Pidal himself admitted that the *Poema* as written down could date no earlier than 1140, he was still convinced that the poem was contemporary with the Cid, since it could have been composed and sung in pure oral form while he was yet alive. Pidal's "modern philological criticism" thus led him to accept the poem and other later narratives as legitimate sources of historical information, just as accurate as the Latin and Arabic histories which we know from internal evidence to have been written during or shortly after the Cid's lifetime. Indeed, Pidal was inclined to treat the *Poema* as his most important source. As he writes in the introduction to *La España del Cid*: "The earlier *jongleurs* alone strove to restore to the people that fuller picture of the hero that was familiar to those among whom he had lived and wrought." Yet this position is now badly outdated and is simply unacceptable to most scholars of medieval Spain. The *Poema* was a product of a different era altogether from the Cid's, containing its own bias and agenda.

Nonetheless, Pidal, too, had his agenda, quite apart from the medieval poem he so admired. This was to portray the Cid as "obsessed" with "the idea of a united Spain." As Pidal writes towards the end of his biography of the Cid: "The fact that, contrary to the custom established in the law and poetry of the time, neither the Cid of history nor the Cid of fiction makes war on his king but remains loyal to him, shows the extent to which the hero subordinated personal motives to love of country, thereby betraying a spirit practically unknown to the heroic types of older epic poems." Obviously, Pidal is basing his argument on the *Poema*, but he goes way beyond it, to argue that the Cid embodied a patriotism that found "expression in his famous resolve to reconquer the whole of Spain." It is highly unlikely that the author of the *Poema*, anxious as he was to push the theme of royal supremacy, would have gone quite this far. Nationalism, no less for the twelfth- or thirteenth-century image of the Cid as for that of Saladin and Alexander Nevsky, was an impossibly precocious concept. Even so, Pidal's vision of the Cid as a national hero who lived to unify Spain, which finds no precedent in any medieval source, was the one that was adopted by the film. We have already seen it in the scene where the Cid accepts the crown of Valencia on behalf of a king "of Christians and Moors . . . of Spain!" Although the real Alfonso VI was looking to expand his territories south of Toledo, he would have found it hard to conceive of himself, especially after the reversals he suffered at the hands of the Almoravids, as anything but ruler of two of the many kingdoms on the Peninsula: León and Castile. Still, the theme keeps cropping up in the film: In the scene where the Cid is greeted by an army just as he is about to depart for exile, he responds to their clamor for his leadership with a resounding rallying cry of, "For Spain! Spain!" And again, when Alfonso refuses to assist the Cid in the defense of Valencia against the Almoravids, despite the gift of the city's crown, the Cid's right-hand man, Alvar Fañez, rebukes the king with: "Who has done more, for you and Spain?!" Clearly, it is Pidal and the film that are obsessed with making medieval Spain into a modern nation, forged by a modern national hero, a Spanish Garibaldi or Bismarck.

Pidal had good reason to want to revive Spanish patriotism through his medieval hero. He belonged to the "Generation of 1898," a group of talented writers who individually contributed to a Renaissance of Spanish letters that—whether at an intentional or subconscious level—sought to atone for Spain's humiliating defeat to the United States during the Spanish-American War, or "The Disaster," as it was known by the losing side. What better way to remind Spaniards that they had once before overcome a rude invader of their empire than to recount the glorious career of the *campeador*? Such a hero also had to be a symbol of Old Castilian and Catholic values for the rosy nostalgia to be complete. Pidal's patriotic effort entailed defending the Cid's reputation against any outside observer who dared lay siege to the edifice of his legend. One of these "presumptuous" foreigners, a highly respected scholar with an international reputation, was the Dutch orientalist, Reinhard Dozy. It was Dozy who, in 1849, first drew widespread attention to the Arabic sources, such as those by Ibn Bassam and Ibn 'Alqama, that give a much needed corrective to the overwhelmingly adulatory treatments of the Cid in Christian texts. The Cid that emerges from the other side, and in Dozy's account, is a ruthless mercenary and opportunist, not a fanatically nationalistic crusader and Moor slayer. It was this image of the Cid "as seen by harsh, malevolent critics" that Pidal was determined to destroy, for his hero "could hardly be the man of stupid and purposeless cruelty, the faithless and deceitful knave, the *condottiere* who knew not country, ideals or honor, that Dozy paradoxically portrayed." Anyone who sided with Dozy, in Pidal's mind, was guilty of "Cidophobia." Yet these days it is Dozy's, not Pidal's, version of the Cid that is widely hailed by scholars of medieval Spain as the one that presents its subject in the most balanced and realistic light.

The real paradox was that Pidal himself benefitted from Dozy's scholarship, for his *La España del Cid* could hardly afford to ignore the medieval Arabic sources. Instead, Pidal uses the "hostile" histories very selectively. He quotes verbatim from Ibn 'Alqama's account of a long conciliatory speech the Cid made to the Moors just after his conquest of Valencia, which in Pidal's mind proves that the *campeador* inaugurated a benevolent administration that "was to serve as a model to his immediate successors in the Reconquest." But 'Alqama's ensuing testimony that the city's Muslim inhabitants quickly became disillusioned with the Cid as a result of his harsh and punitive tax policies is dismissed by Pidal on the grounds that the Cid needed to reward his followers and punish those who collaborated with the Almoravids. Also, Pidal admits that the Cid was motivated by a desire to secure al-Qadir's treasure when he executed Valencia's *qadi*, or judge, Ibn Jahhaf, in the cruel fashion as reported by Ibn Bassam. Yet Pidal elides this embarrassing blot on the Cid's pure motivations as "a relic of the lust for wealth that had consumed such heroes of an earlier and more barbaric age." Although Jahhaf's execution was "impolitic," this is only because he then became a martyr which the Almoravids could use to fan "the smouldering embers of Moslem rebellion."

Pidal's vision of the Cid as Spain's unifier goes against not only the above Arabic sources, but also against the best Christian account of the Cid written shortly after his death. The *Historia Roderici* portrays the Cid as a freelance soldier perfectly willing to serve Moorish emirs, such as al-

Mu'tamin of Zaragoza, as well as a man perfectly capable of committing ruthless acts even against Christian territories, such as the author's native Rioja region of Castile. Of course, Pidal once again is at pains to put the best spin on this unflattering testimony. The Cid's services to al-Mu'tamin, for example, are described as those of one employed "not as a mercenary, but as one acting in the interests of Castile." His raiding of the Rioja was an act of personal vengeance against his enemy, García Ordóñez, not an act of treason against his king. According to Pidal, "it never entered the Cid's head to avenge himself on his sovereign for the insults the king had heaped upon him." But the *Historia* is careful to note that the Cid's "harsh and impious devastation" took place in lands "which were in Alfonso's kingdom and subject to his authority." All these instances of special pleading call seriously into question Pidal's self-proclaimed objectivity, his stated goal to write a "new history of the Cid" that would examine the sources free from "any spirit of antagonism against the Cid's detractors."

It is worthwhile to unmask Pidal's motivations and methods behind his history of the Cid, because the Spanish scholar's biases became those of Heston, and of the film. To this day, Heston refuses to budge from Pidal's romanticized conception of the Cid, in spite of the revisionism of Dozy and others that has taken place, both before and after Pidal's time. In my private interview with him, Mr. Heston, when asked if he would play his role any differently in light of recent scholarship that favors a view of the Cid as a mercenary, responded:

> No, I don't think so. Most major figures who possessed power were pretty rough fellas in the 11th century and certainly I think that was true of the Cid. But he did unify Spain, and he did drive the Moors from Valencia. . . . Besides, especially for the film, his marriage to Chimene [Jimena] and his clear love for her, which I don't think has ever been challenged, is crucial, and you have to focus on that too.

Heston here betrays the typical Hollywood temptation to pursue "the romance angle" in any given movie script. In the case of the Cid, that angle is particularly appealing since his love for his wife is given such poignant expression in the *Poema*: Before the Cid departs for exile, he takes leave of Jimena "with such pain as when the fingernail is torn from the flesh." From Heston's point of view, it all makes for "a marvelous love story . . . I really can't think of any love story in film that combines war and love and betrayal as this does that works as well." What is equally revealing is how loyal Heston remains to Pidal's interpretation of the Cid.

Yet when Heston accepted the role in July 1960, he had some misgivings. He writes in his journal that his first impression of the Cid, based on "the rather meager material the Paramount research department turned up," was that the Spanish hero seemed "to have been nearly as often a bad man as a good one." Heston was also perplexed, and justifiably so, as to why such a "rough fella" should have refused "to take for himself the crown he had won back for Alfonso." Unfortunately, Heston's qualms, and any potential complexities he may have brought to the role, were later quashed, perhaps as a result of his personal contact with Pidal once on location. The actor's conservative political leanings have only served to harden his determination to echo Pidal's views. In his autobiography (written in 1995), Heston writes:

> Some modern historians, trying to clear the cloud of Arthurian legend that obscures him, have cast the Cid simply as a ruthless mercenary. Certainly they were endemic in Europe a few centuries later, the Italian *condotieri* [sic], the Spanish *conquistadores* who conquered South America. However politically correct that may be, I don't think it's a realistic view of the Cid.

It is a nice irony, perhaps, that Mr. Heston takes exception to what he sees as an anti-heroic, politically-motivated revisionism of the Cid, when in fact his own view is a highly polemical one that originated in the very anti-American atmosphere of turn-of-the-century Spain.

Pidal influenced the film not only by rejecting whatever did not fit in with a nationalistic vision of the Cid, but also by uncritically accepting legendary tales spun by Spain's "jongleurs," whom Pidal considered to be "chroniclers rather than poets." From an historian's point of view, Pidal's standards of historical authenticity are seriously flawed. Nevertheless, most of the fanciful accretions to the Cid legend, dating at the earliest to the thirteenth century, found their way into the film. These include the story of the Cid's refusal to kiss Alfonso's hand in 1072 until the new king took an oath that he had had no hand in the murder of his predecessor, his own brother, Sancho. In the film, the incident serves to exculpate the Cid from any blame attached to his switch of allegiance to a man whose hands may have been guilty of fratricide. Another legend tells of how the Cid singlehandedly defeated fourteen Leónese knights who had captured King Sancho of Castile at the Battle of Golpejera in 1071. But in the movie, it is Alfonso who benefits from the rescue even though the Cid serves Sancho, a fact that helps establish the Cid's even-handed devotion to justice; meanwhile, the overwhelming odds against him are only slightly reduced to thirteen opponents. In some film scholars' minds, this extraordinary feat of bravado sets up the Cid as the "perfect" male hero, whose refusal to compromise on any point of honor elevates his masculinity to the level of "spectacle." The same goes for the other great fight scene in the film, the Duel for Calahorra, which was so realistic it required Heston to train for two hours each day with the Italian fencing master, Enzo Musumeci Greco. It is at least possible that the real Cid fought such a trial by combat, since his participation in one is attested by both the *Carmen Campi Doctoris* and the *Historia Roderici*.

Reviewers were divided about the success of *El Cid*'s take on its title character. Some criticized Heston for his "marble-monumental style"; others praised the film for breathing into the "demigod" a believable humanity. Nearly all agreed that Heston was the only actor of the time of sufficient stature to inhabit such a larger-than-life historical role. Indeed, Heston's portrayal is so definitive that audiences are likely to forever afterward conjure up the actor's visage whenever they think of the historical Cid. Heston in his autobiography describes his own "handle" on the role as that the Cid was a "biblical Job figure, defiant and enduring"; he got this idea from the film's screenwriter, Philip Yordan, and it was apparently endorsed by Pidal. Even so, Heston informed me in our conversation together that he has found the great men of history to be "interesting, but not easy to find. They're often quite remote, as the Cid was." Thus, capturing a medieval legend on film proved to be a challenge for Heston, even though, as he boasted to me, he had "done more historically great men than any actor I can think of."

Clearly, Heston believes that he captured the real, historical Cid on film. He took his role very seriously, telling me in our interview that, "I think you owe as an actor a responsibility to great men, if you are going to play them." Although some license for invention may be allowed, Heston declares that "the main thing is to try and reach as close to what they were really like as you can." But where should the line between history and legend be drawn in the case of the Cid, about whom we know rather more than the dimly lit figure of King Arthur? As Heston himself reminded me, "It is important to remember that [the Cid] was a real man. This is not King Arthur or something."

Nowhere is this dilemma more telling than at the end of the film, when the Cid dies, only to have his corpse strapped onto his horse by his wife and sent out to win his last, great victory against the Almoravids. The source of this remarkable finale, which a *Time* reviewer called "a vision of chilling weirdness," is a late thirteenth-century account of the Cid's death written by one of the monks of Cardeña, the abbey where the Cid was entombed. According to this legend, which Pidal chose not to include in his biography, the Cid was inspired by a vision of St. Peter, the patron saint of Cardeña, to undergo an autoembalmment by drinking preservatives such as myrrh and balsam during his last days. (A similar embalmment story was told by Albert of Aachen of the second crusader king of Jerusalem,

Baldwin I, who died in 1118.) Heston, while admitting to me that "one can question" the historical accuracy of the legend, still defiantly maintains that the scene "makes a marvelous ending, I can tell you that." He was apparently not bothered by the fudging of history in this particular instance, despite describing himself as being "a bug for historical accuracy." As an actor, Heston was attracted to the Cid's deathbed scene because of its dramatic possibilities. It appealed to him on several levels, as he told me in person:

> It's a) an heroic death; b) it's his determination that somehow his will will be carried out and his insistence that his wife see to that; and then [c)] his reconciliation with Alfonso. It is a marvelous scene, no question, and it was wonderful to play. Actors love death scenes.

The scene had the added bonus of allowing Heston to act from the comfort of a bed, rather than attempting to reenact a violent end, which he has been forced to do for most of his historical roles. "I've usually died," Heston told me, "falling from high places, or being run down or shot at, or beheaded." But when the actor rides out as the Cid's corpse "through the gates of history," accompanied by a swelling organ solo, we know that in this instance history has been trumped by an excessive dramatic license.

No doubt Heston and his fans view the liberties that *El Cid* takes with history as quite harmless. They are wrong. This is not to say that a film is not entitled to alter, conflate, or even invent historical "facts" in order to deliver a coherent narrative on screen. As already stated in the introduction of this book, the conventions unique to film dictate that its visual images, to at least some degree, "fictionalize" history for the sake of its vision. And most historians can probably live with this alternative reality created by the movies, provided that the film's vision contains a core of historical truth about its subject. But in this case, historical truth has been sacrificed for the sake of an extremely dangerous vision, one that has disturbing implications for how medieval history can be manipulated into propaganda, even in a film as apparently harmless as *El Cid*.

This brings us to the third, most sinister agenda of the film. At the time *El Cid* was being made, between September 1960, when Heston first arrived on location, to April 1961, when Heston wrapped up his last sequence—the Duel for Calahorra—on the set of Belmonte Castle, Spain and its film industry were still firmly under the control of Francisco Franco's censors. This was shortly to change with the appointment in 1962 of a new Minister of Information and Tourism, Manuel Fraga Iribarne, who inaugurated a cautious liberalization of the media, and of cinema in particular, through sweeping changes made to the Board of Censors and to its guidelines for film. Nevertheless, Spain at the turn of the decade, according to an historian of the nation's cinema, Peter Besas, "was still in the throes of the strictest cultural, moral, and religious censorship." Besas experienced Franco's repressive atmosphere firsthand during his visit to the country in 1959. He was shocked to find Spain the only European country where one could be fined for kissing in public, where "menacing" Civil Guards patrolled the streets, where one-armed and one-legged beggars served as constant reminders of the nation's brutal Civil War, and where it seemed that "everywhere you went the walls of buildings and the sides of barns on the roads were painted with pro-Franco and pro-Falange slogans and symbols." (The Falange Española, or "Spanish Phalanx," was Spain's Fascist party, similar to the Fascio di Combattimento of Italy and the Nazi party of Germany. Their blue-uniformed thugs played analogous roles to the Black Shirts and the Brown Shirts.)

Bronston's film empire in Spain seems to have been largely exempt from Franco's harsh censorship. Yet "salutary neglect" from the authorities came not without its price. Aside from his commercial productions, Bronston made a number of official films for the Spanish government with the express purpose of promoting Spanish tourism and culture abroad. One of these, a short film entitled *El Valle de los Caídos* (*The Valley of the Fallen*), extols Franco's huge monument to the Civil War, a project that in fact was completed using the slave labor of 20,000 Republicans who had somehow escaped execution. As a matter of fact, *El Cid* itself can be viewed as among Bronston's propaganda "presents" to Franco, a movie designed to put Spain's best face forward on the international stage, at a time when the country's Fascist credentials still compromised it in the eyes of much of the world.

The historical figure of the Cid was one with whom Franco closely identified, on both a personal and public level. Rodrigo's exile from Castile and subsequent triumph at Valencia, for example, could find a parallel in Franco's own political career in 1936. When the Republican Popular Front was narrowly elected to power in February of that year, Franco was forced into "exile" in the Canary Islands and Morocco; by the following summer, however, Franco was back on the mainland at the head of an army that had been transported across the straits of Gibraltar by German aircraft. (Spain's navy remained loyal to the government.) Similarly, Franco could portray himself as leading a second "Reconquest" to liberate Spain from another foreign enemy, in this case, the "Godless Communists" who were backing the Republicans. In due course, Franco was elected *Generalísimo*, or Supreme Commander, of the Nationalist forces and hailed as *Caudillo* and *Jefe del Estado*, honorific titles that conveyed his status as "leader" or "boss" of the Fascist state. *Caudillo* was therefore analogous to *Duce* and

Führer, the Fascist titles, adopted respectively, by Mussolini and Hitler. But in Spain especially, Franco's accolades also evoked the warrior heroes and conquerors of the medieval past, above all, the Cid and *campeador*, Rodrigo Díaz.

Nationalist propaganda followed Franco's lead in marrying his *cruzada* against the Republicans and Communists to the Cid's "crusade" against the Moors. February 1937 saw the first issue of a Nationalist journal, *Mío Cid* (*My Cid*), that was published in Burgos with the professed aim to "raise the standard of the Cid throughout Spain [so that we are] at one with his cause, his spirit, and his example." (In 1941 this manifesto was reprinted and three articles by Pidal included in the issue.) The same year, 1937, also saw the publication of a collection of modern ballads that equated Franco with the Cid. A Nationalist film made of the "liberation" of Barcelona, the last Republican stronghold to fall to the Nationalists during the Civil War, hails Franco as the "Caesar, Cid, Alexander [the Great]" at the head of his victorious army. (The film can currently be viewed as part of Basilio Martín Patino's 1974 documentary, *Caudillo*.) In reality, thousands of pro-Republican sympathizers were summarily shot by the Nationalists when they entered Barcelona, a gruesome pattern of reprisal that was repeated in town after town taken by either side during the Civil War. Even after the war, Franco's shameless appropriation of the Cid's legacy continued. At the dedication of a statute of the Cid at Burgos on July 24, 1955, Franco drew a clear parallel between Spain's medieval and modern history: "The great service of our crusade, the virtue of our *movimiento* is to have awakened an awareness of what we were, of what we are, and what we can be." The Cid, Franco emphasized, was to be the symbol of a "new Spain," for "in him is enshrined all the mystery of the great Spanish epics: service in noble undertakings, duty as norm, struggle in the service of the true God." Perhaps the most brazen identification, in artistic terms, that Franco made with the Cid and the Middle Ages was the enormous mural (approximately 10 by 20 feet) that he commissioned after the Civil War and housed in the *Servicio Histórico Militar* (Military Historical Service), which is now the *Instituto de Historia y Cultura* (Institute of History and Culture). In the foreground is Franco, no longer the dumpy figure he was in real life, decked out in a full suit of medieval plate armor and white robe, holding in both hands a great broadsword, while in the background are his Nationalist forces arrayed in twentieth-century uniforms and bearing modern weaponry, such as guns. Like Hitler, Franco had himself painted as a medieval knight because he saw great propaganda value in associating himself with the heroic ideals of his country's medieval past.

It should be obvious by now that Pidal's vision of the Cid as the man destined to unite Spain lent itself remarkably well to Franco's own Cidian

propaganda. Pidal claimed that the "true" Cid was the Cid of the *Poema* —
the champion of a Catholic, Castilian, royalist Spain; similarly, Franco presented himself as the staunch champion of the Church, the monarchy, and,
in general, of the conservative elements of the population who looked forward to a return to the ways of "Old Castile." Just as nationalism was crucial to Pidal's reconstruction of his medieval hero in the face of hostile foreign criticism, no less did it sustain the Franco regime after the end of
World War II, when Spain was isolated by the victorious Allies. Above all,
both Pidal and Franco were convinced that Spain could be united only by
a single leader, a man of such stature that he admitted of no rivals. For
Pidal, this meant denigrating the character of a king, Alfonso VI, who, in
Heston's words, "treated [the Cid] very badly." Going beyond the *Poema*,
Pidal speculates that the young Alfonso "was of a docile nature and readily deferred to his parents and his elder sister Urraca, so that he became
the favorite son and developed all the selfish traits of a spoilt child." And
this is what we get in the film, as the role is played by the English actor,
John Fraser. For Franco, no less than for Stalin and Hitler, there could be
only one *Caudillo*. In similar fashion to how Pidal relegated Alfonso VI to
a lower place in history than the Cid, Franco ruled out the possibility of a
restoration of the monarchy of Alfonso XIII. From Franco's point of view,
only he could end the bitter factional strife of the Civil War and at the same
time keep Spain free from foreign interference, whether this be
Communist, Fascist, or democratic. The king was bluntly told by Franco
in 1937 that he had no place in "the new Spain which we are forging," since
"your training and old-fashioned political practices [i.e., the former consti-
tutional monarchy] necessarily provoke the anxieties and resentments of
Spaniards."

It is impossible to tell how far Pidal acquiesced in Franco's Fascist
makeover of his Cid. His biographers have portrayed him as the typical
absent-minded professor, a man so consumed with his academic studies
that he was oblivious to politics. Heston himself remarks in his autobiography that Pidal's "tiny house was bursting with books" which covered, he
noted, "every flat surface I saw," including the toilet tank. However much
Pidal may have found Franco's manipulation of his scholarship on the Cid
to be "extremely distasteful," I do not believe that he was entirely blame-
less of it. Although Pidal was certainly no Fascist, he was also no friend of
democracy. The young Pidal beheld the ultraroyalist example of his father,
Juan Menéndez Fernández Cordero, a judge of the Royal Tribunal of
Galicia. When the Bourbon monarchy was toppled and the First Republic
proclaimed in 1869, the year of Pidal's birth, his father lost his post for the
next seven years because he refused to swear allegiance to a liberal constitution that guaranteed religious freedom. (Pidal took his mother's sur-

name, since its lineage was more distinguished.) In 1904 and 1905, Pidal himself served the restored monarchy of King Alfonso XIII as mediator of a boundary dispute between Ecuador and Peru in South America. Most likely, Pidal was a monarchist and a conservative, a faction that, at their most extreme, became known as the Carlists (named after some nineteenth-century kings of Spain) who allied themselves with the Nationalists during the Civil War. He left the Spanish capital, Madrid, in November 1936, the very month when the Republicans rallied to make a successful stand against the encircling Nationalist forces. As might be expected, Pidal chose Valencia as his port of departure the following month for a self-imposed exile of two-and-a-half years. During that time, he lectured at the *Casa Italiana* of Columbia University in New York City. Since the *Casa* had been founded by the Mussolini regime that was lending 50,000 troops to help Franco win the war, this earned Pidal the enmity of the Republican government. When the war ended in 1939, Pidal returned to Spain in July, at the same time that half a million refugees were fleeing the other way, across the Pyrenees mountains into southern France.

It is true that Pidal was not treated very well by the ensuing Franco dictatorship. For a time, he had his bank assets frozen and had to appear weekly before the Tribunal of Political Responsibilities. But this ordeal was probably alleviated by his son, Gonzalo, who after the war worked for the official *Radio Nacional* in Burgos, and by a young Falangist, Antonio Tovar, who had been Pidal's student at the *Centro de Estudios Históricos* (Center of Historical Studies) and who now acted as Pidal's chauffeur to his meetings. In 1947, Pidal was reinstated as director of the Royal Spanish Academy. In the meantime, *La España del Cid* became a set textbook for cadets at Franco's military academies. General Antonio Aranda, director of the *Escuela Superior del Ejército* (Superior School of War), was fond of comparing his Civil War exploits to the Cid's campaigns in the Spanish Levante, and he held up the Cid as a homegrown model of supreme loyalty to a nation and its leader that should be emulated by the entire military staff. According to an historian of the Cid, María Eugenia Lacarra, "It is evident that for the Francoist military, it was an easy transition from the medieval military *Caudillo* to the present *Caudillo*, the *Generalísimo* Francisco Franco. . . . He was for them the most important example of loyalty to the fatherland and the maker of national unity." Moreover, Lacarra claims that Pidal, wittingly or not, was instrumental in this process of identification of Franco with the Cid: "Menéndez Pidal offers his contemporaries a lesson in conformity to the state and of obedience to authority. On the other hand, he also justifies arrogance and ambition on behalf of the supreme power of a military *Caudillo*." In addition, Pidal's interpretation of the Cid, as this was adopted by Francoist ideology, was dispensed by school textbooks in children's classrooms throughout Spain and, at a higher level, was unanimously endorsed by the nation's academic and university professors.

By the very act of turning to Pidal and his son for expert advice, the filmmakers of *El Cid*, rather than improving the historical accuracy of the film, instead present us with a misguided and harmful image of the Cid, one that dishonors the memory of thousands who suffered at the hands of the Franco regime. For the Cid of the film, at an almost subconscious level, is a Fascist vision of what this medieval hero should have been like. There is one place in *El Cid* where its Fascist subtext, for those who choose to scratch beneath the surface, becomes unmistakable. Not surprisingly, this occurs during the portrayal of the Cid's siege and triumphant entry into Valencia, which held such pregnant propaganda possibilities for Franco and Aranda. After building up our expectations by showing the magnificent siege towers being laboriously dragged into place, the film refrains from depicting a full-scale assault. Instead, Heston as the Cid slowly rides to the head of his impressive army, then stands in his stirrups, holds his hand aloft and addresses a long speech to the Valencians, urging them to "rid yourselves of your leaders, join with us!" Rather implausibly, the Cid tries to convince his half-starved victims that "we do not wish to attack you—we are not your enemy." He concludes this remarkable piece of histrionics by assuring the besieged, "We bring you peace. We bring you freedom. We bring you life. We bring you bread!" The last line is the cue for the catapults to let loose a hail of bread loaves, rather than stones, into the city. When the scene was filmed on February 18, 1961, Heston noted in his journal that "the switch of hurling groceries instead of stones from the siege engines looked rather comic to me, though it may read well enough in the script." However comic it now appears on the screen, this anticlimactic ending to the siege would have been positively hilarious had a shot of a cabbage impaling itself on a defender's spiked helmet not been edited from the final cut. By the time Heston wrote his autobiography thirty years later, he praised the scene for having followed the more bland script of history rather than one that might have pleased the crowd with violence and gore. But even Pidal, who places great emphasis on the Cid's humane treatment of his enemies, does not go so far as to say that his hero fed the inhabitants of a city he was trying to starve into submission. Instead, the scene closely follows a characteristic piece of Nationalist propaganda: that its conquering forces were humanitarian "liberators," as evidenced by carefully staged film footage of female members of the Falange distributing bread and food from the back of trucks to the outstretched hands of a grateful crowd. Meanwhile, behind the scenes, male terror squads were conducting mass executions of Franco's political opponents.

Once the Muslim inhabitants of Valencia dispatch their corrupt emir, al-Qadir (played by a suitably oily Frank Thring), the movie reaches a premature climax with the Cid's victory parade into the city. This is the ideological heart of the film, since it is here that the Cid refuses to accept the crown of Valencia except on behalf of his ideal of a unified Spain, albeit one headed by an unworthy king. Heston, quite rightly, judged the scene to be a crucial one. As an actor, he was drawn to the scene's emotional power, which was similar to what he had felt playing Moses' exodus in *The Ten Commandments* (1956), or what he was going to feel playing "Chinese" Gordon's return to the Sudan in *Khartoum* (1966). As Heston recalls in his autobiography, when he passed through the replica city gates as the Cid, he seemed to be magically transported in time to the eleventh century:

> We filmed his [the Cid's] entry into Valencia as bloodless, following Menéndez Pidal's account. The citizens welcomed him in preference to the weak King Alfonso as the abler soldier they needed against the Moors, offering him the crown of Valencia. The Cid, stubbornly unwilling to displace the king who had exiled him and imprisoned his wife and children, refused the crown, surely one of the outstanding examples of loyalty in history.
>
> It was also a key moment in the movie; I thought a lot about how to play it. As sometimes happens in a film, that wasn't necessary. It played itself. I led a mounted troop to the gates of the city, real iron gates set in the real stone wall of a medieval city. The sun and the sea were as they'd been a thousand years ago. The gates swung open, two thousand people screamed welcome. I rode through, Babieca [the Cid's horse] dancing under my hand, both of us aroused by the roar: "Cid! Cid! CID!" I swung off the horse, down into the welling sound, and climbed the steep, time-worn stone steps set in the wall. At the top, I turned, the sea behind me, the city and the people lying below, reaching, entreating, warm and open as a woman. "Cid! Cid! CID!"
>
> You don't have to act that. You can't act it. I was there. It happened to me. I know, in my bones and blood, what it is to take a city. Yes, of course it's like sex. It *is* sex . . . to the power of ten.

A large part of the sensual spell cast by this scene seems to have been the adulation accorded the great men of history. Nonetheless, Heston's libido was not aroused by anything authentically medieval. Regardless of how Valencia's Moorish citizens felt about becoming the subjects of a ruthless Christian mercenary, it never would have occurred to them to cheer on a leader in such a fashion. The same goes for an earlier scene showing the Cid followed into exile by an army of Castilian freebooters, who cry, "Cid! Cid! CID!" as their leader emerges from a barn where he

has just spent the night trysting with his wife. This is not to say that these
scenes are not historical. It's just that the leadership cult they portray is
from the wrong moment in history. Adulation of political figures by adoring crowds chanting simple slogans—whether these be "Franco!" "Duce!"
or "Zieg Heil!"—was peculiar to the Fascist movement of the twentieth
century. The army extras of the film, so accustomed to shouting "Franco!
Franco! FRANCO!" in support of their Caudillo, would have found it an
easy transition to mouth the words "Cid! Cid! CID!" Like the political
rallies staged by the Fascists, the crowd scenes in the film where everyone
calls in perfect unison the Cid's name were choreographed, in this case
under the direction of the movie's military advisor, Commandante Luis
Martin de Pozuelo, who issued his cues from a loudspeaker. (Pozuelo's
appointment as advisor came from the army general staff, not from
Bronston's production company.) Also present was the army minister and
Civil War veteran, General Antonio Barroso y Sánchez Guerra, who
enjoyed visiting the set and was apparently "eager to see his troops perform in a mock medieval battle."

The orgiastic cries of "Cid! Cid! CID!" that seduced Heston into
believing that he was back in the Middle Ages are not found in any
medieval source, not even in Pidal's history. They are entirely modern
inventions, made possible only by the propaganda techniques of crowd
psychology developed by the Nazis and other Fascist parties at their mass
rallies. To this day, Heston seems blissfully unaware that he reenacted on
the set of Peñiscola a Fascist leadership cult. During our personal interview, I asked Mr. Heston whether the Franco government had made any
attempt to influence the film:

> No. I remember the then Prince [Juan] Carlos came to the set and visited,
> and he was appropriately greeted, of course, and seemed to enjoy himself.
> But I never heard from the government or that there had been any involve-
> ment. I don't know why they would. We were telling probably Spain's most
> important story, and it was a story about a warrior.

When queried as to whether the political climate of Fascist Spain inadver-
tently affected the film in any way, the actor seemed genuinely puzzled and
responded, "I can't think how." Heston, like most audiences of his film, did
not have the benefit of an intimate knowledge of Spanish politics or history. The eight months that Heston spent in Spain were no doubt insulated
from the squalid daily life that was witnessed by Besas. (His arrival in the
country was smoothed by the special immigration and customs clearances
that Bronston was able to arrange with the normally strict Franco government.) Heston's only major contact with the Spanish public seems to have

been a "public relations exercise" at a bullfight in Castellón de la Plana, where he paraded with the matadors on the white horse he used to reenact the Cid's battles. For political reasons, Bronston never invited Franco onto the set, although the *Caudillo*'s designated successor, Prince Carlos, was a personal friend and, as Heston testifies, was eagerly invited to meet the stars. In the event, Carlos engineered a peaceful transition to democracy shortly after he became king upon the *Caudillo*'s demise in 1975. But in 1961, it was generally expected that Carlos would continue Franco's legacy, so that a Fascist regime would live on in Spain even after the founder's passing, much like how a corpse leads an army into battle at the conclusion of *El Cid*.

A more subtle point of entry for the Fascist agenda of the film is its portrayal of two kinds of Moors. At the very beginning of the movie, a voiceover narration tells us this about the Cid: "He rose above religious hatreds and called upon all Spaniards, whether Christian or Moor, to face a common enemy who threatened to destroy their land of Spain." This immediately cues the appearance of the film's villain, the Almoravid leader, Yusuf ibn Tashufin, played by Herbert Lom (later of *Pink Panther* fame). Robed all in black, Yusuf delivers a long harangue to the native Muslim emirs concerning both his hatred of civilization and his plans for world conquest:

> The Prophet has commanded us to rule the world! Where in all your land of Spain is the glory of Allah? When men speak of you they speak of poets, music-makers, doctors, scientists. Where are your warriors?! You dare call yourselves sons of the Prophet?!
>
> You have become women! Burn your books. Make warriors of your poets. Let your doctors invent new poisons for our arrows. Let your scientists invent new war machines. And then, kill! Burn! Infidels live on your frontiers. Encourage them to kill each other. And when they are weak and torn, I will sweep up from Africa. And thus the empire of the one God—the true God, Allah—will spread. First, across Spain. Then, across Europe. Then, the whole world!

Yusuf and the Almoravids thus represent the bad Moors, fanatical Muslims who will stop at nothing to slake their lust for power and in the process will destroy everything in their path. The film also makes it clear that Spain is the bulwark of civilization, a buffer zone against the new threat. If Spain falls, so goes Europe and the rest of the world.

Later in the film, we are introduced to the good Moors, the Muslims who choose to ally themselves with the Cid in order to resist the Almoravids. They are led by the emir of Zaragoza, al-Mu'tamin (played by

Douglas Wilmer), who dubs Rodrigo "El Cid" in recognition of the fact that he "has the vision to be just and the courage to be merciful." After a joyous reunion across a river separating their respective territories, the Cid and Mu'tamin converse on their common cause as they gaze on the bonhomie generated by their now combined armies:

> Cid: How can anyone say this is wrong?
> Mu'tamin: They will say so, on both sides.
> Cid: We have so much to give to each other, and to Spain.
> Mu'tamin: If we are not destroyed first.

Good Christians and good Moors, such as the Cid and Mu'tamin, here stand together against bad Christians and bad Moors, such as Alfonso and Yusuf, who wish to divide the country and rule.

This is hardly an accurate picture of the complex relations between the Christian and Muslim inhabitants of medieval Spain. It is true that there existed a certain amount of *convivencia*—literally "living together"—between the adherents of the two religions in eleventh-century Spain. But this was largely on a political level, confined to the country's upper classes. When the Cid soldiered for the *taifa* state of Zaragoza during the 1080s, for example, he did so not because he felt any ideological sympathy for Islamic nationalists, but simply because, as the *Historia Roderici* attests, he was well rewarded for his service. Alfonso VI was no more adverse than Rodrigo to allying himself with Moors when it suited his interests to do so, in contrast to his portrayal as a hard-line Christian in the film. As a matter of fact, Alfonso first exiled the Cid in 1081 because he had offended the king's Muslim client, al-Qadir, at that time emir of Toledo. From 1092, Alfonso's *convivencia* took a more personal turn when he took on a Moorish mistress, Zaida, the widow of the emir of Córdoba, who presented him with the king's only male heir, Sánchez Alonso.

It is also true that the Almoravids were distrusted and despised by Spain's eleventh-century establishment, Christian and Muslim alike, because they were perceived as fanatical outsiders who had little appreciation for the country's unique and sophisticated Mozarabic culture. Yusuf not only defeated Alfonso at Sagrajas in 1086, he also deposed almost all of the southern *taifa* kings in 1090 and 1091. But while Spanish Christians refused to look upon the Almoravids as anything other than "Ishmaelite" barbarians, to use the words of the *Historia Roderici*, the Moorish political leaders of al-Andalus, when push came to shove, still preferred a Moroccan Muslim ruler to a Castilian Christian one. Yusuf and his Almoravid army were highly popular among Spain's Muslim rank and file, and nowhere more so than in Valencia, where they were viewed as liberators from the oppressive tax policies of their emirs and the Cid. The film would have been more accurate, indeed, if it had shown Valencia's populace screaming, "Yusuf! Yusuf! YUSUF!" instead of "Cid! Cid! CID!"

What, then, is the significance behind *El Cid*'s two-faced portrayal of Islam? The film's message is remarkably in sync with the all-pervading fear of Islamic terrorism that has swept the Western political landscape ever since September 11, 2001. Yusuf is a kind of medieval Osama bin Laden figure, out to turn the clock back to a pure, fundamentalist version of Islam unsullied by a corrupt and decadent Western civilization. Meanwhile, the Christian society that is the fanatic's target seeks allies among the more civilized Muslims, who may feel just as threatened by their coreligionist's radicalism. Obviously, global terrorism had not assumed the importance during the making of the film that it has today. What did alarm many in the West when the movie debuted in 1961, a year before the Cuban Missile Crisis, was the seemingly ever-present and omnipotent threat of communism. During the Cold War, the "Red Scare" was seen as a danger that could infiltrate America from both without and within. This was no less true of Spain during the Civil War, when the Popular Front and the Republicans were known to be assisted by the Soviets (among others). Even though Franco was also receiving foreign help—from Fascist Italy and Germany—this was not so objectionable in a country as Catholic as Spain, for whom the openly atheist stance of communism was anathema. Indeed, many in the 1930s considered fascism the only ideology capable of beating off the "Godless Reds." At the very beginning of the Civil War, on July 25, 1936, the same day that his representatives approached Hitler for aid, Franco gave a speech that eerily echoes the opening narration of *El Cid*:

> We are in a war that is resembling more and more the character of a crusade, of a great historical campaign, and of a transcendental struggle of people and civilizations. This war has chosen Spain again in history, like a battlefield of tragedy and honor, to save herself and to bring peace to a world gone mad. . . . In view of the enemy that we are confronting . . . we have decided before God and the Spanish nation to carry out this unification endeavor . . . a mission that has been entrusted to us by God.

Here are all the themes of the movie: the need for unity in the face of a common enemy who threatens to destroy Spain in a struggle that will also decide the fate of world civilization.

There is another, even closer parallel between Nationalist propaganda during the Civil War and *El Cid*'s depiction of the Moors. Franco began his military career in the Spanish Foreign Legion, the *Tercio de Extranjeros*, which was assigned to police the Spanish Protectorate of northern

Morocco. Due to his bravery and iron discipline (legionnaires could be shot if disrespectful to a superior officer), Franco rose rapidly in the ranks, and by 1926 he was, at thirty-three, the youngest general in Europe. It was in the Legion that Franco perfected the terror tactics he was later to turn on his own countrymen. Basically, he employed two types of troops, just like the good and bad Moors of the movie. Franco's "good Moors" were the regular *legionarios* in his reconstituted Army of Africa, who supposedly had returned to Spain to save it from communism. They included the *Guardia Mora*, or Moorish Guard, Franco's personal bodyguard composed of native Moroccans dressed in the flowing white robes of Bedouin tribesmen, who formed an important part of the new leadership cult around the *Caudillo*. On October 1, 1936, the Moorish Guard—mounted on horseback— escorted their leader into the main square of Salamanca to witness Franco's investiture as head of state, just like the Cid paraded with Mu'tamin and other Moorish allies into Valencia during the film. Franco's "bad Moors" were the native Moroccan mercenaries, or *Regulares*, whom he recruited into his African army. Commanded by Spanish officers who spoke their language and knew their culture, the *Regulares* were given the most bar- baric duty on campaign: to loot, rape, murder, and sexually mutilate Republican resisters. Often, Franco delayed his advance and pursued a war of attrition, resulting in heavy casualties among his own troops, in order to mop up the political opposition using these greatly feared foreign forces. A town besieged by the Nationalists was typically told that only the "good Moors" in Franco's army could avert its imminent destruction by the inhuman invader, their "bad Moor" comrades, provided the inhabitants surrendered and handed over all Republican sympathizers to be summar- ily shot. *El Cid*'s portrayal of good and bad Moors makes historical sense only in the context of the two "Moors" Franco used to win the Civil War.

Once again, Mr. Heston seemed clueless as to the Fascist subtext of his film. When I asked him whether he thought the Moors should be por- trayed any differently if the movie were to be made today, he responded, "No, I don't think so. I think they were portrayed correctly. There were good Moors and bad Moors, and it worked out very well." In all fairness to Heston, most everyone outside of Spain at the time of the film's release would also have been unaware of the deeper and darker meanings behind the seemingly innocuous plot. But in Spain itself, the political message would have been unmistakable to a population only a generation removed from the Civil War. To them, the Cid was the Middle Ages' Franco, a medieval justification for the current regime. Ironically, Franco himself was unable to attend *El Cid*'s Madrid premiere on December 27, 1961 as the result of a shooting accident he suffered on Christmas Eve. But Heston, who was present and lamented Franco's absence, recorded in his journal that "the audience reaction was, of course, the best yet." Even on the superficial level that most audiences understood the film, *El Cid* played a crucial role in the rehabilitation of Spain on the international stage. Despite Franco's claims that Spain had remained neutral during the Second World War, the country had supplied the Axis powers with Wolfram, a metal ore used to make armor-piercing artillery shells, and even sent a "Blue Division" of Falangist volunteers to fight alongside the Wehrmacht. As a result of this collaboration, Spain was excluded from the United Nations at the war's end. Yet the ensuing Cold War ensured the survival of any leader—even a Fascist one—who openly declared his country to be "a happy, unified oasis of peace in a troubled world in which the Communist hordes were ceaselessly on the prowl." Franco astutely played on America's new fears of the Red Menace, and the decade prior to the making of *El Cid* was marked by a rapprochement between Spain and the nation that had sent the "Abraham Lincoln" brigade to fight on the Republican side during the Civil War. In 1953, Franco signed the Defense Pacts agreement that gave the United States a military presence on five air bases and countless naval installations throughout Spain. The U.S. president who negotiated the bases agreement, Dwight Eisenhower, set the seal on Spain's reentry into the world community when he paid a state visit to Franco in 1959. *El Cid* was merely the icing on the cake for America's new ally in its anti-Communist crusade.

CHAPTER FOUR

Splendid in Spandex
Robin Hood Films

The Background

The quasi-historical figure of Robin Hood joins Joan of Arc as perhaps the only personalities from the Middle Ages who can rival the popularity of King Arthur. Indeed, it may be that Robin Hood is too popular, for during the writing of this chapter, one of my books on the legendary thief was actually stolen! (Perhaps my muse has an ironic sense of humor.) A surer indication of Robin Hood's legacy is that no less than three dozen films and television shows feature him as their central character. This doesn't count the many other films indebted in some way to the Robin Hood legend: the *Ivanhoe* productions, for instance, in which Robin Hood has a walk-on role; the "son of Robin Hood" sequels; "Robin Hood Westerns," which pursue the outlaw theme in the American Wild West; movies about the "Scottish Robin Hoods," Rob Roy and William Wallace; and brazen Robin Hood knockoffs, such as *The Flame and the Arrow* (1950). Like King Arthur, Robin Hood has become a cultural phenomenon, invading many other mediums in between the medieval ballads and the modern cinema. These include the "Robin Hood Games," a version of the May Games in which whole villages throughout England from the fifteenth to the seventeenth centuries would celebrate a "Robin Hood Daye," most likely culminating in a dramatic presentation of some kind. In addition, there are any number of Robin Hood plays, poems, novels, children's books, comics, illustrations, and other assorted paraphernalia. Unlike the King Arthur corpus, however, none of the modern written versions of the Robin Hood story have quite the memorable power as the cinema's reimagining of his world. Whereas our imaginations about King Arthur are haunted by the words of T.H. White or Alfred Lord Tennyson (who was unable to work the same magic in his Robin Hood drama, *The Foresters*), it is Errol Flynn's portrayal in *The Adventures of Robin Hood* (1938) that rules our recollections of the famous outlaw.

The parallels between Robin Hood and King Arthur can be drawn out even further when one considers their respective origins. Both are shrouded in obscurity, and in each case an academic industry has sprung up to illuminate the darkness. It is no accident that the same sensationalist authors, Graham Phillips and Martin Keatman, who claim to have unearthed "the true story" of King Arthur, have also written an exposé of "the man behind the myth" of Robin Hood. (Their candidate: Robert Fitz Odo of Loxley, Warwickshire, on the sole grounds that an unidentified grave slab in Loxley churchyard is "remarkably similar" to another unidentified grave slab in Yorkshire traditionally associated with Robin Hood.) As noted in Chapter 1, legends have a way of becoming far more potent than reality. The search for the real Robin Hood, like the search for the real King Arthur, is probably a fruitless quest, which isn't to say that historians and antiquarians of great ingenuity haven't tried. Instead, it is the myth of Robin Hood, and the meanings to be mined from it, that seem more real than a flesh and blood figure who may lurk underneath all the layers of legend.

Even so, it is perhaps obligatory to review what evidence there is for the existence of a real Robin Hood. Naturally enough, it has been historians and their antiquarian ancestors of the nineteenth century who have been most interested in pursuing the elusive quarry of an historical figure to correspond to the legend. One notices that the latest literary scholars of the outlaw, such as Stephen Knight and Jeffrey Singman, studiously avoid or downplay the thorny issue of whether there was a real Robin Hood. In this, they are following the lead of *their* nineteenth-century predecessor, Francis Child, who produced a definitive edition of all the Robin Hood ballads as part of his grand survey of the entire English and Scottish ballad genre. Child, none too impressed with attempts thus far to locate a real Robin Hood, declared that such an effort required "an uncommon insensibility to the ludicrous," which would inevitably lead one to the conclusion that Robin Hood was "absolutely a creation of the ballad muse." If one took this advice to heart, one would stop right there and go on to talk about the medieval *Gest of Robyn Hode*. But historians are not ones to be dictated to by cranky literature professors.

So the search continues. Right from the start, it should be pointed out that there is absolutely no credible evidence that the real Robin Hood lived as an outlaw during the reign of Richard the Lionheart (1189–1199) or of his younger brother John (1199–1216), as is retailed in all the movies about him. This fiction is based on an early, very short "biography" of Robin Hood by the Scottish chronicler, John Major, who included it as part of his *Historia Majoris Britanniae* (*History of Great Britain*) published in 1521. Aside from dating Robin Hood's activities to the years 1193–1194, when King Richard was held captive on his way home from the Third Crusade, Major also states that Robin was the "prince of thieves," who "permitted no harm to women nor seized the goods of the poor, but helped them generously with what he took from abbots." As we will see, popular notions that Robin helped restore Richard to the English throne and "stole from the rich to give to the poor" have no basis in any authentic medieval tradition about him. Nevertheless, they were to be endlessly repeated down through the ages by various antiquaries, poets, and playwrights, who embroidered this fantasy by assigning Robin a birthplace, Locksley; a noble title as earl of Huntingdon; and even an elaborate pedigree dating back to the time of William the Conqueror (1066–1087) and a gravestone at Kirklees in Yorkshire, complete with a seven to eight line epitaph.

This is not to say, however, that some of these familiar aspects of Robin's screen persona do not find a firm foundation in the Middle Ages. Hereward the Wake, considered to be the first English outlaw, was a Saxon nobleman dispossessed during the reign of William the Conqueror; it is his story of Saxon resistance to Norman oppression, first written down in the twelfth century, that was later to become enshrined in the Robin Hood tradition, largely through Sir Walter Scott's 1819 novel, *Ivanhoe*. Unlike Robin Hood, Hereward's existence as a real historical character is readily attested to by the medieval records, such as the *Anglo-Saxon Chronicle* and *Domesday Book*. Another historical outlaw, Fulk Fitzwarin, was one of the barons to force King John into signing Magna Carta in 1215. The French prose romance of his career, composed by the late twelfth century, tells of Fulk's struggle to both recover his inheritance and free England from King John's tyranny, two plot elements that became a part of the Robin Hood legend when it received an aristocratic makeover in the plays of Anthony Munday in 1598. The Robin Hood of the silver screen thus does correspond closely with some authentic medieval out-laws—but none of them are Robin Hood.

The closest that medieval records come to disgorging a real Robin Hood who can correspond to the one inhabiting the late twelfth-century setting of most films is the Robert Hod, or Hobbehod, of Yorkshire: He was a fugitive of justice in 1225 and was fined in absentia for the sum of £1.5, according to the pipe rolls of the exchequer for 1226–1234. It is just possible that Hod may be an alias for Robert of Wetherby, an "outlaw and evildoer of our land" who was hunted down and hanged in 1225 by the sheriff of Yorkshire, Eustace de Lowdham. Another Robert Hood, servant of the abbot of Cirencester, is recorded as the slayer of Ralph of Cirencester in 1213–1216; however, this crime took place in Gloucestershire, near the southern border with Wales, and thus is far from the geographical origin of Robin Hood's legend, in Sherwood Forest and Barnsdale. That's all we have on these early "Robin Hoods," and admittedly, it's not much to go on. Yet shadowy as he is, it is the Robert Hod, fugitive, of 1225 who is the one favored by the leading Robin Hood historian, James C. Holt, as the most likely candidate for the real outlaw. There are some good reasons for this. For one thing, he is the only Hood recorded as outlawed by the medieval English courts. Another point in his favor is that his legend seems to have gained some currency during the latter half of the thirteenth century. Between 1261 and 1296, no less than eight men with the surname "Robinhood"—combining the first and last names of the outlaw—are found in various records. According to legal documents, five of these Robinhoods were charged with a crime and two of the five were actually outlawed. The earliest "Robehod," from 1261–1262, was an alias assigned by royal officials to a fugitive whose real name was William, son of Robert le Fevere of Berkshire. If Robinhood nicknames were already being used this far south in England, so the argument goes, then the original man behind the legend, if there was such a person, must have existed some decades earlier. Adding to the dossier of the case is that the only medieval chroniclers to mention Robin Hood, the Scotsmen Andrew de Wyntoun and Walter Bower, both of whom wrote during the first half of the fifteenth century, place the outlaw in the 1200s, between 1266 and 1285. Moreover, the thirteenth century, as James Holt is at pains to point out, was a time when the targets of Robin Hood's wrath—such as sheriffs, royal forest law, and Church land grabbing—were also at the center of England's political debates.

As might be expected, this far from settles the matter. For the setting and cultural milieu of the Robin Hood ballads that survive from the Middle Ages are more in tune with the fourteenth century than with any other period. Their emphasis on archery skills, yeomanry, maintenance of retainers "with cloth and fee," and, above all, on a hero king called Edward—most likely Edward II (1307–1327) or Edward III (1327–1377)—all point to the later Middle Ages. Nor can the ballads' concern with distraint of knighthood, abuses of sheriffs, or oppression of the forest law be taken as exclusive of any one time period, for they were equally omnipresent during the fourteenth as the thirteenth century. But in other respects, the world of Robin Hood—one of rampant corruption throughout the legal hierarchy, ready resorts to retributive violence, and fluid social structures—accords most well with what we know of late medieval England. There is always the danger that our darker picture of the later Middle Ages is simply due to the better survival of unflattering records. And it is always perilous to argue for the historicity of Robin Hood from the ballads, since these share many stock elements with other legends, as another Robin Hood historian, Maurice Keen, has demonstrated. Yet it is also true that Robin Hood's legend has more in common with the later outlaw tradition—especially with the *Tale of Gamelyn*, which is securely dated to the mid-fourteenth century—than with an earlier one.

A fourteenth-century Robin Hood has the distinction of being the first and perhaps the most widely accepted candidate for the honor of being the real outlaw. In 1852, an assistant keeper of records at the Public Record Office in London, Joseph Hunter, announced that he had uncovered a "Robyn Hode" in a household account book, where he is recorded as porter of the king's chamber between March and November 1324. The timing of Robyn's royal service, Hunter argued, tallies well with the *Gest of Robyn Hode* if "Edwarde, our comly king" is identified with Edward II. The king had personally visited Nottingham in November 1323 as part of a tour of the northern counties, during which time he presumably could have pardoned Robyn and invited him to join his household, as he does in the *Gest*. But there is no evidence to suggest that this "Robyn" was ever a fugitive of justice, let alone a criminal. Even so, Hunter's Robyn, to this day, still has his staunch defenders, among them the legal historian, John Bellamy, who has written probably the most detailed investigation into the historical Robin Hood. It was Bellamy who parried Holt's discovery that "Robyn Hode" actually had been in the king's employ earlier than previously thought: by June 1323, five months *before* King Edward visited Nottingham in November. In a chapter devoted to chronology, Bellamy shows that Robyn could have been reconciled with the king during an earlier period of the king's northern tour, when he visited Nottingham in March and possibly again in April 1323, and thus just in time for him to show up in the royal household accounts in June. Bellamy also devotes much space and energy to finding other fourteenth-century historical analogues to the minor characters of the *Gest*, particularly Sir Richard at the Lee, the poor knight whom Robin befriends and succors in the greenwood.

There is also the possibility that the real Robin Hood lived during the 1330s, which was early in the reign of Edward III. These years coincided with the heyday of some notorious outlaw bands, such as the Folvilles and the Coterels, who operated chiefly in the northern counties of Nottinghamshire, Derbyshire, Leicestershire, and Rutland. It was also a time when outlaws consciously imitated the royal style when going about their intimidation and extortion. The most famous example of this is the letter to Richard de Snowshill, parson of Huntingdon, from a Yorkshire criminal who called himself "Lionel, king of the rout of raveners [robbers]," and who signed off with, "given at our castle of the North Wind, in the Green Tower, in the first year of our reign." The young king, Edward III, is likewise a better model for the *Gest*'s "comly kynge" than Edward II. In contrast to his father, he was extremely popular and virile, delighting in tournaments, war, and games of chivalry. One can well believe that this is the king of the *Gest* who gives Robin an ear-ringing buffet for missing his mark and who consents to don Robin's livery of Lincoln green as they shoot arrows together on their way to Nottingham. Moreover, Edward III's reign was long enough to encompass the 22 years during which Robin, according to the *Gest*, lives in the greenwood in "drede of Edwarde our kynge" after leaving the royal service.

In 1330, Edward III did come to Nottingham, where he staged a dramatic coup d'etat against the corrupt regency of his mother, Isabella, and her lover, Roger Mortimer, by taking them prisoner in a nocturnal raid on Nottingham Castle. Obviously, this is highly reminiscent of the later tradition whereby Robin and Richard stage their own coup against the tyrannical regency of Prince John. Edward was also known for his policy of pardoning even notorious criminals, such as the Folvilles and Coterels, in exchange for military service in his Scottish or French wars. In addition, Edward conducted a national enquiry in 1341 that brought to light myriad abuses committed by his officials—sheriffs chief among them—which had given rise to grievances harbored by his subjects stretching back several years. These investigations uncovered a real sheriff of Nottingham, John de Oxford, whom the historian, J.R. Maddicott, notes is an especially good candidate for Robin's archenemy. Especially if one views Robin as a champion of the poor and dispossessed, then Oxford certainly qualifies as a villain, for in 1338 he seized 20 oxen from four "powerless" men and forced them "to hand over their winter seed, on account of which they sold their land and are utterly reduced to nothing." Maddicott also argues that the mention of "rymes of Robyn Hood" in a version of William Langland's poem, *Piers Plowman*, dated to 1377—which is the first reference anywhere to a literature surrounding the outlaw—implies that the real Robin Hood must have lived in the earlier part of the century, when his legend would have had time to germinate—but not too much time to be forgotten—in the decades in between.

After reading all the claims and counterclaims and rampant speculations, one comes away with the distinct impression that the real Robin Hood will never step forward out of the pages of history. At times, it even seems as if historians are more bent on taking aim at their competitors' contenders than advancing constructive arguments for their own champions. Barrie Dobson and John Taylor, who have produced a widely read modern edition of the Robin Hood ballads, asked despairingly in 1989: "Could it be that the time has finally come when it is no longer profitable to search for a fourteenth- or even thirteenth-century Englishman whose real name was Robert or Robin Hood at all?" Eight years later, in a revised edition of their work published in 1997, their conclusion was that, "at the end of the twentieth century Robin Hood remains almost as elusive as ever." Instead, Dobson and Taylor point to a "third way" to Robin's historical identification, that is, that Robin Hood did not actually exist as a real man, but rather as a favorite acronym to be applied to any outlaw whose notoriety drew the attention of legal clerks and lawyers. In place of one real Robin Hood to have graced the stage of medieval history, there may have been several, so that, in essence, all of the candidates put forward as the outlaw have validity. For who's to say that such a legendary figure was simply one man, and not a conglomeration of many, whose reputations and deeds down the centuries became bound up together in a story of Robin Hood?

This brings us to the medieval Robin Hood ballads which, after all, are our only evidence as to how the Middle Ages imagined Robin Hood. In the end, it is these ballads that bring us closest to the real Robin Hood, such as he may have existed in medieval times. It has been argued in recent years that plays about Robin Hood were just as important as ballads in shaping the legend. As early as 1426–1427, a play or "game" of Robin Hood was recorded as performed in Exeter, but of what this performance consisted is not known. Even if the plays were as important as has been claimed, without the original texts to guide us we have no way of determining their influence. The earliest Robin Hood play to survive is a fragment of "Robin Hood and the Sheriff," which was written down on the back of an accountant's ledger circa 1475. However, most literary scholars believe that this play was derived from an earlier ballad, rather than the other way around.

A connection between Robin Hood ballads and plays becomes clear when one realizes that the ballads were meant to be spoken rather than sung in the usual sense. Altogether, there are five verse "ballads" that give us an authentically medieval Robin Hood. By far the longest, most comprehensive, and most studied of the original ballads is *A Gest of Robyn Hode*, first printed towards the end of the fifteenth century but dated on linguistic grounds to an earlier period, between 1400 and 1450. The *Gest* functions for the Robin Hood legend much like Sir Thomas Malory's *Le Morte D'Arthur* does for French Arthurian romance: It unifies and perhaps condenses preexisting tradition in order to produce a coherent linear narrative. Although the literary scholar, David Fowler, calls the *Gest* "the work

of a skilled artist" whose "narrative symmetry" is comparable to the
Arthurian romances, it is, in fact, less sophisticated than those works or
Malory's masterpiece derived from them. One reason for this may be that
Robin Hood's legend had far less time to develop the complexity that cen-
turies of evolution produced in the story of King Arthur. Another possibil-
ity is that the author of the *Gest* strove to make his art more accessible to a
wider audience than the refined tastes of the aristocratic patrons of
Arthurian romance. Of the four other ballads that preserve a medieval
Robin Hood, two of them — *Robin Hood and the Monk* and *Robin Hood and the
Potter* — tell their own unique tales independent of the *Gest*. Unlike the latter, both survive in manuscript copies in a late fifteenth-century hand. The
last two ballads — *Robin Hood's Death* and *Robin Hood and Guy of Gisborne* —
come down to us only in a seventeenth-century manuscript called the
Percy Folio. Nevertheless, they are considered medieval by association:
Robin Hood's Death because it tells essentially the same story as in the eighth
"fytte" of the *Gest*, and *Robin Hood and Guy of Gisborne* because it is strikingly
similar to the 1475 play fragment of "Robin Hood and the Sheriff."

There are two qualities to these early ballads that mark Robin Hood
as a distinctly medieval character. One is the ballads' concern with abuses
of the law and corruption in the judicial system. The target of their complaints is, of course, the sheriff of Nottingham, who embodies all that is
wrong with the administration of the king's justice. This is amply borne out
in the *Gest* when the sheriff is prepared to execute Robin Hood's ally, Sir
Richard at the Lee, without so much as a trial, and shows himself ready to
do the same to Little John in *Robin Hood and Guy of Gisborne*. Revenge is
swift and sure in each case: The sheriff is shot and beheaded by Robin
Hood in the course of his rescue of Sir Richard, while Little John, after he
is freed by Robin, takes "an arrow broade" and aims it so well at the retreat-
ing sheriff that it "did cleave his heart in twinn." Judicial corruption also
rears its ugly head in the *Gest* in the form of the high justice of England.
When Sir Richard begs his aid against the abbot of St. Mary's, who is about
to seize the knight's estates on account of a delinquent loan repayment, the
justice replies, "I am holde with the abbot, both with cloth and fee." This
means that no matter how pitiful his case, the knight will lose in court
because the justice has been bribed with money and liveries to take the
abbot's side. When Sir Richard triumphantly produces the money owed to
the abbot, the justice retains his fee in spite of the abbot's losses.

The perversion of justice by the very men expected to uphold the
law — the judges, sheriffs, and juries who were taking bribes or extorting
money for their own profit — was of particular concern to the political
community of late medieval England. Although plenty of parliamentary
petitions and statutes were put forward to address the problem, none were

effective, as the necessity of repeating these punitive remedies testifies. In their frustration, many no doubt turned to alternative means of redress. In this light, the real-life criminal bands who wreaked vengeance on corrupt officials—just like Robin Hood unleashes on the sheriff of Nottingham— must have assumed an almost heroic aura. The Folville gang, for instance, was notorious for the murder of Roger Bellers, an unpopular baron of the exchequer, and for the kidnaping and holding to ransom of Richard Willoughby, a puisne justice and future chief justice of the king's bench, who was later to be indicted for having "sold the laws as if they had been oxen or cattle." These attacks—which took place in 1326 and 1332, respectively—were directed against judges who were hated as symbols of oppressive justice and seemed to have earned the Folvilles the admiration, rather than condemnation, of their peers. The chronicler Henry Knighton characterizes Richard de Folville as "a fierce, daring, and impudent man" and implies that the kidnaping of Justice Willoughby was in retribution for the excessive outlawry meted out by the judges of trailbaston [courts named after the "baston," a heavy club typically used in assault crimes] the year before. In *Piers Plowman*, William Langland appeals to "Folville's laws" as the only kind of justice that can "recover what was wrongfully taken" by "false men." How far people's approval of outlaws could go was demonstrated at Ipswich, Suffolk in 1344. To celebrate the demise of an unpopular officer of the king's bench, John de Holtby, the townsmen held a party for his murderers, at which they gave them "presents such as food and drink and gold and silver and sang so many songs of rejoicing in their honor there that it was as if God had come down from heaven." It was then recorded in the indictment that the murderers sat on the steps of the town hall and summoned the chief justice, Sir William Shareshull, to appear before them on penalty of £100. Political poems, such as the *Song of the Venality of the Judges* and the *Outlaw's Song of Trailbaston*, both dating to the early fourteenth century, harp on the abuses of the current legal system and, in the case of the *Outlaw's Song*, look for relief to the greenwood of "Belregard," where "there is no deceit there, nor any bad law."

The second main theme of the medieval Robin Hood ballads is the ready and unremorseful resort to violence. We already have noted how the unfortunate sheriff of Nottingham dies in both the *Gest* and *Robin Hood and Guy of Gisborne*. In the latter tale, Robin not only cuts off Gisborne's head, but afterwards sticks "itt on his bowes end" and slashes "Sir Guy in the fface" all over with his "Irish kniffe," so that "never on a woman borne/Cold tell who Sir Guye was." Perhaps the most shocking violence occurs in *Robin Hood and the Monk*. As Little John settles scores with the monk who had turned Robin in to the sheriff at Nottingham, Much the Miller's son murders in cold blood a young boy, the monk's "litull page, for ferd lest he wold tell." This is not the sort of behavior we normally expect of Robin's "merry men," as they are portrayed in most movies and children's books, where the worst that they do is humiliate their enemies with mischievous pranks and daring escapades. Even in the lighthearted *Robin Hood and the Potter*, the duel between the two protagonists gets ugly when the potter gives Robin a hefty blow in the neck with his staff, knocking him to the ground so that his men must intervene before he is slain. In *Robin Hood's Death*, there is an apocalyptic denouement in which Little John wishes to burn down Kirklees Priory, where Robin has been bled to death, an act that is narrowly averted by Robin's chivalry toward the virgin nuns. Not even the seventeenth-century ballad romance of *Robin Hood and Maid Marian*, where Robin's love interest first appears, can escape a bloody tone. The two lovers commence their courtship by fighting an hour-long battle in disguise in the greenwood, after which they get drunk together until they are legless! This veritable celebration of violence in the ballads may have appealed to the militaristic tastes of real-life archers and robbers. One English soldier recorded in the king's pay in 1338 seems to have been so enamored of the outlaw that he adopted the nickname, "Robyn Hode"; a century later, in 1441, a band of yeomen and peasants who practiced highway robbery on the side were known for singing, "We arn Robynhodesmen, war war war!"

Undoubtedly, the violent tenor of the ballads merely reflects what went on in the real underworld. On occasion, the crimes dryly recorded in the medieval legal records can shock, especially when the victims are defenseless children and women. In April 1362, Thomas Porter, a chaplain, came to the house of William Webster of Pocklington, Yorkshire, and assaulted his wife, Agnes, whom he had raped and robbed some months earlier. When she would not consent to have sex with him a second time, he set fire to the Websters' two-year-old son, burning off one of his feet so that the poor child was permanently lame. In general, medieval England, probably like most parts of Europe at this time, was a violent place. The historian James Given, who has studied the prevalence of homicide in England during the thirteenth century, concludes that "the threat of violence and the effects of violence were, if not a common part of the average Englishman's day, something that he could expect to experience, if only as a spectator, at some time in his life." Even when hardened criminals were run to ground, such as happened to that "fierce, daring, and impudent man," Richard de Folville, at Teigh in Rutland in 1340–1341, the cycle of violence was not at an end. For the manner in which Richard was brought to justice was, from a legal point of view, most unsatisfactory. He was dragged out of the church where he had taken sanctuary and summarily beheaded by the local keeper of the peace, Sir Robert de Colville. This not only violated Richard's right to a jury trial, but also, since Richard was a priest, his benefit of clergy, by which he should have been handed over to the bishop of Lincoln to be tried in an ecclesiastical court. Indeed, it may have been his knowledge that Richard would most likely acquit himself through the more lenient standards of a Church court that determined Colville to mete out rough justice on his quarry while he still had him in his power. Colville's only penalty for his vigilante methods was to receive a whipping after being absolved by Bishop Burghersh and the pope.

These themes of outlaw justice and violence are highlighted even more strongly in the *Tale of Gamelyn*, which is roughly contemporary with the Robin Hood ballads. At the end of the tale, Gamelyn avenges himself on his elder brother, the sheriff, who had disinherited him, by violently overturning the whole machinery of justice—to include not only the sheriff but also judge and jury—which is about to unjustly hang Gamelyn's other brother and ally, Sir Ote. Gamelyn strides into the court and, in brutally efficient fashion, changes places with the judge on his high seat. While "the justice sat still," Gamelyn "cleved his cheeke boon" and then "threw him over the barre and his arm to-brak." After the sheriff, judge, and jury are all bound in chains, Gamelyn's outlaws file in to make up a new jury that delivers a swift verdict. The "justice and the scherreve both hanged hye," while the "twelve sisours [jurors]" who had been bribed by Gamelyn's evil brother to convict Sir Ote are "hanged faste by the nekke." Thus, the message of the *Tale of Gamelyn* is quite clear: True justice can only come from outside the corrupt system and only through violent means. Fortunately for Gamelyn, the king approves of his rough and ready reform; he not only pardons him and Sir Ote, but, in a nice twist of irony, he makes Gamelyn his new chief justice of the forest.

Finally, we should ask if there is any medieval basis to the popular image of Robin as the "prince of thieves" who robbed from the rich to give to the poor? The only possible reference to this role in all the medieval ballads comes at the end of the *Gest*, when the last stanza prays for mercy on Robin's soul, "For he was a good outlawe/And dyde pore men moch god." One must be careful, however, to avoid automatically assuming that "pore men" refers to the class of medieval peasants, as opposed to their lords. The beginning of the *Gest* makes it clear that Robin's poor beneficiaries could just as well be impoverished gentry and nobility. In response to Little John's question of "Where we shall robbe, where we shal reve [despoil],/Where we shal bete and bynde," the outlaw chief admonishes his men to not only "loke ye do no husbonde harm/That tylleth with his ploughe," but also:

No more ye shall no gode yeman
That walketh by grene wode shawe [thicket];

Ne no knyght ne no squyer
That wol be a gode felawe.

The very first "guest" that the outlaws convey to the greenwood in order
to dine with them and be robbed is a poor knight with but 10 shillings on
his person. After confessing that he cannot "pay" for his meal, the knight
proceeds to tell his tale of woe: He has been forced to bail out a son convicted of manslaughter for the sum of £400, to raise which he has put his
estate in hock to the abbot of St. Mary's. Sir Richard is, in fact, the only
"pore man" for whom Robin does "moch god." When Much the Miller's
son questions the wisdom of Robin's loan of £400 to the knight, Little John
rebukes him with, "It is almus to helpe a gentyll knyght/That is fal in
poverte." One could call this, perhaps, stealing from the rich to give to the
not so rich. Robin as an agent of class warfare simply will not work in the
medieval ballads.

Nevertheless, the idea of Robin Hood as an instrument of social—and
not just legal—justice was given considerable credibility in an article written in the late 1950s by Rodney Hilton. Hilton broke ranks with his fellow
historians and dismissed the search for a real Robin Hood, whom he
regarded as nothing more than a "literary creation." This was prelude to
Hilton's main argument, that Robin's true identity was "as a by-product of
the agrarian social struggle." As they demonstrated in their revolt of 1381,
late-medieval English peasants had a major grievance with landlords who
attempted to reimpose oppressive rents and services in the aftermath of the
Black Death, a plague that in 1348–1349 wiped out half the population and
thus made surviving peasant labor far more valuable than before. Hilton
claimed that the "history of intertwined economic and social grievances,
affecting rich and poor peasants, the servile, the would-be free and the
free, seems . . . to have generated the Robin Hood ballads." Villains such
as the abbot of St. Mary's were symbols of "unrelenting land lordism" and
of "landowners who tended to be the most tenacious of their rights and the
least sympathetic in face of social demands from below." On this basis,
then, Robin Hood really was a champion of the peasant class who robbed
from the rich to give to the poor. Moreover, the greenwood, according to
Hilton, represented a realm of "equals, under the direction of a leader chosen for his bravery, not imposed because of his wealth and power." It
should be mentioned that Hilton was not the first to advance these arguments, although he certainly did so more skillfully and subtly that his predecessors, such as H.C. Coote, who in 1885 proclaimed with polemic abandon that the Robin Hood ballads constituted "an epic of communism."

In a riposte published two years later, James Holt effectively demol-
ished Hilton's thesis. Holt pointed out that the northern locale of Robin

Hood's story made it unlikely that the ballads had anything to do with peasant upheavals, such as the Rising of 1381, which took place in the south, in and around London. In general, the north was much more conservative—politically, socially, and religiously—than the south, a maxim that was to hold true right through to the early modern period. What is more, the fascination of the ballads with hunting and hospitality, Holt contended, is more indicative of a genteel origin than a rustic one. But the main thrust of Holt's argument focused on the audience of the ballads: Who was listening to, and thereby patronizing, the Robin Hood tales? The internal evidence of the *Gest* strongly suggests an appeal for the attention of an aristocratic, or at least gentrified, audience. In the opening stanza, an anonymous narrator says:

> Lythe [still] and listin, gentilmen,
> That be of frebore blode;
> I shall you tel of a gode yeman,
> His name was Robyn Hode.

Far from having a revolutionary agenda, the *Gest*, according to Holt, betrays a conservative concern to preserve the precedence of a strict social hierarchy. When Robin stands the poor knight, Sir Richard at the Lee, a supper, he demands payment, since "it was never the maner, by dere worthi God,/A yoman to pay for a knyhht." Upon learning of his poverty, Robin wonders if Sir Richard had been "made a knyght of force/Or ellys of yemanry," or in other words, was he a parvenu to the ranks of the lower nobility by virtue of a forced monetary payment? In reply, Sir Richard proudly affirms his noble lineage: "An hundred wynter here before/Myn auncestres knyghtes have be." Even the other members of Robin's band—Little John, Much, and "Scarlock" [Scarlett]—are mindful of maintaining the proper class distinctions, as they press upon the knight all the accouterments they deem his due: colorful livery, boots, gilt spurs, a horse, and servants. This no doubt reflects both the fluidity of social rankings and the sumptuary legislation that tried to prevent such mobility during the later Middle Ages. Holt's arguments were so convincing that Maurice Keen, who originally had sided with Hilton in regarding the ballads as "an expression of peasant discontent," later felt compelled to publish a rather abject "recantation." Yet in contrast to Hilton, Keen always saw Robin Hood as more of a legal, rather than social, protest figure.

If the ballads did not appeal to as wide an audience as had once been thought, how then did Robin Hood eventually become so popular? Keen argued (before his retraction) that the ballads originated as "songs sung at . . . festivals and dances by forgotten country people." Holt took a completely opposite tack and claimed that the legend was disseminated by minstrels performing in the halls of noble or gentry manor-houses "where the entertainment was aimed not only at the master but also at the members and the staff." From there it was a trickle-down effect, as "the stories . . . spread to the kitchen, the scullery and out beyond the walls to the local tavern and the surrounding cottages." But even though an element of chivalry is worked into the *Gest*, so that it can say of Robin that he was unsurpassed in "curteyse," the ballads are not quite so akin to the romances as one would expect in a tradition that sprang from aristocratic households. A compromise between "the alternatives that Robin Hood was the product of peasant protest or of gentlemanly escapism" has been proposed by the modern editors of the ballads, Dobson and Taylor. They believe that Robin's popular appeal was due to the fact that he "was a new type of hero for a new social group, the yeomen," who exemplified the social aspirations of many in the seismic world of the later Middle Ages. Robin's middling status as a yeoman is especially emphasized in *Robin Hood and the Potter*, which starts out by addressing its audience as "god yemen" and ends with the prayer, "saffe all god yemanrey!" Even Holt, in his 1982 book that purports to be "the last word on Robin Hood," somewhat modifies his original position by conceding that the secret to Robin's popularity may lie in the fact that his audience, as well as the form and content of the legend itself, may have changed considerably over time.

An explicit message that Robin "robbed from the rich to give to the poor" was unlikely to have been cultivated by the ballad singers, since this would not necessarily make Robin popular in the Middle Ages, and certainly not to the gentry audience preferred by Holt. The upper classes would have been very sensitive to any socially leveling themes in the aftermath of the Black Death of 1348–1349 and even more so in the wake of the Peasants' Revolt of 1381. As it was, the burgeoning references to Robin Hood during the late medieval period in various literary and legal records did not always mention the outlaw with approval. Even peasants could be socially conservative. Many of them, after all, did not participate in the Peasants' Revolt, and some actually turned in their colleagues during the suppression of the rising in July 1381. Not even the leaders of the rebellion seem to have wished to associate themselves with the outlaw: John Ball, for instance, wrote to his followers instructing them to "chastise wel Hobbe the Robbere." When in 1439 the tenants of Tutbury in Derbyshire compared the gentleman bandit, Piers Venables, and his yeoman gang to "Robyn Hode and his meynee [retinue]," they were intending no compliment, for they were complaining about Venables' depredations in a petition before Parliament. Corruption of the law, on the other hand, was a universal complaint among all classes—free peasants and gentry alike.

Graphic violence, then as now, was also sure to find an eager audience. In addition, it seems that there is a strong current of popular anticlericalism in the ballads, as when Robin tells his men in the *Gest* that "these bisshoppes and these archebishoppes,/Ye shall them bete and bynde." One should not carry this point too far, however, for Robin was no Lollard heretic but a strictly orthodox Catholic. The *Gest* portrays him as absolutely devoted to the cult of the Virgin Mary, while *Robin Hood and the Monk* has him so determined to hear mass that he braves discovery and capture in Nottingham just so that he might kneel "down before the rode [altar]" in St. Mary's Church. Although Robin targets greedy prelates, his religious sensibilities, like his social ones, are actually quite conservative.

Instead, Robin as the people's champion seems to have had its real origin in 1632, with Martin Parker's *True Tale of Robin Hood*. It is here that Robin truly robs the rich "that did the poore oppresse" and disburse their lucre to the needy, so that he was "feared of the rich, loved of the poore." At the same time, Parker followed the tradition established by the sixteenth-century authors, John Leland, Richard Grafton, and Anthony Munday, who made Robin into an aristocratic peer, the earl of Huntingdon, fallen on hard times. Robin's pseudo-noble heritage, of course, only heightened the poignancy of his charitable deeds. An equally important factor in Robin's transformation into a "social bandit" was probably the Robin Hood Games of roughly the same time period, in which Church-sponsored dramas about the outlaw were performed on the village green in order to solicit alms for the poor. By this stage, Robin Hood was a different "resistance to authority" figure from what he had been in the Middle Ages. Not surprisingly, it was to be the early modern interpretation of Robin Hood as a socioeconomic leveler that was to hold more potency for the early 20th-century cinema. Above all, *The Adventures of Robin Hood* set the mold for Robin as the "prince of thieves," as well as setting the standard in terms of production values for all subsequent Robin Hood films. The makers of that 1938 movie had their reasons for showcasing Robin's generosity to the poor, but every generation that has made a Robin Hood film seems to mine fresh meanings from the outlaw's legend. Although only intermittently faithful to the medieval Robin Hood, movies have nonetheless kept him forever relevant.

The Movies

The popularity of the Robin Hood legend on film is attested not only by the sheer number of movies about him, but also by their variety and span of time in which they were made. Robin is a truly international film star, being the subject of countless Hollywood and British productions as well as at least five Italian, two Spanish, and one Russian treatments. Genres in which he has appeared have run the gamut, from drama and comedy to cartoon and even pornography, the last represented by *The Ribald Tales of Robin Hood* (1969), in which Robin Hood's men are certainly merry. By 1913, there had been no less than five English-language films devoted to Robin Hood, focusing either on his relationship with Maid Marian or on daring rescues of his men from the sheriff of Nottingham. In 1991, the enduring vitality of the legend was such that two Robin Hood films—both the product of Hollywood studios—appeared almost simultaneously, each claiming the mantle of reinterpreting the outlaw for the modern age. This was not the end of it, for even more movies about Robin Hood were apparently in the offing for that year, while one of the films that did make it to the screen inspired a parody two years later.

This chapter will mainly address three categories of Robin Hood films. The first category consists of the "classic" movies that implanted the archetypal image of Robin Hood in the popular consciousness during the silent and early sound and technicolor eras of the 1920s and 1930s. A second category is comprised of a major retelling of the legend in the 1970s, when a radical departure was made from the swashbuckling formula that had held true for nearly four decades. And finally, there remain the "politically correct" and "feminized" versions of Robin Hood that have held sway in the 1990s and continue to do so today.

The first major Robin Hood film to lay down its gauntlet before the movie-going public was *Robin Hood* (1922), directed by Allan Dwan and starring the silent-screen star, Douglas Fairbanks Sr., as the outlaw hero. Fairbanks, although he had done similar swashbuckling turns in *The Mark of Zorro* (1920) and *The Three Musketeers* (1921), seems to have been initially reluctant to play Robin Hood. Among his concerns was to avoid looking "like a heavy-footed Englishman tramping around in the woods," but he solved this problem by concealing trampolines in the forest set to help him traipse around Sherwood. He then was daunted by the mammoth, 90-foot high structure—built at a cost of $250,000 while Fairbanks was away on a tour of Europe—that was to stand in for Nottingham Castle. According to Allan Dwan, "Doug took one look at the castle standing nine stories high and promptly went and hid. He said he could never compete with it as an actor." Eventually he overcame these feelings of inadequacy by exploiting the architecture to show off his acrobatic stunts, such as sliding down the curtains from the balcony along a concealed metal slide. Despite his initial uneasiness over the picture, *Robin Hood* vaulted Fairbanks to even greater fame and fortune, earning his United Artists company $5 million out of a $1.4 million investment and drawing a record audience of over 100,000 people at its New York premiere. The only blemish on this success story

Douglas Fairbanks Sr. strikes a pose as the title character in *Robin Hood* (1922). He doesn't appear in outlaw garb until the second half of the film.

was when Fairbanks, attempting to demonstrate his archery prowess on top of the Ritz Hotel in New York City, accidentally shot a Polish furrier in the buttocks. After successfully hitting a gargoyle in the eye from 100 yards, Fairbanks wanted to demonstrate the distance as well as the accuracy of his arrows, so he let one fly "high over the rooftops." As it happened, it fell to earth just as the immigrant was bending over in his factory "to retrieve a scrap of mink." A $5,000 gift from the rich to the poor apparently was enough to preserve Fairbank's reputation as Robin Hood.

Just before the drawbridge is lowered on Nottingham Castle and the action of the film, the following words appear on the screen: "History—in its ideal state—is a compound of legend and chronicle and from out of both we offer you an impression of the Middle Ages." Aside from the fact that most historians would dispute this definition of history, it quickly becomes clear as the story unfolds that as far as Robin Hood is concerned, this film is almost wholly based on legend, and postmedieval legend at that. For the entire first half of the movie, Robin Hood proper, as an outlaw in Sherwood Forest, does not even make an appearance. Instead, we get Fairbanks as the earl of Huntingdon, the right-hand man of King Richard, who jousts, woos Lady Marian Fitzwalter, and embarks on the Third Crusade at the head of Richard's army. All this has absolutely nothing to do with the medieval ballads, but rather seems derived from the Elizabethan plays of Anthony Munday, particularly *The Downfall of Robert, Earl of Huntingdon*, printed in 1598. Nor does Fairbanks seem to have been at all interested in capturing the essence of Robin's original medieval character; on the contrary, he plays him as a bashful "grown-up schoolboy," a stock-in-trade of nearly all his films.

When at last we do get Robin Hood, it is the skipping, jumping, leaping hero that Fairbanks' fans had come to expect. Oddly enough, there is little emphasis on Robin's role as the "prince of thieves" who robs from the rich to give to the poor. Although a brief scene shows Robin distributing money and food to poor villagers at Nottingham, his main task seems to be to rescue Marian from the clutches of Sir Guy of Gisborne and to restore Richard to his throne in place of the evil usurper, Prince John. The main emphasis here is on romance and chivalry, and while the fifteenth-century *Gest of Robyn Hode* could be said to have some of the latter, the former is entirely absent, as Robin in this ballad has no interest in any woman except the Virgin Mary. In this sense, the extreme aversion which Fairbanks' character displays toward women in the first half of the film, going so far as to jump into a moat to escape them, is perhaps his most authentic aspect. Otherwise, Robin is given a highly aristocratic cast which is most unlike both his yeoman quality in the ballads and his reincarnation in later films as the people's champion. A most revealing point in the film comes when Robin approaches the cliff where he thinks Marian has died: Drawing his sword, he pledges himself to "God, to Richard, and to Her." As the film scholar, Jeffrey Richards, has pointed out, "there is no mention of the common people here." The whole visual atmosphere of the film is characterized by Richards as "pure nineteenth-century Romanticism." Robin Hood as a nostalgic emblem of a bygone era was probably what the people wanted in the aftermath of the most destructive war to date in the modern world. Nonetheless, the brutality of the Great War seems to creep into the film in the form of the various atrocities inflicted upon the English people by Prince John and his henchmen. Graphic scenes depict the branding of a poacher on the neck, the lashing of a bare-backed woman who has spurned John's advances, and the excruciatingly prolonged torture of Lady Marian's maid, whose pained grimaces alternate with the gloating visages of her tormentors. *Robin Hood* is now chiefly remembered for its path-breaking spectacle, one that was popular and profitable enough to ensure that many more Robin Hood films would be made.

A decade and a half later came the first sound and color film of Robin Hood and, coincidentally, what most of the public and film scholars consider to be the greatest Robin Hood movie of all time. *The Adventures of Robin Hood* (1938), directed by Michael Curtiz and William Keighley and starring Errol Flynn as the outlaw, has been dubbed "the definitive Robin picture" and "the vulgate text of the Robin Hood tradition." That publicists at Warner Brothers aspired to such dominance already in 1938 is indicated by the fact that they issued special packages to educators in order to assist them in using the film in classroom lectures on medieval feudalism. Nor did it hurt that the movie received nearly universal acclaim from critics as an instant classic, even though the stars, Errol Flynn and Olivia de Havilland (who played Maid Marian), did not come round to this point of view until later. As yet, time has not toppled *The Adventures* from its throne. Four decades after its release, in 1977, it was rated the fifth most popular movie of all time in a *TV Guide* poll of television program directors. Its lush production values, at a cost of over $2 million, has ensured its continuity for successive generations of viewers of television, where the film is still shown as a "mainstream feature," rather than as a "curio from the past."

The Adventures of Robin Hood thus completely eclipsed the silent black and white version of 1922. Flynn is undoubtedly a much more convincing outlaw hero than Fairbanks, but this does not mean that the later film is any more true to the original medieval ballads. Although eschewing the overly romanticized, aristocratic approach of the Fairbanks picture, *The Adventures of Robin Hood* nonetheless garners almost all of its plot elements from seventeenth-century Robin Hood "garlands". This is no accident, for the filmmakers were assisted by a scholar of Elizabethan literature, F.M. Padelford, rather than a medieval specialist. Still firmly in place is the too early historical setting of 1193–1194—when King Richard was on his way home from the Third Crusade—a convention ultimately derived from John Major's 1521 history of the outlaw. Also center stage, as in previous Robin Hood films, is the romance between Robin and Maid Marian. This plot feature seems to go back to sixteenth-century May Games and a seventeenth-century ballad, *Robin Hood and Maid Marian*, but a more direct inspiration for the film was Reginald de Koven's light opera of 1890, *Robin Hood*, which made Marian the object of a rivalry between Robin and Guy of Gisborne. But whereas Fairbanks plays Robin as a cozy member of the Norman establishment—the earl of Huntingdon—Flynn's Robin is a focus of Saxon resistance to Norman oppression—"We Saxons aren't going to take these oppressions much longer"—and remains a lowly knight until the

Errol Flynn and Basil Rathbone confer on a costume design for Rathbone's character
of Guy of Gisborne for the opening scenes of *The Adventures of Robin Hood*. Flynn's
costume as an aristocratic Robin, along with an early script draft calling for a jousting
tournament like that of the Fairbanks film, were subsequently abandoned.

very end of the film, when Richard dubs him baron of Locksley, as well as
earl of Sherwood and Nottingham. This theme may be appropriate for a
tale such as *Hereward the Wake*, set in the immediate aftermath of William's
Norman Conquest of England in 1066, but it hardly makes sense a century
and a half later, by which time Normans and Saxons had thoroughly assimilated with each other. The Norman-Saxon angle is indebted to Sir Walter
Scott's 1819 novel, *Ivanhoe*, which Hollywood had turned into a widely
admired film in 1913 and included Robin Hood as a bit part.

At least in *The Adventures*, Flynn's Robin must share the stage with
other characters from the legend, such as Little John, Will Scarlett, Much
the Miller's son, and Friar Tuck, something that Fairbanks' ego seemingly
could not abide. All these minor figures can be traced back to the Middle

Ages, even "Frere Tuk," who does not appear in the original ballads but was a pseudonym assumed by Robert Stafford, chaplain of Lindfield in east Sussex, when he was outlawed in 1417. Even so, their identities in the film are instead lifted from the seventeenth-century garlands: Robin's quarterstaff fight with Little John on the narrow bridge, for example, is straight out of *Robin Hood and Little John*, a ballad first recorded in 1624. A later episode showing Robin recruiting Friar Tuck by riding piggyback across a stream is from *Robin Hood and the Curtal Friar*, a ballad popular in England from the mid-seventeenth century.

There are only three plot elements that owe their origins ultimately to the medieval ballads. One is the archery contest at Nottingham, which in the *Gest of Robyn Hode* has Robin shoot at wands, or long sticks stuck in the ground, against "Gylberte wyth the whyte hande" for the prize of a gold and silver arrow. When Robin is unmasked by the sheriff, he manages to escape by shooting his way out, although Little John is injured in the melee. (In the film, Robin is instead apprehended by Prince John after having split his opponent's arrow on a round target—a twist that is again based on *Ivanhoe*.) A climactic duel between Robin and Sir Guy of Gisborne toward the close of the film is also medieval in origin, being the centerpiece of the ballad, *Robin Hood and Guy of Gisborne*. The cause of the enmity between the two antagonists is never explained in the ballad, although it is clearly delineated in the film. (Robin prevents Guy from punishing a poacher of the king's deer, Much the Miller's son.) Finally, there is the familiar encounter in the forest between Robin and the king disguised as an abbot, which is retailed in the seventh and eighth fyttes of the *Gest*. Although this makes perfect sense in terms of the dramatic action of the original ballad—the king is in disguise because he wishes to apprehend an elusive outlaw—it doesn't in the film. Why would a king, having been away from his realm for four years and facing a potential usurpation from his younger brother, wish to cast doubt on his legitimacy by entering the country in stealth? Historically speaking, Richard, upon his return from crusade and a year-long imprisonment as hostage to Emperor Henry VI of Germany, made a state entry into his capital city of London on March 23, 1194, followed by a second coronation on April 17 to set the seal on his restoration. It is true, however, that in the meantime Richard had to go north to retake Nottingham Castle from the supporters of Prince John, who, according to the chronicler Roger of Hoveden, was eventually reconciled with his brother through "the mediation of Queen Eleanor," their mother. We also know from the *Itinerarium Regis Ricardi* (*Itinerary of King Richard*) that on April 2, Richard rode to his hunting lodge at Clipstone in Sherwood Forest, where he had never been and which "pleased him greatly." But all this seems to have been done without the help of Robin Hood.

Yet in spite of all the inaccuracies and modern accretions, *The Adventures* does accomplish the impressive feat of convincing its audience that here is the one and only Robin Hood, such as he may have existed in the Middle Ages. Largely, the credit for this must go to Errol Flynn and his bravura performance, who inhabits his role to such an extent that one reviewer exclaims that he "might well have been Robin Hood in another life." And indeed he may have been, for in real life Flynn was known as something of a renegade cutup, who flouted moral and social conventions through his countless extramarital affairs and who courted needless danger and risk, to the exasperated consternation of his studio bosses. (His autobiography is entitled, *My Wicked, Wicked Ways*.) Shortly before beginning work on *The Adventures* in the summer of 1937, he had had his own adventures in Spain, where he had gone to be a spectator of that country's Civil War, over Warner Brothers' strenuous objections. He apparently was knocked unconscious when an artillery shell took out the balcony on which he was standing in a hotel in Algeciras. This reckless behavior continued during filming, when Flynn not only insisted on performing his own stunts on the set, but also on performing other hijinks when off duty as well. In a case of art imitating life, or perhaps vice-versa, the actor who played Robin's right-hand man, Will Scarlett, was Patric Knowles, Flynn's boon companion in debauchery. In between flying through the old oak trees of Bidwell Park in Chico, California, which doubled as Sherwood Forest, Knowles gave his pal some flying lessons at the local airport, so that soon Flynn was performing his own daredevil stunts in the air. Word quickly got back to the studio about the pair's "joyriding in planes," and they were urgently asked to "cut out the flying, at least until the picture is finished." Flynn, therefore, did not have to even act the part of the defiantly independent, devil-may-care outlaw that seems to capture the essence of the medieval Robin Hood. For what makes the Robin of the original ballads so appealing is that he is ever his own man, whether he be defying his own men by going into Nottingham alone or defying his king by leaving court to go back to the greenwood. The irony is that Flynn, who in retrospect was so perfect for the part, was nearly passed over by Warner Brothers for the role, since their first choice fell on their popular "gangster" star, James Cagney.

Like many great historical films, *The Adventures of Robin Hood* is successful not just because it achieves a core authenticity, but also because it aims at making medieval history relevant to modern events in a way that is supple enough not to overwhelm the period atmosphere of the film. In a perceptive essay on the movie's "visual politics," Ina Rae Hark identifies two agendas in the film that pertain to the sociopolitical concerns of the 1930s. One is democracy's coming struggle with Nazism and Fascist ideology, symbolized in the film by the contrasting settings of the "corrupt court world" ruled (until the very end of the movie) by Prince John, and the "healing green world" presided over by Robin Hood. Differences between the two worlds are highlighted throughout the film using contrasting elements of the mise-en-scene, as well as parallel characters and events. The Norman oppressors, for example, are, in Hark's words, "controlled by an inflexible protocol, visually expressed through geometrical symmetry," which makes them appear "rigid and artificial" in whatever surroundings they happen to be in, whether it be feasting in Nottingham Castle or marching through Sherwood Forest. They sit or stand at perpendicular right angles to their furniture and the floor and seem positively alien to the natural environs of the greenwood. Their "rows of banners on straight poles" and soldiers marching "in strictly drilled ranks" are perhaps deliberately evocative of Leni Riefenstahl's notorious propaganda film, *Triumph of the Will* (1935), whose scripted parades and rallies enacted by the Nazi Party Congress in 1934 became the cinematic embodiment of fascism. Hollywood certainly was aware of Riefenstahl's work, for it gave "Hitler's Honey" the cold shoulder during her tour of the United States in 1938, which coincided with the infamous *Kristallnacht* pogrom. Warner Brothers may have had a personal motive in anticipating the anti-Nazi films that were to come into vogue during World War II: Its Jewish agent in Berlin, Joseph Kauffman, had been lynched by a Nazi mob in 1935.

In contrast to the humorless, sadistic Normans, Robin Hood and his merry men "possess an enormous sense of fun concerning life and themselves." They are also, notes Hark, "spontaneous," "dynamic," and "unrestrained," as if they refuse to be confined by the tyranny of any spatial constructs within the film frame. Moreover, they seem in perfect harmony with nature and at ease in their environment. These differences are highlighted during the outlaws' ambush of the Norman tax caravan and the ensuing forest banquet scene, which serves to point up the Normans' forced efforts at jollity during their own, earlier feast in Nottingham Castle. (Film scholars also note that Keighley and Curtiz, who supervised the forest and castle sequences, respectively, had vastly different directing styles.) As Robin and his men prepare for the ambush, they literally become one with their natural surroundings. Encasing themselves in branches and leaves as camouflage, they seem to metamorphosis into "huge insects," to borrow Scott Nollen's description, as they scale the huge oak trees of Sherwood Forest. At a signal from Robin, they waylay the caravan effortlessly and bloodlessly, as though, in the words of Stephen Knight, the trees themselves "come to life and entrap the Normans by the forces of nature." In a burst of boundless energy, the merry men explode onto the screen, cascading, swinging, vaulting out of the foliage onto the backs of the unsuspecting Norman soldiers. The ambush climaxes when Robin, with an aptitude rivaling Tarzan's or Peter Pan's, swings onto a low oak branch in order to greet his captives with the famous line, "Welcome to Sherwood!" Amplified by Erich Wolfgang Korngold's prancing music, the whole scene has the air of a lighthearted, boyish prank, rather than a deadly serious military operation. The irony is that the "nature myth" or "green man" quality of this much-admired sequence was created with the help of artificial rocks and shrubbery that were strategically placed on the set by the film's art director, Carl Jules Weyl, who won an Oscar for his efforts.

The elemental democracy of the outlaws, whose bonhomie and joie de vivre is so much more attractive than the Normans' oppressive fascism, continues to be on display during the forest banquet that directly follows the ambush. Equality is the order of the day, as the Normans (except for Maid Marian) are divested of their expensive raiment and given shabby rags to wear. In the earlier, Norman banquet at Nottingham Castle, Robin—a lone, anarchic figure—manages to utterly disrupt the festivities by dumping a dead stag on the table, refusing to respect the knights' seating arrangements, and finally making his escape amid general mayhem. By contrast, all the sour-faced Normans fail to make even a dent in the joyous celebration of the Saxon feast, where people seem to dance and laugh continuously. Rather than spit out his food, as he had done in the face of Prince John, Robin here displays a hearty appetite for "honest meat," even if the poor editing of the scene makes it seem as if he devours a huge mutton leg instantaneously! Yet the scene works, not only because it ties in with modern democratic and environmental values, but also because it is authentically medieval. Robin's feasting is given great emphasis in the *Gest*, for it is the raison d'être behind his robberies:

> Than bespake hym gode Robyn:
> "To dyne have I noo lust,
> Till that I have som bolde baron,
> Or some unketh [unknown] gest."

The film also taps into a strong appreciation of and delight in nature that can be detected in the original Robin Hood ballads, such as these opening stanzas of *Robin Hood and the Monk*:

> In somer, when the shawes be sheyne [woods are bright]
> And leves be large and long,
> Hit is full mery in feyre foreste
> To here the foulys song.

To se the dere draw to the dale,
And leve the hilles hee,
And shadow hem in the leves grene,
Under the grene wode tre.

Although the film's image of a dead deer draped over Robin's shoulders may not seem to accord much with nature worship, hunting is an important aspect of Robin's identity in the medieval ballads. When, toward the end of the *Gest*, Robin returns to the greenwood on a "mery mornynge" amidst "the notes small of byrdes mery syngynge," what should he do but slay "a full grete herte" and blow his hunting horn in order to gather round him once again his outlaw band.

The other modern message of *The Adventures of Robin Hood* is a conservative socialism that, especially in the late 1930s, tied in well with America's domestic mood as President Franklin Delano Roosevelt was enacting the New Deal program in response to the Great Depression. Studio president, Jack Warner, despite his Republican sympathies, supported FDR's election campaign in 1932, and according to Ina Hark, Warner Brothers pushed the New Deal social agenda in its Depression-era films. A redistribution of wealth theme receives more play in *The Adventures* than it does in any other Robin Hood movie, and the film must be considered responsible for instilling in the public consciousness the well-worn notion that Robin "robbed from the rich to give to the poor." This theme comes through very clearly in the oath Robin has his outlaws swear at Gallows Oak, where they promise "to despoil the rich only to give to the poor, to shelter the old and the helpless, to protect all women, rich or poor, Norman or Saxon." A little later, in the midst of their forest banquet, Robin has the opportunity to show Marian his "forest hospital," which immediately strikes a somber note to the boisterous proceedings. As the camera pans over the "poor devils" who come up to Robin to bless him for his generosity, we could just as well be viewing one of the government-run work camps celebrated in Depression films such as 20th Century Fox's *The Grapes of Wrath* (1940), based on the John Steinbeck novel. In the latter film, the Joad family is sheltered at one point in their wanderings by the Department of Agriculture's Farmworkers' Wheat Patch Camp, whose benign, bespectacled caretaker (played by Grant Mitchell) bears more than a passing resemblance, physically to FDR, and spiritually to Robin Hood. In *The Adventures*, Robin justifies to Marian the handouts that are sponsored by this medieval version of the New Deal:

Marian: You're a strange man.
Robin: Strange? Because I can feel for beaten, helpless people?

Marian: No, you're strange because you want to do something
about it. You're willing to defy Sir Guy, even Prince John himself to risk your own life. And none of those men was a
Norman.

Robin: Norman or Saxon. What's that matter? It's injustice I
hate, not the Normans.

Marian: But it's lost you your rank, your lands. It's made you a
hunted outlaw when you might have lived in comfort and security. What's your reward for all this?

Robin: Reward? You just don't understand, do you?

Marian: [gripping Robin's arm] I'm sorry. I do begin to see . . . a
little, now.

By the time Maid Marian leaves the outlaw camp, she is a convinced New
Dealer.

Prince John's predatory tax gatherers can thus be compared to the
"callous bankers or Wall Street businessmen" who were considered
responsible for the Great Depression and became the new villains in
Hollywood's socially aware movies of the 1930s. The protagonists, on the
other hand—Robin Hood and Maid Marian—are willing to sacrifice their
personal happiness for a greater good, a theme that anticipates the message
of later films set during the war, such as *Casablanca* (1942). At the same
time, reform does not come at the expense of an essentially conservative
social and political order. By the end of *The Adventures*, King Richard still
reigns and Robin is ennobled in order to allow him to marry Marian. As
Hark observes, in Warner Brothers' films "the true remedy for society's
brutalities must come from above, not below." Like in the ballads, the
Robin of the film embodies resistance to abusive authority, not to authority in general. This does not preclude the possibility that radical sympathies—even Communist ones—may have been held by some working on
the movie. After all, this was the same studio and director who five years
later made *Mission to Moscow* (1943) that whitewashed the Stalin regime.
But the team of screenwriters—including Rowland Leigh (uncredited),
Norman Reilly Raine, and Seton I. Miller—who worked on *The Adventures*
script had to balance competing priorities. As chronicled by the film's historian, Rudy Behlmer, the screenplay went through numerous rewrites
and changes, some of which tried, unsuccessfully, to remain true to the
early ballads, such as by omitting the Maid Marian character altogether.
But inevitably the script succumbed to Hollywood's preconceived notions
of the legend. In the end, the film wants it both ways: social justice and
some limited social leveling, but without the attendant political rebellion
and instability.

The filmmakers also seem to have been anxious not to offend religious sensibilities. As in the ballads, they had to walk a fine line between Robin's targeting of powerful and corrupt churchmen and his bedrock piety. According to Leigh's notes to an early draft of the script:

> There is no doubt about it that Robin Hood's chief antagonists were the bishops, abbots, and friars who bled the poor in order to enrich themselves. This point is insisted upon again and again by every reliable expert on Robin Hood lore. Undoubtedly in medieval times the church took unwarranted liberties with its power and influence. Equally undoubtedly we have no desire to offend either the Catholic or Protestant church of today, and I feel that a tactful compromise will have to be arrived at.

Once again, the original script of *The Adventures* displays a commendable effort to remain true to the medieval ballads, but that effort must be partially sacrificed to a perceived need to provide a modern reinterpretation of the legend. The filmmakers' solution was to create a new role—the bishop of the Black Canons (played by Montagu Love)—that has no basis either in literature or history and thus can offend no one, except perhaps historical purists. (Bishops can only be heads of territorial dioceses, not groups of persons.)

Ultimately, it is the film's message of social justice, not its anti-Fascist theme, that has proved to be the most powerful and enduring. No doubt this was equally true for audiences of 1938 as for those of the present day. War was still a year away at the time of the film's release, while neutrality laws and high unemployment continued to be the order of the day in the United States. A hero who could right social wrongs and inequities simply by "robbing from the rich to give to the poor" was just what the world needed as it struggled to come out of the Great Depression. Robin Hood had demonstrated a stalwart appeal in turbulent times, and this was not to change in later films.

Nonetheless, any movie about Robin Hood that came after *The Adventures* had to labor under its formidable shadow. Some successors adopted the strategy of telling a different tale altogether. *The Prince of Thieves* (1948), adapted from the Alexandre Dumas novel of 1872, has Robin play matchmaker to Sir Allan Claire and Lady Christabel and seems a reprieve of a silent film entitled *Robin Hood* that came out in 1913. Two more films, *The Bandit of Sherwood Forest* (1946) and *Rogues of Sherwood Forest* (1950), relegate Robin Hood to the sidelines and instead focus on his son, respectively Robert of Nottingham and Robin, earl of Huntingdon. The latter film borrowed not only some stock footage from the classic of 1938 but also one its actors, Alan Hale, who played Little John for the third time, after his previous turns opposite Fairbanks and Flynn. These films faced the further disadvantage of having to compete with a tenth-anniversary rerelease of *The Adventures* in 1948.

In 1952 Disney stepped into the Robin Hood ring with its own version, *The Story of Robin Hood and his Merrie Men*, which, according to Jeffrey Richards, was brave enough to attempt the "third major retelling of the legend" after the seemingly unbeatable successes of 1922 and 1938. Although shot on location in England and incorporating some historically accurate details—such as that Robin shoots at wands instead of targets and that in Richard's absence England was run by Eleanor of Aquitaine and William Longchamp, bishop of Ely, not by Prince John—the film lacks the panache of its predecessors. It seems less successful, in fact, than Disney's animated *Robin Hood* that came out two decades later in 1973, in which the characters are depicted as forest animals. Robin Hood made a second screen appearance in 1952 in MGM's *Ivanhoe*, based on the Scott novel. Even though the outlaw is relegated, like in the book, to a minor character, the movie did establish a tradition of associating Robin Hood with the Jews—Isaac of York and his beautiful daughter, Rebecca—who help Ivanhoe ransom Richard back from Germany. Although the history of the Jews during Richard's reign was a tragic one—a wave of anti-Semitic pogroms swept England in 1189–1190 after the king's coronation—the relationship between Robin and the Jews was to be developed for its comic potential in later film parodies of the legend.

The 1950s also saw the first television production of the legend, the first Hammer schlock films that preyed on the popularity of the outlaw, and the first female Robin Hood. Preceded by a failed American pilot, *Tales of Robin Hood* (1951–1952), a black-and-white British series produced by Sapphire Films and unimaginatively titled *The Adventures of Robin Hood* ran from 1955 to 1958. Despite its minimalist production values, the series was popular in Britain and preserved the episodic character of the ballads, as well as delivering some useful history lessons about the medieval manorial system. At the same time, the series' Marxist authors—Ring Lardner Jr., Ian McLellan, and Bill Blake—having been blacklisted in America as suspected Communists, seem to have used the script as an opportunity to expand upon the previous *Adventures'* social message. Robin here becomes a mouthpiece for explaining the evils of class oppression and the benefits of a welfare state. In 1957, Hammer Films produced *Men of Sherwood Forest*, the first of what was to be four entirely forgettable, low-budget treatments of the legend. The best of these was perhaps *Sword of Sherwood Forest* (1960), which starred Richard Greene as Robin, who had also played him in the earlier television series, and Peter Cushing as the sheriff of Nottingham. Also at this time, Robin's offspring made yet another appearance in *Son of*

Robin Hood (1958), whose title disguised the surprise twist that Robin's son, Deering Hood, was actually a daughter, played by June Laverick. Although the plucky female is actually allowed to kill someone with her bow and arrow, the leadership of the outlaw band and climactic duel is left up to her male lover, Jamie, brother of the earl of Chester.

Before leaving this largely derivative period of Robin Hood films, mention should be made of one movie that imaginatively attempts to revitalize the legend: *Robbo and the Seven Hoods* (1964). Although the title is a spinoff of Disney's *Snow White and the Seven Dwarfs* (1937), this film musical is really a modern updating of the Robin Hood story, set during the era of Prohibition and the gang wars of 1920s Chicago. Featuring Frank Sinatra as Robbo and his "Rat Pack" pals, Dean Martin and Sammy Davis Jr. as, respectively, Little John and Will Scarlett, the film pays homage to the "robbing from the rich to give to the poor" theme by having Robbo donate his speakeasy and casino earnings to a local orphanage. Yet this is the only film I am aware of that incorporates the original message of the medieval ballads, namely that of Robin as antidote to legal corruption. Bribery and intimidation of police, judges, and juries by real-life ganglords, such as Al Capone, during the 1920s in Chicago was rampant, and in a funny scene from the film, the point is driven home when the corrupt Sheriff Glick is encased in concrete by a rival gang leader, Guy Gisborne (played by Peter Falk) and literally made "the cornerstone of justice" at a dedication ceremony of the new police building. When Robbo takes the fall for Gisborne's crime and seems about to be convicted in court on the basis of false testimony, his only recourse is to take Gisborne "for a ride." *Robbo and the Seven Hoods*, while ostensibly not about the Middle Ages at all, demonstrates that the medieval significance of Robin Hood—as an outlaw of an abusive judicial system who is the only one capable of upholding the law—can still be made relevant in a modern context. But no other film seems to have taken up this challenge.

Our second major category of Robin Hood films is represented by *Robin and Marian* (1976), directed by Richard Lester and starring Sean Connery as Robin and Audrey Hepburn as Marian. This has been characterized by Stephen Knight as "the most serious of all the outlaw films," as well as being the most realistic and "a radical reworking of the tradition." As Jeffrey Richards notes, it was "the first major Robin Hood film for over twenty years," if one counts the Disney movie of 1952 as a major film. Otherwise, it is the first major Robin Hood film in nearly four decades.

Rather than deliver what most audiences expect from a typical Robin Hood film—defined by Stephen Knight as "youth, melodrama, amazing success, happy futures, fantasy"—*Robin and Marian* chooses to focus on the "autumnal" or declining years of Robin's life, when he is disillusioned with fighting, estranged from his king, on the rocks with Marian, and no longer so nimble in the greenwood. Originally the movie was to be called *The Death of Robin Hood*, but the title was changed by Columbia Studios in order to give the film a more marketable "adventurous love story" appeal. But that is certainly not how the director, Richard Lester, saw things. Although he had made his name directing the widely admired *The Three Musketeers* (1974), which reinvigorated that particular swashbuckling genre, Lester took a different approach in *Robin and Marian*. The film may be considered a powerful antidote to all the romantic hubris that had accrued to the Robin Hood legend over the years, and Lester has been accused of imprisoning the myth "within a cage of credibility." Lester remained bitter over the name change, precisely because he believed it gave the audience false expectations about the kind of movie it was. As he told Curtis Bill Pepper in 1976:

> I felt it was wrong to advertise the film as Columbia did. People expected another *Three Musketeers*, and when it ends up with the leading characters dead on a bed, they were confused. I always felt the one thing you have to do is to advertise a film accurately, so the audience knows what it's going to see. When they don't, there is a built-in resentment. Jim [Goldman]'s original title was *The Death of Robin*. Everybody said, "You can't have a film with 'Death' in the title—it's depressing." But that's what people were going to see. "Love is the greatest adventure of all" [the publicity slogan] was not what it was about.

In fact, Lester apparently scrapped many of the romantic lines between Robin and Marian in the original script, over Hepburn's objections, in order to cut down on the love angle. He later told Andrew Yule: "The title should have been left as *The Death of Robin Hood*. . . . To me, the movie was not a 'comedy adventure,' but people kept asking me where the jokes were. . . . But Robin was straight, I always saw it like that, and because of the connotations of the changed title, it prompted the wrong reaction." In another interview that he gave in 1983 to *Sight and Sound*, Lester described his partly realized vision of Robin Hood as a tragic, ineffectual, almost buffoonish Don Quixote figure, in contrast to the triumphant hero portrayed in earlier films:

> He [Robin] has come back to find that the world has passed him by. In fact the only person who has become anything since he left is the sheriff. But Robin ends up making a general nuisance of himself, he keeps charging off dramatically through fields of crops, destroying things for the sake of a quixotic attitude and he kills the only person who is doing something for the

country, the sheriff. I got about 30 percent of that into the finished picture, but I like it.

Although other films depicted Robin as an older man, they avoided the implications of his age by shifting the plot focus in favor of his son (or daughter). *Robin and Marian*, by contrast, does not flinch from addressing Robin's midlife crisis head on.

The film dismantles the edifice of romance and myth early: In the opening scene, Robin falls out with King Richard, played by Richard Harris, because he refuses the king's command to massacre the defenseless garrison—consisting of "some children and a mad old man"—inside a French castle suspected of hiding a fabulous treasure. Instead of the warrior hero of legend, Richard is here portrayed as a cruel, greedy, and bloodthirsty tyrant. Robin, although loyal to his king, does not follow him unquestioningly. As he tells Richard, "I've followed you for twenty years. I've fought for you in the crusades. I've fought for you here in France. Show me a soldier and I'll fight him now. But I won't slaughter children for a piece of gold that never was." After Richard dies as a result of a freak accident—an arrow lodged in his neck that was thrown at him by the mad old man—Robin and Little John (played by Nicol Williamson) return to England and Sherwood Forest. They wheeze and hack their way through the greenwood, until they meet up with their now-geriatric friends, Will Scarlett and Friar Tuck (played respectively by Denholm Elliott and Ronnie Barker). Meanwhile, Marian, in Robin's absence, has become a nun and under the pseudonym, "Mother Janet," is now the abbess of Kirklees Abbey. She has made her peace with God, so that, as she tells her former lover, "I'm not your Marian. . . . I don't dream about you anymore, Robin." Nonetheless, Robin still attempts one last deed of chivalric derring-do, rescuing Marian and her nuns from the clutches of the sheriff of Nottingham (played by Robert Shaw), who has been ordered by King John to arrest all the high churchmen of England in retaliation for his dispute with the pope. Robin and his band accomplish the rescue, albeit none too nimbly, and toward the end of the film, Robin and the sheriff fight a climactic duel. Perhaps in a nod to the King Arthur legend, Robin defeats his archenemy but is himself mortally wounded in the process, having to be carried off the field by Little John and Marian, who at last has rekindled her love for the outlaw. The film ends in a kind of Arthurian apocalypse, with Robin's band scattered by Norman soldiers, Will and Friar Tuck arrested, and Robin and Marian both dead, killed by poison that Marian has administered to Robin to make him die painlessly and which she has also taken herself. Its final image is of the arrow that Robin fires out of the window to mark his and Marian's grave. Rotten apples on a window sill frame both the beginning and end of the picture in order to symbolize mortality and earthly decay.

The screenplay is by James Goldman, who is better known for the play that served as the film script for *The Lion in Winter* (1968), about the tempestuous relationship between the first Plantagenet king of England, Henry II (1154–1189), and his wife, Eleanor of Aquitaine, and their three surviving sons. Goldman seems to be the only screenwriter to have turned to the original medieval ballads, rather than to early modern garlands, for inspiration about Robin Hood. The theme of the entire movie—focusing on the twilight period of Robin's life—is taken from the eighth fytte of *A Gest of Robyn Hode* and a related ballad fragment, *Robin Hood's Death*. In the *Gest*, Robin leaves the king's court after fifteen months of service in order to go back to "Bernysdale" and spend the remaining twenty-two years of his life in the greenwood. At this point, the *Gest* kills Robin off rather abruptly, through the wiles of "a wycked woman, the pryoresse of Kyrkesly" and her lover, "Syr Roger of Donkesly," who ambushes Robin as he is bled by the prioress. *Robin Hood's Death* elaborates on these few stanzas with some additional details, such as that the prioress had a direct hand in Robin's demise by poisoning his "blood irons" [instruments used to bleed the patient]; that her lover, Red Roger, mortally wounded Robin in the side but at the price of losing his head; and that Little John threatened to burn down the priory to avenge Robin, but was forestalled from doing so with Robin's dying breath. The film, of course, freely adapts all these plot elements, as well as incorporating the later tradition that Robin marked his grave with an arrow. But it provides a plausible explanation for why Robin should have been so gullible as to trust the prioress with his life: She kills Robin, her real lover, out of love. This also exonerates the prioress, and by implication all women, from the age-old stigma of the femme fatale.

Throughout the rest of the movie, one recognizes a clear attempt to demythologize Robin's legend. At one point about a third of the way into the film, Will Scarlett sings for Robin one of the ballads that has been written about him during his absence on crusade. When he finishes, Robin immediately debunks his heroic status:

> Robin: Well, they've turned us into heroes, Johnny. Will, you didn't make it up?
> Will: These songs, I don't know where they come from, but that you hear them everywhere. We go from town to town and . . .
> Robin: What do you do for a living?
> Tuck: Well, I take confessions. He [Will Scarlett] takes the horses.

Will: And everywhere we go, they want to hear about the things
  you did.
Robin: We didn't do them!
Will: I know that!

Robin and Marian lays claim here to giving us the historical truth, rather
than the legendary myth, of Robin Hood. In this respect, it is remarkably
similar to *King Arthur: The Young Warlord*, which came out as a movie a year
earlier. There are a couple of other nice touches of realism in this scene,
such as Robin's discovery of his old hunting horn, now bunged up with
accumulated dirt, and Little John's wish to "go to Barnsdale in the morning [and] see my dad." Both details are straight out of the *Gest:* In the
eighth fytte, Robin summons back his band upon returning to the greenwood by blowing upon a "horne" so that "all the outlawes of that
forest/That horne could they knowe," whereas in the first and second
fyttes, Barnsdale (not Sherwood Forest) is the only place specifically mentioned as the home of Robin and Little John, beginning with the famous
line, "Robyn stode in Bernesdale" (adapted as a limerick, "Robin Hood in
Barnsdale stood").
   Other plot elements of the film that are indebted to the medieval ballads include Robin and Little John waylaying a pot maker and assuming
his identity in order to enter Nottingham, which is lifted from *Robin Hood
and the Potter*. In addition, the film's long, drawn-out duel between Robin
and the sheriff seems choreographed on the basis of the "two howers" long
fight between Robin and Sir Guy in *Robin Hood and Guy of Gisborne*. As in
the movie, the ballad has Robin stumble and then be struck on "the left
side" by a "quicke and nimble" opponent. But just when it seemed that
Robin was doomed, he "leapt up againe" and came at Sir Guy "with an
awkward stroke," slaying him. The treacherous Syr Roger of Donkesly
from the *Gest* is apparently the inspiration for the movie's only villain, Sir
Ranulf of Pudesly, who violates the sheriff's word of honor given to Robin
that his men would "leave the field" should he be defeated by him. Instead,
the sheriff's fall spurs Pudesly to immediately launch an attack that dis-
perses Robin's band, although the knight himself is clubbed to death by
Little John. Shaw's interpretation of the sheriff of Nottingham, on the
other hand, is a departure from both the ballad tradition and earlier film
portrayals. Rather than the inveterately evil villain of the ballads, or
Melville Cooper's comically bungling sycophant in *The Adventures of Robin
Hood*, the sheriff in *Robin and Marian* is a complex, sympathetic figure. He
is more than a match in wit and swordplay for Robin, and, underneath his
haughty and aloof demeanor, he cares for his men and is "almost sorry" to
have to hunt down his old adversary. Since he can read and write (unlike

Robin Hood (Sean Connery) and Little John (Nicol Williamson) ride to Nottingham in a stolen potter's cart in *Robin and Marian*. The scene is based on a medieval ballad, *Robin Hood and the Potter*.

Robin), he is one of the few men around who can competently rule in the king's name, and Lester has even characterized the role as that, "The sheriff is basically a liberal: He's become a genuine grass-roots politician." Perhaps because their enmity has such a long history, Robin respects and feels some kinship with his foe. This is touchingly expressed in the film when, after they pray together with their swords uplifted like crosses, Robin helps the more heavily armored sheriff to get up before commencing their duel to the death.

Aside from mining authentic medieval ballads, *Robin and Marian* also makes an effort to reference real historical events from the time period. This should be no surprise, as Goldman was thoroughly familiar with the Plantagenet family from his play, *The Lion in Winter*, which featured both Richard and John as younger characters. It is true, for example, that Richard died besieging a castle at Châlus, near Limoges in the Limousin region of France, which he believed harbored a gold statue, when what had actually been discovered was a pot of Roman coins in a ploughed field.

The king was fatally wounded in the arm—not the neck—on March 26, 1199, by a crossbowman, Bertram de Gurdun, whose family had been annihilated by the Lionheart. As is shown in the film, it was the botched operation to extract the arrow that killed Richard. Historically, the king did forgive his murderer, but his mercenary captain, Mercadier (who makes a brief appearance in the movie), later apprehended Bertram and had him beaten and then hanged. During Robin's reunion in the film with the remnants of his outlaw band, Friar Tuck makes reference to King John's investiture controversy with Pope Innocent III, in which the king refused to accept the pope's choice of Stephen Langton as archbishop of Canterbury. The pope then placed England under interdict, which, as Tuck explains, means that "you can't hear mass or take holy communion anywhere." Timewise, this would locate the film sometime between 1208 and 1213. The former date is more realistic if John's wife, Isabel of Angoulême—who married the king in 1200 when in her early teens—is to be portrayed as a young, sexually predatory newlywed. The latter date, however, is preferable if one accepts Will Scarlett's complaint of John that "even his own kind have turned against him . . . the kingdom's falling apart," since this would be but two years away from the political crisis that resulted in Magna Carta. For the sake of narrative clarity, *Robin and Marian* compresses several historical events in John's reign into a narrow time frame, whereas Robin's service to King Richard, which can only have lasted from 1190 to 1199, is inflated to twenty years.

Royal authority of any kind does not come off very well in *Robin and Marian*, nor, for that matter, does the violent culture associated with the Middle Ages. From the very beginning of the movie, Robin announces to his band that he hasn't come back to England to rally the people and fight the king, and in a later scene with Marian, he describes his war weariness as a result of his crusading experience:

Marian: You went crusading, didn't you?
Robin: There's some things worth dying for.
Marian: They had souls too, the heathen that you killed. If I
    should die in prison—I'd rather not—but if it comes, it's for a
    reason. I'll have stood for something. But I won't have taken
    another life to do it. What will you do now? Fight the sheriff?
    More causes? Aren't you sick of it?
Robin: On the 12th of July, 1191, the mighty fortress that was
    Acre fell to Richard, his one great victory in the Holy Land.
    He was sick in bed and never struck a blow. And on the 20th of
    August, John and I were standing on the plain outside of the
    city watching, while every Muslim left alive was marched out

in chains. King Richard spared the richest for ransom, took the
strong for slaves, and he took the children—all the children—
and had them chopped apart. When that was done, he had the
mothers killed. When they were all dead—3,000 bodies on the
plain—he had them all opened up so the guts could be
explored for gold and precious stones. Our churchmen on the
scene—and there were many—took it for a triumph. One
bishop put on his miter and led us all in prayer. And you ask
me if I'm sick of it.
Marian: Why didn't you come home then?
Robin: Because . . . he was my king.

This is a far cry from the lighthearted bravado of Errol Flynn. Robin's long
diatribe seems largely based on the *Sultanly Anecdotes* of Baha al-Din,
Saladin's army judge. But the film completely ignores a contemporary
Christian account, the *Itinerarium Regis Ricardi* (*Itinerary of King Richard*),
that is more favorable to the crusaders. At the same time, it amplifies the
massacre with horrors—the killing of even women and children and
searching their corpses for swallowed coins—that are lifted from a completely different event altogether: the crusader conquest of Jerusalem in
July 1099, as told in Fulcher of Chartres' chronicle of the First Crusade.
Thus, two incidents separated by nearly a century are conflated in order to
create a medieval equivalent to the famous My Lai Massacre of 1968 from
the Vietnam War, which became an icon of war's unjustifiable brutality to
the generation of the late '60s and early '70s who were protesting U.S.
involvement in that conflict. (The burning of Châlus castle with the women
and children inside that is shown at the very beginning of the film serves
as a visual premonition of this horror.) Marian, then, in her determination
to go to jail rather than forcefully resist, is a kind of medieval conscientious
objector, analogous to those who went to prison or exile in Canada rather
than be drafted to fight America's "dirty war." Audrey Hepburn, a committed pacifist, agreed to do the film after a eight-year hiatus from the
movies, partly on the strength of the script's antiwar sentiments, such as
expressed above. (She also admired Goldman's other medieval effort, *Lion
in Winter*.) The age-old message of Robin Hood's defiance of corrupt and
abusive political authority likewise takes on new meaning in the post-
Watergate atmosphere of the mid-1970s.

   With all of *Robin and Marian*'s jaded bucking of tradition, the movie
barely pays homage to the familiar themes of romance, righting of wrongs,
and loyalty to "good King Richard" that had sustained previous films in the
Robin Hood genre. Yet the basic elements are still there, including the climactic battle sequence we have come to expect in a Robin Hood film. In

line with the no-holds-barred realism of the rest of the movie, the duel between Robin and the sheriff is perhaps the most accurately staged medieval trial-by-combat on film, with the two sides exhausted from hacking away at each other in hot, cumbersome armor and wielding heavy broadswords and battle-axes. A nice bit of period detail has Robin, prior to the duel, lead out his peasant army wearing a rustic-looking, leather jerkin covered in round brass plates, while this is intercut with the sheriff being waited on by his attendants, who arm him in more costly chain mail leggings and mail shirt. *Robin and Marian* is full of such authentic touches, from the makeshift camp in the greenwood where the outlaws wake, "creaking and groaning," after a night spent sleeping on the ground, to the austere architecture of the Kirklees Priory and Nottingham Castle sets, the latter surrounded by bucolic grape vines that just may have been possible in the English midlands during the warmer climes of the thirteenth century. (The movie was filmed at Pamplona, Spain, which was experiencing its own heat wave at the time that seriously inconvenienced many of the British actors.) Together, all these details lend *Robin and Marian* a gritty, lived-in look that truly transports you back to the Middle Ages and is much imitated by more recent Robin Hood films.

Robin and Marian is probably the most accomplished film of the Robin Hood genre. In the opinion of Lester's filmographer, Neil Sinyard, it is the director's greatest work, one that "does not debunk a legend but humanizes it, in the process giving an old tale new heart and fresh dimensions of heroism." Certainly of all the Robin Hood movies, it is the one that is the most historically accurate, the most respectful of the medieval ballad tradition, and the most authentic and realistic looking in terms of its production values, despite being filmed in a lightning thirty-six days. At the time of its release, it received respectful reviews from most critics. Why, then, was *Robin and Marian* a box-office failure? (It only returned $4 million out of a $5 million investment.) Undoubtedly this is because it was not the Robin Hood that most filmgoers had come to see. The film dared to take a beloved, timeless, mythical hero and lock him "within the passing of human time," thus consigning his legend to "obsolescence." As a consequence, observes Stephen Knight, *Robin and Marian* "is to a substantial degree excluded by viewers from the tradition, simply because of its difference." Perhaps its radical revisionism goes too far, committing, in effect, *hari kari* by turning its merciless, unforgiving glare even onto the hero and heroine who must carry the film. If so, then *Robin and Marian* would be very much a product of its times: For the bitter cynicism and deep disillusionment of the 1960s and 1970s also turned inward and helped undermine America's political and social culture. In an interview with Andrew Yule, Sean Connery astutely recognized this fatal flaw, if it can be called that, in his movie:

The climactic duel between Robin Hood (Sean Connery) and the sheriff of Nottingham (Robert Shaw) from *Robin and Marian*. The choreography of the scene is derived from the medieval ballad, *Robin Hood and Guy of Gisborne*.

> The whole thing was very much anti-mythic. This guy comes galloping back after eighteen years away in the Crusades and he shouts, "Hey, I'm back." And of course no one much cares any more. And he's getting up each morning in the forest, creaking and groaning and coughing and having a leak in the bushes and it's all too much for a man of his age. They hated that idea in the States. They can't take the idea that their hero might be over the hill and falling apart.

But it was precisely this mortal quality to Robin Hood that had attracted Connery to the role, as he told Liz Smith when on location: "I like films that dispel time, and this appealed to me because not only it's an interesting legend, but also an examination of the legend. It's tremendously concerned with dying." One should note, however, that Connery himself didn't like being pegged as "middle-aged" any better than his fans: He objected to the term when it came up during the studio's physical prior to filming. (Connery was 45 at the time; Hepburn was 46.) *Robin and Marian* suffered the same fate as *King Arthur: The Young Warlord*, another 1970s film that used ruthless realism to try to whittle down to historical size a popular British hero of legendary proportions (see Chapter 1). Despite its greater polish and casting of stars with far more name recognition, *Robin and Marian* was no more successful than *King Arthur* in peddling to an unappreciative audience a new and innovative approach to an overexposed and seemingly worn-out legend.

Robin and Marian was to be the last major Robin Hood movie for fifteen years, and to date it has been the last film to have anything interesting to say about the Robin Hood of history or legend. Meanwhile, in 1984, another television series about Robin Hood, called *Robin of Sherwood*, aired in Britain and still retains a loyal fan club on the Internet. Although claims have been made for the series having a radical political subtext along the lines of *Robin and Marian*, these are not convincing. Instead, *Robin of Sherwood* eschews any kind of historical or literary focus in favor of an altogether different approach, one that dabbles in the occult and black magic. This much is made clear from the very first episode, "Robin Hood and the Sorcerer," in which Robin, an orphaned peasant lad, receives his new identity as "the Hooded Man" from a horned forest deity, Herne the Hunter. There are shades of the King Arthur legend here, for Herne is a kind of Merlin figure who gives Robin a magical bow and a sword, Albion. Another completely new character introduced to the Robin Hood legend is Nazir, Robin's Arab sidekick who is freed by Robin from the spell of the evil enchanter, the baron de Belleme. Perhaps this was a Robin Hood for the growing Wiccan market. Nonetheless, magic is not entirely foreign to the medieval outlaw tradition. It makes an appearance, for example, in the thirteenth-century tales of Fulk Fitzwarin and Eustace the Monk, but is nowhere to be found in the ballads of Robin Hood. At the end of its second season, the series had to cope with the departure of its star, Michael Praed, who was replaced with Jason Connery in the lead role. Before his brainchild was prematurely canceled for lack of funding, Richard Carpenter, the scriptwriter, apparently intended to end *Robin of Sherwood* by killing off all its characters, which at least would have been a blessing to those of us who were no fans of the series and would have paid homage to the better film that starred Jason's father, Sean.

As did the first British television series of the 1950s, *Robin of Sherwood* spawned a flurry of new Robin Hood films for the silver screen. The most indebted of these productions is *Robin Hood: Prince of Thieves* (1991), directed by Kevin Reynolds and starring Kevin Costner as the outlaw. Its producers and screenwriters made ambitious claims for their movie, calling it "a fresh incarnation of the Sherwood rebel" that "adds some new characters, some fresh twists, and some real surprises!" Hardly. In reality, nearly all the plot elements of *Robin Hood: Prince of Thieves* are ripped off from *Robin of Sherwood*. Chief among them is the film's "innovative" center-piece in which Robin befriends a Moor named Azeem (played by Morgan Freedman) during a jailbreak from an Arab prison and then takes him back to England. Although producer John Watson called this "a fresh and exciting way of re-introducing the Robin Hood story," we have already seen how a Moorish character named Nazir had first made his appearance in *Robin of Sherwood*, which Watson clearly expected most American audiences to have never seen. But the plagiarism does not stop there. *Prince of Thieves* serves up plenty of other rewarmed leftovers from the British series, including black magic—now represented by the sheriff of Nottingham's witch, Mortiana; the bad-guy duo of the sheriff and Guy of Gisborne; and even the same burning of villages and siege of Robin's Tree House Camp by a mercenary army of wild Celts hired by the sheriff. The filmmakers were very dishonest in the way they marketed their "fresh and different" version of the legend: that honor more truly belongs to Carpenter's uncredited TV show.

But while *Prince of Thieves* hijacks *Robin of Sherwood*'s original contributions, it also copies the series' drawbacks, namely that it is insufficiently grounded in the history or legend of Robin Hood. This is readily apparent from a perusal of the opening pages of the official movie book that was issued to coincide with the release of *Prince of Thieves*. Although Garth Pearce, the author of the book, demonstrates a firm grasp of the cinematic history of Robin Hood, his knowledge of medieval history is more shaky. Although the "Robert Hood, fugitive," from the exchequer pipe rolls of "1230" receives a mention, Walter Bower's chronicle history of the outlaw from the 1440s is assigned to the wrong author and the wrong century, namely to John of Fordun in 1341.

The most serious liability faced by the film during its production stages was that it was rushed, allowing not nearly enough time for preparation and research into historical aspects of its subject. Because the production company, Morgan Creek, wanted to catapult its product into the market ahead of at least two other competitors—20th Century Fox and TriStar— who were also planning the release of a Robin Hood film in 1991, it gave director Kevin Reynolds a draconian 100-day shooting schedule. (In the end, Fox released its film, *Robin Hood*, a month ahead of its rival.) The film became Reynolds' Waterloo, as he started shooting with only weeks, instead of the usual months, of prep time, and as he fought the uncooperative British weather and fading autumn light on location at Burnham Beeches, Buckinghamshire, and Shepperton Studios in London. Yet these were not insurmountable obstacles, for Michael Curtiz directed *The Adventures of Robin Hood* within similar time constraints. But it became evident during filming that Reynolds' work lacked drive and direction, to the point where his friend and namesake, Costner, began taking over behind the camera. Above all, *Prince of Thieves* suffers from a lack of conviction, since its director never seems to have known why he was making the picture. When asked by Garth Pearce why the medieval outlaw had suddenly become so popular as to have competing movies made about him, Reynolds replied nonchalantly, "I try not to think about it, to be honest."

Most of the major stars of the movie seem to have followed their director's lead in adopting a noncerebral approach to their roles. Costner, in particular, saw himself as primarily an action figure and cites this element as what attracted him to playing Robin Hood. (Morgan Creek's first choice for the title role was Mel Gibson, who would have been the second Australian to have played Robin Hood, after Flynn.) As he told Garth Pearce: "I am physical in my acting. I consider that it's part of what I have to offer. . . . So the chance of shooting bows and arrows and fighting with staves and swords is terrific. It is like being in a sports situation every day." To the consternation of his wife, Cindy, and the stunt coordinator, Paul Weston, he insisted on doing many of his own stunts, whether swinging from trees, galloping on horseback, or dueling with "John Little" in the rapids of Aysgarth Falls, Yorkshire. Although this energetic athleticism is in the best tradition of Fairbanks and Flynn, Costner's wooden and uninspiring acting style could not deliver the panache and bonhomie of his predecessors. Aside from perhaps making Robin the staunch champion of an extremely laid-back pacifism, Costner is unable to find new meaning in the legend or a new way to interpret a timeworn role. Instead, he plays Robin Hood simply as Kevin Costner. This straight-arrow approach was apparently blessed by the film's executive producer, James Robinson, who famously remarked: "Have Kevin Costner play Kevin Costner. We'll fix it at dubbing stage." Adding to this fundamental defect is Costner's glaringly American drawl, which the actor could not shed despite weeks of work with a dialect coach. The miscast accent is made only more apparent by the fact that it is surrounded by genuine British ones from a bevy of native-born actors, including Brian Blessed, who plays the elder Locksley but is fortunately killed off before accents can collide in a father/son reunion. Perhaps the best thing Costner does is to eschew spandex-style tights in favor of more realistic, dun-colored trousers, but of course, it's not what's on the outside that counts. (Sean Connery went one better in *Robin and Marian*: He wore nothing on his legs underneath his surcoat.) Far from living up to expectations of being "his greatest screen success yet," *Prince of Thieves* marked a definitive downturn in Costner's career.

Following in the footsteps of the two Kevins, the other American actors in the film were determined to see their roles in strictly contemporary terms, oblivious to the historical and legendary background of the subject. Robin Hood's story here becomes an excuse to push a modern, politically correct agenda, which includes multiculturalism and feminism. Morgan Freedman's character of Azeem is the one through which much of the movie's political correctness and anachronisms are forced onto the screen. As we have seen in the Viking film, *The 13th Warrior* (Chapter 2), it was not unknown for Muslims like Ibn Fadlan to travel to the "northern climes," which Arabs generally regarded as filthy, backward, savage, and cold. According to another Muslim author, al-Idrisi (d. 1165), England was in the northernmost, seventh clime of the world and was an island shaped like an ostrich's head, whose "inhabitants are courageous, vigorous, and enterprising, but a continual winter prevails there." Although Muslims at this time were more advanced than Europeans in such fields as mathematics, medicine, and philosophy, they, too, like everyone else, had their prejudices and limitations. It is obvious from al-Idrisi's account that medieval Muslims were ignorant about European geography and culture, and this hurt them when they encountered the superior warfare that was waged by the "Franks" during the crusades. But at least Freedman plays Azeem with the right mix of bewilderment and condescension, such as a medieval Muslim may have felt when he encountered a "cursed country" where all the people "smell of garlic." Strange to say, the English seem remarkably nonplused by a black Arab in their midst, except for Mortiana, whose dreams are haunted by the "painted man." Ironically, though, Azeem must pass himself off as Robin's slave in order to be accepted in England, so it's hard to see how this character liberates the film.

Even more of a strain on our credibility is that a twelfth-century man, even if he is a more civilized Muslim, has a knowledge of Caesarean births, optical telescopes, and gunpowder. Although the thirteenth-century Chinese, according to Marco Polo, had a knowledge of the last innovation, they did not harness it as a weapon, and it was to be several centuries before any of these inventions were to be introduced to the West. But Freedman seems to have been attracted to the role as a chance to broaden the horizons of the audience. He told Garth Pearce that he was "pleasantly surprised" to be offered the part, complaining that "casting directors in Hollywood don't have too much imagination."

The characters of Maid Marian and Will Scarlett also suffer badly from what has been called the film's "historical amnesia." Mary Elizabeth Mastrantonio, who was a last-minute replacement for a pregnant Robin Wright, plays Marian as the soul of late-twentieth-century feminism transported back to the Middle Ages. Although Robin and Marian do fight in the seventeenth-century ballad, *Robin Hood and Maid Marian*, to knee Robin in the balls is perhaps going a little too far for even this feisty wench.

Mastrantonio evinced not the slightest interest in doing any homework for her part. As she confessed to Garth Pearce: "Acting is about just getting on with doing it. The story was new—Robin Hood to me was just Errol Flynn in tights—so there was much to learn and absorb. I think it is far better to just turn up and start work. . . . Once I realized that this Maid Marian has plenty of guts I was into the part." The same sloppy anachronisms were committed by Christian Slater as Will Scarlett, who does no credit here to his earlier and better medieval turn as the novice Adso in *The Name of the Rose* (1986). Slater, whose California twang is even more whiney and grating than Costner's, was given free rein to interpret his role as a modern-day, maladjusted teenager:

> Several things were put into the script after I was cast. For instance, the fact that Robin Hood really screwed up my life when I was younger. His father dated my mother and I was the result. I came forth into the world as Robin's half-brother. There is one point in the film when I have to tell Robin the truth. So it adds an edge to the whole movie for me.

Although this is, in fact, the only truly original plot element in the film and gives Costner his most memorable line—"I have a brother! I have a brother!"—it reduces the powerful social message of the Robin Hood story to simply one of "family values."

Instead, the English actors must carry the dramatic weight of the film. They include Nick Bremble as Little John, Alan Rickman as the sheriff of Nottingham, Geraldine McEwan as Mortiana, and an American expatriate, Michael McShane, as Friar Tuck. In general, they seem to have given more thought and tried to bring more authenticity to their roles than their American colleagues. Above all, it was Rickman's "hilariously over-the-top" performance as the sheriff—especially when compared to the bland, somnolent acting of Costner—that dazzled both critics and audiences in 1991. His approach to the role was to ham it up as though the film were a burlesque or a farce. After all, how can one take seriously a sheriff who obsesses over his own statue and who tells his coerced concubines: "You, Mauron, 10:30 tonight, you [pointing to another], 10:45 . . . and bring a friend." Since the release of the movie, however, film scholars have reassessed Rickman's manic contribution. Stephen Knight, for instance, takes the actor to task for unbalancing *Prince of Thieves* with his "ripe style," in contrast to Rathbone's professionalism on *The Adventures* set. Similar criticisms are voiced by Scott Nollen, who indicts Rickman's performance as overacted, "outrageous," "unbearable," and "out of control," especially when compared to the "subtle villainy" of Rathbone. But in all fairness to the actor, Rickman is not entirely to blame for stealing the picture. Not

A publicity ensemble photo of the cast from the greenwood scenes of *Robin Hood: Prince of Thieves*. Main actors from left to right are Christian Slater as Will Scarlett, Nick Bremble as Little John, Morgan Freeman as Azeem, Kevin Costner as Robin Hood, and Michael McShane as Friar Tuck.

only was Reynolds' direction too permissive, but the role of sheriff was scripted as an historically implausible, oversized figure who displaces Prince John as the one threatening to take over the kingdom. (The sheriff's obsequious squire addresses him as "sire.") His character was also given the juiciest lines, such as, "Locksley, I'm going to cut your heart out—with a spoon!" or "That's it—cancel the kitchen scraps for lepers and orphans, no more merciful beheadings, and call off Christmas!" As the sheriff later explains to Gisborne, a spoon is his murder weapon of choice because, "It's dull . . . it will hurt more." On an historical note, the English Parliament did actually outlaw Christmas, in 1644, on the grounds that it was a "popish holiday."

Rather late in the day, the filmmakers realized their mistake. When *Prince of Thieves* was screened before test audiences, Rickman's "gleeful villainy" was overwhelmingly preferred to Costner's "sanctimonious Robin." Over Reynolds' objections, Morgan Creek attempted to correct the imbalance by recutting the film before its release, removing scenes with Rickman and restoring footage featuring Costner. This film surgery seems to have backfired, since, according to Stephen Knight, it only heightens the sheriff's remaining impact, and it turns the film into a cookie-cutter action adventure along the lines of Spielberg's *Indiana Jones* films or previous Costner vehicles. (Hollywood wags dubbed the movie *Indiana Hood and the Raiders of the Greenwood* and *Dances with Deer*.) Yet, in fact, the filmmakers may have missed an accidental opportunity to contribute a unique addition to the Robin Hood genre, one that switches the audiences' usual sympathies from a hero it can't bring itself to like to a villain it can't bring itself to hate. This is something that would mirror historians' own recent shift of focus in their study of Robin Hood: from fruitless attempts to reveal the elusive identity of the outlaw, to the more possible potentialities of unmasking the real sheriff. It is Rickman who brings a healthy and much-needed dose of irreverence to the movie's hectoring, overly serious liberalism; indeed, he seems to be the only actor who actually has any fun in the film.

The other Robin Hood movie of 1991, called simply *Robin Hood*, was directed by John Irvin and starred Patrick Bergin as the outlaw. Although it was released by 20th Century Fox ahead of its rival—in the meantime TriStar bowed out of the Robin Hood hunt altogether—*Robin Hood* almost immediately slipped underneath the public radar, since it was screened in the United States only on television and was massively outpromoted by Morgan Creek, which spent $30 million alone on advertising *Prince of Thieves*—one third of the film's total budget. Nevertheless, *Robin Hood* went on to garner the greater critical acclaim, benefitting from more authentic sets—located in Cheshire and Wales, a more straightforward storyline, and, above all, American actors who could muster English accents. Not the least of its advantages was the fact that Sir James Holt, a leading historian on Robin Hood, served as historical adviser to the film. (*Prince of Thieves*, apparently, consulted Jim Lees, who served as past president of the Robin Hood Society based in Nottingham, but is not a professional historian and is virtually unknown in the field of Robin Hood scholarship.) Yet although *Robin Hood* is certainly a better film than *Prince of Thieves*, it is no more notable as an addition to the Robin Hood genre. From the opening scene of the film, it is evident that *Robin Hood* is basically a more realistic remake of *The Adventures of Robin Hood* from 1938.

One significant departure from its predecessor, however, is the film's portrayal of Maid Marian (played by Uma Thurman). In another nod to modern feminism, Marian enjoys a more active role in *Robin Hood* than in most previous films. Just like Deering does in *Son of Robin Hood*, she disguises herself as a boy in order to join Robin Hood's band, but during the climactic duel between Robin and Sir Miles Falconet, she refuses to stand by and watch; instead, she actually lends a hand to the swordplay. At the end of the film, instead of meekly accepting Robin's hand "with all my heart," as she does in *The Adventures*, Marian weds Robin because he "brings spring-time to my heart" (which is the cue for the sun to come out), thus signifying that she will not accept any husband but on her own terms. Even though Normans and Saxons are also reconciled by the film's close, *Robin Hood* eschews the easy ending of having King Richard arrive on the scene to right all the wrongs of his dastardly brother, Prince John.

If for nothing else, we should be grateful to this latest round of high-brow Robin Hood films for being midwife to the birth of what many consider to be the lowest of the low-brow outlaw movies: Mel Brooks' *Robin Hood: Men in Tights* (1993), starring Cary Elwes as perhaps the most irreverent Robin yet. Although many critics and film scholars deride this parody as offensive, crude, and hopelessly anachronistic, it delivers a visceral humor that many audiences, myself included, do find funny. Moreover, as one brave defender of the movie, Stephen Knight, points out, *Men in Tights* does fit the Robin Hood tradition "snugly," being part of what Knight calls a "carnivalization" of the legend going all the way back to the medieval May Games and more recently encapsulated in several parodies of the 1980s. In 1981, *Time Bandits* had the Monty Python comedian, John Cleese, make a brief appearance as a class-conscious Robin Hood who, in the script's words, was to be "played like the Duke of Kent." In contrast to their genteel leader, Robin Hood's not-so-merry men dole out vicious face punches to the poor after receiving their handouts. Later, in 1984, came *The Zany Adventures of Robin Hood*, which features Jewish humor in the form of characters lifted straight out of *Ivanhoe* and an "Entebbe Raid" on Nottingham Castle, complete with Israeli commandos. Then in 1988–1989 came the gender-bending *Maid Marian and her Merry Men*, a British TV series for children written by Tony Robinson (who plays Baldrick in the better-known *Black Adder* series) and narrated by a Rastafarian rapper named Barrington.

Men in Tights is indebted to at least the latter two films, reproducing *Zany Adventure's* Jewish references—with Mel Brooks taking a turn as a circumcision-obsessed "Rabbi Tuckman"—and mimicking *Maid Marian's* Barrington in its opening rap number that sets the wacky tone for the rest of the movie. Mainly, however, *Men in Tights* is a spinoff of *Prince of Thieves*, with mock impersonations of many of the latter's characters and scenes. Its funniest parodies come from "Asneeze" and his son, "Ahchoo," while at one point in the film, Robin Hood boasts to Prince John that, "Unlike some other Robin Hoods, I can speak with an English accent." References to other Robin Hood movies include the unceremonious dumping of a wild pig (or "boor") on Prince John's banquet table in imitation of the famous scene with the stag from *The Adventures of Robin Hood*, or villagers protesting the use of flaming arrows to introduce the opening credits, which mocks the special effects pioneered by *Robin of Sherwood*. *Men in Tights* also makes free play with various aspects of American popular culture that seem to have absolutely nothing to do with Robin Hood, such as the "tom-ahawk chop" and chorus made famous by Atlanta Braves fans, which the spectators adopt at Robin's archery contest. Amazingly enough, this anachronism is played straight in a recent film about medieval jousting, *A Knight's Tale* (2001), which has the crowd chant to the tune of "We will rock you!" by a popular rock group from the 1970s, Queen. A more intel-ligent intrusion of contemporary culture into *Men in Tights* is Ahchoo's passing reference to the beating of a black man, Rodney King, by Los Angeles police. As he is manhandled by the sheriff of Nottingham's men, Ahchoo exclaims, "Man, I hope somebody's getting a video of this thing!" The Rodney King episode—recorded on a bystander's home video recorder in 1992—is an uncomfortable reminder that even in a modern, progressive society, justice can shockingly miscarry. And really, this is pre-cisely what the original medieval ballads of Robin Hood are all about.

One may well wonder with some trepidation what's next in store for Robin Hood films? For the moment, it seems that Hollywood will continue to pursue the "feminization" of Robin Hood, as is also being done to the King Arthur legend. In 2001, the same year that TNT Films came out with its miniseries, *Mists of Avalon*, Disney produced a short TV movie geared for the young teenager market, *Princess of Thieves*. The plot revolves around Robin Hood's daughter, Gwyn, who helps Prince Philip, son of Richard the Lionheart, succeed to the throne in spite of the machinations of Prince John. Meanwhile, she has issues to work out with her father, Robin, who has been an absent "deadbeat dad" for five years, leaving her to be raised by her uncle. This idea of turning the outlaw into a girl is not new, since we have already encountered it in *Son of Robin Hood* from 1958, and it makes an even earlier appearance in the silent film, *Lady Robin Hood* from 1925, which stars Evelyn Brent in the dual role of Catalina/La Ortiga, described as a "female hybrid of Robin Hood and Zorro." As a matter of historical note, Richard had no heirs, and even if he did, he certainly wouldn't have called him Philip, the name of his archrival, Philip Augustus, king of France.

Who knows? Perhaps in the future we'll see Robin Hood reincarnated as a New Age champion of environmentalism. Whatever lies ahead, we can be sure that Robin Hood will always be in vogue.

CHAPTER FIVE

Welcome to the Apocalypse
Black Death Films

The Background

Toward the end of the year 1347, some merchants who had been trading in the Black Sea region returned to their home ports in Italy. Unbeknownst to their friends and family, and perhaps even to themselves, they brought back with them a most unwelcome commodity: the dreaded plague or pestilence, a disease that had not been seen in Europe and the Mediterranean for nine centuries. According to the apocryphal account of Gabriele de Mussis, a contemporary chronicler from Piacenza, Italy, these first victims and carriers of the Black Death into Europe had contracted the disease as the result of a primitive form of germ warfare. In 1346, the Mongol armies of the Kipchak khan, Janibeg, attempted to expel the infidel Christian presence from his recently converted Muslim lands. As the Mongols were besieging the Genoese at Caffa (now Feodosiya), an important trading post on the north coast of the Black Sea, the besiegers suddenly found themselves besieged by the plague. Before leaving, the Mongols decided to give their enemies a taste of their own affliction. Loading their dead, plague-ridden comrades onto their catapults, they then lobbed these human missiles "into the city of Caffa in order that the intolerable stench of those bodies might extinguish everyone." Although it is unlikely that the disease was first communicated from East to West in such a highly dramatic fashion, it is entirely possible that the Mongols did transmit the plague to Europeans by the more peaceful means of trade. One of the most coveted export products from the Black Sea region were luxurious animal furs, such as ermine and marten. These furs—even when skinned—made ideal homes for fleas that carried within their stomachs the bacteria causing bubonic plague. When Italian merchants brought their exclusive wares home, to be draped around their wives' lovely necks or sold at some high-end market, little did they know how costly their imports were to become.

By 1348 the Black Death had a firm grip on Italy, Spain, France, England, and perhaps western Germany and Norway. By 1349 and 1350, it had spread to almost all the rest of Europe, including the Low Countries, Austria, Ireland, Wales, Scotland, and the whole of Germany and Scandinavia. Only Poland and Bohemia seem to have been relatively spared by the disease, perhaps because of few trading contacts there. The consequences for Europe's population were catastrophic. Best estimates that can be made from a variety of records to survive from this period indicate that, on average, 50 percent of the inhabitants of any given city, town, or village succumbed, although of course there was considerable variation depending on time and place. Our most accurate records of mortality, for instance, are the registers kept by bishops that record every vacancy that occurred in every parish church in their dioceses. Ten plague registers survive from England, which yield an average mortality of 45 percent among the priesthood in 1349, while a register that survives from Barcelona in Spain points to an even higher, 60 percent death rate between May 1348 and April 1349. It may be argued that priests had better living standards than most peasants, but if they were doing their duty of administering last rites, which their high death rate indicates, then in fact their exposure may have been greater. We also have other records that can tell us how many peasants died from plague, and these rates tend to be no lower than that of their priests. Lords kept annual accounts of how many tenants there were on their manors and what rents and services they owed, and these survive in good number—especially from ecclesiastical institutions—throughout England. Manorial account rolls yield death rates during the plague ranging from 40 to 70 percent. On the Continent, a parish register at Givry in France records a 50 percent mortality in the second half of 1348, while at San Gimignano in Italy, household census returns tell us that population there declined by 59 percent in the city and by 45 percent in the *contado*, or surrounding countryside, as a result of the first outbreak of the Black Death.

This was indeed the "Golden Age of the Germ," for plague came not just once but again and again, revisiting Europe's beleaguered population about once a decade throughout the second half of the fourteenth and throughout the fifteenth centuries. Nor was it only plague that killed. Other diseases that put in an appearance include smallpox, tuberculosis, the "stich" (pleurisy), the "flux" (dysentery), the "sweat" (influenza), and a horrible venereal disease—perhaps gonorrhea—that was known as the "French Pox," in which men's penises acquired a burning sensation before these rotted off and the victims died. The effect of all this mortality was to keep Europe's population low until the very end of the Middle Ages. A telling testimony to the late medieval demographic crisis is to plot the life expectancy of the monks at Christ Church Priory in Canterbury and at Westminster Abbey in London, both of which have left detailed obituary records. Despite the fact that the monks at these prestigious and wealthy institutions were extremely well fed and medically cared for, their life expectancy from birth fell precipitously throughout the fifteenth century, by as much as a decade, until it reached a nadir in the low twenties. Other dramatic statistics can be compiled from the tax records for several Tuscan towns in Italy, which reveal that population there declined over the course of the fourteenth and fifteenth centuries by anywhere from 62 to 75 percent. Meanwhile, in eastern Normandy (which was ravaged by war as well as plague), the century between 1347 and 1442 saw its population falling, according to its tax records, by a whopping 130 percent.

The Black Death can therefore be called the defining event of the late Middle Ages, one that changed, and extinguished, the lives of millions of Europeans. But what exactly was the Black Death? First of all, it should be pointed out that the disease was never called by that name during the Middle Ages. Instead, it was most commonly known as the "plague," the "pestilence," or the "great mortality." The designation of the 1348 outbreak as the "Black Death" only became current among historians during the eighteenth and nineteenth centuries, and even then it was a mistranslation of *pestis atra* or *atra mors*, Latin for "dreadful disease" or "dreadful death." These terms date back to the writings of Seneca during the first century A.D. but were reintroduced by Scandinavian chroniclers during the sixteenth and seventeenth centuries.

We are indebted to the Victorian era not only for giving a name to this remarkable historical phenomenon, but also for bequeathing to us the first modern medical analysis of how plague kills and why. During the 1850s, a French biologist called Louis Pasteur first discovered that diseases like plague were caused by parasitic organisms known as bacteria, which were so small that they could only be seen under a microscope. One of Pasteur's proteges who studied at his institute in Paris, Alexandre Yersin, later had a unique opportunity to put this microbiotic theory into practice when he attempted to contain a plague outbreak in the crowded Chinese port of Hong Kong in 1894. Unfortunately, Yersin was not entirely successful, for by the end of the century, the plague had spread to Bombay and other parts of India, where it was to rage intermittently until the middle of the twentieth century, killing a total of nearly 13 million persons. Reports of

the disease that filtered back to Britain from its Third World colonies contributed to the horror that plague continued to hold for the modern
Western consciousness. Sir Arthur Conan Doyle's Sherlock Holmes story,
"The Giant Rat of Sumatra," plays upon this fear: Holmes must foil the
agents of his archenemy, Professor Moriarity, who attempt to raise the
specter of the medieval holocaust in Victorian Britain by importing a
plague-infested rat from southeast Asia. Even as recently as 1994, medical
newsletters in the U.S. and Europe reported the alarming news that both
bubonic and pneumonic plague were once again striking down thousands
in the Indian subcontinent.

Yet out of this turn-of-the-century experience with plague came the
first systematic study of the disease. The Plague Research Commission,
appointed by the British Home Office in 1905, published regular reports
in the *Journal of Hygiene* on the epidemic in India from 1906 until 1917,
when mortalities began to abate. Based on these observations, we know
that the symptoms of plague are caused by the invasion and multiplication
inside the human body of the bacterium, *Pasteurella pestis* or *Yersinia pestis*
(named after Pasteur and Yersin) and that the symptoms can take three
forms, depending on the mode of transmission of the bacteria. The most
common type of plague is bubonic, named after *bubon*, originally a Greek
word for groin, which is where the swellings associated with this form of
the disease usually appear (at least according to the modern diagnosis of
the disease). In bubonic plague, the bacteria invade the body through the
bite of a flea, which lives off the blood of animals, such as cats, dogs, and
rats. A flea that is "blocked" by plague bacilli—in other words, whose
stomach is filled with bacteria—is constantly hungry and none too dis-
criminating about its host. It will happily feed on humans once its animal
host has grown cold after dying from the plague. Since its stomach is
already full, the flea is also forced to regurgitate its blood meal back into
its victim, along with perhaps thousands of bacteria. These then multiply
in the patient's bloodstream during an incubation period of between two to
eight days, at the end of which time they collect in the lymph nodes located
in the groin, armpits, or the neck, depending on which is closest to the original point of entry. It is then that the first symptoms appear, starting with
a high fever and shortly followed by the signature swellings, or buboes, of
the lymph glands, which is actually a sign that the body is trying to expel
the infection. Other symptoms include violent headaches; subcutaneous
bleeding that produces large livid spots on the skin; and loss of nervous
and motor control, which can manifest itself in a variety of ways, including
convulsions, dizziness, restlessness, stupor, and delirium. If the patent dies,
usually of heart failure or internal hemorrhaging, these symptoms typically
last from three to six days. However, a significant proportion of victims of

bubonic plague—anywhere from 10 to 40 percent—do recover naturally from the disease during the second week after the onset of symptoms, by which time the buboes have burst open and released their pus.

The two other forms of the plague are the pneumonic and septicemic varieties, which are even more deadly than the bubonic kind. In pneumonic plague, an especially virulent form of the disease, the bacteria are spread through airborne droplets, much like the common cold, which then invade the lungs and produce a bloody sputum. Victims succumb in 100 percent of the cases within three days of the infection. Septicemic plague is a most rare and mysterious form of the disease. Here, the plague bacilli invade and multiply within the patient's bloodstream so rapidly that he or she may die within hours, without ever evincing any symptoms. We don't know exactly how septicemic plague was spread. It may have been caused by the bite of a human flea, *Pulex irritans*, that was capable of transmitting extraordinarily large numbers of bacteria after feeding on an already infected host. On the other hand, the septicemia may also have been spread much like modern hepatitis—through dirty instruments, such as a scalpel tainted with the blood or pus of a plague victim. Hygiene was none too good in the Middle Ages, and a knife that was used to lance a plague boil may then have been applied to "bleed" a patient, ironically in the hopes that this would prevent or cure the disease.

In several parts of the world, the plague bacteria are what is called "endemic," that is, they are perpetually present in the bloodstream of the rodent and their attendant flea populations within a given locality. Such plague "reservoirs" seem to have existed since ancient times in the Himalayan foothills between India and Tibet, and since the second half of the thirteenth century in the Central Asian steppes in Mongolia and Kazakstan. Today, endemic plague also persists in isolated regions of the western United States, where signs warn visitors to national parks not to feed squirrels, since they may give them the plague. Even so, at least a dozen outbreaks still occur in the U.S. annually, such as when a man from Santa Fe, New Mexico, who had camped out in a flea- or rodent-infested sleeping bag, nearly died of bubonic plague while on vacation in New York City in November 2002. Since rodents are not normally migratory, the disease can become "pandemic," or contagious throughout a wide geographical area, only when it makes the leap from animals to humans, who then carry it further afield. Conditions for a pandemic outbreak of plague were created in the century prior to 1348 with the establishment of the Mongol Empire that stretched from China in the east to Russia in the west. As Marco Polo testifies in his *Travels*—based on a journey he had made to Cambulac, or modern-day Beijing, in the second half of the thirteenth century—a relatively safe, fast, and efficient overland route now linked the endemic areas of Asia with Europe. When Polo's Italian countrymen rushed to establish lucrative trade links with the Mongol Empire in the early fourteenth century, they laid the groundwork for a most deadly import. A similar process seems to have happened with the recent AIDS epidemic, which first made the jump from monkeys to humans in Africa and then traveled around the world through the almost unlimited modern methods of transport.

There are a couple of theories as to where the Black Death may have originated. A number of European chroniclers point to China or India, and native Chinese annals actually record disease epidemics raging through several provinces during the 1330s. Also in these years, the annals record a series of ecological disasters—including floods, famines, droughts, and earthquakes—that alternated with the epidemics. It might seem that these natural occurrences are unrelated to disease, but in reality climactic and terrestrial upheavals may have displaced the Manchurian marmot and other plague-bearing rodents from their mountain homelands down into lower elevation areas closer to human habitation. The Muslim world traveler, Ibn Battuta, bears witness to a disease in southern India that he personally contracted, and from which he fortunately recovered, in 1344. Yet it is not certain that any of these epidemics recorded in the Far East were plague, as not enough information about them survives. Another, more likely possibility is that the Black Death started in the 1330s in Central Asia. This theory is supported by another contemporary Muslim chronicler, Ibn al-Wardi, who was writing from Aleppo in northen Syria. He claims that the plague "began in the land of darkness," which probably refers to Mongolia, since al-Wardi's patrons, the Mamluk rulers of Syria, had been locked in bitter rivalry with the Mongol hordes for nearly a century. Also supporting a Central Asian origin is the archeological evidence of several hundred Nestorian gravestones that were discovered in 1885 in what is now the northern border region of Kyrgyzstan, a republic carved out of the former Soviet Union that straddles northwestern China. In 1338–1339, over 100 deaths were recorded on the gravestones, and on three of them, 10 victims are listed as dying from "plague" or "pestilence." Whatever its origins, the Black Death made its way to the Black Sea ports that provided the first point of contact with Europeans. From there, the plague spread rapidly throughout Europe along an extensive and well-established network of sea and land trade routes.

These days, plague—if it is caught early enough—can be easily cured by a dose of penicillin, which was developed from fungus, or plant mold, by Sir Alexander Fleming in 1928 and first injected into humans in 1940. Obviously, our medieval ancestors did not have the benefit of our modern medical knowledge, but this does not mean that they had no response to the disease. In general, medieval chroniclers and physicians advanced two explanations for the Black Death. Above all, they said, the plague came from God and was a mighty blow sent down from on high as a chastisement for man's excessive wickedness and sin. In a sense, this gave humans some control over the disease, since by reforming their lives or performing some extraordinary penance, God could be induced to take His divine anger and retribution away. But most fourteenth-century doctors, particularly those attached to universities, also admitted of natural causes of epidemic disease, and this explanation had come into vogue during the previous century when Christian thinkers rediscovered the works of classical philosophers and attempted to harmonize rationalism with faith. Their most important authorities included Hippocrates and Aristotle from the fifth and fourth centuries B.C., Ptolemy and Galen from the second century A.D., and Avicenna from the early eleventh century. Out of this mostly ancient tradition came the miasmatic theory of contagion: that a plague was spread by "evil vapors," or a miasma, which, when introduced into the air, corrupted it and changed its substance. Such evil vapors could be attributed either to a "universal and distant cause," namely to a conjunction of the planets, Saturn, Jupiter, and Mars, in which the close proximity of their opposing properties produced atmospheric disturbances, or to a "particular and near cause," in which the vapors came from sources closer to hand, such as earthquakes, swamps, or rotting corpses. The medical faculty at the University of Paris issued a most authoritative, and conventional, enunciation of the miasmatic theory in October 1348: It favored the astrological explanation for the vapors and dated the all-important planetary conjunction to precisely 1:00 p.m. on March 20, 1345. Allied to the belief in an aerial spread of the plague was the theory, also derived from the ancients, of person to person contagion, usually by breath or touch. It was not until the pioneering work of Pasteur in the 19th century that the germ theory of disease replaced the miasmatic legacy of the Middle Ages.

The miasmatic and interpersonal methods of contagion conditioned doctors' prescriptions for preventing an outbreak of the pestilence, and sometimes their advice was adopted by civic authorities in special ordinances drawn up to combat the disease. Eminently practical was their recommendation to flee from or quarantine the sick, and this seems to have led to the first recorded practice of using wooden coffins, instead of the usual cloth shrouds, to bury the dead. Also patients were urged to seal the doors and windows of their homes and treat the air with fragrant herbs, vinegar, or the smoke from aromatic woods. One prescription that may have caused more harm than good was the precaution against bathing, which was thought to open the body's pores to the miasma. In reality, medieval people's poor hygiene contributed substantially to the virulence of bubonic plague, since fewer baths meant more fleas. Even without this misguided advice, it is unlikely that many Christians would have bathed anyway, since bathing was equated with immorality and prostitution. Muslims may have had an advantage here, since their religion emphasized purity, and they inherited the regular use of baths from the Romans. Indeed, their superior cleanliness was a point of pride for Arabic authors when describing the filthy habits of their enemies. The Muslim encyclopedist, al-Qazwini, writing in the latter half of the thirteenth century, complained that European Christians "do not cleanse or bathe themselves more than once or twice a year." This is probably true, since monastic regulations, such as those at the prestigious Benedictine abbey of Cluny in France, provided for only two baths at most for each monk per year. Al-Qazwini also said that Christians do not wash or change their clothes until these "fall to pieces." On the other hand, Muslims were at a disadvantage in that they were forbidden by Islamic law from fleeing a plague area, since the disease was considered a mercy or "martyrdom" from God, rather than a straightforward case of human infection.

During the first epidemic of 1348, both Christian and Muslim doctors had to rely on classical authorities in order to treat plague. Later, however, by the end of the fourteenth century, physicians may have resorted more to practical measures, such as better hygiene and quarantine, that were based instead on their own experience in combating the disease. The most popular cure for any ailment during the Middle Ages was to bleed the patient, called, in medical parlance, a phlebotomy, in order to release the poison and restore the proper balance of the body's humors, which Hippocrates and Galen had taught was essential for good health. Bleeding was in fact to prevail as a general remedy for illness until the nineteenth century. Alternatively, patients could take a theriac—a treacle or syrup— that was thought to have the power to neutralize the plague poison within the body. Such medieval "miracle cures" were composed of various elements aged for a number of years, and they usually included chopped-up snakes and other exotic ingredients, such as Armenian clay, rare herbs, powdered gems, and precious metals. Surgeons also treated the plague boils with special plasters or attempted to hasten their demise by burning or cutting them open.

Although later doctors believed they enjoyed better success in curing their patients (probably due to the advent of natural immunity or lower virulence rather than effective treatment), members of the medical profession who faced the Black Death of 1348 often seemed helpless, and frankly admitted the fact. The pope's personal physician, Gui de Chauliac, testified that the first plague outbreak "rendered doctors powerless and put them to shame. . . . When they did visit [the sick] they did hardly anything for them." Some modern scholars have seized upon medieval impotency as an excuse to ignore altogether contemporary writings about the disease. This is a mistake. Although medieval authors were certainly respectful of authority and tradition—whether this be biblical or classical—they also relied on their own observations, especially in the context of an unprecedented event such as the Black Death. Giovanni Boccaccio, for instance, describes himself as an eyewitness to the plague's ravages in the city of Florence, which he would "scarcely dare to believe," he says, "were it not for the fact that I am one of many people who saw it with their own eyes." The Moorish physician from Almería in Spain, Ibn Khatima, gives in his plague treatise of 1349 a clinical—and judging by modern standards, most accurate—description of bubonic and pneumonic plague and expresses great confidence in the cure of bloodletting, which he backs up by citing specific case studies. Even Gui de Chauliac, who contracted but survived the disease in 1348, drops his fatalistic attitude when discussing a second plague outbreak in 1360, in response to which he prescribes detailed recipes for theriacs and custom treatments for buboes appearing on different parts of the human body.

Although they universally subscribed to the miasmatic theory, most medical authorities of the time attempted to relate it to some unusual phenomenon that they had observed or experienced, whether this be thunder and lightning, a comet, or an earthquake. Some medieval theories about the plague are unique and owe nothing to older sources. An anonymous physician from Montpellier in France, for instance, believed that the plague could pass from one person to another by sight alone, "when an aerial spirit leaves the eyes of a sick person and strikes the eyes of a healthy man attending him, especially when he is looking at the sick man in his death throes." Other theories, although widely accepted back then, nowadays may strike us as, quite frankly, bizarre. The medical faculty at the University of Paris gave credence to the "accidents of the soul" theory, that one could contract the plague merely "by imagination," or just by thinking about it. Gentile da Foligno, a highly respected Italian physician attached to the University of Perugia, was convinced that powdered emeralds taken internally was a surefire remedy, as the gem was known to crack the eyes of a toad. He also advised drinking liquid gold and wearing a gold ring set with an amethyst inscribed with the figure of a man holding a serpent. Yet at the same time, some medieval medical theories make perfect sense. The principle behind a theriac, that one can neutralize a poison by ingesting it in harmless quantities (hence snakeskin was a popular ingredient), is the same one that was used to develop the smallpox vaccine during the eighteenth century. Medieval doctors also believed that a victim's breath was highly contagious, which is actually true in the case of pneumonic plague.

Contemporary descriptions of the symptoms experienced during the Black Death—which usually were written down by chroniclers rather than by physicians, who were more concerned with explaining the causes and cures of the disease—are quite full and enable one to make an accurate diagnosis. There was a long historiographical tradition for describing plague symptoms, going back to Thucydides' account of the "plague" (probably typhus fever) in Athens in 430–429 B.C. and Procopius' history of an outbreak of bubonic plague in the Mediterranean during the sixth century A.D. (It was Procopius who bequeathed the word "boubon" to describe this form of the disease.) Fourteenth-century chroniclers of the Black Death seemed to realize that here was a unique historical event, which they must record for posterity so that, in the words of John Clynn of Ireland, "by chance a man, or anyone descended from Adam, should remain behind in the future who can escape this pestilence and continue the work I have begun." (Clynn himself died of the plague in 1349.) Their accounts are descriptive enough that we can be fairly confident they were made from first-hand, or at least contemporary, information.

Taken together, these descriptions, despite occasional eccentricities, are remarkably similar in their diagnoses of plague. Nearly all chroniclers, for example, mention the buboes or swellings that appear in bubonic plague. Although many symptoms are not unique to plague—lymphatic swelling and subcutaneous bleeding are also present in typhus, and violent fever heralds anthrax—plague is the best fit when these symptoms occur in conjunction with each other. Sometimes the diagnosis is unmistakable. Michele da Piazza, a Sicilian chronicler, records the progressive stages that modern doctors have observed in bubonic plague, starting with small swellings or pustules at the site of infection that Piazza describes as "the size of a lentil" (a description also used by Procopius) and progressing to larger buboes the size of a nut or egg. Louis Sanctus, writing from Avignon, mentions that the pope's surgeons performed autopsies that revealed the presence of pneumonic plague in the victims' lungs, and several other chroniclers, including Piazza, likewise distinguish between the bubonic and pneumonic forms. A few authors, Sanctus among them, even bear witness to the rare variety of plague—septicemic—that they noted killed victims very suddenly, causing them to fall down dead in the street or never waken from their slumbers. It is most unlikely that any other disease but plague would take on these three forms, as they are described in the chronicles.

Nevertheless, some modern scholars persist in doubting whether people in 1348 suffered and died from plague. The skeptics usually are scientists—bacteriologists or zoologists—with little to no historical training, but occasionally they are joined by historians, who really should know better than to be taken in by their theories. Typically, they use the latest scientific knowledge as an excuse to shortcut slogging through the medieval sources in order to cut right to the chase of their biological objections. These center on the claim that bubonic plague must be preceded by a large mortality among rats, where plague bacilli incubate, but which is not thought to be noted by any medieval source. (In actuality, several contemporary chroniclers, including Giovanni Villani, Fritsche Closener and Nicephorus Gregoras, do associate the advent of the Black Death with rats.) This is accompanied by an almost obsessive concern with biological factors, such as the migrating habits of the black rat, the density of the creatures per household necessary to sustain an "epizootic," or epidemic level of the disease, and the density of fleas per rat. The biological experts seem to forget that plenty of other animals who lived in close proximity to humans carry fleas, and that fleas do not need animal carriers to migrate but can hitch a ride in traveling merchandise, such as furs, wool packs, and straw, and live for long periods without a host on grain. If bubonic plague is not virulent enough, then pneumonic plague certainly will do, and the fact that Marseilles in southern France and several dioceses in the south of England experienced their highest mortalities during the winter and spring months indicates that pneumonic plague can travel ahead of or independently from the bubonic variety. Furthermore, the cold, wet summers and warm winters reported for 1348 may have made it possible for the two forms to invade each other's seasonal cycles. It is the height of arrogance to assume that we moderns, at six and a half centuries' remove from the event, are in a better position to diagnose the disease than our medieval ancestors, who actually lived through it. Although biological experts have undoubtedly done a service by making modern medical knowledge about the plague more accessible, it may be just as anachronistic to apply that knowledge to the Middle Ages as it is Marxist theory. The historian Sam Cohn argues on the basis of a combination of medieval and modern evidence that the Black Death differed substantially in terms of transmission, symptoms, virulence, immunity, and demographic patterns from its modern counterpart. But even granting Cohn's argument, which can be challenged on grounds too numerous to mention here, still does not dethrone plague from its place as the most likely candidate to fit the diagnoses of most chroniclers and doctors who witnessed the Black Death. (Significantly, Cohn offers no alternative disease to replace plague.) Modern tests done on bacterial DNA extracted from related strains to *Yersinia pestis* suggest that it can mutate over time and thus drastically alter plague's epidemiological behavior. Recently, forensic techniques have been successful in extracting *Yersinia* DNA from the dental pulp of fourteenth- and sixteenth-century plague victims. As future laboratory work may show, the plague of our ancestors may not have been the same one we know today.

Nonetheless, one alternative disease to plague has gained alarming currency in the popular consciousness of late: anthrax. Championing this alternative is currently trendy because of the recent bioterrorism using anthrax powder. Norman Cantor, the author of a popular new book on the Black Death, makes ambitious claims that anthrax must be accorded at least equal responsibility to plague for the rampant mortality of 1348. Cantor is a medieval historian, but the main sources of his medical analysis seem to be modern scientific reports. Citing the "smoking gun" of anthrax spores recovered from an archeological excavation of a medieval plague graveyard, as well as fourteenth-century evidence of cattle murrains (epidemics that targeted farm animals), he theorizes that the "rapid dissemination" of the disease was due to the eating of anthrax-tainted meat.

There are some powerful historical objections to the anthrax theory, however, that should once and for all drive a stake through the heart of this monstrosity. First of all, surviving manorial records testify to ample supplies of meat and grain during the Black Death, and several chroniclers record that there were so many animals per capita that they wandered aimlessly through the fields. There was no reason anyone should have had to eat tainted meat during the plague. Second, some cities, attempting to forestall the disease, did take elaborate precautions with regard to the handling of meat. Pistoia in Italy, for example, enacted no less than seven ordinances regulating how the city's butchers could select, slaughter, and sell their produce. All animals before they were slaughtered had to be checked by a city official to make sure they were healthy. Yet this did not save Pistoia: By 1415, the city had lost 65 percent of its population since the advent of plague in 1348. Finally, there *was* a time shortly before the Black Death when conditions were ripe for a rapid outbreak of anthrax: the Great Famine that struck northern Europe between 1315 and 1322. Widespread murrains, or animal diseases, occurred, and chroniclers in both England and Holland report that poor people were reduced to eating dead and raw "carcasses of cattle like dogs." Even so, mortality during the famine averaged only around 10 percent, according to a variety of urban and manorial records. Assuming that all these deaths were due to anthrax and not to starvation or some other disease, this is hardly in keeping with the astronomical mortality of 50 percent recorded during the Black Death.

In the end, the quest to know the exact nature of the disease that struck in 1348 may be irrelevant. It is clear from the surviving evidence that, whatever it was, the epidemic killed an awful lot of people. The removal of so many in such a short space of time—which our modern, germ-slaying society still makes possible through the cataclysmic technology of war—was bound to have a myriad of attendant effects. Because films about the Black Death tend to focus on the social and psychological, as well as religious and artistic, fallout of the plague, the economic consequences are only mentioned briefly here. A severe shortage of peasant labor ensued in the wake of the Black Death. Some lords seem to have accommodated to the new situation, but by and large, the response of the upper classes was a collective denial of economic realities. Throughout Europe—in England, France, Italy, and the Spanish kingdoms of Castile and Aragon—legislation was enacted by royal councils and representative assemblies that tried to turn the clock back on the Black Death. Peasant freedom of movement was to be strictly curtailed, vagabonds put to work, and wages fixed to the low level they had been before the plague. Thus, it should not be assumed that postplague serfs automatically benefitted from the laws of supply and demand in a free-market economy. Instead, the medieval manorial and guild system was a highly regulated one. Evidence of enforcement of these laws, which survives in the ample legal records of England, suggests that there was widespread evasion but also strenuous efforts to make them stick. This seems to have led to rising tensions in society, which flared up in peasant revolts, such as occurred in France in 1358 and in England in 1381. By the end of the Middle Ages, direct exploitation of peasant labor had given way in most parts of Europe to a land of rent-paying free tenants.

In social terms, many chroniclers of the Black Death complained that during and after the plague, the normative customs of society broke down. Priests and doctors refused to visit the sick, laws and dress codes were disregarded, and, what shocked contemporaries the most, even family ties were set aside. The great Florentine author, Giovanni Boccaccio, noted that "this scourge had implanted so great a terror in the hearts of men and women that brothers abandoned brothers, uncles their nephews, sisters their brothers, and in many cases wives deserted their husbands. But even worse, and almost incredible, was the fact that fathers and mothers refused to nurse and assist their own children, as though they did not belong to them." A refrain along similar lines occurs in chronicle after chronicle. Gabriele de Mussis seems to capture the authentic anguish of family members on their deathbeds when he has them cry out: "Mother, where have you gone? Why are you now so cruel to me when only yesterday you were so kind?" or "My children, whom I brought up with toil and sweat, why have you run away?" The fear of dying, alone and forgotten, which comes through very strongly in these accounts, seems a reliable bellwether of the plague's severe social impact on medieval Europe.

Yet it is hard to know how accurate other lamentations of social failings are, since many of these are a standard feature of the earlier plague accounts by Thucydides and Procopius, and one can find medieval authors making the same complaints even before the Black Death. An innovative argument was advanced by the American sociologist, James Westfall Thompson, in 1921, which was that the social response of the shell-shocked survivors of World War I could provide an analogue for what happened in 1348. The comparison falters, though, when one realizes that the nihilism of the "Lost Generation" was altogether different from the certainties of the "Age of Faith." A modern secular outlook that could contemplate the notion that "God is dead" never would have occurred to the medieval mind. None of the authors writing in the midst of the Black Death doubted for a moment that their terrible ordeal served a higher purpose, even if they could not fathom what that was.

Psychological reactions to the Black Death were famously recorded by Boccaccio, who just prior to the plague had written what is considered to be the first psychological novel, the *Elegia di Madonna Fiammetta* (*Elegy for Lady Fiammetta*). In the introduction to his most famous work, *The Decameron*, he notes three psychic responses to the disease: isolation, denial, and moderation. Boccaccio, who was writing in 1350 when the plague's impact would have been still fresh in his mind, was astute enough to recognize some basic instinctual strategies for coping with fatal infection that hold true for any generation. We see these same responses, for example, in modern Western society's sexual behavior in the immediate aftermath of the AIDS crisis during the mid-1980s.

But a couple of psychological reactions were unique to the Middle Ages. One of these was the Flagellant Movement that swept Austria, Germany, and Flanders in 1348 and 1349. Named after the *flagella*, or whips, they used to scourge their bare bodies, the Flagellants and their spectators hoped that their extreme penance would appease an angry God who was using the plague as a great scourge on a sinful mankind. By the autumn of 1349, the movement had grown to alarming proportions and was condemned by the pope, but even the Flagellants' detractors testify to the emotional power that their performances held. A hostile German chronicler, Henry of Herford, nonetheless claims that when the Flagellants came to town, "One would need a heart of stone to be able to watch this without tears." The emotional fervor they whipped up seems to have mirrored their physical excesses. Herford observes that they would get so carried away that: "the scourged skin swelled up black and blue and blood flowed down to their lower members and even spattered the walls nearby. I have seen, when they whipped themselves, how the iron points [of their whips] became so embedded in the flesh that sometimes one pull, sometimes two, was not enough to extract them."

Another instrument of psychic release for medieval sufferers of the Black Death was a favorite scapegoat: the Jews. Between September

1348 and February 1351, as many as 100 towns and cities in Germany and Switzerland massacred their Jewish populations. The total death toll may have been as high as 16,000. In one city alone, Strasbourg, 2,000 Jews were burnt alive all at once in the town square on Valentine's Day, February 14, 1349. Invariably, Jews were tortured into falsely confessing that they had poisoned drinking wells used by Christians—one of these the now famous source of bottled water, Évian-lès-Bains. Medieval pogroms against the Jews had their own religious and economic logic. Jews were denounced as Christian-hating "Christ killers" and grasping moneylenders; but doctors also lent a hand to this effort, because they gave credence to "artificial" causes of the plague, such as poisoning of the air or water, which conferred a comforting sense of human control over the disease. Most disturbing about the pogroms is the way in which they anticipate the twentieth-century Holocaust. Evidence exists that even in the Middle Ages, there was both the desire and the means to eliminate every Jew alive. Mass exterminations were devised, such as the specially constructed wooden houses that were used to cremate hundreds of victims at Constance and Basel. The German chroniclers, Heinrich Dapifer von Diessenhoven and Herman Gigas, both gave vent to a popular will to annihilate the Jews, and transcripts of the first confessions to well poisoning extracted from Jews at Chillon and Châtel in Switzerland in September and October 1348 were circulated to other Swiss and German towns as trumped-up proof of an international Jewish conspiracy. During their confession and execution, several Jews at Chillon were forced to implicate their entire race by saying "that all Jews from the age of seven on could not acquit themselves of this charge [of poisoning], since they all alike knew and were guilty of the said matter." Yet the confessions that were dragged out of them by torture are contradictory and, quite simply, unbelievable.

The medieval psychological response to the Black Death was, of course, bound up with religious attitudes. In the case of the Jewish pogroms, medieval Christianity had its ugly side. Indeed, one scholar of medieval anti-Semitism, Gavin Langmuir, argues that even though "blood libels" against the Jews, such as well poisoning, contained irrational accusations of crimes no one had seen any Jew commit, they were, nonetheless, a product of Christians' quite rational doubts about their religion. Jews, for example, denied fundamental Christian tenets such as the Trinity, which had to be taken on faith. Perhaps Christian doubts were exacerbated by the climate of uncertainty in the wake of the Black Death. On the whole, however, medieval religious belief proved remarkably resilient in the face of the plague and was a key factor in Europeans' psychological and cultural recovery from the disease.

A popular argument to make is that the Black Death ushered in a more secular outlook that anticipated the Renaissance and a widespread criticism and disillusionment with the Church that foreshadowed the Reformation. In general, so the argument goes, medieval culture was on the wane, or in decline, during the century and a half after the Black Death, and a vibrant, modern society was poised to take its place. These days, the "waning of the Middle Ages" thesis, named after the popular book by the Dutch historian, Johan Huizinga, carries very little weight. Huizinga, who first published his book in 1919, largely interpreted the later Middle Ages from the vantage point of the deep disillusionment that set into European society in the immediate aftermath of World War I. Like Thompson's analysis, his work is more valuable as a reflection of the pessimistic outlook of the "Lost Generation," rather than as an historical reconstruction of the resilient medieval attitudes that weathered the Black Death.

It is true that there was plenty of contemporary complaint about "leapfrogging" priests who abandoned their parishes for more lucrative posts opened up by the plague mortality, but those who complained the loudest were themselves clerical reformers. Some parishes were simply too destitute of churchgoers after the plague to support a full-time rector, while the high death rate among the priesthood during the Black Death is in itself a testimony to their dedication and courage during the crisis. So many priests could not have died if they were not ministering to their flocks. As for their parishioners, there is also ample complaint, again largely coming from clerical authors, that religious fervor had fallen off in the aftermath of the disease. Some bishops bemoaned lack of attendance at church and lack of respect for holy ceremonies and precincts when parishioners did attend. But the evidence of wills, when ordinary people, more so than at any other time of their lives, reveal their religious attitudes, show that medieval faith remained strong and conventionally pious. Testaments survive in good number from the late Middle Ages in the archives of several cities throughout England and Italy. Overwhelmingly, those approaching their end still wanted to be buried in or around the parish church and have priests say masses for their souls and for the souls of their kin. Commemoration and perpetual remembrance of the dead also comforted the living by reassuring them of a degree of immortality even after death.

It is indeed possible that late medieval Europe saw a religious revival, not a decline. Mysticism, defined as a supernatural experience of the Godhead in this life, underwent a renaissance during the late fourteenth and fifteenth centuries. Movements such as the *Devotio Moderna* in Germany and the Brethren of the Common Life in Flanders were complemented by powerful individual figures, many of them women, such as St. Catherine of Siena, St. Birgitta of Sweden, and Julian of Norwich. Perhaps mystics helped their society cope with plague by holding out the hope that the Author of this calamity was not so inscrutable and wrathful after all. The English anchoress (meaning someone who lives in isolation in a private cell), Julian of Norwich, lived through no less than eight outbreaks of plague between the 1340s and the second or third decade of the fifteenth century. In her *Revelations of Divine Love*, she develops an unique vision of a maternal, nurturing God that undoubtedly was part of the solace she gave visitors who came to her cell for spiritual advice. A woman who almost willed herself into a near-death illness as part of her mystical journey, Julian seems to have plague in mind when she writes: "people suffer such terrible evils that it does not seem as though any good will ever come of them." Yet no matter how much we suffer, Julian reminds us, there is always the love of God, who holds out the promise of redemption whereby "terrible evils" will be justified. In place of the angry, vengeful God whom most chroniclers depicted as sending down the pestilence as retribution for human wickedness, Julian substitutes a merciful, forgiving deity who is "never angry and never will be angry, for He is God's goodness, life, truth, love, peace." Julian's optimistic faith that "all shall be well" even in a world poised at the brink of oblivion may be the best clue we have as to how Western civilization survived the painful ordeal of the Black Death.

Perhaps the most eloquent expression of late medieval Europe's religious and cultural renewal is to be found in its art. As this relates to the Black Death, an obvious starting point is the varied representation of the corpse or cadaver, an art form sometimes collectively known as the *memento mori*, or remembrance of death, theme. Medieval death imagery can be horribly gruesome, displaying such details of decay as the worms that crawl through the flesh rotting off the bones. (Worms were also believed to herald plague, either falling in a "pestilential rain" from the sky or appearing spontaneously out of diseased corpses.) Many have accused the late Middle Ages of having a morbid obsession or fascination with death. *Memento mori* art, for example, is the centerpiece of Huizinga's "waning" thesis, in which he argues that "the abused imagery of skeletons and worms" drained all art of humanity and "living emotion" as the death figures began to conform to a rigid stereotype. His argument was taken one step further in 1951 by the art historian, Millard Meiss. He contends that even Italian art, which unlike that of northern Europe generally eschewed *memento mori* images, moved away from humanistic values in the aftermath of the Black Death, just when it was supposedly entering the dynamic, early phase of the Renaissance. But if one looks closely at cadaver images on their own terms, without our modern aversion to death, one can find a hopeful, even uplifting message amidst all the skeletons and worms.

Artistic depictions of death began well before 1348. Around 1280, a group of English manuscript illuminators portrayed the Fourth Rider of the Apocalypse as a shrouded skeleton or cadaver in order to make his entry within the Book of Revelation more dramatic. The image was to go on to have a most vivid and even terrifying representation, which seems a reflection of the apocalyptic scenarios fashionable among chroniclers of the Black Death, for whom the incredible mortality was convincing proof that the end was nigh. In passages reminiscent of the Revelation, Louis Sanctus, Gabriele de Mussis, Heinrich of Herford, and an anonymous Austrian chronicler all attribute the origins of the plague to exotic regions in the East where it supposedly had rained frogs, toads, snakes, lizards, scorpions, worms, as well as large hailstones, blood, and burning fire. Plenty of other apocalyptic signs were reported, such as earthquakes, comets or "bright stars," a black dog "carrying a naked sword in its paw," and a Siamese twin. Some claimed that the Antichrist was abroad at this time, or that his reign was heralded by the Flagellants, the "race without a head" (since they had no leader) predicted by the popular Cedar of Lebanon prophecy. Others saw signs of a new age in the fact that post-plague children had fewer teeth than before.

Yet at the same time that the Fourth Rider of the Apocalypse was holding sway in medieval art, a very different depiction of the corpse was emerging by the end of the thirteenth century. Here, the awesome power of death is mitigated to some degree by allowing the living to engage in a dialogue with the dead. Appropriately titled, the Three Living and the Three Dead, the legend describes how three walking corpses, who were kings in former days, warn their living counterparts to prepare for the fate they see before them. A version of the legend in which the dead lie mute in their tombs is famously rendered in the *Triumph of Death* fresco in the Camposanto of Pisa, attributed to Francesco Traini. Dated to around the time of the Black Death (the fresco may in fact predate the plague), Traini's masterpiece succeeds in making the legend, painted on the left side of the mural, proceed as a natural corollary to an apocalyptic figure of Death on the right.

Without a doubt, the image most readily associated with the Black Death is the Dance of Death. It may have been inspired by a nervous disorder symptomatic of bubonic plague called chorea, or St. Vitus' Dance, in which the sufferer's uncontrollable physical movements appear to be dancing. Chroniclers in France and Germany also report that people danced to try to ward off or cure themselves of the disease. The Dance was later acted out for didactic purposes, for its message that everyone, from pope and emperor on down to the hermit and the poor, must "dance" with Death would have hit home in time of plague. A mural on the theme was first painted in the 1420s along one side of the cloister of the cemetery of Les Innocents in Paris (which no longer survives). In subsequent centuries, the Dance of Death continued to be a popular artistic subject. Not long after the Middle Ages, Shakespeare worked it into his play, *Measure for Measure*, while in the nineteenth century, Camille Saint-Saëns expressed it musically in his tone poem, *La Danse Macabre*. Most recently, Ingmar Bergman imagined it cinematically in the finale to his film, *The Seventh Seal* (1957).

The Dance of Death may have Death interacting with social types, but what could have possessed individual patrons to masquerade as dead—in the form of a gruesome cadaver or corpse—on their tombs? One of the earliest such monuments is that of François de la Sarra of Switzerland, who memorialized himself around 1390 as a dead man being devoured by frogs and worms. In 1424–1425, Archbishop Henry Chichele in England commissioned the first "double-decker" tomb that contrasts a resplendent effigy of himself on the upper level of the monument with a horribly emaciated, naked representation below. These *transi* images (from the Latin word *transire*, meaning to "pass away") were evidently quite fashionable among northern Europe's upper classes, as hundreds of them survive from the late fourteenth to the seventeenth centuries. They seem to be excellent illustrations of the late medieval obsession with death, but what are the tombs actually saying? Worms appear to wriggle into the arms and legs of François de la Sarra, for example, as a symbol of death and decay. But could not the worms also be wriggling *out* of the body, as it is being remade at the Resurrection? This idea is strengthened when one remembers that worms are associated with the Resurrection in the Book of Job: "And though after my skin worms destroy this body, yet in my flesh shall I see God" (Job 19:27). Chichele's tomb presents even more of a conundrum, since he was not to die until 1443, and thus for nearly 20 years he could contemplate a portrait of his own dead self. Yet instead of drawing his eyes downward toward his corpse, the tomb may have directed his gaze upward to his upper effigy—not as an image of himself in life, but in the afterlife, as is indicated by the angels who hold the pillow cradling his head. His cadaver image, which is so realistic that some observers even today wonder aloud whether it is not the real thing, then becomes a transitional figure in which the terror of death gives way to the triumph over death at the Resurrection.

That this is indeed how Chichele would have "read" his tomb is demonstrated by a contemporary English poem entitled, *A Disputacioun Betwyx the Body and Wormes*. The opening lines of the poem tell of a pilgrim wandering into a church to escape the plague and falling asleep beside the tomb of a great lady. In a marginal illustration of the manuscript, the tomb is pictured in Chichele's "double-decker" style, with a cadaver riddled with worms and other assorted creatures lying in its shroud underneath the effigy. The pilgrim-poet proceeds to dream of a surreal dialogue taking place between the lady's corpse and the worms that devour it. Although the worms are deaf to the body's pleas for a halt to the process of decay, by the end of the poem, the body and worms literally kiss and make up because the lady has realized that the deplorable corruption of her body doesn't matter in the end: For at "the day of dome," her body "sal agayn upryse" in all its original "glorified" beauty. Medieval men like Chichele could calmly contemplate their future deaths and face it squarely—even imagine themselves as dead—because they firmly believed that death was not the end, but merely a beginning. When the last trumpet sounds at the end of the world, even bodies ruptured by plague boils will be reborn, whole and sound, once more.

The Movies

The Seventh Seal (1957), directed by Ingmar Bergman, is not only considered the best film about the Black Death, it is also one of the most admired films about the Middle Ages and, quite possibly, the greatest movie of all time. Certainly, it is the film most written about: Well over seventy reviews, articles, essays, and books have made it their subject. To pardon a pun, it is perhaps a film that has been analyzed to death. But *The Seventh Seal* is not appreciated in academic circles only; it has succeeded in penetrating our popular culture as well. One Bergman filmographer, Hubert Cohen, has quipped that Bengst Ekerot's personification of Death in the film is so convincing that "at times we even may half-imagine that a black-cloaked figure wearing a stocking-tight, black cowl around his chalk-white face is going to attend our own expiring, and that he will be speaking Swedish—with English subtitles across his waist." (One wonders how the actor himself, who died in 1971, conceived his own reckoning—or did he pay a special penalty for imitating Death?) This conceit has actually been realized in the self-referential Arnold Schwarzenegger vehicle, *Last Action Hero* (1993). The main character, Jack Slater, in addition to confronting Arnold playing himself as his real-life actor persona, also comes face to face with Ekerot's death figure, who, courtesy of a magical movie ticket, glides out of the screen on which *The Seventh Seal* is playing to fully emerge from cinematic black and white to living color. In this case, however, the "real Death" supposedly speaks with a British accent and wields a scythe (a prop that only appears at the end of the film during the Dance of Death).

At the same time, even a film so well regarded as this one, that has insinuated itself into our popular consciousness about death and plague, is

During the plague, the knight, Antonius Block (Max von Sydow), plays a game of chess with Death (Bengst Ekerot) in *The Seventh Seal*. The scene was inspired by a medieval wall painting that Ingmar Bergman had seen on one of his father's preaching missions in Sweden.

by no means a perfect historical reconstruction of the Black Death. Aside from the appropriateness of its cinematic techniques, which is also the subject of some debate, the film only partially succeeds in conveying the period atmosphere and thought world of the fourteenth century. Bergman would probably counter that it was never his intention to make an historical or period film. As he wrote in a program note that accompanied the movie's premiere: "It is a modern poem, presented with medieval material that has been very freely handled." The script in particular—which is sometimes labored, an effect that apparently is even more noticeable in the original Swedish—embodies a mid-twentieth century existentialist angst that is entirely out of place in the Middle Ages. Still, to be fair to Bergman, one must allow him his artistic license, and the script's modernisms may be justified as giving the movie's medieval theme a compelling and urgent contemporary relevance that has not diminished with time. Yet the film succeeds to a large degree because it is set in the Middle Ages, a time that can seem both very remote and very immediate to us living in the modern world. While the dialogue has afforded critics a rich diet for analysis, the images on the screen are equally famous for bringing to life the medieval wall paintings that inspired Bergman to make his film, and which play their own role in the action. Ultimately, *The Seventh Seal* should be judged as an historical film by how well it balances the medieval and the modern — as perhaps a cinematic lesson in the connections to be made between the cultural attitudes and preoccupations of the two eras.

The plot of the film has been described as being simple and straight-forward, like a medieval morality play. A knight, Antonius Block (played by Max von Sydow), and his squire, Jöns (played by Gunnar Björnstrand), return home to Sweden after ten years on crusade. On the desolate seashore the knight encounters Death, but he persuades him to stay his hand as long as they play a game of chess, with the prize being the knight's life. The knight uses his reprieve to try to penetrate the ultimate secret of what lies beyond death and to perform "one meaningful deed" that can redeem his futile life. On his journey home, he and his squire encounter various signs of a country wracked by the Black Death, includ-ing rotting corpses, deserted homesteads, the Flagellants, a witch being burned as a scapegoat for the plague, and the gruesome, horrifying spec-tacle of a man dying from the disease. When the knight and his squire finally come home to his castle, from which all have fled during the plague except for his wife, he faces his final reckoning with Death in an apoca-lyptic denouement, where all succumb to the disease, including the knight, his wife and squire, and his guests — a blacksmith and his wife and a peas-ant girl whom the squire had rescued along the way. Only a holy trinity of an acting troupe family — Jof, Mia, and their son, Mikael (Joseph, Mary, and Michael) — survive the Apocalypse, minus their colleague, Skat, who in the meantime has also fallen victim to Death. The film ends with a reen-actment of a medieval Dance of Death along the horizon of a "dark, stormy sky," as the survivors walk away into the brightening dawn of a new day.

Before the action begins, a brief title card sets the stage of this historical time period: "It is the middle of the 14th century. Antonius Block and his squire, after long years as crusaders in the Holy Land, have at last returned to their native Sweden, a land ravaged by the Black Plague." More precisely, this would date the action to 1350, the year that the Black Death arrived in Sweden, probably from the neighboring country of Norway, where the dis-ease had taken hold in 1348 and again in 1349 as a result of trade contacts with England. Magnus Ericsson, king of Sweden and Norway, sent out a circular letter in the spring of 1350 in which he warned that:

> Every Christian man and woman must sorely fear, for God, because of the
> sins of men, has sent a great plague upon the whole world, so that the

greater part of the people who live in the lands [England] lying to the west of our land, have died a swift death. And now this flying sickness is all over Norway and Holland and will soon be here, and it takes such a hold that before they are sick, people fall down and die without the sacraments, and wherever it comes, there are not so many people left that they can bury the dead.

Meanwhile, the Vadstena Diary confirms that a "great mortality" struck Sweden in 1350. It is not known exactly how many people in Sweden died from the disease. A later chronicle records, rather implausibly, that five-sixths of the population succumbed, but a record of payment of Peter's pence after 1350 suggests a plague mortality of around 40 percent. In addition, land prices, as recorded in Östergötland in 1353, were halved "because the great mortality . . . had left many holdings desolate and tenants hardly could be found."

As far as crusading goes, the most likely arena for the knight's activities before the opening of the film was Russia, not Jerusalem or the Holy Land. Sweden had been fighting a long-running battle with the Russian republic of Novgorod on its eastern border, as the thirteenth-century career of Alexander Nevsky, discussed in Chapter 3, testifies. Hostilities between the two sides broke out again in the second decade of the fourteenth century, and in 1348 King Magnus organized a crusade against Novgorod that culminated in the battle, and Swedish defeat, at Toads' Field on July 23.

Historical quibbles aside, *The Seventh Seal* serves up some of the most convincing images that imagine the Middle Ages. From its opening frames, we are fully taken in by the illusion that we are back in the fourteenth century. The main reason for this is that, visually at least, Bergman completely surrenders his film to a late medieval artistic milieu. Nearly all of the most memorable scenes have their parallels in original art and literature. The first appearance of Death in the film, described as "one of the most dramatic entrances in cinema," is straight out of the fifteenth-century morality play, *Everyman*, which originated in England or Flanders and, like the mystery play cycles, was performed as street theater by the trade guilds of major towns. Everyman, like Block in the film, obtains a brief reprieve from Death so that the play can go on. Bergman recalls his opening sequence as the most daring and accomplished in the whole movie:

It was a delicate and dangerous artistic move, which could have failed. Suddenly, an actor appears in whiteface, dressed all in black, and announces that he is Death. Everyone accepted the dramatic feat that he was Death, instead of saying, "Come on now, don't try to put something over on us! You

can't fool us! We can see that you are just a talented actor who is painted
white and clad in black! You're not Death at all!" But nobody protested.
That made me feel triumphant and joyous.

In reality, the illusion is not so hard to understand. It plugs into a
deepseated psychological need in humans, especially developed in the
Middle Ages, to converse with Death and thus humanize him in order to
take some of the terror out of his coming. We can trace this theme in a variety of medieval garbs aside from *Everyman*, including the Three Living and
the Three Dead, the Dance of Death, and *transi* tomb sculpture.

At first, Bergman effectively conveys the terror of Death through the
use of extreme close-up and shot/reverse shot techniques. Death opens his
cloak to receive both the knight and us, the audience, as he approaches the
camera until his blackness fills our entire field of vision. Then, our next
angle of vision on Death is from behind, as if he had walked right through
us. Scholars of the film, such as Hubert Cohen and Egil Törnqvist, note that
by this means, Bergman forces the audience to identify with Block's visceral
fear of death. But then the knight's wits recover and the dialogue resumes,
with Death betraying some personality, and even a sense of humor:

> Block: Wait a moment.
> Death: That's what they all say. I grant no reprieves.
> Block: You play chess, don't you?
> Death: How did you know that?
> Block: I have seen it in paintings and heard it sung in ballads.
> Death: Yes, in fact I'm quite a good chess player.
> Block: But you can't be better than I am.
> Death: Why do you want to play chess with me?
> Block: I have my reasons.
> Death: That is your privilege.
> Block: The condition is that I may live as long as I hold out
>   against you. If I win, you will release me. Is it agreed? [The
>   knight holds out his two fists to Death, who smiles at him sud-
>   denly. Death points to one of the knight's hands; it contains a
>   black pawn.] You drew black!
> Death: Very appropriate. Don't you think so?

The exchange is almost a direct paraphrase of *Everyman*, and once again it
taps into an age-old compulsion to personify Death. Bergman, no less than
his medieval ancestors, felt an urgent need to make Death more approach-
able in order to reconcile himself to his own, personal death. As he writes
in his autobiographical discussion of the film:

As far back as I can remember, I carried a grim fear of death, which during puberty and my early twenties accelerated into something unbearable. The fact that I, through dying, would no longer exist, that I would walk through the dark portal, that there was something that I could not control, arrange, or foresee, was for me a source of constant horror. That I plucked up my courage and depicted Death as a white clown, a figure who conversed, played chess, and had no secrets, was the first step in my struggle against my monumental fear of death.

One of his formative experiences as an adolescent came when he happened to be trapped inside a mortuary. At first terrified by being alone with a half-dozen corpses, the ten-year-old Bergman gradually became sexually aroused by the naked, still firm body of a dead young girl.

There are plenty of other images in the film that seem lifted straight out of the Middle Ages and thereby lend an impressive historical authenticity. Block's chess game with Death—which forms the unifying conceit of the film, Jof's vision of the Virgin Mary teaching the Christ child how to walk, Death sawing down the tree that shelters Skat, and Jof's final vision of his former companions dancing with Death, all were inspired by medieval wall paintings that Bergman had seen in his youth when he had accompanied his father, a Lutheran pastor and court chaplain to the king of Sweden, on his preaching tours to the country churches around Stockholm. As he writes in his program note to *The Seventh Seal*:

While Father preached away in the pulpit and the congregation prayed, sang or listened, I devoted my interest to the church's mysterious world of low arches, thick walls, the smell of eternity, the colored sunlight quivering above the strangest vegetation of medieval paintings and carved figures on ceiling and walls. There was everything that one's imagination could desire: angels, saints, dragons, prophets, devils, humans. There were very frightening animals: serpents in paradise, Balaam's ass, Jonah's whale, the eagle of the Revelation. All this was surrounded by a heavenly, earthly and subterranean landscape of a strange yet familiar beauty. In a wood sat Death, playing chess with the Crusader. Clutching the branch of a tree was a naked man with staring eyes, while down below stood Death, sawing away to his heart's content. Across gentle hills Death led the final dance towards the dark lands. But in the other arch the holy Virgin was walking in a rose-garden, supporting the Child's faltering steps, and her hands were those of a peasant woman. Her face was grave and birds' wings fluttered round her head. The medieval painters had portrayed all this with great tenderness, skill and joy. It moved me in a spontaneous and enticing way, and that world became as real to me as the everyday world with Father, Mother and brothers and sisters.

The Dance of Death motif is closely associated with the Black Death, since its message that all social classes must dance with Death would seem especially apropos during a time of plague, and since some people seemed to have tried to ward off or mask the disease by dancing. But the visual image does not actually belong to the time-setting of the film. The earliest painting of the Dance is the fresco that once adorned the southern cloister of the cemetery of Les Innocents in Paris, completed by 1424–1425. This is also true of the chess-playing Death, which occurs in conjunction with the Dance. A stained-glass window of Death checkmating a bishop on a chessboard survives as part of a Dance series at St. Andrew's Church in Norwich from the late fifteenth century and also occurs in John Lydgate's English poem, the *Dance of Death*, from the 1430s. Bergman's inspiration is medieval, but not quite so contemporary with the mid-fourteenth century plague as he would have us believe.

Even without the benefit of Bergman's program notes, it is made clear about a third of the way into the film that the moving images take their cue from medieval wall painting. At one point, Jöns enters a church and strikes up a conversation with the painter, Albertus Pictor (1445–1509), who is finishing a fresco on the subject of the Black Death. All of the painted images—the Flagellants, the screaming plague victim trying to rip out his boils, the Dance of Death—will subsequently be reenacted on the screen. Pictor explains, to an almost nauseating degree, each detail of his creation to Jöns and at the same time cues us in to the historical as well as artistic milieu of the film. It is even possible that the painter serves as a mouthpiece for Bergman's private concerns as a filmmaker, especially as to how movies such as *The Seventh Seal* will be received by his audience:

> Jöns: Why do you paint such nonsense?
> Pictor: I thought it would serve to remind people that they must die.
> Jöns: Well, it's not going to make them feel any happier.
> Pictor: Why should one always make people happy? It might not be a bad idea to scare them a little once in a while.
> Jöns: Then they'll close their eyes and refuse to look at your painting.
> Pictor: Oh, they'll look. A skull is almost more interesting than a naked woman.
> Jöns: If you do scare them . . .
> Pictor: They'll think.
> Jöns: And if they think . . .
> Pictor: They'll become still more scared.
> Jöns: And then they'll run right into the arms of the priests.

Pictor: That's not my business.

Jöns: You're only painting your Dance of Death.

Pictor: I'm only painting things as they are. Everyone else can do
as he likes.

Jöns: Just think how some people will curse you.

Pictor: Maybe. But then I'll paint something amusing for them to
look at. I have to make a living — at least until the plague takes
me.

Jöns quells his fear by drinking some of Pictor's brandy and painting
a funny picture of himself, which could be considered an allegory of how
Bergman himself uses humor in the film to counterbalance his terrifying
images. As the director writes in his memoirs: "In a joyful scene with the
painter of churches, Albertus Pictor, I present without any embarrassment
my own artistic conviction. Albertus insists that he is in show business. To
survive in this business, it's important to avoid making people too mad." A
good example of Bergman's tension-releasing humor is Jöns' encounter
with a "sleeping man" lying with his dog by the roadside. When the squire
prods him for directions and eventually lifts his head, it is to gaze into a
corpse face "with empty eye sockets and white teeth" (stage direction from
screenplay). Jöns then tells his master that the man was mute, but "quite
eloquent . . . the trouble is that what he had to say was most depressing."
Bergman also had his private joke when he sent this bit player, a production assistant named Ove Svensson, to the studio's canteen just to watch
people's reactions to the gruesome makeup.

Another joke at the expense of his own profession is when Bergman
stages the death of the actor, Skat. After play acting at death with a "stage
dagger" that has a retractable blade, Skat dies for real when Death saws
down his tree, up which he has taken refuge from the creatures of the
night. The scene may have been inspired by a wall painting, but the dialogue is reminiscent of the play, *Everyman*:

Death: I'm sawing down your tree because your time is
up.

Skat: It won't do. I haven't got time.

Death: So you haven't got time.

Skat: No, I have my performance.

Death: Then it's been canceled because of death.

Skat: My contract.

Death: Your contract is terminated.

Skat: My children, my family.

Death: Shame on you, Skat!

Skat: Yes, I'm ashamed. Isn't there any way to get off? Aren't
there any special rules for actors?
Death: No, not in this case.

Skat's ham acting may fool others, but not Death, who inexorably punc-
tures the rarefied atmosphere in which movie stars and their flunkies live.

The fact that Bergman shot his film in black and white (as he did in his
thirty other productions until 1963), gives *The Seventh Seal* a grainy texture
and seems well suited to a medieval subject, particularly one about the
Black Death. Perhaps this is because black and white conveys a sense of
"otherness" and the more earthy, elemental tones associated with the
Middle Ages. Students of the film have also noted that black and white
brings out the stark contrasts between light and dark, and between life and
death, that lie at the heart of the movie's identity. The fidelity of the film's
period atmosphere is even more remarkable when one considers that it was
shot in only 35 days on a shoestring budget—$150,000 (not very much
even in 1956). Aside from the costumes, the sets are highly evocative of a
time and place appropriate to the fourteenth century: the church with its
painted walls and affective carving of a Christ suffering on the cross; the
deserted long houses and the village Embarrassment Inn, where domestic
animals rub elbows with people; the knight's drafty, inhospitable "black
boulder" of a castle. Much credit is due to the set designer, P.A. Lundgren,
who accompanied Bergman to medieval sites, such as Härkeberga
Church—scene of the famous murals by Albertus Pictor from the 1480s—
in order to realize the director's vision. Even nature seemed to cooperate
during the filming. There is the famous story, for example, of how
Bergman improvised the film's indelible final image—the Dance of
Death—to coincide with a dark storm cloud that suddenly appeared over
the horizon on location at Hovs Haller, which necessitated the impress-
ment of some passing tourists, since all the actors had gone home!
Bergman also had a stroke of good fortune when filming the plague death
agony of Raval in the forest glen, a scene that is almost unbearable to
watch in all its naked, brutal realism. (Bergman himself says that the scene
"used to fill me with fear and, at the same time, fascination.") Yet a wonderful sense of peace and benediction steals over the scene at the moment
of Raval's demise, as a shaft of sunlight suddenly breaks through and
bathes the body in its "pale" light. Bergman captured the effect at the end
of the take when he "let the camera keep rolling, for some reason."

Above all, *The Seventh Seal* empathizes magnificently with the apocalyptic fantasies and anticipations that hung over Europe during the Black
Death. The film is framed by a reading from the Book of Revelation at
both the beginning and end of the knight's tale. At the start of the film, a

voiceover, presumably Death's, reads from chapter 8, verse 1, as we look out over a desolate, rugged sea coast: "And when the Lamb had opened the seventh seal, there was silence in heaven about the space of half an hour." The visuals and the dialogue seem to be in perfect harmony at this point, and together they create, in the words of Peter Cowie, "a mythic country of death". (In reality the location was Hovs Haller, on the southwest coast of Sweden.) Just prior to the reading, a sea eagle is shown hovering in a stormy sky as the soundtrack of a *Dies irae* plays to a *Carmina Burana*-like crescendo. This suggests, without need for any words, Revelation 8:13: "Then I looked, and I heard an eagle calling with a loud cry as it flew in mid-heaven: 'Woe, woe, woe to the inhabitants of the earth when the trumpets sound which the three last angels must now blow!'" The stage is now set for Death's dramatic entrance. Critics of the film have usually interpreted the entire rest of the movie as taking place within that half hour of silence, although in real time, the action seems to extend from morning to evening of one day (roughly twelve hours).

The closing sequence, in which Block's wife, Karin, reads from the Book of Revelation at the "last supper" of the knight and his companions in the great hall of his empty, echoing castle, hits another artistic high point that can only be described as "film poetry." A tense, hushed air of anticipation hangs over the scene, as the wife picks up the reading from where Death left off at the beginning of the film and intones from chapter 8, verses 7–11:

> The first angel sounded, and there followed hail and fire mingled with blood, and they were cast upon the earth; and the third part of the trees was burnt up and all the green grass was burnt up. And the second angel sounded, and as it were a great mountain burning with fire was cast into the sea; and a third part of the sea became blood. . . . And the third angel sounded, and there fell a great star from heaven, burning as it were a torch, and it fell upon the third part of the rivers and upon the fountains of waters; and the name of the star is called Wormwood. . . .

At this point, Death himself enters the hall, and the guests assemble to dance away with him "toward the dark lands."

In a world where half the population was dying from the plague, it would have been only natural to assume that the Apocalypse was at hand. Agnolo di Tura of Siena, who buried his five children with his own hands in 1348, wrote that "so many have died that everyone believes it is the end of the world." Many chroniclers describe the advent of the Black Death in words borrowed from the Book of Revelation. Gabriele de Mussis, for example, characterizes the origin of the plague as "the angel hurling vials of poison into the sea," which evokes Revelation 16, where seven angels pour out seven bowls of God's wrath upon the earth. Revelation 8:7–11, as quoted at the end of the film, is powerfully echoed in Louis Sanctus' account of how the plague arrived in India in 1347:

> On the first day it rained frogs, serpents, lizards, scorpions, and many venomous beasts of that sort. On the second day thunder was heard, and lightning flashes mixed with hailstones of marvelous size fell upon the land, which killed almost all men, from the greatest to the least. On the third day there fell fire together with stinking smoke from the heavens, which consumed all the rest of men and beasts, and burned up all the cities and castles of those parts.

A rain of apocalyptic signs heralding plague occurs in many medieval accounts of the Black Death of 1348. Similarly, *The Seventh Seal* is replete with "evil omens": Jöns tells his lord of rumors concerning cannibalistic horses and four suns in the sky, and later the villagers at the Embarrassment Inn gossip of monstrosities pouring out of an old woman and another giving birth to a calf's head. The "four suns" is analogous to the "big and very bright star" that Jean de Venette claims to have seen in the western horizon of Paris in August 1348, while a monstrous birth actually was reported by Thomas Burton, abbot of Meux Abbey in Yorkshire, who writes that "shortly before this time [1348], there was a certain human monster in England, divided from the navel upwards and both masculine and feminine, and joined in the lower part." (The "monster" was probably a Siamese twin.) That people could believe in such superstitions may seem farfetched to our modern sensibilities, but Bergman has tapped into a quite authentic medieval outlook here.

Although he "paints" a nearly flawless picture of the late Middle Ages using stunning visual imagery, Bergman seems to mar his film's beauty by having some of his characters—particularly Antonius Block and Jöns— speak what is, in the opinion of many, very awkward, convoluted, and modern-sounding dialogue. Both the knight and his squire serve as mouthpieces throughout the movie for a nihilistic angst and doubt concerning the existence of God, sentiments that owe much to the famous French apostles of existentialism during the 1950s, Jean Paul Sartre and Albert Camus. As defined by Charles Ketcham, who interprets several of Bergman's films in light of this philosophy, existentialism is "a radical method of acknowledging life in terms of one's existence rather than one's essence, one's individuality rather than one's commonality, one's choices rather than one's conformity." In other words, existentialism turns away from beliefs that unify man—religion, existence of a soul, morality, and the like—to instead embrace the heroism of the individual, whose life acquires meaning only in terms of the actions he performs during the brief time allotted to him in the here and now. In a nod to stoicism, existentialism also believes that free will does not really exist for man, but that each person will simply act out what already has been decreed by one's moral and psychological makeup. Therefore, existentialism rejects almost all of what the Middle Ages holds most dear, and consequently, it sounds very odd coming out of the mouths of medieval characters.

Why, then, did Bergman choose an existentialist theme for a film set in premodern times? One good reason for the anachronism is that it adds greatly to the continued relevance of *The Seventh Seal*, despite its historical setting. In the 1950s, the world had fully entered the atomic age. By 1952 and 1953, both the U.S. and the Soviet Union had each tested a hydrogen bomb, which had a destructive capacity up to 1,000 times that of the uranium and plutonium bombs dropped on Hiroshima and Nagasaki in 1945. With the rapid buildup and deployment of nuclear arsenals, the atomic arms race was demonstrated to be dramatically different from previous military conflicts. This one had the apocalyptic potential to destroy all life and to engulf the entire world. Bergman makes the comparison between the destructive capacity of the Black Death and atomic weapons quite explicit in his program note to *The Seventh Seal*:

> In my film the crusader returns from the Crusades as the soldier returns from the war today. In the Middle Ages, men lived in terror of the plague. Today they live in fear of the atomic bomb. *The Seventh Seal* is an allegory with a theme that is quite simple: man, his eternal search for God, with death as his only certainty.

It has been noted by the film's admirers that recent events have by no means diminished the urgency that *The Seventh Seal*'s cataclysmic message holds for our times. Although the threat of atomic annihilation may have abated with the end of the Cold War, this has been replaced by plenty of other candidates for the role of inaugurating agent of the Apocalypse: incurable diseases like AIDS, Ebola, SARS, and Mad Cow's Disease; the ecological catastrophe of global warming; and now, the threat of global terrorism.

Some historians, such as Barbara Tuchman in *The Distant Mirror*, have taken a cue from Bergman and tried to push the comparison between the Black Death and nuclear holocaust as a way for modern readers to creatively reimagine what life must have been like for our fourteenth-century forebears. Lately, Norman Cantor has peddled this approach in his book, *In the Wake of the Plague*:

The pestilence deeply affected individual and family behavior and consciousness. It put severe strains on the social, political, and economic systems. It
threatened the stability and viability of civilization. It was as if a neutron
bomb had been detonated. Nothing like this has happened before or since in
the recorded history of mankind, and the men and women of the fourteenth
century would never be the same.

Cantor uses the neutron bomb analogy presumably because this weapon
destroys people but not buildings, as the plague had done. But a neutron
bomb does not worm its way into the social and familial fabric of society,
which Cantor claims is so distinctive about the Black Death. A bomb represents a threat from without, whereas plague wreaks its havoc from within.
What was so frightening about the Black Death was that even medieval
people believed, as we now know, that they could contract the disease from
absolutely anyone, even their closest friends and family. Death was all
around them: There was no escape. Another important difference between
the Black Death and the Atomic Age is that, while both engender an apocalyptic scenario, the modern Apocalypse is tinged with nihilism, in which
the senseless destruction acquires a far greater sense of terror because, in
an existentialist world, it is perceived to be so meaningless. This is an
unbridgeable gap between medieval and modern sensibilities.

The Seventh Seal flaunts its existentialist anachronisms in three, almost
equidistant places at the beginning, middle, and end of the movie. First
comes the famous confessional scene between Antonius Block and Death:

> Block: Through my indifference to my fellow men, I have iso-
>   lated myself from their company. Now I live in a world of
>   phantoms. I am imprisoned in my dreams and fantasies.
> Death: And yet you don't want to die?
> Block: Yes, I do.
> Death: What are you waiting for?
> Block: I want knowledge.
> Death: You want guarantees?
> Block: Call it whatever you like. Is it so cruelly inconceivable to
>   grasp God with the senses? Why should He hide himself in a
>   mist of half-spoken promises and unseen miracles? [Death
>   doesn't answer.] How can we have faith in those who believe
>   when we can't have faith in ourselves? What is going to hap-
>   pen to those of us who want to believe but aren't able to? And
>   what is to become of those who neither want to nor are capa-
>   ble of believing? [The knight stops and waits for a reply, but
>   no one speaks or answers him. There is complete silence.] Why

can't I kill God within me? Why does He live on in this painful
and humiliating way even though I curse Him and want to tear
Him out of my heart? Why, in spite of everything, is He a baf-
fling reality that I can't shake off? Do you hear me?

Death: Yes, I hear you.

Block: I want knowledge, not faith, not suppositions, but knowledge. I want God to stretch out His hand toward me, reveal
Himself and speak to me.

Death: But He remains silent.

Block: I call out to Him in the dark, but no one seems to be
there.

Death: Perhaps no one is there.

Block: Then life is an outrageous horror. No one can live in the
face of death, knowing that all is nothingness.

Death: Most people never reflect about either death or the futil-
ity of life.

Block: But one day they will have to stand at that last moment of
life and look toward the darkness.

Death: When that day comes . . .

Block: In our fear, we make an image, and that image we call
God.

Meanwhile, Jöns conducts his own dialogue with the church painter,
Albertus Pictor:

Jöns: Me and my master have been abroad and have just come
home. Do you understand, you little pictor?

Pictor: The Crusade.

Jöns: [drunk] Precisely. For ten years we sat in the Holy Land
and let snakes bite us, flies stings us, wild animals eat us, heathens butcher us, the wine poison us, the women give us lice,
the lice devour us, the fevers rot us, all for the Glory of God.
[He and painter make an ironic sign of cross.] Our crusade
was such madness that only a real idealist could have thought
it up. But what you said about the plague was horrible.

Pictor: It's worse than that.

Jöns: Ah me. No matter which way you turn, you have your
rump behind you. That's the truth.

Pictor: The rump behind you, the rump behind you—there's a
profound truth. [Jöns paints a small figure that is supposed to
represent himself.]

Jöns: This is Squire Jöns. He grins at Death, mocks the Lord, laughs at himself and leers at the girls. His world is a Jöns-world, believable only to himself, ridiculous to all including himself, meaningless to Heaven and of no interest to Hell.

The scene marks a radical departure from the *Everyman* allegory. In the medieval play, Death makes no bones about the fact that he is God's messenger, and Everyman uses the time allotted to him to set his spiritual accounts in order in anticipation of the afterlife, not in a fruitless quest for proof of God's existence. In *The Seventh Seal*, on the other hand, Death seems to be reduced from an invincible agent of God's reckoning to a kind of shrink from the minimalist school of psychoanalysis—one who listens but refuses to give any answers. He must use deception—pretending to be a father confessor—in order to extract the knight's stratagems and so win the chess game, and when it is over, he admits to the knight that he has no secrets to divulge—"I have nothing to tell." Some critics regard this scene as a confusing twist from our initial perception at the beginning of the film, where Death seems to be an almighty and terrifying figure; others praise it for increasing the drama of the movie and giving Death a more complex, almost human quality.

The second main entry point for modern existentialism into *The Seventh Seal* comes when the knight and squire witness the burning of the witch, Tyan:

> Jöns: What does she see? Can you tell me?
> Block: [shaking his head] She feels no more pain.
> Jöns: You don't answer my question. Who watches over that child? Is it the angels, or God, or the Devil, or only the emptiness? Emptiness, my lord!
> Block: This cannot be.
> Jöns: Look at her eyes, my lord. Her poor brain has just made a discovery. Emptiness under the moon.
> Block: No.
> Jöns: We stand powerless, our arms hanging at our sides, because we see what she sees, and our terror and hers are the same.

Finally, when Death arrives at the knight's castle, there comes a resolution not only of Block's chess game with Death, but also of the existentialist debate between him and Jöns, with the knight's wife acting as referee:

> Block: From our darkness, we call out to Thee, Lord. Have mercy on us because we are small and frightened and ignorant.

Jöns: [bitterly] In the darkness where You [God] are supposed
to be, where all of us probably are. . . . In the darkness You
will find no one to listen to Your cries or be touched by Your
sufferings. Wash Your tears and mirror Yourself in Your indifference.
Block: God, You who are somewhere, who *must* be somewhere,
have mercy upon us.
Jöns: I could have given you [Block] an herb to purge you of
your worries about eternity. Now it seems to be too late. But in
any case, feel the immense triumph of this last minute when
you can still roll your eyes and move your toes.
Karin: Quiet, quiet.
Jöns: I shall be silent, but under protest.

Much of the dialogue in these three scenes, especially as spoken by
Jöns, already had been developed by Bergman two years previously in his
one-act play, *Wood Painting*, which served as the basis for the film. In great
contrast to Sydow's role, the knight of the play speaks almost no dialogue,
since the actor who played him in the original production at the Malmö
City Theatre was, as described by Bergman, "very handsome, but as soon
as he opened his mouth, it was a catastrophe." Instead, Jöns must carry the
weight of the play's existentialism, much of which is transferred verbatim
to the film, such as when he muses contentedly outside the Embarrassment
Inn: "My little stomach is my world, my head is my eternity, and my hands,
two wonderful suns. My legs are time's damned pendulums, and my dirty
feet are two splendid starting points for my philosophy." In the case of the
film, however, the squire's unalloyed existentialism is now counterbalanced
by the knight's more ambivalent approach to this modern, antimedieval
creed.
   The knight and the squire are often described by film scholars as rep-
resenting two poles of, respectively, intellect and action, but their actual
portrayal doesn't always fall neatly into these categories. The knight, for
example, confesses to Death that he will use his reprieve to perform "one
meaningful deed," and after he discovers that it has been Death in the confessional all along, he recites what could be considered the existentialist
credo: "This is my hand. I can move it, feel the blood pulsing through it.
The sun is still high in the sky and I, Antonius Block, am playing chess
with Death." Later, the knight does carry through with his "one meaningful deed," when he distracts Death long enough during their chess game to
allow Jof, Mia, and baby Mikael to escape from Death's clutches. (This
premise again militates against Death's supposedly invincible power.)
Block also is the only one who helps the executed witch, Tyan, by giving

her a potion to ease her pain. While Jöns, too, performs his share of meaningful deeds—rescuing both the mute peasant girl and Jof from the seminarian, Raval—he stops short of doing anything for Tyan or Raval as he watches them both die horrible deaths.

A more useful comparison may be to say that the knight symbolizes agnosticism, as someone grappling with doubts about his faith, and the squire atheism, as one who refuses to believe altogether. (At one point, Jöns declares that the Holy Trinity is no more than a "ghost story" to be "accepted without too much emotion.") In terms of Boccaccio's plague psychology, one could say that Jöns responds with denial when confronted with the realities of the disease, while Block opts for moderation, since he acknowledges Death's presence and tries to do something about it. The knight and squire could also be said to represent two different stages in mankind's relationship with God. Jöns is the fully modern man whose disillusionment with life's latest horrors has made him skeptical of any place for religion in human history, but Block is a transitional figure, with one foot in the Middle Ages and the other in the modern world.

A critic of the film, Birgitta Steene, has called the knight's quest for God "blasphemous" because "a desire for ultimate knowledge is treason against God," which can only end in the knight's fall, as he is willing to worship even the Devil, along with Tyan, if this will prove God's existence. While this may be true of an Old Testament interpretation of man's search for God, it is not entirely accurate when applied to the New. To doubt one's faith is not out of place even in the Gospels. Jesus himself said on the cross, "My God, why hast thou forsaken me?" [Matthew 27:46], and Thomas, the doubting disciple, declared of the risen Christ, "Unless I see the mark of the nails on his hands, unless I put my finger into the place where the nails were, and my hand into his side, I will not believe it" [John 20:25]. The great medieval Church fathers, St. Anselm and St. Thomas Aquinas, did attempt to address doubts about God's existence, such as are expressed by the knight, by applying rational thought to faith. But, as Charles Ketcham points out, Anselm's ontological proof—or proof by definition—and Aquinas' Aristotelian proof by causation would only have been scorned by the knight as man's clever, circular arguments to justify his psychological need to believe in the supernatural.

The Middle Ages had yet another response to Antonius Block's tormented struggle to penetrate the silence of God: mysticism. In the "negative" tradition of mysticism going back to the anonymous figure of Pseudo-Dionysius in the sixth century A.D., the "dark night of the soul"—wherein God appears to be a silent, mysterious, unknowable being—is fully acknowledged as the first stage of the mystical quest for a direct experience of the divine. A popular fourteenth-century mystical manual called

The Cloud of Unknowing, among the first works to be written in vernacular English prose, gives this advice about how to penetrate the "cloud of unknowing" surrounding God:

> But now you will ask me, "How am I to think of God himself, and what is He?" and I cannot answer you except to say, "I do not know!" For with this question you have brought me into the same darkness, the same cloud of unknowing where I want you to be! For though we, through the grace of God, can know fully about all other matters, and think about them—yes, even the very works of God himself—yet of God himself can no man think.
> . . . Therefore, though it may be good sometimes to think particularly about God's kindness and worth, and though it may be enlightening too, and a part of contemplation, yet in the work now before us it must be put down and covered with a cloud of forgetting. And you are to step over it resolutely and eagerly, with a devout and kindling love, and try to penetrate that darkness above you. Strike that thick cloud of unknowing with the sharp dart of long-ing love, and on no account whatever think of giving up.

Of course, God's existence is already taken for granted by the mystic, who trusts that the cloud of unknowing will be parted once his loving faith has been sufficiently demonstrated (even though revelation is completely up to God's will). The knight does not have the faith to even begin the mystical journey, and while the medieval belief in God could be said to be self-jus-tifying, the same could be said of Block's agnosticism. Because he is unwill-ing to trust implicitly that God is ever present, he can never experience the mystical union with the divine that would give him the proof he so desper-ately craves.

Aside from its larger concerns with existentialism, *The Seventh Seal* is also a very personal film for Bergman. It was a way for him to work out his own inner conflict about his faith. As he writes in his autobiographical memoirs about the movie:

> *The Seventh Seal* is one of the few films really close to my heart. . . . Since at the time I was still very much in a quandary over religious faith, I placed my two opposing beliefs side by side, allowing each to state its case in its own way. In this manner, a virtual cease-fire could exist between my childhood piety and my newfound harsh rationalism. . . . I still held on to some of the withered remains of my childish piety. I had until then held a totally naive idea of what one would call a preternatural salvation. My present conviction manifested itself during this time. I believe a human being carries his or her own holiness, which lies within the realm of the earth; there are no other-worldly explanations. So in the film lives a remnant of my honest, childish

piety lying peacefully alongside a harsh and rational perception of reality.

The Seventh Seal is definitely one of my last films to manifest my conceptions of faith, conceptions that I had inherited from my father and carried along with me from childhood.

Bergman then explains how later, apparently after he had completed *The Seventh Seal*, he lost his belief in the afterlife, and paradoxically, his fear of death:

> My fear of death was to a great degree linked to my religious concepts. Later on, I underwent minor surgery. By mistake, I was given too much anesthesia. I felt as if I had disappeared out of reality. Where did the hours go? They flashed by in a microsecond.
>
> Suddenly I realized *that is how it is*. That one could be transformed from *being* to *not-being*—it was hard to grasp. But for a person with a constant anxiety about death, now liberating. Yet at the same time it seems a bit sad. You say to yourself that it would have been fun to encounter new experiences once your soul had had a little rest and grown accustomed to being separated from your body. But I don't think that is what happens to you. First you *are*, then you are *not*. This I find deeply satisfying.

Bergman's operation experience therefore became his religious epiphany: definitive proof, not of God's existence, but of his absence. In an interview he gave in 1968, Bergman was brutally dismissive of even his former agnosticism, his very quest for faith that he had expressed in *The Seventh Seal*:

> I've always felt sympathy for the Jönses and the Jofs and the Skats and the Mias. But it's with something more like desperation I've experienced the Blocks inside myself. I can really never get shot of them, the fanatics. Whether they appear as religious fanatics or vegetarian fanatics makes no odds. They're catastrophic people. These types whose whole cast of mind as it were looks beyond mere human beings toward some unknown goal. The terrible thing is the great power they often wield over their fellow human beings. Apart from the fact that I believe they suffer like the very devil, I've no sympathy for them.

The Seventh Seal therefore became the perfect sounding board for Bergman's rebellion against his paternally imposed piety. Indeed, one is tempted to see Raval, the evil seminarian who set the knight on the path of his fruitless crusade, as a subliminal portrayal of Erik Bergman, a dour pastor who was, according to his son's account, an even harsher father.

There is one other personal experience of Bergman's that impinges upon the film. This was his flirtation with Nazism at the age of sixteen, when he was sent to Haina, Germany, as a summer exchange student. In his autobiography, Bergman records that the enthusiasm of his German peers for the Hitler Youth and the Nazi Party was so infectious that he began giving the Heil greeting at every opportunity and that he once attended a Nazi rally in Weimar. He was not alone, for his brother, Dag, was a founder of the Swedish Nazi Party, and his father duly voted for them. After the war, when he was confronted by the evidence of the Holocaust, Bergman was "overcome by despair, and my self-contempt, already a severe burden, accelerated beyond the borders of endurance." Although *The Seventh Seal* does not directly address the Jewish pogroms that took place during the Black Death, Bergman does seems to exorcize some of his guilt-laden demons from his anti-Semitic past through a pull-no-punches portrayal of the execution of the witch, Tyan. Like the Jews, she has been made a scapegoat for the plague, and, also like them, she is put to death by cremation. Significantly, Jöns wishes to rescue her but then realizes that this is futile and, as he stands by helplessly watching her funeral pyre, cries out: "That poor little child. I can't stand it. I can't stand it!" Bergman claims in his autobiography that he only came to grips with the Holocaust when he realized that he was "guilty by association only." In a revealing passage, Bergman recalls how the religion teacher at the German school he attended in Haina read from the Nazi newspaper, *Der Stürmer* and "repeated in a factual tone of voice, *von den Juden vergiftet* [poisoned by the Jews]." Clearly, the Nazis were reviving the blood libels leveled against the Jews during the Middle Ages. It is even possible that Bergman's teacher was quoting from the May 1, 1934 issue of *Der Stürmer*, which ran an infamous front-page article that featured an illustration of Jewish rabbis collecting blood from Christian children, who were being slaughtered with long knives.

Balancing the tormented skepticism and bitter cynicism of Block and Jöns are the simple faith and love between Jof and Mia. As with the existentialist theme, there are three scenes in *The Seventh Seal* where their uplifting message is on display. One takes place early in the film, when the actor troupe of Jof, Mia, and Skat wake up in their touring wagon. Jof gets up first, roused by a mosquito which he smacks against his forehead, smearing it with blood. This seems yet another cryptic reference to the Book of Revelation, where the angel of the East carries "the seal of the living God" and cries out: "Do no damage to sea or land or trees until we have set the seal of our God upon the foreheads of his servants" [Revelation 7:3]. Already Bergman signals that Jof and Mia represent something more than the triumph of the human spirit; they also point to the triumph of the heavenly host over death at the Resurrection. Such an interpretation is strengthened by other symbolic aspects of this scene: Jof's vision of the Virgin Mary teaching the Christ child how to walk, inspired, as we know, by a medieval wall painting Bergman had seen as a child; Jof's boast to Mia that their child, Mikael, will do the "one impossible trick" of acrobats, "to make one of the balls stand absolutely still in the air"; and a skull-like mask, which Skat has used to rehearse the part of Death, hanging impotently from the wagon as Mia declares her love for her husband while he remains "silent as a grave" (stage direction from screenplay).

Bergman's second affirmation of faith comes at roughly the midpoint of the film, just after Jof's excruciatingly cruel humiliation at the aptly named Embarrassment Inn, where he has been forced by Raval at knife point to dance like a bear. The scene starts out with Antonius Block and Mia talking together on a sunny hillside. Eventually, they are joined by Jof, Jöns, and his girl. A bowl of fresh milk and some wild strawberries are passed around by Mia to the company. Birgitta Steene has called this "the most crucial sequence in the film" because it takes on an Eucharistic symbolism. For the knight, it is a turning point in his quest for faith. It is at this moment that he has the closest thing to a religious epiphany:

> I shall remember this moment. The silence, the twilight, the
> bowls of strawberries and milk, your faces in the evening light.
> Mikael sleeping, Jof with his lyre. I'll try to remember what
> we have talked about. I'll carry this memory between my
> hands as carefully as if it were a bowl filled to the brim with
> fresh milk. And it will be an adequate sign—it will be enough
> for me.

Immediately thereafter Block wanders down to the beach to resume his chess game with Death, with Jof and Mia's caravan in the background. It is here that the knight learns of Death's designs on the "holy family" and forms his resolve to perform his "one meaningful deed" by saving them.

At the end of the film, of course, we have Jof's vision of his former companions dancing with Death. With a shock of recognition, he describes the dancers to his wife:

> I see them, Mia! I see them! Over there against the dark,
> stormy sky. They are all there. The smith and Lisa and the
> knight and Raval and Jöns and Skat. And Death, the severe
> master, invites them to dance. He tells them to hold each
> other's hands and then they must tread the dance in a long
> row. And first goes the master with his scythe and hourglass,

but Skat dangles at the end with his lyre. They dance away
from the dawn and it's a solemn dance toward the dark lands,
while the rain washes their faces and cleans the salt of the tears
from their cheeks.

The last line again points to the Resurrection at the Last Judgment, for it
recalls the words of St. John in the last chapter of his Revelation, when he
sees a vision of the new Jerusalem, accompanied by: "a loud voice pro-
claiming from the throne: 'Now at last God has his dwelling among men!
He will dwell among them and they shall be his people, and God himself
will be with them. He will wipe every tear from their eyes; there shall be
an end to death, and to mourning and crying and pain; for the old order
has passed away!'" [Revelation 21:3–4] Perhaps, too, there is something
significant about the fact that the knight's wife, Karin, and Jöns' girl are
both omitted from the Dance.

It's pretty clear that these scenes represent Bergman's "childish piety,"
the pure, innocent faith as it is supposed to have existed in the Middle
Ages. Equally obvious is that this piety leans heavily toward the "feminine"
side of God's nature—His nurturing, redemptive, forgiving aspects—that
found ample expression in the writings of late medieval female mystics.
The cult of the Virgin Mary—embodied in Jof's first vision—is one example of this "feminization of devotion" that can be traced back to the
Mariology of St. Bernard of Clairvaux in the twelfth century. Even more
evocative is the hillside "communion" of strawberries and milk. In late
medieval Scandinavian lore, strawberries are symbols of the Virgin and
also are associated with Sweden's most beloved Catholic saint, St. Birgitta
of Sweden (1303–1373). One story has it that a dying child and namesake
of the saint pleaded for strawberries in the dead of winter and was granted
them through a vision of the holy woman's spirit. St. Birgitta is said to have
predicted the Black Death in a famous prophecy from her *Revelations*, written in 1347:

> Then said our Lord: "Therefore it is just that I go with my
> plough upon all the earth and world, both heathen and
> Christian. I shall neither spare the old nor the young, neither
> the poor nor the rich. But each shall be judged according to
> justice and each shall die in his sin; and their houses shall be
> left without inhabitants; and yet I shall not make an end of the
> world."

Although Birgitta insists that there will be judgment for man's sins, she is
not nearly so apocalyptic as male chroniclers who try to fathom God's plan

behind the plague. Milk, naturally, is also symbolic of the Virgin Mother, and it likewise evokes the "Jesus as Mother" concept that is beautifully expressed by another fourteenth-century female mystic, Julian of Norwich. In Chapter 60 of the long text of her own *Revelations*, Julian writes: "The mother can give her child her milk to suck, but our dear Mother Jesus can feed us with himself, and He does so most generously and most tenderly with the holy sacrament, which is the precious food of life itself."

Regardless of whether Bergman consciously references all these meanings in his film, we know at the very least that the above scenes reflect some powerful feminine influences on his own life. Aside from his mother, Karin Bergman, there was his maternal grandmother, Anna Åkerblom, at whose country house in Dalarna, Sweden, he picked wild strawberries every summer. Indeed, the milk and strawberries of the second scene have been called "private symbols in Bergman's world, the Eucharist in a communion between human beings." Bergman himself has said: "Whenever I am in doubt or uncertain, I take refuge in the vision of a simple and pure love. I find this love in those spontaneous women who . . . are the incarnation of purity." Although the character of Mia is an obvious embodiment of this purity, the knight's wife and Jöns' girl also play this role. The name of the knight's wife, Karin, not only recalls Bergman's mother but also St. Birgitta's daughter, Catherine, who followed her mother in becoming a mystic and saint. Both the wife and the girl are selfless in their willingness to sacrifice themselves for others. The wife has dutifully waited for her husband to return in spite of the fact that all her household has fled from the plague; the girl is the only one to attempt to bring water to the dying, gasping Raval, despite the fact that he had earlier tried to rape her. Both also resign themselves to Death: The wife welcomes him "courteously" into her house, and the girl utters the last words of Jesus on the cross: "It is finished" [John 19:30]. Finally, both are spared the Dance of Death as seen by Jof in his vision. What has happened to them? Have they gone directly to heaven? Do they perhaps symbolize the triumph over death at the Resurrection, when the body—a crucial component of late medieval female mysticism—will be fully restored and joined with the soul at the end of time? Marc Gervais, one of Bergman's filmographers, notes that we, the audience, "scarcely notice" the women's absence from the Dance of Death, yet their fate still seems significant, as if "the two women are conscious of something the others ignore." I suspect that this something has to do with the power of love and redemption that Bergman believes women can offer in the face of overwhelming suffering—precisely what female mystics offered in the aftermath of the Black Death. Here again, as with the inspiration provided by the medieval wall paintings of his childhood, Bergman's personal vision coincides with an authentic historical touch.

The famously emotive Flagellant sequence from *The Seventh Seal*. The image of the crucified Christ in the upper right is the same one that we see in an earlier scene of Antonius Block's confession to Death.

This brings us back to our original question: Does Bergman sufficiently balance his medieval and modern approaches to faith? I believe that, when all is said and done, he does not. *The Seventh Seal* is altogether too dark, too pessimistic a film to adequately convey how late medieval society was able to overcome the Black Death, and thus make the transition to the modern world. Bergman himself confessed in his film memoirs that "what attracted me [to *The Seventh Seal*] was the whole idea of people traveling through the downfall of civilization and culture." Shortly after its release, some reviewers picked up on the film's overwhelming darkness. John Russell Taylor, for instance, judged it a failure because "it never finally convinces us, as it obviously intends to, that all its horrors, the rapes, tortures, flagellations, burnings, are valid expressions of a pessimistic world picture only lightly touched with hope." One comes away from *The Seventh Seal* more powerfully impressed by images that show a "waning" civilization, as opposed to the lighter scenes that point to late medieval culture's recovery and renewal. Albertus Pictor's prophecy that people are more fascinated by a skull seems to be self-fulfilled by Bergman, as he imbues more dynamism and direction into the darker scenes.

A good example of the director's privileging of pessimism is the famous Flagellant sequence. This was by no means the first time that the Flagellants had been portrayed on film. A Swedish silent classic from 1921, *Häxan* (also known by its English title as *Witchcraft Through the Ages*), "unflinchingly presents," according to the film scholar, Kevin Harty, "the squalor, cruelty, and superstitions of the Middle Ages" in the form of a documentary-like account of medieval persecutions of witches, which are then compared with modern treatments of the insane. Among the film's macabre demonstrations of medieval "barbarism" is a procession of nude Flagellants. *Häxan*, which was produced by Svensk Filmindustri, the same company that produced nearly all of Bergman's most famous films, including *The Seventh Seal*, was undoubtedly known to Bergman and perhaps inspired his own Flagellant and witch-burning scenes. It also seems that Bergman borrowed from a Flagellant scene in August Strindberg's play, *The Saga of the Folkungs*.

The portrayal of the Flagellants in *The Seventh Seal* is remarkable for capturing the hysterical emotionalism that they literally whipped up and which was attested to by plenty of medieval chroniclers. Yet when the monk who leads the procession stands up to deliver a sermon, a jarring, fanatical note is sounded that is not entirely fair to the real, historical Flagellants. Bergman has stated that he modeled the sermon on that of the fiery preacher, Father Paneloux, in Albert Camus' existentialist novel, *The Plague*. Set during a modern outbreak of plague in Oran, Algeria, during the 1940s, the novel contrasts Paneloux's flagellating faith with the heroic medical efforts of Dr. Bernard Rieux, practically the only character who does anything constructive to alleviate people's suffering during the epidemic. In the same way, the monk's sermon is played in the film as a futile rant against man's stupidity, arousing only self-loathing and contempt. As the Flagellants process into the village, everyone weeps, bows, and prays in response to the spectacle of extreme humiliation, except for the knight, squire, and his girl, all of whom look on with detached, slightly condescending faces, as if in sympathy with the sentiments of the audience. After the procession leaves, Jöns remarks: "This damned ranting about doom. Is that food for the minds of modern people? Do they really expect us to take them seriously?" The Flagellants, therefore, acquire in the film a voyeuristic tinge as a strange, surreal sect that is alien to our better selves, even during the Middle Ages.

By and large, medieval chroniclers of the Flagellants—who were almost always members of the Church—do betray a scornful hostility to what they regarded as a dangerous and newfangled religious movement.

But at least it cannot be said that anyone was indifferent to them. Most people of the time were divided about how to react to the Flagellants: The common people seem to have staunchly supported them, while the authorities, both civil and ecclesiastic, were extremely wary. It was apparently not unknown for the medieval Flagellants, in their sermons and songs, to preach a doom-laden message. Two chroniclers from Strasbourg, Mathias of Neuenburg and Fritsche Closener, record that a centerpiece of Flagellant ceremonies was the reading of a "heavenly letter," in which such fire and brimstone sentiments as "Christ is displeased at the wickedness of the world!" were dispensed in the course of the sermon. But at the same time, it is undeniable that crowds of medieval onlookers welcomed the Flagellants with open arms and rejoiced in their coming; they did so because they believed that the Flagellants' extraordinary penance would help ward off the plague, not because their preachers would tell them what they already knew, that is, that everyone was in imminent danger of death. So venerated were the Flagellants in some places that the blood that rained down their bodies during their excessive whipping performances was reverently collected and preserved as miracle-working relics. Housewives in Flanders reportedly wiped up their blood with rags, which they then used to dab "their eyes and those of others." A Flagellant preacher in Tournai compared the redemptive power of the Flagellants' blood to that of Christ on the cross, a position backed by the townsfolk but one that most churchmen denounced as perilously close to heresy. Flagellants would not have enjoyed the popularity that they had among the common people if their message was entirely nugatory.

When *The Seventh Seal* follows up the Flagellant scene with the burning of the witch, Tyan, and then by the plague death of Raval, the overall impression conveyed of medieval cruelty, depravity, and demoralization is complete. It is hard to see how the "joyous" scenes featuring Jof and Mia can compete with such searing images. This is not to say that these uplifting sequences, as explained above, cannot be interpreted as holding a profound meaning within a medieval context. Yet their symbolism, such as it is, is sometimes elusive and overly subtle. Nor is it unambiguous. Many of Bergman's symbols are perfectly capable of bearing more than one interpretation. To take one example, the squirrel that appears on the tree stump after Skat's death seems to be a straightforward allegory of the continuity of life and of Christian Resurrection. But it is also quite possible that the image has an entirely pagan meaning, as a personification of Ratatosk the Squirrel, who in Viking mythology runs up and down the world tree, Yggdrasill, trading insults between the eagle resting in the topmost branches and Nidhogg, the corpse-devouring dragon dwelling in the lowest root called Niflheim, land of the dead. A double, and contradictory, meaning may also be assigned to Jof and Mia. When asked in a 1968 inter-view if the names of Jof and Mia were mere chance, Bergman replied: "No, not at all. Naturally, they're Joseph and Maria, it's as simple as that." But these characters, who do not appear in Bergman's original play, *Wood Painting*, may not be so simple after all. Rather than being allegories for the holy family, Jof and Mia may just as well be a latter-day Adam and Eve or Noah and his wife: People simply fortunate enough to have been spared the Apocalypse and left behind to repopulate the earth.

All in all, Bergman seems unwilling to endorse the lighter passages of his film with the same confidence and reliability on faith that existed in the Middle Ages. Instead, modern skepticism and existentialism are allowed to seep through, even here. Jof's glowing epiphany of the Virgin Mary, for instance, is undermined by his confession to Mia that he has made up visions in the past, such as of the Devil painting their wagon wheels red. Similarly, we do not know whether to trust his last vision, of the Dance of Death, since he names only one female dancer—the smith's wife, Lisa—while the image on the screen clearly delineates two women dancing. Although Jof is a kind of saintly Everyman figure—he has to play the "soul of man" opposite Skat's Death at the saints' feast in Elsinore—he is also often derided in the film as a buffoonish fool or clown, who must play the cuckold in the troupe's performance before the Embarrassment Inn. Despite the fact that Antonius Block has his "adequate sign" in his com-munion of strawberries and milk on the sunny hillside, his comforting reas-surance utterly evaporates at the end of the film, when he cries out to a God who is "somewhere, who must be somewhere." Bergman's ensuing closeup of the girl's radiant, tear-stained face overshadowed by Death's approach may very well, as Marc Gervais surmises, capture in her "enrap-tured gaze . . . the vision of further mysteries, further mystical experiences" to be glimpsed in a far-off time and place. Yet the dissolve and graphic match from her face to Mia's, as the latter peeks out at a world that has weathered the passing storm, seems to symbolize instead an existentialist belief that the only eternity is the rhythmic ebb and flow of life's continu-ous cycle. Bergman indicates as much when he writes in his memoirs: "I infused the characters of Jof and Mia with something that was very impor-tant to me: the concept of the holiness of the human being. If you peel off the layers of various theologies, the holy always remains." But Bergman's light is not clear enough, nor forceful enough, to keep out the dark. In the struggle between his two "pieties," the medieval-based one is never given the chance of a fair fight. This seems especially true when one compares *The Seventh Seal* to Bergman's other medieval film, *The Virgin Spring* (1959), a lesser-known production but one that ends on a far more affirmative note on medieval faith. After viewing *The Seventh Seal*, one can be forgiven for wondering how in the world postplague Europe managed to have a Renaissance.

Nevertheless, *The Seventh Seal* would go on to become a much imitated classic. Its Flagellant sequence, for instance, probably inspired a similar scene in the Polish film, *Krzyzacy (Knights of the Teutonic Order)*, released in 1960, while a more comedic take on the scene—one where monks beat their heads with wooden boards—occurs in *Monty Python and the Holy Grail*, from 1975. The latter film also has a famous "Bring out your dead!" sketch, set during a plague in a medieval village, which actually has some basis in historical fact. According to Giovanni Boccaccio, Florence during the Black Death was plagued by the depredations of the *Becchini*, a grave-digging fraternity that blackmailed survivors by threatening to take them away while still alive if they did not pay them more money to dispose of their dead. Also in 1975, the American comedian, Woody Allen, who has nominated *The Seventh Seal* as his favorite film, paid homage to Bergman's Dance of Death with his own version at the end of his comedy, *Love and Death*. Then in 1983, the Monty Python troupe mined *The Seventh Seal* once again for comedic gold in their fourth film, *The Meaning of Life*, which also parodies the Dance of Death sequence. In a scene highly reminiscent of Death's arrival at the knight's castle, Mr. Death, in Monty Python's version, comes knocking on the door as an uninvited guest at a posh dinner party in progress at a quaint country cottage. Rather than inspire a hushed awe in his victims, Mr. Death must instead listen to the interminable table talk of some American visitors, who engage in a metaphysical debate about the meaning of death. Meanwhile, the wind howls and the hearth blazes, atmospherics that are lifted straight out of Bergman's film. After Mr. Death points to the demise of all from the salmon mousse (botulism), the soiree embarks on a Dance with Death from the convenience of their cars. Other films, such as *The Masque of the Red Death* or *The Pied Piper of Hamelin*, both of which exist in several versions, refer to the plague but without being too specific as to the historical time period or setting. *Die Pest in Florenz* (1919) depicts the plague in Florence during the time of Savonarola (1452–1498), while a Norwegian film, *Trollsyn* (1994), is set during the Black Death in Norway.

There are two other, more notable films that take the Black Death as their main subject and, what is more, use *The Seventh Seal*'s plot device of contrasting medieval and modern approaches to catastrophe. One is *The Navigator: An Odyssey Across Time* (1988), which is usually relegated to the science fiction section of video stores, even though it could equally qualify as an historical film. A New Zealand production, *The Navigator* was directed by the reclusive Vincent Ward, who also created the film's story line and cowrote the screenplay. Until he was eclipsed by Peter Jackson, director of the *Lord of the Rings* trilogy (2001–2003), Ward was perhaps his country's best known and most highly regarded filmmaker. His film also stars a bunch of New Zealand actors who are virtually unknown in the United States.

Taking its cue from other movies in the time-travel genre, such as *A Connecticut Yankee in King Arthur's Court*, *The Navigator* imagines what it would be like for modern, everyday people to encounter their distant medieval ancestors. Only this time, the twist is that instead of having modern man travel back to the past, *The Navigator* brings medieval people forward to the present. More recently, in 2000, this concept was turned into a comedy called *Just Visiting* (a remake of the French film, *Les Visiteurs*, from 1993), in which a French nobleman, Count Thibault, and his trusty servant, André, are transported to modern-day Chicago.

Time travel has been accomplished in the movies in a number of ways. *Just Visiting* relies on special effects and suspension of disbelief. (Thibault's wizard concocts a magical time-travel potion.) *The Navigator*, on the other hand, makes this possible through the dream vision, a plot device also used in the *Connecticut Yankee* films, which in turn borrowed it from Mark Twain, who in his novel has Hank Morgan knocked over the head in order to wake up in King Arthur's court. In this case, the time "navigator" is a young boy called Griffin (played by Hamish McFarlane), who lives in a hillside mining village in Cumbria in northwest England. An introductory title card informs us that the Black Death is about to invade England from Europe and that one-third of Europe's population has already succumbed to the disease. The real mortality rate was more like one-half, and, in spite of the subtitle, "Cumbria, March 1348," it would be far more likely to be 1349 before the plague reached this far north in England. But these historical quibbles do not detract from the rest of this excellent film.

The Navigator opens with a closeup of Griffin's face in a trance-like state, an image that is intercut with snippets from his dream: a long tunnel, a cathedral, a Celtic-style cross being fixed to the spire, and a falling glove. Griffin's second trance is triggered by the long-awaited homecoming of his beloved brother, Connor (played by Bruce Lyons), who comes back to the village after an absence of 26 days. Nonetheless, the villagers have been anxious about his return, and Connor confirms the stories they have been hearing about a deadly pestilence abroad in the land. A village conference is held, at which it is decided that the best miners will follow Griffin's dream, as well as local rumor, which tell them to journey down the deepest mine shaft to "the far side of the earth," where they expect to find a great church to make an offering of a cross spike forged from their local copper, so that the village will be spared the pestilence. The conference is interrupted by the sudden arrival of strangers on the lake. At first believing them to be pillagers from "the stone-cutting village across the cliffs," the miners discover that they are in fact "refugees from the East" who are fleeing the plague, albeit too late. To keep the infected people from wading ashore, they attack the ships with long poles and flaming arrows. The scene seems lifted straight out of the plague chronicle of Louis Sanctus, who describes how three Genoese galleys brought plague back from the Crimea at the end of 1347 and "were expelled from that port with flaming arrows and diverse engines of war, because anyone who dared touch them or have any business dealings with them immediately died."

Ward does a superb job in this first part of the film in recreating the authentic atmospherics of the Middle Ages. Shot in grainy black and white, these scenes show grimy, unwashed peasants dressed in rags, living in wooden hovels, and being lowered by hand-turned cranks down rough-hewn mine pits. The muted lighting reveals a desolate, claustrophobic, almost alien landscape, but one that is comfortingly familiar to the medieval villagers, for whom Connor's absence of little less than a month seems like an eternity. Even the actors' faces are transformed into Middle Aged versions, which in Arno's case is accomplished through a false set of teeth applied to Chris Haywood's mouth in order to make them look rotten. Obviously, Ward owes a debt to Bergman (even though his favorite Bergman film is *Persona*, not *The Seventh Seal*), but the illusion that we are actually in the Middle Ages seems to surpass even *The Seventh Seal* and *The Virgin Spring*, and it remains unmatched, except perhaps by Chris Newby's *The Anchoress* (discussed in the Afterword). Here, equal empathy is accorded to the medieval, as well as to the modern, mindset. The villagers fervently believe in their "superstitions," such as that the Black Death will "skip right over" their community if only they put "witches' spikes" atop their roofs or if they catch a glimpse of holy relics, such as "St. Augustine's fingerbone and feathers from the Angel Gabriel." Their simple, yet powerful and enduring, faith contrasts with their primitive scientific knowledge: Connor tells them that the plague is spread by the full moon, which "bears contagion before it like a sack; at sunrise she lets it fall . . . on us." Ward is never condescending toward these odd people, who seem so far removed from us moderns. Instead, we are so fully immersed in their thought world that gradually we come to accept it, implicitly.

The film even attempts to recreate the medieval English language and its rhythms, although it sounds remarkably close to Jordie slang, the well-neigh incomprehensible dialect of Newcastle (compare to *Stormy Monday*, a film set in the modern-day version of the city). Hard to follow at first, *The Navigator*'s dialogue requires close attention and gradual acclamation. For the benefit of frustrated viewers, here is a "translation," as near as I can make out, of the crucial opening exchange during the village conference:

Martin: All right, all right, all right. There's a powerful evil on
    the move. Connor's seen it. A pestilence which ups further
    than the full moon, he said. Do we panic, or do we plan? Tell
    them Arno.
Arno: A week back, I found a monk across the lake. He spoke of
    a great church being built in the West. He says it's highest in
    Christendom. There's builders coming from everywhere, tim-
    ber for its construction. You make offering, you stop Death.
Searle: No! Church is too far! Beyond further reaches of earth I
    hear. Across mountains, across seas. Across horrors there
    aren't even names for.
Arno: We've got to go, Searle. There's pilgrims on every road.
Martin: With Connor to lead the party, we'll do it. He knows the
    outside world better than anyone. What do you say, Connor?
Connor: I've seen pilgrims, Martin. I've seen so many bodies
    there weren't enough living to bury the dead. I've seen mobs
    chasing monks from their abbeys for refusing last rites to
    dying. It's these same monks that head west as pilgrims,
    Martin. There are people no more than animals. You can trust
    no one. Children . . . begged me for food. I didn't dare go near
    them. And black boils under their armpits ready to burst and
    they denied plague was upon them! All the churches are
    empty. It's still not satisfied, the evil keeps striding forward
    with each full moon. We've got a month, maybe two, but that's
    with a scrap of God's grace.
Martin: We can do it! Reach the church and raise a spike of
    Cumbrian copper, with you and Searle to lead our party.
Grandma: I deserve this chance. Show the faith!
Grandpa: [holding aloft the spike] Here's to taking it to a jour-
    ney!
Connor: Then Searle must do it. I'm sick of all the death.

Again, the plague references here are quite authentic and are taken almost
directly from the medieval chronicles. Aside from Connor's description of
bubonic plague symptoms, his allusion to mass graves of victims mirrors a
refrain of the English chronicles, that "the living were hardly able to bury
the dead." It should be noted that even though Connor describes the
Church as under attack, this only happens because medieval people place
so high a value on its sacraments: The churches are empty, we are given to
understand, because of mortality, not abandonment of faith.

The transitional stage of the film occurs as the search party—consisting of Connor, Griffin, Martin, Arno, Searle, and his half-witted brother,

Ulf—tunnel to "God's city" on the other side of the world. Unbeknownst to them, they have actually ended up in Auckland, New Zealand, in the late twentieth century (perhaps Ward's private joke, since along with Australia this is the land "down under"). It is made clear, both at the beginning and at the end of the episode, that it takes place entirely within Griffin's dream vision. As the party frantically tunnels down "six times the length" of Arno's rope, going faster than the plague-bearing moon with the aid of a windlass-powered "engine," a winged skeleton blows a trumpet and shrieks across the sky. As in *The Seventh Seal*, these are a people at the brink of the Apocalypse, facing their Last Judgment. Slowly, almost imperceptibly, the film changes over from black and white to color: its cue for the "time warp" from a medieval to modern setting. (A precredit notice warns viewers not to adjust their sets at this point.) Similarly, Griffin here seems to undergo his own transformation—from local visionary who can predict "last year's corn" or a "vein of copper in pit" to a Nostradamus-style prophet who can see into the future.

Once in the twentieth century, our medieval time travelers encounter all the technological paraphernalia of modern civilization: sewers, electricity, cars, submarines, construction equipment, subway trains, and televisions. Ward once more displays a sure touch as we see this familiar technology through medieval eyes. At some point in our childhoods, nearly every one of us in the audience has played with toy versions of these modern machines. Yet now they appear frightening, alien, monstrous—a kind of mirror image of what Ward has done to us in the first part of the film, when he acclimatized us to the medieval world. The sense of wonder and terror generated by the encounter is nowhere better portrayed than in the first scene, where Ulf is caught like a "deer in the headlights" and left stranded in a sea of cross-flowing traffic as he tries to cross the road. (Apparently the scene was inspired by Ward's own experience backpacking across the German autobahn.) A car callously runs over and breaks Ulf's treasured statue of the Virgin Mary, which he clutches to his chest like a security blanket. In this fast-paced world, there is no regard for the innocent, childlike faith of our ancestors. At a later point in the film, the jaws of an earth-moving machine masticate menacingly above Connor like some prehistoric monster. Meanwhile, the rest of the party comes face to face with a submarine as they cross the bay in a little dinghy. (The scene has acquired new meaning in the wake of the tragic collision off the coast of Hawaii between the USS Greeneville and a Japanese fishing ship, Ehime Maru, in February 2001.) As they impotently flail their oars against the ironclad sides of the "dragon," the modern-day horse they have brought along for the ride stands by unfazed, a symbolic link between these two realms. It seems that Ward is making some comment here on the doomsday threat of nuclear annihilation, in the face of which even modern man is powerless. Another reference to a modern "plague" comes when Griffin and Searle come face to face with a bank of televisions in a shop window. At the last second of this scene, attentive viewers will catch a glimpse of a hooded skull flashing across all the TV screens. For those in the know, or who stay tuned to the very end of the credits, this is from the "Grim Reaper" commercial put out by Australia's National Advisory Committee on AIDS, which the government set up under the auspices of the Department of Community Services and Health.

The one encounter between medieval and modern people occurs when the search party stumbles upon some workers at a foundry which is staying open late on its last night of operation. Thinking them "Hari-bloody-Krishnas" or bush people, the foundry workers struggle to understand the strange language of their medieval visitors (an endeavor that we, the audience, can empathize with). For their part, Searle and Griffin attempt to convince the kindly "smithy" and his companions, Tom and Jay, to cast one more job. A surreal dialogue ensues:

Searle: We've brought copper.
Smithy: Fresh off the boat, are you boy?
Searle: Copper! Cast it! Now!
Griffin: Connor said you'd cast a spike. You've got to help us or the village is lost. Please! Cast it!
Smithy: Shh, shh! [To Tom and Jay] Can you understand these buggers?
Tom: Copper?
Searle: Aye, aye! Copper. You must cast it for us. [Arno and Martin try to hand-turn an electric millstone, which Jay turns on for them.]
Griffin: Smithy! You've got to help us. Please Smithy! Cast the spike!
Smithy: If it's casting you're after, sorry son. We're being closed down. [He gazes at the Celtic cross he has taken from Arno] Oh, the church. Hang on. It's over here. Church wanted us to cast a pinnacle, put the scaffold up. We had this bed lying around here for months, waiting for them to scratch around in getting some money. No money.
Martin: The Church . . . is poor?!
Tom: Yeah well, like any other business, eh? When they don't want what you're selling.
Martin: Selling? [Tom and Jay laugh.]

A hushed, mystical aura then steals over the scene when Smithy lowers the medieval Celtic cross into the modern bed, fitting it perfectly. Tom and Jay are no longer laughing. In the end, the foundrymen do cast a new spike, and the film reaches an emotional climax as a small river of molten medieval metal flows down into the modern casting bed, accompanied by rousing vocal and organ music on the soundtrack. As the fully cast cross glows with a white-hot fire, Martin leads the medieval party in a Latin prayer, while the modern foundrymen stand by abashed, uncertain what to do except bow their heads out of respect. Surely, Ward intends this scene to carry the main message of his movie. Despite their simple way of life, medieval people, the director dares to suggest, had something that we in the modern age sorely lack — a confident assurance of faith that gave our ancestors a psychological edge when faced with overwhelming crises such as the Black Death. In the course of our headlong embrace of technology, we in the modern world have lost touch with a way of life that is elemental and unimaginatively powerful. Unlike *The Seventh Seal*, *The Navigator* accords its more privileged and sympathetic portrayal to the blind faith of the Middle Ages, rather than to the cynicism and skepticism of our jaded modern era.

This note is struck a second time when medieval miners and modern blacksmiths join forces to put the spike up on the abandoned church tower before dawn breaks. Suddenly, the mechanical windlass on Jay's truck breaks down, and they are forced back upon good old-fashioned horsepower to pulley the spike up along the scaffold. Symbolically, as well as literally, technology has failed modern man in his hour of need (i.e., there is still no cure for AIDS), and Ward seems to saying here that we moderns desperately need something to fill our spiritual void. By contrast, medieval man had the advantage of spiritual "inoculation" against our modern nihilistic despair. But when Griffin finally guides the pinnacle down into the base of the spire, this is the cue for a second, even greater emotional high-point in the film, as bells ring out and denizens of both the present and past — shown in intercuts of modern Auckland and medieval Cumbria, all in color — celebrate their mutual triumph.

The nightmare of falling from a great height is perhaps the oldest in the book. Griffin's fall, however, takes on new meaning as the villagers celebrate their escape from the "Death." The boy's jig on the hilltop becomes a Dance of Death when he begins to suffer from dizziness and feels a plague boil on his armpit. He runs down to the lake to confront Connor, who experienced the same symptoms during the night but whose boil appeared on his neck and has since burst and released its pus, signifying his recovery. Despite the fact that Connor kept his distance from the others — symbolized in Griffin's dream by his going off on his own — he unwittingly communicated the disease to his younger brother when he lifted him up under his armpits at his homecoming. Connor's glove, which in the dream seems to mark him as the victim who is to fall from the spire, until he gives it to Griffin to help him ascend the ladder to the top, now has become the agent of spreading bubonic plague. Ward stretches our credulity a bit in this scene. It's hard to imagine fleas living on a leather glove; also, the timing of the illness is off, for it normally takes about a week—not a day and a half, as is depicted in the film—for bubonic plague to incubate. Nonetheless, the scene taps into a great fear of dying alone that was genuinely felt by plague sufferers and can be traced in the chronicles. Connor is impelled to stay in the mine pit with the others, even after he first learns that plague is upon him, because, as he explains plaintively to Griffin: "I was afraid. There was nothing else I could do, you understand, there was nowhere for me to go." This is an authentic cry of anguish that could have been written by any number of medieval authors who witnessed first hand the cruel social dislocations created by the Black Death.

The final scene, where Connor pushes Griffin off into the lake in his plague coffin, carries great pathos. A myriad of themes pursued throughout the film come together at this moment. Griffin's powers of prophecy have come true: Without realizing it, he foresaw his own death when he dreamed the Celtic cross in the water—the same one which now adorns his coffin. He also is here portrayed as a sacrificial, Christ-like figure, who gave his life to spare others. The continuity of life is symbolized by the baby to which Linnet, Connor's wife, has given birth within the five or six days it would have taken Griffin to die. As his coffin floats away, Searle wishes him a tender "Godspeed," since Griffin's real journey into the afterlife is just about to take place. *The Navigator* may be classified as a science fiction film, but in actuality, it is a moving testament to the enduring power of a 2,000-year-old faith.

Finally, there is the enigmatic *Book of Days*, which was written and directed by the New York performance artist, Meredith Monk. *Book of Days* not only came out in the same year as *The Navigator*, 1988, it also uses the same time-travel conceit, only in reverse. In this instance, it is the modern world that intrudes upon the Middle Ages, as construction workers detonate a brick wall, behind which lurks a monochromatic medieval world, whereupon the film suddenly switches to black and white. The two films even share the same feature character: the child prophet. Here it is a young Jewish girl called Eva (played by Toby Newman) who can see into the future and has visions of the modern world. However, as is typical of most of Monk's work, *Book of Days* does not have a plot or a story line per se. Instead, it can be considered a collage, montage, or, to use Monk's own choice of words, "a tapestry" that interweaves both medieval and modern images. One of the ways in which the director does this is to have modern reporters, heard off camera, interview various medieval "talking heads": a peasant shepherdess, a Jewish storyteller, a madwoman, an apostate monk, a Jewish grandfather, a doctor, and a knight. As you can probably guess, this is not a typical film. Instead, it belongs to that eclectic category known as experimental, or avant garde, cinema. Indeed, *Book of Days* was never intended for commercial release. It was shown at the New York, Montreal, and Berlin film festivals in 1988 and 1989, and at the same time, a version formatted for television was aired on PBS. Its $1.4 million budget was financed partly by a grant from the National Endowment of the Arts. Nowadays, it is only available on VHS copies distributed by Monk herself.

Much of the film is strange and on the surface seems to have nothing to do with the Black Death. Halfway through the movie, we get a series of "entertainments," including the sawing of a woman in half and the story of Frankenstein that is continued when the Jewish storyteller switches on an old-style, 1930s radio. All this could be Monk's tribute to street theater; yet the latter scene could also be a cryptic reference to the Golem, the Frankenstein-like monster created by Rabbi Loew of Prague that in olden times was believed to protect the Jewish quarter from anti-Semitic pogroms, such as occurred during the Black Death. But at the core of the film are some powerful scenes which, like those in *The Seventh Seal* and *The Navigator*, invite the audience to compare medieval plagues with their modern equivalents. One obvious parallel is between the Black Death and AIDS. During the interview with the Flemish physician, "Philippus Groetius," the doctor is asked at one point by his modern questioner: "What is a virus? How do you treat stress?"—to which his puzzled reply is, "Stress what?" Monk then intercuts the interview with images of a cell dividing as magnified under an electron microscope. The message seems to be that even with our biomedical technology, we can be just as stumped as the medieval physician by new diseases such as AIDS (which unlike plague is caused by a virus, not a bacterium). Later, when Eva has become the protege of the madwoman (played by Meredith Monk herself), who teaches Eva to trust her visions, she tells her mentor of: "a place I've never seen before. They walk on gray ground. I hear an intent noise. Many people are falling. They can't breathe. There's no air. Everyone is sick. It is hot. I'm afraid. I'm afraid." The camera then pans left, with no editing transition, directly from the medieval setting of the madwoman's cave to the modern streets of New York. Eva seems to be channeling modern fears of nuclear holocaust, a twentieth-century parallel to medieval plague that we have already seen referenced in both *The Seventh Seal* and *The Navigator*.

If *Book of Days* has a plot at all, it concerns the pogroms against the Jews during the Black Death. This is one of the few films to address the subject of Christian persecution of Jews during the Middle Ages, and it certainly gives a more probing portrayal than the Hollywood treatment in *Ivanhoe* (1952). Shortly after blasting through to the Middle Ages, we are introduced to the Jewish community in town. An overhead shot of the town clearly delineates the "Jewish Quarter," located outside the town walls, where Jews are segregated from Christians. Monk also imposes a stark contrast in their clothing—white for Christians and black for Jews— to drive home the point that these are separate communities. (As Eisenstein did in *Alexander Nevsky*, Monk seems to be reversing the symbolic connotations associated with these colors.) The Jews wear the "sign of infamy," or the Jewish badge, which is here depicted as a yellow circle, which had been mandated by Pope Innocent III from 1215. A slow pan down a proclamation pasted to a wall sets forth the medieval proscriptions against Jews. In addition to the ghettos and the badges, Jews are also segregated by trade: The only profession open to them is moneylending. These scenes will naturally make most audiences think of the Nuremberg Laws and the yellow star of David imposed upon Jewish citizens in Nazi Germany. Although Jews and Christians mingle amicably enough in the market, we sense a coming storm. When Eva draws water from the village well, this both anticipates and refutes the accusation of well poisoning made against the Jews during the Black Death.

We are then taken inside a Jewish household, where we are shown simple furnishings and food. After a communal meal at a long table attended by the extended family (a "last supper"?), there commences a talking-head interview with the patriarch, a kindly Jewish grandfather named Jacob Benabrum (played by Pablo Vela). His sense of "otherness" from the Christian community is quickly established when the interviewer asks him if this is his "hometown"? Jacob subtly corrects him by saying, "My home is in this town, yes." He informs us that he is a merchant and that he is defenseless, since he owns no weapons. A touch of humor is introduced when Jacob at first denies, then reluctantly admits, after heckling from his family, that he once got drunk "by accident" (probably during the Festival of Purim, a Jewish holiday celebrating misrule). In the background, we see the family both at work—counting out money on a scale—and at play—the men at dice and the women at cat's cradle. Suddenly the interview takes on an ominous tone:

> Interviewer: What's the worst thing you can imagine happening?
> Benabrum: Well, I've thought of this many times. The worst
>   thing that could happen is to die alone and away from my fam-
>   ily and in a strange town. I don't like talking about this if you
>   don't mind.

bent on scapegoating the Jews. He exhorts them to, "Go home," but
avail. Suddenly the interviewer's microphone is shoved into his face:

nterviewer: Brother, brother. What's going on here?
Monk: They don't know what they're doing. They want to go to
the Jewish Quarter but they don't know what they want.
They're just full of hatred. They're completely mad. They say
the Jews are guilty for all this. But everyone's dying: Jews,
Christians, men, women. I'm sorry I can't talk to you anymore.

onk then turns back to the crowd in another futile attempt to per-
them to disperse. We then see the Jews being held prisoner in a
age, as the rampaging Christian mob tramples to death a Jewish vic-
eanwhile, the Black Death spreads, which is indicated by the red
n the overhead plan of the town that keep getting bigger and big-
til they cover nearly the entire surface. These images are intercut
strange figure in black who gesticulates wildly while checking his
Most students of the film interpret him as Father Time, or Death.
, we enter once more into the home of the Jewish family that was
wed earlier. Whereas once there had been the busy hum of life,
ere is a desolate silence, broken only by the buzzing of flies around
gue-ridden corpses. The camera slowly pans over all the members
ousehold (just as it had panned over them at their communal meal),
ast comes to rest upon Grandfather Jacob and Eva, who lie in bed
r in a tender last embrace.

ard the end of the film, Monk closes the circle by returning to the
scene of the construction workers. This recapitulation device was
loyed in *The Seventh Seal* and *The Navigator*, where it is represented
ectively, a reading from the Book of Revelation and Griffin's dream
a Celtic cross in the water. In *Book of Days*, the construction crew
a team of amateur archeologists (a metaphor Monk has used in
ns), as they enter through the beckoning doorway of the Jewish
d explore the dark, empty room with their flashlight. They even-
ht upon Eva's markings: In addition to the plane and the car, there
ched on the wall a gun, a briefcase, and a pair of eyeglasses. On
dtrack we hear once again the song Eva sang with her grandfa-
signals that we should interpret these images like Eva did of her
e gun, perhaps, as a symbol of the future technology of mass
tion; and the eyeglasses and suitcase to represent the piles of pos-
hat were confiscated from the Jews upon their arrival at the
ps. Medieval pogroms during the Black Death, Monk implies,
wed the greater tragedy of the Holocaust, for in both atrocities

Interviewer: I hear rumors of trouble in neighl
   you think the trouble will spread to this tow
Benabrum: Trouble always spreads, my friend
   Always.
Interviewer: What is a radiator?
Benabrum: A radiator? I think you must be r
   young man who makes our candles.
Interviewer: Are you happy?
Benabrum: At this moment, I'm very happy,

Grandfather Jacob is then called away by
Monk next cuts to them sitting together in a Jew
grandfather about a recurring dream, in which
the sky that leaves a trail of smoke"; a "woman
who is "not wearing many clothes" (at this point
base of her head); and a "big carriage with no h
out of it." She also draws a plane and a car in t
grandfather someone taking pictures with
Nostradamus figure, Eva seems to foresee
Holocaust: the Luftwaffe bombers, the victim
cars to the concentration camps, the "processin
before being sent to the gas chambers, even the
pagandists or Allied liberators. The cemetery
this vision, for it spells mass death. Her gran
interpret her dream biblically: The woman is
the horseless carriage is Noah's ark. But eve
forting view that Eva's signs are "very ancien
lished tradition of the Old Testament, he seem
ing catastrophe, which he prefers to ignore
alone, away from his family, a tragedy that
during both the Black Death and the Holoc
nations a bit, the radiator—a device that co
gas chambers or the crematoria. Benabrum
that trouble will inevitably come (perhaps
pogrom), no matter how happy one may l
inside the carriage/ark are "trying to escape
succeed." Grandfather Jacob then teaches
thematic link later in the film. After some i
scratching the images of her futuristic visic
   The last third of *Book of Days* drama
Jewish community of the Black Death. A
dead of the plague, the apostate monk tries

mob
to n

The
suade
large
tim. l
areas
ger, u
with a
watch
Finall
interv
now th
the pla
of the
and at
togethe
  To
openin
also em
by, resp
vision o
acts lik
other f
home a
tually li
is now
the sou
ther. Th
dream:
extermi
sessions
death ca
foreshac

the perpetrators evinced a desire to eliminate all the Jews by whatever means at their disposal.

But Monk is making another, even more powerful point here. It may be all well and good to have the gift of prophecy, as Eva has, but it is equally important to look back into the past and try to learn from it. Only in this way, Monk suggests, can we prevent the tragic events of history from repeating themselves. As Monk said in an interview about *Book of Days*: "Basic human nature remains the same, no matter what the overall environment in society is like." The study of history is not an academic exercise for Monk, but an extremely urgent means of addressing our social ills. We are clearly invited to draw parallels not only between the pogroms against the Jews during the Black Death and the Holocaust, but also between the former event and the scapegoating of homosexuals during the AIDS crisis, an issue that was very much to the fore in the late 1980s. Today's audiences may also bring to mind the "ethnic cleansing" that has occurred since the release of the film in the former Yugoslavia during its civil war in the 1990s. Monk's film is not simply entertainment; it is a call and incitement to activism. Her message seems to be that, unlike the interviewers in the film, we cannot simply stand by and dispassionately watch as an atrocity takes place. *Book of Days* thus acquires a relevance that extends well beyond the date of its release.

It is remarkable how all three directors who tackle the Black Death— Bergman, Ward, and Monk—use a common fund of themes, film techniques, and even characters. Nonetheless, each filmmaker comes to dramatically different conclusions about the meaning that this apocalyptic event holds for history. The Black Death may not be a particularly prolific subject for film. Yet in spite of this, it has proved to be one of the most rich and rewarding topics of the cinematic arts.

CHAPTER SIX

Movies and the Maid
Joan of Arc Films

The Background

Like other iconic figures of medieval legend, such as King Arthur and Robin Hood, Joan of Arc endures as a perennially favorite subject of the cinema. To date, there have been no less than forty-one films and TV movies on Joan of Arc, a total that rivals that of the Robin Hood genre. Cinematic interest in Joan began early, with two pioneering French film-makers, Georges Méliès and Georges Hatot, each coming out with a film entitled *Jeanne d'Arc* in 1897–1898, at the dawn of the film industry. Nor has recent history shown any slackening of interest in the Maid. Just as 1991 produced a spate of Robin Hood films, so 1999 saw the almost simultaneous release of two movies about Joan. She has also enjoyed an international appeal. In addition to the Hollywood and other English-language productions, movies about Joan of Arc have been made in French (in equal number to English films), Italian, and one each in German and Russian. Many of these films have been inspired by an abundant literature on Joan that includes — aside from historical works — novels, plays, poems, operas and oratorios. To an even greater degree perhaps than King Arthur, Joan of Arc has attracted the highest literary talent, although this does not necessarily translate into works of high literary merit. In plays alone, Joan has enjoyed the attentions of Shakespeare, Schiller, Péguy, Shaw, Brecht, and Anouilh; this does not count the eclectic contributions of Christine de Pizan (the only author contemporary with Joan), Voltaire, and Mark Twain. One reason for the special fascination with Joan may be that — unlike King Arthur or Robin Hood — she is a legend with a highly distinct personality, probably the single-most documented individual to emerge from the Middle Ages. As if this was not enough, she was also a transvestite, she claimed to hear voices, and she died extremely young.

The career of this remarkable woman is well known and can be briefly told. She was born in perhaps January 1412 in Domrémy, a town in Lorraine near Vaucouleurs on the eastern border of France. Vaucouleurs and its immediate environs constituted an isolated bastion of loyalty to Charles VII, the Valois claimant to the French crown, within a sea of English- and Burgundian-controlled territory. Although Joan came from a region that was peripheral to the French kingdom, she was on the front lines of the nearly 100-year-old struggle between England and France. In 1428, her village was burnt to the ground, and she and her family had to flee for safety to the nearest walled town, Neufchâteau. As Joan was growing up, the Hundred Years War took a dire turn for the French. Ever since their celebrated victory at Agincourt in 1415, the English pursued a strategy that went beyond the mere feudalistic aims of the previous century, in favor of a nationalistic, far more ambitious goal of conquest of the entire country. This was made possible by two developments that had occurred a decade before Joan first came to the attention of her contemporaries in 1429. One was the assassination of the duke of Burgundy, John the Fearless, by partisans of Charles VII on the bridge of Montereau on September 14, 1419; this drove John's son and successor, Philip the Good, into the arms of the English and thus handed them a most powerful ally on France's eastern border, where Joan lived. The other was the Treaty of Troyes of 1420, which purported to change the dynastic history of France by replacing the Valois line — since 1422 headed by Charles VII — with the English Lancastrian dynasty of Henry V (1413–1422) and his son, Henry VI (1422–1461). This gave the English legitimate pretensions as rightful rulers of France.

The first public notice of Joan was in February 1429, when she was on her way to Chinon to meet "her dauphin," the traditional name given to the heir to the French throne. She had somehow persuaded the captain of Vaucouleurs, Robert de Baudricourt, to lend her an escort, and she was already wearing men's clothes. Baudricourt's endorsement was essential to Joan's "mission," for without it, she never would have been received by Charles VII. After her first meeting with him on March 6, 1429, Joan managed to gain the future king's confidence and trust. This was no mean feat, as the young Charles seems to have been of flighty and suspicious temperament. Legend has it that at their first interview, Joan picked Charles out from a crowd, and Joan herself testified that she gave the king a "sign" by which to believe in her, though what this was will probably always remain a mystery. Whatever marvels she may have performed, Joan was required to undergo a theological examination at Poitiers by a board of churchmen loyal to Charles—as well as submit to a physical confirmation of her virginity by some ladies at court—before she was entrusted with men-at-arms. Although the register of the so-called "Poitiers trial" does not survive, it seems on second-hand evidence to have examined Joan on some of the same issues that were later raised at her trial for heresy in 1431: namely, the inspiration of her "voices" and, possibly, her adoption of male dress.

After that, events proceeded quickly for Joan during the next year of her life. Toward the end of April 1429, she arrived at Orléans, which had been under siege from the English since October 1428. Orléans was a most strategic city: Its fall could have opened up the whole south of France below the Loire River to the English advance and linked English-held territories in the north with Guyenne, an English duchy in the southwest. But it was not to be, for Joan officially liberated Orléans on May 8, after the English bastide of the Tourelles at the southern end of the city bridge over the Loire had been taken the previous day. In June, the English were dislodged from several smaller towns near Orléans along the Loire, culminating in a major battlefield defeat of the English army on June 18 at Patay, where it is estimated that 2,000 English died to only three of the French. This cleared the way for Charles' coronation procession to Reims, where, in accordance with ancient custom, he was solemnly crowned king of France on July 17. Even though the English were to stage a rival coronation ceremony for the nine-year-old Henry VI at Paris in December 1431, it was at last Charles' turn to enjoy an air of legitimacy that effectively erased the Treaty of Troyes.

Reims can be considered the high watermark of Joan's brief career. Thereafter, her fortunes quickly faded as her influence at the French court seemed to wane. An attack on Paris at the Saint-Honoré Gate on September 8 failed and was called off two days later. During the attack, Joan was struck by a crossbow bolt in the thigh, her second battle scar after the famous arrow wound she had received above the breast at the siege of the Tourelles on May 7. Meanwhile, the king had negotiated a series of truces with the duke of Burgundy, leading him to formally disband his army on September 21, which reduced Joan to the role of conducting petty skirmishes against local robber barons, such as Perrinet Gressart of La Charité-sur-Loire. It was not until May 6, 1430 that Charles acknowledged his mistake of abandoning Joan's aggressive war strategy. But by that time it was too late: The English and Burgundians had used the breathing space to cement their alliance, and Joan was captured on May 23 outside Compiègne as she was attempting to relieve the town from a much larger Anglo-Burgundian force. For the next 6 months, she was a prisoner of John of Luxembourg, a staunch partisan of the duke of Burgundy, although Joan's captivity may have been alleviated by the companionship and support of three namesakes: Joan of Luxembourg, John's aunt; Joan of Béthune, the count's wife; and Joan of Bar, his stepdaughter. Finally, in November 1430, Joan was sold and handed over to the English for 10,000 *livres tournois*—with apparently no attempt made by Charles VII to ransom his erstwhile champion. Joan's trial at Rouen in English-held Normandy could now begin.

That remarkable trial lasted altogether a little under five months, from January 9 to May 30, 1431. It was presided over by Pierre Cauchon, bishop of Beauvais, a former rector of the University of Paris and a lifelong supporter of the Anglo-Burgundian cause. In the end, Joan was formally charged with 12 articles of accusation (reduced from an original 70), in which four main counts of heresy were leveled against her: (1) that she was falsely and demonically inspired by her "voices;" (2) that she wore male dress; (3) that she expected divine aid to favor the French against the English and Burgundians; and (4) that she defied the Church Militant (i.e., the hierarchical Church here on earth headed by the pope) with regard to all of the above. Under extreme pressure, which included the threat of torture, Joan acknowledged and abjured a generalized form of these charges on May 24 before a very public assembly held at the cemetery of the abbey of Saint-Ouen. Upon her confession, she was sentenced by Cauchon to life imprisonment and remanded to the English jailers, who had had custody of her throughout the trial. She also, for the first time, resumed women's clothing. Three days later, on May 27, it was reported that Joan was once more wearing male dress, and this was confirmed the following day when Cauchon and several other assessors visited her in person in her cell. On May 29, Cauchon held a very brief trial of relapse, in which it was declared that Joan had gone back to her original heresy. With no secular judgment that was considered procedurally necessary in such cases, Cauchon straightaway handed Joan over to be burned at the stake in the Old Market of Rouen, which took place on May 30, 1431. Just over 20 years later, in 1455–1456, the original verdict of condemnation against Joan was nullified at a "trial of rehabilitation" presided over by churchmen now loyal to Charles VII. In 1920, Joan was officially canonized as a saint (after yet another, "Devil's advocate" trial) by Pope Benedict XV and the Catholic Church.

There are several mysteries about Joan of Arc that need to be addressed—if not fully answered—before one can begin to understand her. A main conundrum concerns her voices. What are we to make of them? Modern interpretations of the voices have run the gamut from acceptance of them as real (either of earthly or supernatural origin) to dismissal of them as psychosensual hallucinations. To accept Joan as a divinely inspired figure is ultimately an act of faith. Otherwise, a number of physiological explanations have been advanced to account for Joan's voices: Ménière's syndrome (a disease of the inner ear, producing dizziness), amenorrhea (inability to menstruate), and a tubercular lesion of the brain. (Joan was struck on the head by a stone at the siege of Jargeau in June 1429.) This does not count psychoanalytic theories, which have tended toward the Freudian (i.e., St. Michael's lance was a phallus). However, all the evidence indicates that this girl, who was not yet out of her teens, was remarkably healthy and had a sharp and retentive mind. It must be noted that in the Middle Ages, supernatural revelations were considered to be entirely plausible and when subjected to investigation, were almost entirely approached on spiritual rather than physical grounds. Plenty of female mystics, especially in the late medieval period when their writings were becoming more autobiographical and more prolific, testified to experiencing paranormal sights, sounds, and sensations. Not even Joan's judges at Rouen questioned the fact that Joan had visions—their only concern was to prove their diabolical, rather than heavenly, origin.

Aside from her birth, Joan's first encounter with her voices is among the earliest historical events to come down to us from her life. She told the tribunal at Rouen on February 22, 1431:

> that from the age of 13, she received revelation from Our Lord by a voice which taught her how to behave. And the first time she was greatly afraid. And she said that the voice came that time at noon, on a summer's day, a fast day, when she was in her father's garden, and that the voice came on her right side, in the direction of the church. And she said that the voice was hardly ever without a light, which was always in the direction of the voice.

A week later, on February 27, Joan identified the voices as those of St. Michael (who reportedly came to her first), St. Catherine, and St. Margaret; modern scholars have assumed that these angelic figures correspond to St. Michael the Archangel, St. Catherine of Alexandria, and St. Margaret of Antioch. But Karen Sullivan has argued that one must be wary of trusting the trial record with regard to the voices, since it reflects what the assessors wanted to hear and is not confirmed by any testimony from the trial of rehabilitation. On the other hand, Joan identified her voices early in the trial, when she apparently still felt free to answer "boldly" and had not yet been worn down by her interrogators' relentless questions. Moreover, she invited the assessors to "send to Poitiers where I have been previously examined" if they doubted her word on this score. Whatever the exact nature of her inspiration, it is clear that Joan and many of her contemporaries, at least on the French side, sincerely believed in the reality of her voices. There is probably no other way to explain how Joan was consistently able throughout her career to defy the incredible odds ranged against her.

Another source of fecund speculation concerns Joan's relationship with Charles VII and the "sign" exchanged between them. Conspiracy theorists and amateur historians claim that Joan had a secret blood tie to the king as his half-sister, the daughter of the queen mother, Isabeau of Bavaria, and Duke Louis of Orléans, which she may have revealed to him at Chinon (the "bastardy" school). Since Louis was assassinated in 1407, this would make Joan 24 years old at the time of her death, and it would assume that Isabeau had given birth to a twin daughter alongside the practically stillborn son delivered in November of that year. It would also require that Joan, her mother, Isabelle Romée, and numerous godparents and neighbors had all perjured themselves at their respective trials. An even more ridiculous hypothesis is that Joan, because of her royal ancestry, was saved from the stake by Cauchon and her jailer, the earl of Warwick (the "survivalist" school). This theory is not helped by the claim that Joan reappeared some years after her purported execution. Several imposters, in fact, tried to pass themselves off as the Maid in the decades following her death, the most notorious of which was Claude des Armoises, a widow with two children.

Joan herself testified at her trial "that the sign was that the angel, in bringing her king the crown, assured him that he would have the whole and entire realm of France through the help of God and her efforts." She then goes on to describe in detail the crown and the manner of the angel's presentation of it to Charles. The whole testimony of this tenth session on March 13 has an air of allegory about it, as if it is not meant to be taken literally, and it may be that Joan, after persistent badgering on this point from her judges, confessed to the surreal episode out of sheer exhaustion. According to the "posthumous informations," drawn up by Cauchon in June 1431 shortly after the execution, Joan had acknowledged that: "It was I who brought the message of the crown to my king. I was the angel and there was no other, and the crown was no more than the promise of the king's coronation which I made to him." Although the notary of the trial, Guillaume Manchon, refused to authenticate the posthumous informations with his signature, the retraction does ring true, considering that Joan until then had refused to reveal the sign or was vague about it. Even on the very day of the session in question, March 13, she declared when first pressed that, "I have sworn and promised not to reveal this sign," and she rhetorically asked her interrogators, with perhaps a touch of mockery, "Do you wish me to perjure myself?" Without the above explanation, her abrupt volte-face and volubility about the sign are extremely puzzling.

Most scholars assume that Joan's "sign" was to assure Charles that he was the "true heir" to the disputed crown of France. Some such message was reported by Simon Charles, president of the royal treasury, and by Jean Pasquerel, Joan's confessor. The chronicle of Pierre Sala, repeating the testimony of the king's chamberlain, Guillaume Gouffier, alleges that Joan recited to Charles a secret prayer that only he knew, in which he begged for the Lord's protection "if it were true that he was His heir, descendant of the noble House of France, and that the kingdom should in justice belong to him." A theory proposed in the 1990s by the French historian, Bernard Guenée, asserts that Charles' doubts about the legitimacy of his inheritance arose not from questions concerning his paternity (his mother, Isabeau of Bavaria, was notoriously dissolute), but rather from his remorse over his involvement in the murder of the duke of Burgundy at Montereau in 1419. Other recent scholars of the "sign," such as Jean Fraikin, seem more prepared than their predecessors to accept as genuine the elaborate masquerade that Charles is said to have staged in order to test Joan. According to the court chronicler, Jean Chartier, Joan was first presented to Charles of Bourbon, count of Clermont, and then to a squire, both pretending to be the dauphin, but that Joan easily saw through these ruses. Fraikin believes that, since the date of Joan's meeting with the king — March 6 — happened to fall on Laetare Sunday or mid-Lent, a traditional occasion for merrymaking and festivities, that the masquerade, for all its theatricality, would have been a natural and logical occurrence.

Another mystery connected with this stage of Joan's career is the lost transcript of Poitiers. Why is there no surviving record of it? That one did indeed exist during Joan's lifetime is made clear by her reference at her heresy trial to a "register of Poitiers," in which her answers were "written down." Assuming that such things do not go missing by accident, what was in the register that would cause Charles or his advisers to want to destroy it before it could be entered as evidence at the rehabilitation trial of the 1450s? There are really only two occasions when the Poitiers record would have been destroyed: either in 1430–1431, when Joan was captured and put on trial by the English, or shortly before the rehabilitation trial itself. The historian, Charles Wood, who has speculated at length on this subject, seems to favor the latter alternative. By this time, Charles VII was extremely anxious to prove his paternity in response to an English effort to discredit it, and he badly wanted to enlist Joan's mission in his support. But that original mission had been to simply raise the siege of Orléans, Wood contends, so that the record had to be manipulated to include the additional goal of leading Charles to his coronation at Reims, something that would be far easier to do if the only evidence available was in oral form. The weakness of this argument is that it would imply that Charles exercised a much greater control over the rehabilitation testimony than he did. One of the witnesses allowed to testify in 1452, during the early stages of the rehabilitation proceedings, was Jean Beaupere, one of Joan's judges at her Rouen trial who was still hostile to Joan. He remained convinced, for example, that her voices derived "more from natural cause and human invention than supernatural," and he characterized Joan as "very subtle, with a woman's subtlety." Another weakness of Wood's thesis is that he argues from the silence of the record, a most dangerous thing to do in the case of the condemnation trial. He reads much into the fact that Joan did not jump at her judges' offer to submit her case to Poitiers, indicating that, like Charles, she finally realized that its register was not all that favorable to her cause. But it may be that her response at this juncture was simply left out by Cauchon. One assessor sympathetic to Joan, Friar Isambart de la Pierre, testified at the rehabilitation that Joan did offer to submit to the Council of Basle, on Pierre's advice that there would be "as many of her party as of the English," but that Cauchon angrily ordered the notary to not record her answer. It is more likely, on the whole, that if Charles did destroy the Poitiers register, he did so in 1430–1431, when it seemed possible that Cauchon's tribunal would, in fact, subpoena this damning record and expose the king' support for what now appeared to all to be a lost cause.

Joan's exploits in the military field—at Orleans and elsewhere—have been a source of wonder, to both medieval and modern observers alike. Her military skills are attested, above all, by John, the duke of Alençon, a close associate of Joan's on the battlefield:

> In everything that she did, apart from the conduct of the war, Joan was young and simple; but in the conduct of war she was most skillful, both in carrying a lance herself, in drawing up the army in battle order, and in placing the artillery. And everyone was astonished that she acted with such prudence and clear-sightedness in military matters, as cleverly as some great captain with twenty or thirty years experience; and especially in the placing of artillery, for in that she acquitted herself magnificently.

Part of the secret of her military success is that, just like teenagers today, she had an aptitude for the latest technology, in this case, gunpowder. Where and how she learned the military art, such as the ability to tilt— normally a skill only taught to noble sons and acquired after long training—is a mystery. She probably was accustomed to riding a horse on her father's farm, but it may be that she simply had a natural calling for war.

A woman who led men into battle was, of course, highly unusual in the Middle Ages, and it remains so today. Yet Joan would not have been considered by her contemporaries to be unprecedented. Two authors writing in her support in 1429, Jean Gerson and Christine de Pizan, both compare her to the Old Testament "amazons," Esther, Judith, and Deborah. The puzzle is why men followed her when she did not offer them the typical blandishments provided by most military captains, such as plunder and booty. (Joan, in fact, expressly forbade looting and would not touch anything she felt had been taken unjustly.) The military historian, Kelly DeVries, speculates that French soldiers nonetheless welcomed Joan's leadership and participation because of her mystical and semidivine status as a *mulier sancta*, or holy woman. Joan brought to the fray something more powerful than any weapon of war—the favor of God—which medieval men knew could turn the tide of battle. John, count of Dunois, the "Bastard" of Orléans, testified at the rehabilitation trial that Joan's arrival at his beleaguered city on April 29, 1429 coincided with a miraculous change in the wind that allowed relief convoys to sail up the Loire River. He and others also bore witness to Joan's military élan, in which she consistently advised attack as opposed to the more cautious approach of the more seasoned commanders. Another celebrated "miracle" associated with Joan's battlefield exploits is that, despite the twin disadvantages of her youth and her gender, she was able to gain acceptance as an equal among her hardened companions. Her squire, Jean d'Aulon, reported at the rehabilitation that "never, despite any sight or contact I had with the Maid, was my body moved to any carnal desire for her, nor were any of her soldiers or squires moved in this way, as I have heard them say and tell many times." Feminist historians have had a field day with this testimony, but it seems that for Joan, it was an eminently practical matter: In the heat of battle, it was simply more expedient to dress like those around her. Still, it is probable that male dress played an important role in preserving Joan's virginity, which was a crucial component of her status as *mulier sancta*.

Another reason Joan was able to raise morale among her troops is that she imposed upon them a great sense of discipline and professionalism. As DeVries notes, "Joan set an elevated moral tone for her soldiers" by leading them in regular confession and forbidding gambling and swearing. (She famously exhorted Etienne de Vignolles, known as La Hire, to swear "by his staff.") Also unusual for the time was to drive away the camp followers, or prostitutes, which both Alençon and Joan's page, Louis de Coutes, witnessed her do with a drawn sword. Joan can thus be compared, in military terms, to Oliver Cromwell: Someone who helped fashion a medieval version of the "New Model Army" that combined esprit d'corps, tight discipline, the latest technology, and a moral certitude that God was on their side. These were almost irresistible ingredients for victory.

Eventually, Joan's military brilliance faded, but not until the army and leaders with whom she had won her victories were disbanded by Charles.

Even so, the English evidently still felt threatened enough by her military reputation to exult in the capture of the "whore of the Armagnacs." They, no less than the French, were awed by her military prowess, even though they interpreted the reasons for her success quite differently. At this stage, another issue for historical debate has arisen over whether Joan was betrayed by Guillaume de Flavy, the captain of Compiègne, when he locked her out of the city on May 23, 1430. While some contemporary chroniclers hint at the betrayal, modern scholarly opinion is divided on this point—indeed, one of the most respected historians of Joan of Arc, Régine Pernoud, has changed her mind on the subject, first rejecting and then entertaining the possibility of Flavy's treason. Even though Flavy kept Compiègne loyal to the French crown, it seems that he did not have to shut the bridge gate against Joan in order to save the city. The English and Burgundian attackers would still have had to cross the River Oise before they reached the main gate of Notre Dame. Joan's retreat could have been covered and the city still easily defended. A formal accusation was later made against Flavy in the French Parlement, that he had been bribed by the duke of Burgundy in order to surrender both Compiègne and the Maid. But the jury, both then and now, is still out on the truth of this charge.

This brings us to Joan's trial at Rouen, the most controversial subject of all. Once again, Joan astounds us with her indomitable spirit in the face of daunting odds. A teenage girl—alone and bereft of legal counsel, barely literate, and daily subjected to the mockery of hostile jailers and confined in iron shackles—nonetheless was able to parry and occasionally flummox as many as forty-four learned judges ranged against her, who brought with them a battery of doctorates and other degrees in theology and canon and civil law. No less than her liberation of Orléans and crowning of Charles VII, it has all the trappings of a miracle.

Despite Cauchon's boast to his fellow assessors that he would engineer a "beautiful trial," the end result of the whole process was to be determined by Joan herself. Since she was an anomaly—the *Journal of the Bourgeois of Paris* pointedly pondered of her, "what *it* was, God only knows"—the trial was also bound to be quixotic. Although ostensibly conducted as an investigation into the crime of heresy under the auspices of the Inquisition and the Church, Joan's trial flagrantly violated a number of rules of inquisitorial procedure. As a suspected heretic, Joan did *not* have the right to legal counsel, nor to know who had accused her in the "preliminary informations," contrary to what the twenty-seven articles of the rehabilitation trial and many modern commentators have claimed. But, as Régine Pernoud points out, normal protocol did call for her to be tried in the diocese where she was born or where the heresy had been committed (whatever Joan's "heresy" was), and for her to be kept in a Church prison guarded by female jailers. Cauchon failed to adhere to both of the above conditions, and he got around the rules on technicalities. He received a "commission of territory" from the Rouen cathedral chapter that allowed him to try the case in this staunchly pro-English venue, and the keys to Joan's prison cell were in the custody of ecclesiastics, one of whom was Cauchon himself. The latter arrangement did not in the least bar English jailers from complete access to Joan's person, since three of them regularly slept in the same cell with her at night. Other peculiarities occurred at the end of the trial. According to the court usher, Jean Massieu, who testified at the rehabilitation, Joan was given communion by a Dominican friar, Martin Ladvenu, on the morning of her execution. However, reception of this most holy sacrament implied that one was orthodox enough to receive God's grace and was thus completely incompatible with Joan's presumed status as a relapsed heretic. Nevertheless, it was done with the express permission of Cauchon, who instructed Ladvenu to "give her the sacrament of the Eucharist and anything she asks." Another irregularity was that Joan received no secular judgment before being burnt at the stake, a formality that was required upon relaxation of heretics by the Church to the secular arm. In his haste to burn her, Cauchon practically admitted that he and his tribunal were directly responsible for Joan's death.

But by far the most bizarre peculiarity of all, and one that is often passed over by modern commentators, is that when the trial began on January 9, 1431 — opening with the *procès d'office*, or the judges' preliminary investigations — Cauchon still had not formulated an accusation specifying the heresy of which Joan was accused! This was completely unprecedented, for no other case in the whole annals of the medieval Inquisition, so far as I know, thus proceeded without a formal charge to hand. Manuals consulted by medieval inquisitors clearly specified that an individual summoned to appear before the Holy Office was to be informed beforehand of the "reasons for the summons" and of the specific offense for which he was "to answer for his faith." Even the case that is most like Joan's in terms of abuses of procedure — the trial of the Knights Templar in 1307–1314, where the victims were also kept in secular rather than ecclesiastical jails and confessions extracted by intimidation and torture — at least had a series of offenses, albeit manufactured, with which to charge the accused, consisting of sodomy, idolatry, denial of Christ, and spitting on the crucifix. From the rehabilitation trial, we learn that Cauchon had sent agents to Joan's hometown of Domrémy and other neighboring parishes in order to gather denunciations against her, out of which he had hoped to manufacture a charge by the time of the first public session and interrogation of Joan on February 21, but that they "had found nothing about Joan that he [Nicolas Bailly] would not wish to find about his own sister." As a result, a frustrated Cauchon accused Bailly of being "a traitor and a bad man" and refused to pay his expenses. An effort to charge Joan with witchcraft met with even less success. Although the promoter, Jean d'Estivet, accused her of "carrying a mandrake in her bosom" and other fanciful charges in his original seventy articles, they were later dropped when the list was reduced to twelve.

It goes without saying that Joan's trial was, above all, a political one and had little to do with heresy. This inescapable fact was made more than clear when the English crown, on January 3, 1431, issued its official commission to Cauchon to proceed in his trial of Joan. At the end of the commission, it was baldly stated that "it is our intention to bring back before us the said Jeanne, if it should not be that she is convicted or found guilty of the said crimes [of heresy] or any of them, or of other crimes touching our faith." No matter what the outcome of her trial, Joan could not escape the consequences of the political (and military) threat she posed to her enemies. It was an anomalous situation that did not go unnoticed by contemporaries. A trial for heresy naturally required the presence of the Inquisition, but the vice-inquisitor, the Dominican Jean Lemaître, who was acting as representative of the grand inquisitor of France, Jean Graverent, was most reluctant to participate. He told Cauchon on February 20 that "as much for the serenity of his conscience as for a more certain conduct of the trial, he did not wish to be involved in this present affair," and he did not make a public appearance until the second session, on February 22, when he expressed grave reservations about the "borrowed jurisdiction" of Cauchon in Rouen, which made him "doubtful of joining in the matter." That he was appearing at all was apparently due to the fact that Graverent, at Cauchon's urging, ordered him to do so, but even then he seems to have maintained only a fitful presence throughout the trial. No doubt Lemaître was extremely embarrassed, and quite possibly appalled, by the other irregularities that opened the proceedings.

Essentially, the case against Joan had to be formulated ad hoc out of her replies to her interrogators' questions. This was, again, an extremely unusual way of going about a heresy trial, since most inquisitors had an interrogatory formula prepared based on the specific kind of heresy of which the subject was accused. Even with their advantages of scholastic learning and of deception (it was not uncommon for inquisitors to introduce spies into prisoners' cells, as was done in this case), the assessors still had a hard time catching out Joan. To hear voices by no means marked one as a heretic; plenty of late medieval male and female mystics claimed very similar supernatural experiences. Nor was cross-dressing necessarily incompatible with holiness. Several early Christian female saints, including Saint Margaret, whom Joan, perhaps not coincidentally, identified as one of her voices, crossed gender lines in order to preserve their virginity and sanctity. But it was when her judges were questioning her on the subject of her voices that they nearly entrapped her, and she stepped perilously close to the precipice on the morning of March 14:

> Asked whether, since her voices have told her that in the end she will come to the Kingdom of Heaven, she believes herself assured of salvation, and that she will not be damned in hell, she said that she will be saved, as firmly as if she were already there. And when they told her that this answer had great weight, she answered that she, too, accounted it a great treasure. Questioned as to whether, after this revelation, she believes that she cannot commit mortal sin, she answered: As to this I know nothing; but commit myself in all things to Our Lord.

This is the closest Joan ever came to admitting of an actual heresy—the heresy of the Free Spirit. It had led the beguine, Marguerite Porete, to the stake in 1310 on the (contested) charge that she claimed to have attained a state of grace that rendered her incapable of sin. But Joan seems to have stepped back from the brink. Earlier, on February 24, Joan had been interrogated along similar lines when she was "asked if she knew whether she were in the grace of God, [to which] she answered: 'If I am not, may God put me there; if I am, may He keep me there.'" The notary, Boisguillaume, testified at the rehabilitation trial that this perfectly orthodox answer "stupefied" her judges.

In the end, the main charge against Joan was that she defied the Church Militant. It was on this point that she received her "charitable admonition" on the last day of her trial of condemnation, May 23, when her judges compared her to a rebellious knight who refused to obey his king. Although the Church Militant had been explained to her on March 17 as consisting of the ecclesiastical hierarchy and Christian community here on earth, Joan seems to have persisted in associating it exclusively with the tribunal that was assembled before her. According to Friar Isambart de la Pierre, who testified at the rehabilitation:

> When Joan was asked whether she wished to submit herself to our father the Pope, she said that she did, provided that she could be led and taken to him, but that she did not wish to submit herself to those there present—that is to say, to the Bishop of Beauvais [Cauchon]—since they were her mortal enemies. And when I pleaded with her to submit to the General Council then assembled [at Basle], at which were many prelates and doctors of the French king's party, Joan said, on hearing this, that she submitted to the Council. Then the Bishop of Beauvais interrupted me violently, saying: "Be

quiet, in the devil's name!" On hearing this, Master Guillaume Manchon, who was writing the proceedings, asked the Bishop whether he should record her submission. The Bishop answered no, that it was not necessary. And Joan said to him: "Oh, you write down everything that is against me all right, but you will not record anything in my favor." And I do not believe that remark was written down either, though it aroused a great uproar in the court.

Joan repeated her appeal to the pope on the day of her abjuration, May 24, but "she was told that this did not suffice, for it was not possible to send to the Holy Father, being so far away, and that the ordinaries were each one judge in his own diocese, and that therefore she must submit to our Mother, Holy Church." In actual fact, participants in any Church trial, especially one as important as this was, had the right of appeal to Rome, which was unfairly denied to Joan.

As the foregoing exchange witnessed by Isambart de la Pierre proves, Joan clearly recognized that a political undercurrent ran through her whole trial, despite the mirage of its ecclesiastical purpose. At the same time, however, she was no ordinary political prisoner. Although Joan's family had been ennobled by Charles VII in December 1429, it was in no position to ransom her back from the English, nor was the king eager to do this, a sad fact that Joan herself must have realized during her long months in prison. Even if her ransom could have been paid, it does not seem that the English would have been willing to let her go, for she represented a much graver threat than a mere soldier of war. Joan professed to accord Charles and the French cause the favor of God, and it was this, above all else, that had to be destroyed through a trumped-up charge of heresy. This much was made clear in Guillaume Erard's sermon at Joan's abjuration, when, according to Jean Massieu's testimony at the rehabilitation, he called Charles a "heretic and schismatic" because he adhered "to the words and deeds of a woman, vain and defamed and of all dishonor full." This neatly summed up the whole purpose of Joan's trial. In reply, Joan defended Charles, despite his abandonment of her. "He is," she swore, "the noblest Christian of all the Christians, and who better loves the faith and the Church, and is not such as you say." So effective was this riposte that Erard ordered Massieu to, "Make her be silent." If Joan was too political a prisoner to be heretical, she was also, in the challenge she posed to the English, too spiritual an enemy to be only political.

There has been some attempt in recent years among French scholars to rehabilitate Cauchon; according to Régine Pernoud, her colleagues now portray him "as a sincere and educated cleric with high if somewhat rigid professional standards, for whom Joan the Maid and her supporters embodied everything from which he wished to save his country." This position seems to owe its ultimate inspiration to George Bernard Shaw, who sympathetically reevaluated the bishop in his 1923 play, *Saint Joan*. For Shaw, Cauchon had been unfairly demonized, first by the rehabilitation trial of the 1450s, and then by more modern historians, such as Andrew Lang, whose rabidly pro-Joan biography, *The Maid of France*, had appeared in 1908. Instead, Shaw depicts Cauchon in his play as a conscientious, well-meaning ecclesiastic determined to give Joan as fair a trial as he can within the limits of medieval jurisprudence. Joan, according to Shaw, really was a heretic who posed a very real threat to the Church as a kind of proto-Protestant seeking to replace the pope at Rome with "Pope Joan." Moreover, Shaw denies that there was any political motivation to Joan's trial, stating in his lengthy preface to the play that "it is unreasonable to suppose that the political bias of a body of Frenchmen like the assessors would on this point have run strongly in favor of the English foreigners . . . against a Frenchwoman who had vanquished them."

This is an astoundingly naive view, and Shaw's usually perceptive and even-handed judgment on display in the preface seems to desert him here. Those seeking to exonerate Cauchon as a man who acted in good faith throughout Joan's trial are engaged in a doomed exercise. Apologetics on behalf of the bishop can go too far. They completely ignore the fact that throughout his career—before, during, and after Joan's trial—Cauchon was a staunch adherent of the English and Burgundian cause. He played a crucial role, for example, in the Cabochian revolt of 1413 that attacked the dauphin and his partisans, for which he was subsequently banished from the French capital by the Armagnac party. He also was a creature of the University of Paris, which had its own reasons for opposing Joan and Charles—as part of its effort to expand its role in French government and Church affairs. The only justification for a forgiving view of Cauchon seems to be the fact that he secured Joan's abjuration, and consequently her temporary escape from the stake, on May 24, for which he apparently endured some abuse from the Englishmen present. But this is counterbalanced, and indeed overwhelmed, by contradictory testimony, most of which comes from the rehabilitation trial which Shaw dismissed as politically "corrupt." Admittedly, it was in Charles' interests to discredit Cauchon, but the bias of the rehabilitation was of no greater degree than that of the original trial of condemnation, and its evidence should not be discarded altogether.

We have already seen that the few assessors who were sympathetic to Joan, such as Isambart de la Pierre, testified to Cauchon's attempted efforts to manipulate the trial record, and this was confirmed by the testimony of the notary, Guillaume Manchon, who, to his credit, refused to go along with Cauchon's designs. De la Pierre also reported that the English "threatened me horribly that if I did not keep quiet, they would throw me in the Seine." According to another witness, Friar Guillaume Duval, this threat was uttered by the earl of Warwick. Nor did Cauchon himself refrain from outbursts of intimidation. Guillaume Manchon stated that when the bishop learned that Jean de la Fontaine, who presided over the trial in Cauchon's absence, as well as Isambart de la Pierre and Martin Ladvenu, were advising Joan in public and privately in prison to submit to the pope and council, he "stormed most angrily against Jean Lemaître, the Inquisitor's vicar, and threatened to do them a mischief." When he got wind of this, a frightened La Fontaine fled the city, while the others were protected only by the good graces of Lemaître, who warned Cauchon that he would no longer take part in the trial "if any mischief were done to them." Even so, Cauchon did manage to have another Rouen cleric, Nicolas de Houppeville, arrested and thrown into prison for expressing opposition to the trial.

The abjuration, in which Cauchon supposedly demonstrated his clemency, is cloaked in confusion and mystery. Witnesses present at the event who later testified at the rehabilitation, such as Jean Massieu, noted that the letter of abjuration that Joan signed was a very general and brief denial of her "errors," and that the entire schedule was only six to eight lines long; but the abjuration recorded in the official trial record consists of forty-four lines (in the Latin translation). Another puzzling detail is that, according to another witness, Aimond de Macy, it was an Englishman, Laurence Calot, secretary to King Henry VI, who handed Joan her cedula of abjuration and helped her sign it, despite the fact that the other Englishmen present were reported to be indignant at Joan's escape from the fire. It would not be surprising if the whole thing was stage managed by Cauchon in order to induce Joan to relapse, which could then make for a much stronger case for condemnation and execution (and a correspond-ingly lesser one for Joan's martyrdom). Especially suspicious is an exchange that was reported by Jean Favé to have occurred between the earl of Warwick and one of the assessors just after Cauchon had finished reading Joan's sentence: "When the earl of Warwick complained to the bishop and to the doctors, saying that it would go badly for the king [of England] because Joan would escape them, one among them answered: 'My lord, do not worry; we will catch her again.'"

The real proof of Cauchon's good intentions should be found in what he did with Joan after her abjuration. She was sentenced to "perpetual imprisonment," but according to Guillaume Manchon, Joan expected to spend it in a Church prison guarded by women instead of obnoxious English jailers. This was, after all, only proper protocol for an inquisitorial trial. When one of the assessors, Nicolas Loiseleur, commended Joan for having "saved your soul," she replied, "Well, as to that, some of you men of the Church, take me into your prison so that I be no longer in the hands of these Englishmen." (Manchon also testified that Loiseleur had earlier acted as Cauchon's spy, by pretending to befriend Joan in her cell and offering to hear her confession.) Instead, Cauchon cruelly ordered her guards, "Take her back to where you found her," or in other words, back to her secular jail in the castle of Rouen. As Joan was now expected to wear a woman's dress as a symbol of her repentance, Cauchon must have known that this could have but one outcome. It was an open invitation to rape to Joan's uncouth English jailers, and it was bound to trigger her resumption of men's clothes which would signify, in her judges' minds, her relapse. That this is indeed what happened is testified by Isambart de la Pierre, who was present at the trial for relapse on May 28:

> After her renunciation and abjuration, when she had put on male clothes again, she excused herself for having done so in the presence of myself and several others. She said and publicly affirmed that when she put on women's clothes the English had done her great wrongs and violence in her prison. And indeed I saw her weeping, with her face running with tears, and so outraged and disfigured that I felt pity and compassion for her.
>
> When she was labeled an obstinate and relapsed heretic, she publicly answered before the whole court: "If you, lords of the Church, had taken me and kept me in your own prison, perhaps things would not be like this with me."
>
> After the final conclusion of that session and of the suit, the lord Bishop of Beauvais said to the English: "Farewell, be of good cheer. It is done."

Another Dominican, Martin Ladvenu, who was also with Joan in her last days, gave very similar testimony. At the rehabilitation, he accused Cauchon of "two signs of partiality." One was that the bishop kept her in a secular prison "in the hands of her mortal enemies" where she was "tormented and ill-treated," even though Cauchon "could easily have had her kept and guarded in an ecclesiastical prison." The latter course, in fact, was advised by the other assessors, "but the bishop answered that he would not do that for fear of displeasing the English." The other sign of partiality was that, after Joan's relapse, Cauchon was heard by Ladvenu to remark loudly and laughingly to the earl of Warwick: "Farewell, farewell, it is done. Be of good cheer!" This is almost word for word what De la Pierre reported. Ladvenu likewise testified that Joan had told him that, after her abjuration, "she was violently tormented, worried, beaten, and ill-treated in her prison" and "that this was the reason why she had resumed male clothing." Finally, Joan is alleged by Ladvenu to have confronted Cauchon with his treachery: "Alas, it is through your fault that I am to die. For if you had had me kept in a Church prison, I should not be in this plight." Joan, no less than a modern reader of the evidence 600 years later, clearly recognized that Cauchon had desired her death from the very beginning.

And what of Joan herself? What was in her mind toward the end? There are a number of possible explanations for why Joan took the fatal step of renouncing her abjuration, which she must have known could only end in her death by burning at the stake. (Her judges were very explicit on this point in their "charitable admonition.") First, we should ask why Joan abjured at all? On May 23, the day before her abjuration, she famously boasted to her judges after having been read her charitable admonition: "And if I were to be condemned and saw the fire lit and the wood prepared and the executioner who was to burn me ready to cast me into the fire, still in the fire would I not say anything other than I have said. And I will maintain what I have said until death." But it may be, when it came down to it, that Joan did abjure "through fear of the fire," as she stated at her relapse. In addition, she may have sincerely believed that she was not retracting the substance of her abjuration, such as she had originally made it in its abstract form and under confused circumstances. When confronted at her trial for relapse with the fact that she had promised to renounce her voices, "she answered that she never intended to have denied her apparitions, that is that they were Saint Catherine and Saint Margaret. And what she said, she said for fear of the fire. And if she recanted, it was untrue." She also claimed "that she had never intended to take an oath not to take man's dress again." Nonetheless, she declared herself willing to put a woman's dress back on "if the judges desire it," but as "for the rest, she knows no more."

There is always the possibility that Joan was suicidal. The assessors explored this avenue during the trial of condemnation, and in particular, they interrogated her concerning her attempted escape from John of Luxembourg's castle at Beaurevoir, where she was held between June and November 1430. As part of this escape attempt, which probably took place sometime in November, Joan leaped from a window in the castle that was sixty to seventy feet from the ground. Incredibly, she survived the leap, and, after being knocked unconscious, she recovered in a few days. On March 14, the assessors inquired as to "the reason she leaped from the tower of Beaurevoir." Joan gave two explanations: one being that she wished to go to the aid of the besieged city of Compiègne, which was being hard pressed by Burgundian forces; the other, to avoid being handed over to the English, which she had also heard was about to happen. In both cases, she declared that "she would rather die" than live to see the worst that would befall, either the "destruction of good people" at Compiègne, or that she "be in the hands of her enemies, the English."

Granted, Joan was desperate about her current situation, but not necessarily suicidal. She tried to escape once before, at her prison at Beaulieu-lès-Fontaines by slipping "between two pieces of wood," but on this occasion without endangering her life. Since Joan could not expect to be ransomed by her family or friends, she was willing to try any means of escape, and she forthrightly told her judges on March 14 that "I have never been a prisoner in any place but I would try to escape from it." When asked point blank if "when she leaped, she expected to kill herself, she answered no. But in leaping she recommended herself to God, and believed that by means of this leap she could escape and avoid being handed over to the English." Later that same afternoon, she elaborated on her leap from the tower of Beaurevoir: "I did not do it out of despair, but in the hope of saving my life and of going to the help of a number of good people who were in need." The leap was, in fact, against the advice of Joan's voices, and since "she believes that she did wrong in making the leap," she confessed herself and asked pardon of Saint Catherine and our Lord for what she had done. Her penance, she said, was "the hurt she received in falling." (From the Church's point of view, this confession and penance had no merit, since it had not been made to a priest.) Joan here reveals her ever pragmatic side: She wished to evade the English because they inevitably would treat her harshly, and this indicates that, ultimately, she was trying to prolong her life, not prematurely end it. (The fact that she abjured for "fear of the fire" also confirms this.) Her testimony convinced George Bernard Shaw to absolve her of suicidal tendencies, but not the University of Paris, who, in response to Article 8 of the accusation, declared that Joan's leap from the tower of Beaurevoir "was cowardice tending to despair and to suicide." But then, the learned clerks were not psychologists, nor by any means unbiased observers.

It is undeniable, however, that Joan made a conscious choice to relapse. When her judges asked her why she had resumed a man's dress and if anyone had induced her to do so, "she said [that she did it] of her own will. And that nobody had forced her to do so." This was in spite of the evidence given at the rehabilitation by Isambart de la Pierre and Martin Ladvenu that Joan had been practically forced to reassume male clothes in order to preserve her chastity. Even more extenuating circumstances were reported by the usher, Jean Massieu, who testified that on Sunday, May 27, Joan asked her jailers to have her chains removed "in order to fulfill a physical need," but that one of the English guards pulled off her woman's clothes and gave her back her old male ones, which included a tunic, cape, and short robe. Since they refused to give her anything else to wear, Joan "was compelled to go out . . . and to wear those clothes," in spite of her pleas to the guards that this was forbidden her. Either we must believe that the record of the relapse was tampered with and Joan's true answers not recorded, or that she finally reconciled herself to her death. When she was asked if she had heard her voices since her abjuration on the 24th, she replied: "God has expressed through St. Catherine and St. Margaret His great sorrow at the strong treason to which I consented in abjuring and making a revocation to save my life, and said that I was damning myself to save my life." At this point, the scribe noted in the margin, "A deadly reply," which Joan must have known she was making.

One popular theory for why Joan decided to relapse is that she could no longer bear to be in prison, especially under the conditions she had endured throughout the trial, which were now to last to the end of her days. At her trial for relapse, she declared to her judges: "I took it [men's clothes] again because it was more lawful and convenient than to have women's clothes because I am with men; I began to wear them again because what was promised me was not observed, to wit that I should go to mass and receive the body of Christ and be freed from these irons. . . . I would rather die than stay in these irons; but if it is permitted for me to go to mass, and if I could be freed of these irons, and if I could be put in a decent prison and if I could have a woman to help me, I would be good and do what the Church wishes." This testimony, like that mentioned above, is at odds with a free-will choice to abandon female dress, and it must have embarrassed Cauchon. But by now, Joan must have realized that as a political prisoner, she had little hope of her prison sentence being commuted, as was usual in such cases before a true tribunal of the Inquisition. She had only to think of the sad example of Duke Charles of Orléans, who had been a prisoner in England since his capture at Agincourt in 1415 and was to remain so until 1440. (His release apparently had been one of Joan's four "missions" stated at her examination at Poitiers in 1429.) As part of his characterization of Joan as a down-to-earth ingenue, George Bernard Shaw makes her supposed dread of life in prison the primary reason for her relapse. In one of his more fanciful departures from the trial record, Shaw has Joan declare to the assessors that she cannot live without hearing "the wind in the trees, the larks in the sunshine, the young lambs crying through the healthy frost, and the blessed blessed church bells that send my angel voices floating to me on the wind." But there is no evidence, and indeed it seems unlikely, that Joan ever expected to be set free once she abjured, which Shaw has his character naively believe as the setup to her relapsed outburst. The real Joan's only expectation seems to have been to enjoy slightly more lenient conditions in a Church prison.

I am convinced that there is something more going on here than simply Joan's disappointment at the hard manner in which Cauchon carried out her abjuration sentence. Joan herself gives us a clue as to what this something was in some crucial testimony she gave on March 14. In the first part of her statement, she elaborates on the famously defiant declaration she had made to Cauchon on February 24, that he "take good heed of what you do, for in truth I am sent from God and you are putting yourself in great peril"; now she interprets the "great peril" as the possibility that she will be rescued through "some disturbance" at her prison. Immediately thereafter, Joan makes the following revelation to the court:

> And furthermore, the voices have told her that she would be delivered by a great victory. And later, her voices said to her: "Take it all cheerfully. Do not despair on account of your martyrdom, for in the end you will come to the Kingdom of Heaven." This her voices told her simply and definitely, without faltering. And her martyrdom she called the pain and suffering that she was undergoing in prison; and she does not know whether she will suffer still more, but puts all her faith in Our Lord.

Once again, Joan interprets her voices' message prosaically (at least for the benefit of the court), but in the back of her mind, could she not have read a more profound meaning that related to her coming death at the stake, which perhaps she foresaw? She would not have been the first saint to choose sacrificial martyrdom as a way out of an impossible political situation. Ironically, it was an Englishman, Thomas à Becket, who provided the model for Joan: On December 29, 1170, he preferred to remain at the altar celebrating mass in Canterbury Cathedral when confronted by four murderous knights who believed themselves to have been sent by King Henry II to "rid me of this turbulent priest." Like Becket, Joan may have realized that her greatest weapon, and the surest way to triumph over her enemies, was to die an heroic death that would in the future provide a rallying point for her cause and which was far preferable to a long, slow decline into oblivion. (Coincidentally, Isambart de la Pierre quoted Becket in support of his decision to urge Joan to appeal to "the Pope and the General Council.") That this is what Joan ultimately understood as her martyrdom is indicated by the fact that, on the last day of her life, according to almost all the witnesses present, she called several times the name of "Jesus!" For what better model of selfless sacrifice is there than Christ? If this is indeed what Joan intended by her relapse, and I believe that it is, then she proved that, even to the very end, she had not lost her prescient power to see the "peril" that her judges would suffer at the hands of posterity.

The Movies

The earliest films on Joan of Arc, which are largely a series of staged tableaus depicting the main events of her life, focus primarily on her role as the national savior of France. Any suggestion of her religious status as a saint, which only began to be recognized by the Church at her beatification in 1909, is relegated to a concluding afterthought, as Joan is burning at the stake. This tradition was continued by the first Hollywood film on the subject, Paramount's *Joan the Woman* (1917), directed by Cecil B. DeMille. Considering the character of DeMille's subsequent work, it should come as no surprise that the film is called "the first cinematic spectacle about Joan." DeMille himself wrote in his autobiography that *Joan the Woman* began the "DeMille formula for the historical pictures." However, the film is hardly concerned with history.

Jeanie Macpherson's screenplay for *Joan the Woman* is based on the Friedrich Schiller play from 1801, *Die Jungfrau von Orléans* (*The Maid of Orléans*), which preposterously has Joan fall in love with an English soldier, Lionel (changed in the film to Eric Trent). But at least DeMille's epic makes Joan die correctly, at the stake, instead of on the battlefield, as in Schiller's play. Since the film was intended as a propaganda piece to induce America to enter World War I, the love angle was essential as a means to elide the rivalry between two countries who were now brothers in arms. To further emphasize the point, *Joan the Woman* begins and ends with scenes of Eric Trent in his modern reincarnation as an English tommy in the trenches, who is inspired by Joan's example to go on a suicide bombing mission. In his autobiography, DeMille conceded that this framing device was "the greatest dramatic fault" of his film.

Although a brief scene dramatizes her voices, *Joan the Woman*, as the title implies, is almost entirely concerned with Joan as a romantic, rather than religious, figure. The opening title card of the movie proclaims that it is "founded on the life of Joan of Arc, the girl patriot, who fought with men, was loved by men, and killed by men—yet withal retained the heart of a woman." One can say with confidence that this was diametrically opposed to how Joan herself interpreted her life, and it is doubly ironic given that she adopted male dress in order to remain a virgin. Joan's transvestitism is discreetly overlooked by the film, even to the point of dressing up her armor with a skirt. But oddly enough, the stocky, heavy-set features of Geraldine Farrar, the opera diva whom DeMille recruited to star in his film, make for a distinctly masculine, unattractive Joan. When the critic, Alexander Woollcott, objected to Farrar's casting, an oblivious DeMille found the criticism "surprising." The director was also blindsided by the negative reaction to his demonization of churchmen in the movie, especially of Pierre Cauchon, who functions as the film's consummate villain. Even though I believe that Cauchon was guilty of conspiring to kill Joan, DeMille's treatment of him is heavyhanded in the extreme. Without any historical foundation whatsoever, Cauchon is portrayed as a poisoner, attempting to murder Charles VII, and, in another over-the-top scene, he receives the inspiration to burn Joan by accidentally setting fire to a statute of the Virgin. Before her execution, white-robed Klansmen-looka-likes torture Joan as Cauchon gleefully looks on. No wonder that this characterization "caused flutterings of resentment in some religious circles," as DeMille ruefully admits in his autobiography.

One of the last silent films made about Joan of Arc happens to be, in the opinion of many, the best and most spiritual depiction of the saint. *La Passion de Jeanne d'Arc* (*The Passion of Joan of Arc*), directed by the Danish filmmaker, Carl Theodor Dreyer, and released by the Société Général des Films in 1928, is enshrined as a classic of world cinema, often cited by critics as one of the greatest films of all time, and fully the equal of Ingmar Bergman's *The Seventh Seal* or Sergei Eisenstein's *Alexander Nevsky*. Indeed, Dreyer's masterpiece towers over any other film portrayal of Joan, dominating the genre to an even more oppressive degree than *The Adventures of Robin Hood* does for its realm. Although the film is justly celebrated for its pioneering and eclectic cinematic techniques, the *Passion* is also, I believe, the most historically true portrait of Joan to date in the cinema.

How did Dreyer achieve such a feat? Like Eisenstein, Dreyer had his method, which he characterized as "abstraction." As he explained in a famous essay he wrote in 1955 on the "craft" of filmmaking:

> In order not to be misunderstood, I must at once define abstraction as something that demands of the artist to abstract himself from reality in order to strengthen the spiritual content of his work. More concisely: the artist must describe inner, not outer, life. The capacity to abstract is essential to all artistic creation. Abstraction allows the director to get outside the fence with which naturalism has surrounded his medium. It allows his films to be not merely visual, but spiritual. The director must share his own artistic and spiritual experiences with the audience. Abstraction will give him a chance of doing it, of replacing objective reality with his own subjective interpretation.

Even though Dreyer clearly intended that his theory receive wide circulation, abstraction remained his own personal vision, unique to his films. It is not easy, in fact, to determine from the above definition precisely what Dreyer meant by abstraction. The best sense one can make of it is that the director intended to strip away all the accretions of props, makeup, cos-

tumes, and all the other paraphernalia that traditionally go into an historical costume drama. In this way, the audience is forced to focus on the
actors' facial expressions and gestures, which can reveal the real, secret
history behind the facade.

Abstraction is equated in Dreyer's mind with simplification, as he
writes further in the same essay:

> The closest road at hand is the road of simplification. Every creative artist is
> confronted by the same task. He must be inspired by reality, then move
> away from it in order to give his work the form provoked by his inspiration.
> The director must be free to transform reality so that it becomes consistent
> with the inspired, simplified image left in his mind. Reality must obey the
> director's aesthetic sense. This abstraction through simplification, so that a
> purified form emerges in a kind of timeless, psychological realism, can be
> practiced by the director in a modest way in the actual rooms of his films.
> . . . The director can give his rooms a soul through simplification, by remov-
> ing all that is superfluous, by making a few significant articles and objects
> psychological witnesses of the inmate's personality.

There is the famous story, for example, of how Dreyer filled the set of
Ordet, or *The Word* (1954), with all the implements of a country kitchen and
then personally went around removing the props one by one until he had
achieved the simplicity he wanted. Dreyer, therefore, aimed for a kind of
"pure cinema," one in which, especially in the age before sound, the visual
texture was all important.

Abstraction and simplification were achieved in the *Passion* first by
streamlining the storyline. Instead of telling the whole story of Joan's
career, Dreyer focuses only on her trial and execution in 1431. This is further compressed into the space of a single day (although the marking of
time in the film is extremely ambiguous), so that the five months of Joan's
interrogation, abjuration, and execution at Rouen take place within almost
one fluid scene. The action shifts seamlessly among just five sets: the court
of Rouen Castle, where Joan's initial interrogation occurs; Joan's cell,
where she suffers further interrogation and persecution from spies and jailers; the torture chamber, where her judges unsuccessfully try to persuade
her to recant; the cemetery, where Joan abjures under threat of imminent
death; and finally, the castle courtyard, where Joan is burned at the stake.
(Historically, the last scene was staged in Rouen's marketplace.) Note that
although the time line is compressed, it faithfully reproduces the sequence
of events at Joan's trial. The realistic sets built at Billancourt Studios and
at a site in Clamart, France, allowed the cast to faithfully recreate, and
almost relive, Joan's original experience. Indeed, the shooting of the film

lasted five months, from May to October 1927, exactly the same length of time as it took for Joan's actual trial.

Another reason why the *Passion* succeeds as an historical film is that Dreyer, despite his protestations on simplification, made elaborate preparations and conducted extensive research into Joan's trial before filming. According to one of Dreyer's filmographers, Ebbe Neergaard, the director spent eight months preparing the script, beginning in October 1926, and his set designers, Jean Hugo and Herman Warm, worked from fifteenth-century illuminated manuscripts housed in the Bibliothèque Nationale. They constructed for him a monumental set at Clamart, just south of Paris, which consisted of:

> a great septagonal or octagonal castle with a very tall tower in each of the corners and a high wall running between the towers. Inside there were little houses built very simply, but with crooked angles and windows set out of line, like those in the miniatures. In the center of the courtyard, opposite the drawbridge, was the church or chapel, and at the side [was] the entrance to the churchyard, where the burning took place. The walls consisted of a cement shell ten centimeters thick, enough to carry the weight of the actors and technicians during the shooting. The whole construction was painted pink to give it a grey effect against the sky, which stood out white in the film.

New technologies such as panchromatic film stock, which can record different shades of grey, and "nitraphoto" floodlights, which provide more even, brighter lighting than carbon arc lamps, allowed cinematographer, Rudolph Maté, to give the film's striking images, despite being shot in black and white, an "etched relief" and "high contrast" that have been compared by admiring critics to a Hieronymus Bosch painting, a late Gothic view of the world come to life.

Nevertheless, Dreyer never allowed his authentic props, sets, or costumes to overwhelm the film. Instead, their purpose seems to have been to disappear into the background, to become such a natural and accepted part of the film frame that viewers could then focus on what was important: the struggle for Joan's soul. As Dreyer wrote in 1929 shortly after the release of the film:

> A thorough study of the documents from the rehabilitation process was necessary; I did not study the clothes of the time, and things like that. The year of the event seemed as inessential to me as its distance from the present. I wanted to interpret a hymn to the triumph of the soul over life. What streams out to the possibly moved spectator in strange close-ups is not acci-

dentally chosen. All these pictures express the character of the person they show and the spirit of that time. In order to give the truth, I dispensed with "beautification." My actors were not allowed to touch make-up and powder puffs. I also broke with the traditions of constructing a set. Right from the beginning of shooting, I let the scene architects build all the sets and make all the other preparations, and from the first to the last scene everything was shot in the right order. Rudolf Maté, who manned the camera, understood the demands of psychological drama in the close-ups and he gave me what I wanted, my feeling and my thought: realized mysticism.

Unlike the makers of so many Hollywood spectacles, Dreyer recognized that it was not the period details that mattered. In fact, authentic detail was occasionally allowed to lapse, as when Warwick and his soldiers are shown wearing World War I-style helmets, or when one of the priests at Joan's preexecution mass is depicted wearing glasses. Rather, it was the essence of Joan's historical significance, and the meaning of her ultimate sacrifice, that Dreyer sought to convey.

Dreyer was greatly aided in this task by the words of Joan herself, as these were recorded at her trial. Originally, the film was to be based on two novels by Joseph Delteil, but Dreyer wisely scrapped fiction for the real thing: the actual transcript of Joan's trial, as edited by Pierre Champion. (In the film credits, Delteil, who had written a tentative screenplay that was never used, is listed with the director as coauthor, while Champion is credited as historical consultant.) The *Passion* was also slated at first to be a talking picture, but Dreyer had to abandon the idea because film studios in Europe were not yet equipped for sound. Some critics, such as Tom Milne and David Bordwell, actually regard the film's silence as a blessing, since it plays into Dreyer's stated purpose of simplification by forcing the audience—especially at the not-infrequent moments when actors speak but no title cards are provided—to abstract meaning from faces and gestures alone. Despite its lack of sound, it is the dialogue, almost always lifted straight out of the trial transcript, that dictates the ebb and flow of the film. As Dreyer reported to Michael Delahaye in an interview conducted for the film magazine, *Cahiers du Cinéma*, in 1965:

> For me, it was before all else the technique of the official report that governed. There was, to start with, this trial, with its ways, its own technique, and that technique is what I tried to transpose to the film. There were the questions, there were the answers—very short, very crisp. There was, therefore, no other solution than to place close-ups behind these replies. Each question, each answer, quite naturally called for a close-up. It was the only possibility. All of that stemmed from the technique of the official report. In

A poster for the English language version of *La Passion de Jeanne d'Arc*, which was
re-released by Gaumont with the addition of sound by Lo Duca in 1952.

addition, the result of the close-ups was that the spectator was shocked as
Joan was, receiving the questions, tortured by them. And, in fact, it was my
intention to get this result.

An opening shot of an invisible hand turning over the leaves of a manuscript copy of the trial record sets up an authentic, documentary-like tone
for the rest of the film. Meanwhile, the title card reads: "At the
Bibliothèque Nationale in Paris it is possible to see one of the most famous
documents in the history of the world—the official record of the trial of
Joan of Arc." This firmly establishes the film's factual credentials. Yet
Dreyer goes on to transcend historical docudrama by having his actors
give visual expression to the stark words up on the screen. The result—a

strange hybrid of a silent and a talkie—is a film that impresses as both historically true and soulfully timeless.

This brings us to Dreyer's cinematic technique, primarily his use of close-ups, that contribute to the *Passion*'s unique status as a movie admired as much for its "film poetry" as for its historical veracity. For Dreyer, it was above all the human face and its endless possibilities of expression that served as his artifact, his source "document" of choice in which to excavate all the historical meanings of his film. As he wrote in 1955:

> Nothing in the world can be compared to the human face. It is a land one can never tire of exploring. There is no greater experience in a studio than to witness the expression of a sensitive face under the mysterious power of inspiration. To see it animated from inside, and turning into poetry.

Even though Dreyer considered film to be a subjective art medium, the *Passion* revolves around the historical record of Joan's trial, so that the actors' faces are made to reflect the internal dynamics of the transcript. The physical deformities on the faces of many judges—warts on the face of Cauchon, folds of fat on the face of the promoter, Jean d'Estivet, and wisps of hair like devil's horns on the head of the vice-inquisitor, Jean Lemaître—all bespeak of a tribunal whose justice is distorted, complacent, and perverted for evil ends, as indeed the evidence, especially from the rehabilitation, can be cited in support.

The famous scene of the judges conferring to ask one of their entrapping questions, passing off the loaded interrogatory from one to another as the camera follows their conniving faces, drives home the point that Joan faced a conspiracy of judges, whose number and learning were designed to overawe and break her down, as they eventually did. Dreyer also demonstrates a grasp of the central historical fact behind Joan's trial, which was that it was primarily political, rather than religious, in motivation. The "iron mask" worn by the earl of Warwick (played by an unknown Russian café proprietor), who is often shown conferring with one of the judges, Nicolas Loiseleur, illustrates the English determination to manipulate the trial behind the scenes in order to obtain the desired outcome. At the same time, the clear-complexioned faces of Nicolas de Houppeville and Jean Massieu (the latter played by the 25-year-old avant-garde artist, Antonin Artaud) communicate these judges' more equanimous and sympathetic stance toward the accused.

Above all, it is the face of the French actress who plays Joan, Renée or Maria Falconetti (her middle name happened to be Jeanne), that carries the film. Her tear-stained, chapped, bewildered, suffering, beatific face registers in minute detail the emotionally complex progress of Joan's trial.

As a result, it is her visage, more than that of any other actress who has played Joan throughout cinematic history, that comes to mind as embodying the real Joan, at least for those who have seen the film. In his interview with Delahaye, Dreyer recalls how he stumbled upon this remarkable woman and the defining moment when he realized that she alone was right for the part:

> I went to see her [Falconetti] one afternoon and we spoke together for an hour or two. I had seen her at the theater. A little boulevard theater whose name I have forgotten. She was playing there in a light, modern comedy and she was very elegant in it, a bit giddy, but charming. She didn't conquer me at once and I didn't have confidence in her immediately. I simply asked her if I could come to see her the next day. And during that visit, we talked. That is when I sensed that there was something in her to which one could make an appeal. Something that she could give; something, therefore, that I could take.
>
> For behind the make-up, the pose, behind that modern and ravishing appearance, there was something. There was a soul behind that facade. If I could see her remove the facade it would suffice me. So I told her that I would very much like, starting the next day, to do a screen test with her. "But without make-up," I added, "with your face completely naked."
>
> She came, therefore, the next day ready and willing. She had taken off her make-up, we made the tests, and I found on her face exactly what I had been seeking for Joan of Arc: a rustic woman, very sincere, who was also a woman who had suffered. But even so, this discovery did not represent a total surprise to me for, from our first meeting, this woman was very frank and, always, very surprising.

Stories abound that Dreyer, already known for his extremely demanding and uncompromising direction, put the stage actress—who was making her first, and what would end up being her last, screen performance— through a second "martyrdom" in order to achieve her almost painfully emotive performance: making her kneel for long periods of time on stone floors, playing rushes over and over again—as much as seven or eight times—until the precise facial expression was found, and subjecting her to a real bloodletting. During the abjuration scene, Falconetti's real hair was shorn, which required the actress to wear a wig off the set. (The other actors sported real tonsures.) It is even rumored that for some scenes, the director put his star under hypnosis! But in actuality, it seems that Falconetti was a willing collaborator in Dreyer's obsessive perfectionism. Several times, he paid public tribute to her massive contribution, without which the film would never have been possible. During the final days of

Renée Falconetti as Joan, about to face her judges in the torture chamber sequence
from *La Passion de Jeanne d'Arc*. Note the off-kilter, trapezoidal shape of the doorway,
with the door jambs slanting slightly toward each other at the top.

shooting, for example, he brought the actress' real tears to his lips as her
head was being shaved, and in 1964, at the Paris premiere of his last film,
Gertrud, he laid a bouquet of flowers on Falconetti's grave.

In his interview with Delahaye, Dreyer does more concrete homage to
the special relationship he enjoyed with "his Joan":

> With Falconetti, it often happened that, after having worked all afternoon,
> we hadn't succeeded in getting exactly what was required. We said to our-
> selves then: tomorrow we will begin again. And the next day, we would have
> the bad take from the day before projected, we would examine it, we would
> search and we always ended by finding, in that bad take, some little frag-
> ments, some little light that rendered the exact expression, the tonality we
> had been looking for.
>
> It is from there that we would set out again, taking the best and aban-
> doning the remainder. . . .
>
> I therefore took her for the film, we always understood each other very
> well, we constantly worked very well. It has been said that it was I who
> squeezed the lemon.

I have never squeezed the lemon. I never squeezed anything. She always gave freely, with all her heart. For her heart was always committed to what she was doing.

Similarly, Dreyer's filmographer, Ebbe Neergaard, testifies to the interdependence of these two artists, when at times it was Falconetti who had to give expression to what Dreyer could not:

> When Dreyer was about to shoot an important scene with Falconetti, everyone not directly concerned was banished from the set, and absolute silence was demanded. . . . Sometimes he would put screens up round the group so as to be completely undisturbed. When he was describing what he wanted, he would stammer and go red in the face, not from shyness or any hesitation as to what he meant, but simply from eagerness to make his feelings and intentions completely understood. The blotchy red face and the feelings and the disjointed speech were evidence of his unswerving belief that there is only one expression that is right, that can and must be found. But just because it seemed so difficult for him to express himself clearly, the actress was fired to work in with him with all her power. She was, as it were, activated into expressing what Dreyer could not show her, for it was something that could only be expressed in action, not speech, and she alone could do it, so she had to help him. And she realized that this could only be done if she dropped all intellectual inhibitions and let her feelings have free access from her subconscious to her facial expression.

From what we know of her personal life, it should perhaps come as no surprise that this comedienne could inhabit so successfully the role of a tragic heroine. In her memoirs, Hélène Falconetti remembers her mother as plagued throughout her life by hereditary depression and a self-destructive impulse. But if Falconetti somehow identified her personal tragedy with Joan's, she was sadly mistaken. Whatever she may have thought, her life was not imitating art when she committed suicide in Buenos Aires in 1946.

It is possible to dissect the *Passion* frame by frame, as the film historian, David Bordwell, has done, in order to discover the abundant idiosyncracies of Dreyer's camera. There are numerous examples of what Bordwell calls Dreyer's "eccentric" method: lack of depth cues, canted or tilted camera angles, off-center framings, and disjointed editing. In addition, there are some special Dreyer touches: the zooming in and out of an English soldier assaulting Joan, the extreme low angle shots of Cauchon and the other judges (achieved by digging holes for the camera throughout the set), the dizzying whirl of the torture wheel, the upside-down shot of

English soldiers and the crowd entering Rouen Castle, and the rhythmic tracking of maces handed down from a tower to a waiting soldier. These are just as innovative as anything produced by Dreyer's contemporaries, Eisenstein and Riefenstahl, but because they are in service to the director's coherent personal vision internalized throughout the film, rather than to an externally imposed ideology, they do not nearly draw as much attention to themselves as the more self-conscious techniques of the other directors.

There are several possible explanations for Dreyer's persistent violation of film convention. Bordwell has explored the film as expression of the subjective point of view of Joan, either from her spiritual attitude or her actual physical perception. Lately, however, he has opted for seeing the film as embodying a constant struggle between the contradictory impulses of discontinuity and unity, in what he calls "a dialogue of texts," perhaps because Dreyer wished to push to the limit the boundaries of film art.

Almost miraculously, Dreyer has managed to conjure up the illusion of a medieval point of view. Despite the fact that film is a modern invention, when viewing the *Passion*, one gets the strangest feeling that one is intruding upon another world. The off-kilter camera angles, mirroring the off-kilter architecture copied from medieval manuscripts, is perhaps how the movie would have been filmed if this technology had been available to the Middle Ages. It refuses to obey modern conventions of perspective and naturalism that imposed themselves on late medieval art with the dawn of the Renaissance.

Finally, Dreyer exhibits a close empathy with the spiritual yearnings of the real Joan and her interpretation of the significance of her "martyrdom." We have already discussed in the background section how Joan, at the point of her relapse, probably judged that her cause would be better served by her death rather than her life. As she was being consumed by fire at the stake, she was heard to utter the name of Jesus several times, indicating that she intended her sacrifice to be a selfless one that would accomplish for posterity what her continued presence on earth could not. Dreyer seems very much in tune with this last act of Joan's and makes it the centerpiece of his "hymn to the triumph of the soul over life." The message is hammered home repeatedly in the film through indelible images: the cross formed by the shadow of the window on the floor of Joan's cell; her plaiting of a straw "crown of thorns"; her jailers' mock crowning of her with her own handiwork; the skull crawling with worms in the cemetery that is associated with Golgotha; the executioner's sweeping up of the discarded crown that triggers Joan's recantation; the old woman, a kind of Simon the Cyrene figure, who brings Joan a cup of milk as she is led out for execution; and the birds flying away from the church dome and the baby suckling at its mother's breast as Joan dies. These last images could perhaps symbolize, respectively, the Holy Ghost and "Jesus as Mother." According to a rehabilitation witness, Isambart de la Pierre, an Englishman, formerly an inveterate enemy of Joan's, claimed to see "a white dove flying from the direction of France at the moment when she was giving up the ghost."

The scenes of Joan's death are made all the more poignant when some of the judges and English soldiers—who now gaze up instead of down at their victim—join in mourning the passing of so indomitable a spirit. (This also has historical foundation, according to evidence given at the rehabilitation.) Additionally, it completes the emotional progress of the film, since the same judges who weep at her decision to accept her death, such as Jean d'Estivet, are also the ones who had earlier been her bitterest adversaries. As David Bordwell writes, "Dreyer will not withhold humanity even from these corrupt men: they are at least capable of recognizing the grace they lack." Dreyer then distills the meaning of his film into the "final interrogation" between Joan and Jean Massieu (erroneously identified in the screenplay as Martin Ladvenu):

Massieu: How can you still believe that you are sent by God?
Joan: His ways are not our ways! . . . Yes, I am His child!
Massieu: And the great victory?
Joan: My martyrdom.
Massieu: And your deliverence?
Joan: Death!

Dreyer is also right to devote an extended scene to Joan's last communion (amplified here by the unhistorical addition of choirboys), since this symbolizes Joan's ultimate vindication and exoneration from heresy. While Joan's picking up of the rope dropped by the executioner and handing it to him to finish binding her to the stake may be, in Bordwell's phrase, "an abstract sign of utter resignation," it also serves as a touching symbol of Joan's forgiveness of her enemies. The last scenes are of the English army—triggered by a man who defiantly shouts at Warwick, "You have burnt a saint!"—mercilessly driving the crowd out of Rouen, intercut with images of Joan's lifeless body being reduced to a flaming heap of ashes. Although this may be a rather bleak message that God has abandoned His people and His champion to slaughter and death, it also foreshadows a resistance to oppression—largely inspired by Joan's example —that eventually was to result in France's liberation at the end of the Hundred Years War in 1453. Immediately after the final shot, which shows the stake foregrounded against a cross hovering in the distance, a title card proclaims that Joan "has become the incarnation of imperishable France." In Bordwell's analysis, the theme of "spiritual deliverance" has trumped "political repression," and the end result, like the history of these times itself, "is a complex mixture of despair and affirmation."

After the *Passion*, it is almost pointless to talk of any other Joan of Arc film. Even so, there exists yet another worthy French silent feature about Joan, *La Merveilleuse Vie de Jeanne d'Arc* (*The Marvelous Life of Joan of Arc*), which was directed by Marco de Gastyne and was released by Natan Productions in the same year, 1928, as Dreyer's *Passion*. Although Dreyer's film was to go on to become more famous and celebrated, it was the *Merveilleuse Vie* that did better at the box office. This is perhaps because Gastyne was a more conventional film director (he had formerly been an academic painter and set designer) who fulfilled national expectations of Joan's iconography; by contrast, the *Passion*, with its unorthodox closeups, seems to have wrongfooted French reviewers. They complained that the film was "too true for sensitive viewers" and was "nearly physically tortuous for the spectator." One critic even opined that "Joan suffers, but the spectator suffers no less." This was no accident, for Dreyer confessed to *Avant-Scène Cinéma* that, "Such was the role of the close-ups: to move the viewers so that they would feel in their own flesh the suffering endured by Joan."

The *Merveilleuse Vie* is a different film altogether from the *Passion*, since it aims to tell the whole story of Joan's career, from her first hearing of voices at Domrémy until her death. Although some scenes have a static quality since they are derived from readily recognizable artistic images of Joan, the battle scenes, in particular, are staged with an energy and realism that remain unsurpassed. Despite being made in a more straitlaced, censored era than today, the film does not spare the gory details, such as of a soldier impaled on a stake at the foot of the Tourelles outside Orléans. De Gastyne also benefitted from a "cast of thousands," which included four regiments of the French army lent by President Raymond Poincaré, and from authentic medieval locations, such as the walled town of Carcassonne and Reims Cathedral (both heavily restored), and the abbey of Mont-Saint-Michel. If the trial scenes, which were to be left out of the film altogether in its original conception, do not measure up to the *Passion*'s, at least the *Merveilleuse Vie* correctly portrays Joan's persecution at Rouen as a logical extension of her political struggle with the English.

From the heights of these classic films about Joan, the genre descended to the depths of blatant propaganda in the next major movie about her, *Das Mädchen Johanna* (*Joan the Maid*), directed by the Nazi filmmaker, Gustav Ucicky, and released in 1935. Here, it is Charles VII, rather than Joan herself, who is the hero of the film. He is played by Gustav Gründgens as a Machiavellian, all-wise leader who is willing to sacrifice everything—even Joan's life—for the greater goal of a united nation. As he says in the film: "Alive she [Joan] does us no more good; dead she is a martyr. . . . She is a thousand times stronger dead. . . . I want her to burn; it is necessary that she burn." This message has a chilling impact in light of the massacre of SA leaders that Hitler engineered on June 30, 1934, the so-called Night of the Long Knives. Strange to say, almost all of the contemporary reviewers of the film, with the single exception of Graham Greene, were completely oblivious to its sinister import. The mild critical reception of *Das Mädchen Johanna* seems to foreshadow the Allied appeasement of Nazi aggression that was to contribute to the outbreak of World War II. These days, Joan's symbolism has once again been coopted by ultra-rightist groups, such as Jean-Marie Le Pen's National Front party, where Joan's nationalistic mission to drive the English from France has been transmuted into a xenophobic attack upon racial and ethnic groups deemed "non-French."

The ensuing hiatus of wartime in the 1940s put a hold on a film project that was to star the Swedish actress, Ingrid Bergman, as Joan. According to her autobiography, Bergman had been "obsessed" with playing the saint since childhood. She was to get her chance after the war in RKO's 1948 production, *Joan of Arc*, directed by Victor Fleming. This was theoretically based on Maxwell Anderson's play, *Joan of Lorraine*, in which Bergman had starred on Broadway in 1946. As it was, Anderson's premise, about an actress playing Joan in a "play within a play," was scrapped in favor of a straightforward historical narrative about Joan of Arc. This was probably for the best, as Anderson's play has been criticized for being intellectually pretentious and long-winded. Despite the publicity hoopla surrounding the film—which included Bergman retracing Joan's steps in France, a cover on *Life* magazine, and a 75–foot high replica of the actress in white plastic armor that graced the film's N.Y. premiere—most critics judged *Joan of Arc* dull and uninspiring. As Bosley Crowther noted in *The New York Times*, Bergman is a radiant Joan, but as an actress she lacks the depth and pathos to bring Joan's spirituality to the screen. Four years later, Bergman admitted as much when she commented, "I would never have agreed to play the role if I had then seen Dreyer's *La Passion de Jeanne d'Arc*." (In actuality, she had lobbied actively for the part and even helped finance the film's production.) Her one saving grace in *Joan of Arc*, oddly enough, is her heavily inflected speech, which is probably the most authentic of any English language film about Joan. Since she came from Lorraine, on France's eastern border with Germany, Joan more than likely spoke French with a German accent.

Joan of Arc will go down as the quintessential Hollywood film of the genre. Even though it relies on historical records for much of its inspiration, particularly during the trial scenes, it takes the usual Hollywood lib-

Ingrid Bergman in the title role is about to be burned at the stake for the conclusion of RKO's *Joan of Arc* (1948). Crew members callously nicknamed the scene, "The Barbecue."

erties. The most notorious of these is the romance angle that is imposed upon Joan and the duke of Alençon: As the rest of the army disbands, Joan and her "gentle duke" exchange lovesick glances worthy of Schiller's play. Historically speaking, the scene is preposterous, since Joan's treasured status as a virgin precluded any such attachments, let alone with a married man. Alençon himself testified at the rehabilitation that he "never had any carnal desire for her," even when he saw Joan's naked body. Nonetheless, even Hollywood's version of Joan must remain a virgin, and this is perhaps what contributes to the lack of empathy between the actress and her subject. Bergman prepared for the role with her usual stint on the casting couch, in this case conducting a clandestine love affair with the film's director, Victor Fleming. Only here there was no sexual outlet on the screen for the extramarital energies she was expending off the set.

The release of *Joan of Arc* was soon eclipsed by Bergman's scandalous elopement with the Italian director, Roberto Rossellini. In a letter she wrote (but did not send) to the film's historical adviser and promoter, Father Paul Donceur, Bergman blamed *Joan of Arc's* failure at the box office on the undue attention aroused by her private life. Perhaps Bergman felt compensated by the fact that she got to play Joan yet again, in the 1954 film her new husband directed, *Giovanna d'Arco al Rogo* (*Joan at the Stake*). This was based on the 1939 oratorio by Paul Claudel and Arthur Honnegger, which Bergman and Rossellini staged concurrently with the film on a theatrical tour of Europe. Bergman's second film about Joan is much different from her first: It eschews Hollywood-style spectacle in favor of a "neo-realistic" approach which Rossellini characterized as "pure cinema." As she burns at the stake, Joan confesses to Fra Domenico and reviews her life in flashbacks, which includes a surreal scene where Joan's judges interrogate her while wearing animal heads. Despite such artistic pretensions, the film was not well received by the critics, although it has subsequently found its defenders. Commercially, the film fared even worse, joining a lengthening list of failed Bergman/Rossellini collaborations.

Joan of Arc was to be the graveyard of other talents in Hollywood. In 1957, she ensnared the great Austrian-born director, Otto Preminger, who attempted a film version of the George Bernard Shaw play, *Saint Joan*. How a film that employed so much talent—Preminger as director, Graham Greene as screenwriter, and venerable actors such as John Gielgud, Felix Aylmer, and Finlay Currie—could end up being so awful is a mystery. According to a publicity film about the making of *Saint Joan*, "A tremendous amount of research was done to ensure historical accuracy and . . . to achieve authenticity." Yet period details do not a great movie make. In his autobiography, Preminger describes himself as having a "lifelong love affair" with the play, but after the release of the film, he came to realize—I believe correctly—that Shaw's "deep but cool intellectual examination of the role religion plays in the history of man" is not quite right for the cinema. Early on in the production, he got bogged down in a well-publicized talent hunt for the role of Joan. After personally screening thousands of applicants in America and Europe—among the rejects was Barbara Streisand—Preminger settled on a complete unknown 17-year-old from Marshalltown, Iowa, Jean Seberg. Employing an actual teenager to play the teenage Joan was not new: Simone Genevois was also 17 when she starred in Marco de Gastyne's *La Merveilleuse Vie de Jeanne d'Arc* in 1928. But the ingenue Seberg was completely out of her depth mouthing the intellectual acrobatics of Shaw, no matter how hard Preminger coached her. The director's masochistic control over his protege was legendary: Seberg became so inured to the rigors of filming that she wanted to continue acting even after one of the gas jets used to simulate the flames at Joan's burning at the stake got too high and singed off her eyebrows. (The accident is shown on the publicity film in order to dispel rumors that Preminger took his realism too far.) Nor was Seberg the only one miscast; Richard Widmark, an actor more at home in Westerns, gives an overly comic performance as the dauphin, Charles. Even Graham Greene was criticized for emasculating much of the meaning from Shaw's original play in the film's dialogue. Preminger seems never to have realized that Shaw himself wrote a screenplay to translate his drama from stage to screen. Apparently, the great playwright was fascinated by the visual possibilities that film offered over the static backdrops and small casts of the theater, especially in crowd scenes such as the siege of Orléans.

Five years later, in 1962, we get a sharp swing away from the overexposed methods of Hollywood directors like Fleming and Preminger in Robert Bresson's *Le Procès de Jeanne d'Arc* (*The Trial of Joan of Arc*), starring Florenz Carrez in the title role. Like Bresson's Arthurian film, *Lancelot du Lac* (1974), *Le Procès* is an abstract, metaphorical film that treats cinematic images as symbols. The film historian, Kevin Harty, characterizes both of Bresson's medieval productions as the director's "personal meditation on the nature and possibility of goodness in the world." Following in the footsteps of Dreyer, Bresson chooses to dramatize only the last stage of Joan's life — her trial and execution, based scrupulously on the records of her condemnation and rehabilitation. But unlike his Danish predecessor, Bresson never allows his camera to come face to face with Joan's soul. Instead, his film technique has been described as distant and "voyeuristic," so that the audience never becomes involved in Joan's drama emotionally but must accept her spiritual conviction on faith. When Bresson does employ closeups, it is of Joan's hands and feet, which are apparently intended as a kind of "surface" symbol of her ordeal and, in the words of an admiring critic, serve "to dehierarchize images of the face." The result, however, must be judged as far less effective than Dreyer's *Passion*.

Finally, we come to the most recent films about Joan, made during the 1990s. The first of these is the marathon rendition directed by Jacques Rivette called *Jeanne la Pucelle* (*Joan the Maid*), released in 1994 and starring Sandrine Bonnaire as Joan. Perhaps only French filmmakers have the audacity to expect their audiences to sit through nearly six hours of cinema. To make the viewing more palatable, Rivette has divided his film into two equal parts, one entitled "The Battles," and the other, "The Prisons." *Jeanne la Pucelle* has the spare, static look of a documentary. Rather than offering up a dramatic presentation of Joan's life and vision, the film alternates reenactment sequences with "talking head" cameos of the actors delivering lines taken verbatim from their historical characters' testimonies, almost all from the rehabilitation. This approach is established at the very beginning of the film when Rivette, borrowing a page from Bresson, shows Joan's mother, Isabelle Romée, being escorted into a hall between two nuns and then making her official request for a trial of nullification of the previous sentence passed against her daughter. *Jeanne la Pucelle's* historical credentials are superb. The closing credits cite the works of the grande dame of Joan of Arc studies, Régine Pernoud, as inspiration. At times the film is painstaking in its adherence to historical detail. This is the only Joan of Arc film I know of, for example, which reenacts Joan first "trial" concerning her voices, at Poitiers in March 1429. Yet surprisingly, in a film of this length, Rivette omits entirely Joan's second trial at Rouen. Instead, Cauchon confronts Joan in her prison at Beaurevoir shortly before she is to be handed over to the English. When Joan recognizes the bishop as her inveterate enemy, the rest is assumed to be a foregone conclusion. *Jeanne la Pucelle* therefore pushes Pernoud's interpretation of Cauchon, which I believe is the correct one, as a politically motivated judge who engineered Joan's death from the very beginning, rendering her actual trial superfluous.

One cannot ask for any better effort from an historical film than what is delivered by *Jeanne la Pucelle*: strict adherence to the records in consultation with the leading historian of the subject. But still there is something missing from *Jeanne la Pucelle* that can make it a great film on a par with Dreyer's *Passion*. It lacks that spark of spirituality, an indefinable, transcendent quality that lets us see into Joan's soul. When Bonnaire as Joan is led to the stake in a heretic's dunce cap, she seems to be a figure ridiculous rather than sublime. Her last cry of "Jesus!" is, as Kevin Harty points out, a bitter one full "of anger and of pain." This makes her all too human. Consequently, one can hardly believe that here is the sacrificial, Christ-like Joan who has gone to meet her Maker.

The enduring popularity of Joan as a subject for film is attested by the fact that no less than two movies about her were released in 1999. A four-hour television miniseries, called simply *Joan of Arc*, got first exposure when it was aired on CBS in May of that year. Despite being a TV film, the *Joan of Arc* miniseries was invested with the high-profile billing of any blockbuster at the box office, including a $20 million budget and an "all-star" cast. It was directed by Christian Duguay and starred Leelee Sobieski as Joan, with cameo roles by Peter O'Toole as Bishop Cauchon and Shirley Maclaine as Joan of Luxembourg, Joan's kindly jailer in Beaurevoir Castle. But the film has not been received kindly by the critics. A recent historian of Joan of Arc, Mary Gordon, has compared Sobieski's bland delivery of her lines to that "of a depressed teenager telling her parents she's on the way to the mall." Indeed, *Joan of Arc* could greatly benefit from the panache and perhaps even risqué quality of a European lead. Instead, the film opts for portraying Joan as simply a very nice person, so nice, in fact, that she is loathe to attack the English in the Tourelles and must be compelled to do so by La Hire. (Sobieski commented in an interview that she was attracted to the role "because she [Joan] was such a good person, and I felt playing her made me a better person.") But we know from rehabilitation testimony of those who fought alongside Joan at Orléans, such as the Bastard, Dunois, that she was constantly goading her fellow commanders on to the attack. Another historical reviewer, Kathryn Norberg, has accused the film's producers of pushing the "likeable" portrayal of Joan so far as to invent wholly fictitious scenarios, such as that Joan set up a soup kitchen in Vaucouleurs and organized public works projects to help displaced peasants "rebuild their lives."

Other historical blunders committed by the film include: Cauchon introduced early on as a member of Charles VII's entourage, even though he must later preside at Joan's trial—which makes absolutely no sense politically; Joan's former comrades-in-arms attempting to rescue her just as she is being burned at Rouen—which most definitely did not happen; and staging Joan's execution in the depths of winter, while it is snowing— when in fact this took place well into springtime at the end of May. No doubt this last distortion was done for a kind of "fire and ice" visual effect, although I think an even more poignant message would have been conveyed if Joan's life had been cut short just as nature's cycle was being reborn. But then, this conceit had already been employed by *A Man for All Seasons* (1966), about the Catholic martyr during the English Reformation, Sir Thomas More. The one intriguing thing about this production is that, with the exception of *Das Mädchen Johanna*, it provides the most sympathetic portrayal of King Charles of any Joan of Arc film. In the 1999 production, Charles (played by Neil Patrick Harris, of *Doogie Howser, MD* fame), just before he sends Joan off on her last expedition, in the course of which she will be captured at Compiègne, offers her a chance to save herself by assuring her, "Joan, you don't have to do this." Joan's fatalistic reply is to tell the king: "The day we met, we spoke of God's plan, and we still have to play our parts. Whatever you do, you do by the will of God. Know that I know that." Charles is therefore absolved by Joan herself of any culpability in her coming death.

If one was looking for a more dynamic Joan of Arc, he certainly got it later that same year with the portrayal by Milla Jovovich, a Ukranian-born model and rock star turned actress, in *The Messenger: The Story of Joan of Arc*, directed by Luc Besson, who is better known for his New Age science fiction films. Once again, a movie about Joan of Arc is able to boast of a big budget—$60 million—and of some high-wattage star power, including John Malkovich as King Charles, Faye Dunaway as his mother-in-law, Yolanda of Aragon, and a brief appearance by Dustin Hoffman as Joan's "Conscience" during her trial. This time, the Americans are ably assisted by French actors, who lend a welcome international flavor to the production in the roles of Dunois, Alençon, and La Hire. Unfortunately, Jovovich plays Joan as if she were a hyperkinetic, crazed psychotic on speed, or quite possibly, acid. Here there is no doubt, as in the miniseries, that Joan is a bloodthirsty warrior. When she is not screaming frantically at anyone who happens to be within a 100-decibel range, she is having weird, psychedelic visions, such as of quasi-sexual encounters in the forest with St. Michael (or is it Christ?) and of stained-glass windows morphing into angels. In an interview with *Le Monde* magazine, Besson confessed that he chose Jovovich, his wife at the time, to play Joan because she was "sexy" and looked like the saint, both of which are impossible criteria since there is no authentic portrait of Joan and she aspired to be a virgin. The star herself summed up her interpretation of the role in her own interview, with *Vanity Fair* magazine, as that "Joan was really a mover and a shaker. She was a real Tasmanian devil."

Nonetheless, there is an interesting, if horribly flawed, agenda at work in *The Messenger*. Besson is a member of the notoriously secret, conservative Catholic organization, Opus Dei (meaning "the work of God"), which advocates a return to the Latin mass and, within its own hierarchy only, lay control over liturgy and ritual. In its espousal of lay piety through a secular "prelature" of business professionals, who take vows of chastity and poverty (members are expected to donate all their earnings to the order), Opus Dei is remarkably similar to the medieval movement of the beguines, who flirted dangerously with heresy in the late Middle Ages. In the context of such sympathies, it is no surprise to find Besson inventing a scene where a younger Joan, impatient to hear mass, bursts into the church at Domrémy and takes communion with her own hand, the sacramental wine spilling like blood down her face. This potentially subversive message— that if the clergy cannot satisfy lay people's spiritual yearnings, they must help themselves—also seems to be behind the climactic sequence of the film, where Joan is interrogated by her "Conscience," personified by Dustin Hoffman. When Cauchon, who is otherwise a sympathetic character, learns of Joan's retraction, he refuses to hear her last confession, and she is instead absolved (in Latin, no less!) by her Conscience. By the time the priests raise a cross before her eyes at her execution, it is of no use, because Joan is already burnt flesh. In most films, and according to the rehabilitation testimony of both Isambart de la Pierre and Martin Ladvenu, the cross was held in front of Joan while she was still very much alive. Joan also was allowed to make a last confession, which she did to Ladvenu.

The implications of the film's conclusion for the meaning of Joan's legacy are even more disturbing. In a scene of breathtaking cynicism, Joan's "voices" are subjected to an unflinching analysis by Conscience, who, speaking in a flat, monotonal voice, judges them to be no more than superstition and delusion. (In this regard, *The Messenger* boldly bucks film tradition.) The "miracle" of Joan finding a sword in a field, for example, is contrasted with more probable, earthbound scenarios, such as that it was flung, dropped, or simply cast aside by a passing soldier. This kind of New Age, pop psychology greatly appeals to some audiences, and the effectiveness of the scene is largely due to editing that crisply cross-cuts among the different "possibilities," as Conscience relentlessly pursues his argument like a lawyer making a legal brief. In a low-angle closeup of Hoffman's nostrils, Conscience towers over Joan and portentously intones: "You didn't see what was, Jeanne. You saw what you wanted to see." Later, the judges' ruthless questioning about whether Joan killed anyone is continued by Conscience, who forces Joan to admit that she fought only for herself, rather than for God and took pleasure in shedding blood, until she begs to be "set free" from her guilt. Even Joan's very belief in God is challenged by Conscience, who tells her after she has signed her abjuration: "You know what you just signed? You just signed away His existence. . . . For you, He's a lie. An illusion. . . . In the end, it was you who abandoned Him."

All this is meant to be a clever "trial within a trial," with Conscience's verdict, delivered within the privacy of Joan's cell, privileged by the film far more than the public one handed down by the judges outside. But the end result is that Conscience convicts Joan of being "proud," "stubborn," "selfish," and "cruel," exactly the same accusations that were leveled against her by her judges and other political enemies during her trial. Joan's mission, according to the film, all boils down to an act of personal revenge for the brutal murder and rape (committed in that order) of Joan's sister, which is shown in a graphic scene at the very beginning of the movie. This premise is sheer historical nonsense, since Joan had no sister, while her two real siblings—Pierre and Jean—were able throughout their lives to bask in their sister's glory and suffered no misfortune, that we know of, that would justify such terrible vengeance. *The Messenger* is perhaps the only film in cinematic history to betray its own heroine by condemning her. No movie about Joan of Arc can succeed unless it approaches her on her own terms and pays homage to the faith, courage, and spirit that led her to the stake.

AFTERWORD

It should be obvious by now that there is no one secret, no special formula, for making a great historical film. Rather, classics such as *The Seventh Seal* or *La Passion de Jeanne d'Arc* seem to be the product of an unique and intangible set of circumstances. Similarly, really bad movies such as *The Black Knight* or *Robin Hood: Prince of Thieves* can point to no one, defining moment when the film falls apart. Movie magic (and disaster) remains elusive. The best we can do, perhaps, is dissect how a particular film got things right or wrong after it was made.

Recently a rare opportunity arose for me to delve a little deeper into the makings of a much admired—even by professional historians—film about the Middle Ages. The movie in question is *The War Lord*, released in 1965 and directed by Franklin Schaffner (who twenty-two years later made the far less memorable *Lionheart*, about the Children's Crusade of 1212) and starring Charlton Heston as Chrysagon, the main character of the title. Set in the mid-eleventh century on the sea coast of present-day Belgium, *The War Lord*, as Orson Welles informs us in the opening narration, is about a warrior in service to the duke (actually count) of Flanders, who has been sent to defend a lonely tower and village on the swampy march, or fringes, of the county from Frisian raiders. Almost immediately upon his arrival, the war lord must chase off the heathen invaders with the help of his retinue, which includes his brother, Draco (played by Dean Stockwell), and his trusty lieutenant, Bors (played by Richard Boone). Eventually, however, Chrysagon is defending his tower not only against the Frisians, but even against his own peasants. The latter have been antagonized by their lord's violation of feudal custom, namely the *jus pri-mae noctis*, or right of first night, with a newlywed bride. Chrysagon invokes first night in order to bed Bronwyn (played by Rosemary Forsyth), a beautiful peasant girl who, he believes, has bewitched him with her druidic magic. But the villagers' outrage, led by Mark, Bronwyn's cuckolded groom, only erupts when Chrysagon decides to keep his lover beyond the first night. By the end of the film, the war lord has successfully defended his tower against his rebellious serfs and made peace with the Frisians, only to be mortally wounded by Mark in an ambush. The last we see of Chrysagon, he is riding off with Bors in order to give an account of his actions (which include killing his own brother, Draco) before the duke.

The War Lord is not a perfect rendering of the Middle Ages. The Frisians, who occupied the coast of what is now Holland, were by this time fully integrated into Christian Europe and, already by the early ninth century, had themselves suffered from raids across the North Sea by the heathen Danes. First night was never a feudal right of medieval lords: It in fact was an invention of sixteenth-century dramatists. Pagan druidic customs had long ago died out or been fully assimilated by the triumphant Christian religion. But there is a lot that *War Lord* gets right about medieval history. It gives us, for example, one of the best depictions of the complex culture of feudalism and manorialism on film. In a memorable scene, the villagers file into the lord's castle to lay their grievances at the manor court, which is presided over by Chrysagon in the surly manner of a lord who knows he has obligations (in this case, to dispense justice) as well as privileges of rank. The ambiguous ending—will Chrysagon be punished by the duke as a rebellious vassal?—is appropriate enough, even if the historical count of Flanders, Baldwin V (1035–1067), had a reputation as one of the most powerful rulers of the time (he was styled "prince of the fatherland") who would brook no insubordination. Not even the most politically advanced state in Europe, the duchy of Normandy, Flanders' western neighbor, had a universal and rigid set of expectations regarding feudal obligations, at least until the Conquest of 1066. The uncertainty of what will happen to Chrysagon as he rides away to face the duke accurately reflects this situation.

Aside from refusing to deliver a happy ending, *The War Lord* also bucked Hollywood tradition by portraying a siege rather than a full-scale battle, as was expected in most "sword and sandal" flicks set in ancient or medieval times. In this, too, *The War Lord* anticipated historians, who have now decided that sieges played the most important role in medieval military history, since they ultimately decided control of territory. In addition, the love affair between Chrysagon and Bronwyn accurately reflects medieval attitudes toward women, which vacillated between an ideal, chivalric ethos that was tied to the cult of the Virgin Mary, and the misogynistic stereotype of an evil seductress that was traced back to the biblical Eve. At one point in the film, Chrysagon tears down a medieval wall hanging that depicts the temptation of Adam and Eve; the act seems to symbolize Chrysagon's frustration over his forbidden desire for Bronwyn.

The War Lord is so good that the American Historical Association honored it, along with its leading man, Charlton Heston, at one of its annual meetings, held in Chicago in 1991. Mr. Heston proudly boasted to me that "we got an award for that film about ten years ago . . . from some historical association [that] labeled it, I think, 'the most accurately depicted story of the period of any film,' and I'll settle for that." What made it possible for The War Lord to adhere so closely to historical veracity? I explored this subject with Mr. Heston in my interview with him at his home in Beverly Hills in October 1999 (see also his comments on El Cid in Chapter 3). Heston took a great personal interest in the film, since he had optioned the rights to the original Broadway play, The Lovers, by Leslie Stevens. The play, however, was "largely discarded," according to Heston, when it came time to write the film script, since the actor felt that the story could only work as a movie, not as drama. John Collier, the original screenwriter assigned to the project, was chosen by Heston because he was a good writer and "had a considerable reputation" for his knowledge of the medieval period, even though Heston also recalls that he was a "difficult man" to work with. (Heston's Journals record that Collier stormed out of script meetings.)

Equally crucial for the success of The War Lord was Heston's personal interest in history. Prior to filming, he visited the Sutton Hoo exhibit at the British Museum in London in order to verify that chain mail would have been worn by noble warriors of the time. When asked who or what was responsible for the film's historical accuracy, Heston replied: "Maybe me. I cared about it. As I said, I'm a history buff, and especially if I'm doing a part, you want to do it as right as you can, no question. It's not a hard choice to make. It's hard to do sometimes. . . . " Unlike El Cid, The War Lord does not aim to tell the grand sweep of events, but limits the ambitions of its plot to a given time and place, which is perhaps what allowed Heston to maintain artistic control over its content. As he told me in our interview:

> This is really a small story, it's not a war. He [Chrysagon] is keeping the
> watch on the tower, that's his duty for however long—six months, a year?—
> as long as the duke wants him to. But they expect to be raided, it's much like
> the forts in North America in the early years—they got raided every so
> often, but they could be defended and by and large were successfully
> defended. And I think also you don't see that kind of an assault on a tower.
> Battles are another thing, and everybody's seen them. I think they did that
> very well. Frank Schaffner did a marvelous job on that film.

Heston also paid tribute to the second-unit director, Joe Canutt (son of Yakima Canutt), who supervised all the action sequences:

> I think that's one of the best siege scenes in the history of film, I really do. . . . The tower still stands on the Universal [Studios'] back lot. I remember while we were shooting some of the night footage there, every night—and we'd go 'til 3, 4 in the morning—and almost every night a young guy, a student obviously, would come up and watch, and then after a while I'd throw him off. And finally I said, "Frank [Schaffner], why don't we let him stay, let him watch. He never says anything." And so we did. It was Steven Spielberg.

The War Lord made an impression, obviously, on more than just history buffs.

Nonetheless, *The War Lord* was a disappointment at the box office and failed to recoup its $4 million investment. Heston was also disappointed that in the final cut of the film, Universal eliminated some scenes that he considered crucial to his original vision of the story. This sad fate of worthy historical films—to fade away into oblivion until they are rediscovered by film historians—seems destined to continue. A recent production that shares with *The War Lord* an ability to dazzle critics, but apparently not the moviegoing public, is *The Anchoress* (1993), directed by Chris Newby. Although it was honored at both the Cannes and Sundance film festivals the year of its release, *The Anchoress* may have suffered from the fact that its distribution by the British Film Institute was very limited. It is now more widely available on video and well worth watching. *The Anchoress* tells the story of a 14–year-old peasant girl, Christine, who decides to be immured in a wall next to the parish church of Shere so that she can escape the romantic attentions of the village reeve and be close to a wooden statue of the Virgin Mary, which inspires Christine with ecstatic visions. This is one of the best depictions of medieval women—and the ways in which they both defied and were circumscribed by the dominant male hierarchy—on film. The screenplay by Judith Stanley-Smith is based on actual letters discovered at Shere in Surrey, England, concerning a real-life anchoress, Christine Carpenter, who was enclosed under the direction of the bishop of Winchester in the 1320s. The film does an excellent job of showing the various stages by which Christine becomes an anchoress, beginning with her examination by the parish priest and then the bishop on her suitability for enclosure, and ending with the rain-soaked ceremony of her physical "walling in," so that she is "dead to the world." But *The Anchoress* does not confine itself to Christine' cell, for it also shows us the lives of Christine's mother, Pauline, who wages a bitter struggle with the parish priest over her right to sell home remedies to ailing villagers, and Christine's younger sister, Meg, who does marry the reeve. We also catch a glimpse of the lives of other villagers who come to Christine's window for guidance and advice, which, contrary to the popular image of anchoresses as simply shut off from the rest of society, kept them in constant contact with the outside world. Added to this are some very authentic sets, such as the village church—where parishioners must stand on the dirt floor (there were no pews in the Middle Ages)—and Pauline's wooden hovel, which rival the gritty realism reproduced in *The Seventh Seal* and *The Navigator* (chapter 5). Newby succeeds in capturing some strikingly beautiful images—such as of Christine escaping from her cell by "sprouting" from the ground outside— that are all shot in black and white, which seems to be the obligatory medium for atmospherically true films about the Middle Ages.

By contrast, recently released movies set in medieval times that are popular blockbusters at the box office seem to achieve their broad appeal only at the expense of horrible distortions of history. In 1986, for example, the widely-heralded, *The Name of the Rose*, based on the bestselling novel by Umberto Eco, trumpeted an international effort that included a German production company; a French director, Jean-Jacques Annaud; and a cast of Hollywood stars such as Sean Connery, F. Murray Abraham, and Christian Slater. Yet despite all its fancy trimmings, *Name of the Rose* (like the book) serves up a ghoulish mockery of the Middle Ages whose menagerie of deformed monks belongs more in an 18th-century Gothic novel than in a sophisticated, late 20th-century film. Perhaps the gravest inaccuracies are reserved for Abraham's character, the 14th-century French inquisitor, Bernard Gui, who in real life was no pyromaniac madman: He consigned just 6.5 percent of his victims to the flames and only when they refused or relapsed on their confessions to heresy. In the following year, 1987, an unassuming French production, *Le Moine et la Sorcière* (*The Sorceress*), presented a much more subtle and sympathetic portrayal of Gui's 13th-century predecessor, the inquisitor of France, Etienne de Bourbon, but unfortunately it could not match the exposure or distribution of its big-name rival.

Another popular but problematic production is *Braveheart* (1995), directed by Mel Gibson, who also stars as the turn-of-the-fourteenth century hero of Scottish independence, William Wallace. The film, which won academy awards for best picture and director, has become a favorite of younger (especially male) audiences, chiefly on account of its gory battle scenes. These are, it must be allowed, grittily realistic and accurate portrayals of the new kind of infantry warfare that Wallace helped develop, in which his "schiltrom" hedgehog formations of common footsoldier conscripts armed with long pikes demonstrated that they could defeat cavalry charges. (Ironically, it was the English who were to learn this lesson most effectively, applying it to win their string of victories in France during the Hundred Years War.)

But *Braveheart* commits many, many historical mistakes, and none have been taken more to task by historians and critics than its flawed portrayal of homosexuality. (The film was boycotted in the United States by GLAAD, the Gay and Lesbian Alliance Against Defamation.) Central to the plot of the film is that the king of England's son, Prince Edward (the future Edward II), is a flaming gay who brusquely repulses the attentions of his beautiful wife, the French princess Isabella, in preference for the companionship of his male lover, Philip (in reality the Gascon noble, Piers Gaveston). This inevitably leads to an affair between Isabella and the testosterone-charged Wallace, which results in the conception, unbeknownst to Edward, of the next heir to the throne (the future Edward III). The whole premise is preposterous for a number of reasons, the most practical one being that the real Isabella did not give birth to her only son, Edward, until 1312, seven years after Wallace was hung, drawn, and quartered by the English on a charge of treason in 1305 (at which time Isabella was only nine years old and still in France).

Of more important consideration is the fact that the film does not accurately reflect Edward's sexuality, or the issue of gayness in general during the Middle Ages. As J.S. Hamilton, the modern biographer of Edward's lover, Piers Gaveston, notes, "The difficulty arises in the use of a modern term such as homosexual, a term charged with meaning and evocative of various stereotypes to modern audiences, but unknown and imprecisely applied to medieval figures." (The medieval term for the homosexual act was sodomy, or the "sin against nature," under which were classified a whole host of sexual activities.) Edward was not gay in our modern sense of the term but was more likely bisexual, since he was not adverse to the sexual company of women and proved it by siring no less than four children (including the future Edward III) with Isabella, as well as an illegitimate son by a mistress. When a group of English barons put Gaveston to death in 1312—which the film portrays as committed by Edward I, who throws his victim out of a window—they were responding not to an offensive sexuality, but to an offensive favoritism that they perceived as denying them titles and treasures rightfully theirs. Ironically, the film's stereotypical image of homosexuality finds its almost sole support in the work of John Boswell, the late, preeminent historian of medieval attitudes toward gays. Boswell, who was himself gay, argued that the late Middle Ages, beginning in the thirteenth century, saw the rise of an unprecedented intolerance toward homosexuals; this was in contrast to the earlier medieval period, which was more accepting of "sodomites." (Boswell cites the example of Richard the Lionheart, who is claimed to have loved King Philip Augustus of France since, in the words of one chronicle, "at night their beds did not separate them.") But Boswell's evidence is largely anecdotal and is not borne out by a close study of canon and civil law codes, which up until at least the fourteenth century evince a progressively lower, not higher, concern for sexual offenses. In a modern context, *Braveheart* is even more disturbing, for it seems to insist on sexual conformity as a precondition for national unity and, in the words of one critic, "valorizes gay bashing."

Thus, there is no sure path to the elusive grail of historically accurate, but still entertaining, films about the Middle Ages. Even when respected historians serve as consultants on films—as was the case in *El Cid* or *Robin Hood* (1991)—this is no guarantee that the end result will be faithful to the historical truth. It is not enough to be enthusiastic and interested about the past, as Heston was in *El Cid*, no less than in *The War Lord*. The key difference seems to be to not allow competing motives for making a film—whether these be financial, political, or even artistic—completely eclipse an honest effort to make the audience empathize with our medieval forebears; nor should filmmakers give in to the temptation to stereotype the people of the Middle Ages as either grotesque gargoyles or anachronistic moderns.

It may be all too easy to blame Hollywood movie moguls and their minions for pitching films that sacrifice sensitive treatments of the past for a mass marketing appeal of their product. Undoubtedly, the moguls would respond that they are only "giving the people what they want." And in a sense, this is true. After all, it is we, as audiences, who go in droves to see *El Cid* or *Braveheart*, while ignoring *La Passion de Jeanne d'Arc*, *Robin and Marian*, or *The War Lord*. Perhaps we must bear some of the blame if history goes awry on the silver screen, since filmmakers partly leave it up to the audience to judge whether their movies are successes or failures. If we want a better "knight at the movies," then we must learn to recognize, appreciate, and yes, go to see worthy films that do justice to the Middle Ages.

FOR FURTHER READING

Prologue

David Herlihy's essay, entitled, "Am I a Camera? Other Reflections on Films and History," was published in *American Historical Review* 93 (1988):1186–92. Another important essay in the AHR Forum was Robert Rosenstone's "History in Images/History in Words: Reflections on the Possibility of Really Putting History onto Film," *AHR* 93 (1988):1173–85. There are several other collections of scholarly essays and books that explore the general relationship between film and history: P. Sorlin, *The Film in History: Restaging the Past* (Oxford: Blackwell, 1980); M. Ferro, *Cinema and History*, trans. N. Greene (Detroit: Wayne State University Press, 1988); *Resisting Images: Essays on Cinema and History*, eds. R. Sklar and C. Musser (Philadelphia: Temple University Press, 1990); *Image as Artifact: The Historical Analysis of Film and Television*, ed. J.E. O'Connor (Malabar, FL: Krieger Publishing, 1990); L. Grindon, *Shadows on the Past: Studies in the Historical Fiction Film* (Philadelphia: Temple University Press, 1990); R.A. Rosenstone, *Visions of the Past: The Challenge of Film to Our Idea of History* (Cambridge, MA: Harvard University Press, 1995); *The Persistence of History: Cinema, Television, and the Modern Event*, ed. V. Sobchack (New York: Routledge, 1996); *Screening the Past: Film and the Representation of History*, ed. T. Barta (Westport, CT: Praeger, 1998). A book that is more accessible to the general public is George MacDonald Fraser, *The Hollywood History of the World: From One Million Years B.C. to Apocalypse Now* (New York: Beech Tree Books, 1988). Although entertaining, this work, by a former Hollywood screenwriter and author of the infamous "Flashman" series, seems more concerned with matching stars to their characters' portraits than with history. Readers are better advised to consult: *Past Imperfect: History according to the Movies*, ed. T. Mico, J. Miller-Monzon, and D. Rubel (New York: Henry Holt, 1996), and Joseph Roquemore, *History Goes to the Movies* (New York: Doubleday, 1999), both of which have a few chapters on medieval films.

For a more scholastic definition of "medievalism" than the one I provide here, see J. Simons, "Medievalism as Cultural Process in Pre-industrial Popular Literature," in *Medievalism in England II*, ed. L.J. Workman and K. Verduin (Studies in Medievalism, VII, Cambridge: D. S. Brewer, 1996). Simons applies medievalism to popular English literature from the sixteenth through to the eighteenth centuries, and indeed, the vast majority of scholarly work on medievalism, especially as it pertains to the movies, has been done by literature professors rather than historians. Useful catalogues of all the films ever made on a medieval topic have been compiled by: K.J. Harty, *The Reel Middle Ages: American, Western and Eastern European, Middle Eastern and Asian Films about Medieval*

Europe (Jefferson, NC: McFarland, 1999); and D.J. Williams, "Medieval Movies: A Filmography," *Film and History* 29 (1999):20–32.

The Holy Grail of Hollywood: King Arthur Films

There are more books about Arthurian films than perhaps about any other medieval film genre. Some good collections containing perceptive essays on the subject include: *King Arthur through the Ages*, 2 vols., ed. V.M. Lagorio and M.L. Day (New York: Garland Publishing, 1990); *Cinema Arthuriana: Essays on Arthurian Film*, ed. K.J. Harty (New York: Garland Publishing, 1991); *Popular Arthurian Traditions*, ed. S.K. Slocum (Bowling Green, OH: Bowling Green State University Popular Press, 1992); *King Arthur on Film: New Essays on Arthurian Cinema*, ed. K.J. Harty (Jefferson, NC: McFarland, 1999). Rebecca and Samuel Umland's *The Use of Arthurian Legend in Hollywood Film: From Connecticut Yankees to Fisher Kings* (Westport, CT: Greenwood Press, 1996) is too enamored of postmodernist jargon to be accessible to a general audience. The most authoritative filmography of movies with an Arthurian theme is Bert Olson's *Arthurian Legends on Film and Television* (Jefferson, NC: McFarland, 2000).

My main source on the historical and mythological Arthur was Norris J. Lacy and Geoffrey Ashe, *The Arthurian Handbook*, 2nd ed. (New York: Garland Publishing, 1997). Also exploring various aspects of Arthuriana is *King Arthur in Popular Culture*, eds. Elizabeth S. Sklar and Donald L. Hoffman (Jefferson, NC: McFarland, 2002), which includes a section on television and film. N.J. Higham, *King Arthur: Myth-Making and History* (London and New York: Routledge, 2002) provides an excellent discussion of the historical context of the making of Arthur's legend in Britain during the early and high Middle Ages. A sensational treatment of Arthur's history is Graham Phillips and Martin Keatman, *King Arthur: The True Story* (London: Arrow, 1992). The edition of Malory's *Le Morte D'Arthur* that I have quoted in this chapter is from the edition by Eugene Vinaver, *The Works of Sir Thomas Malory*, 3 vols. (Oxford: Clarendon Press, 1947). For scholarly studies of Malory's life and work, readers should consult: E. Reiss, *Sir Thomas Malory* (New York: Twayne, 1966); P.J.C. Field, *The Life and Times of Sir Thomas Malory* (Cambridge: D. S. Brewer, 1993); and *A Companion to Malory*, ed. E. Archibald and A.S.G. Edwards (Woodbridge, Suffolk: D. S. Brewer, 1996).

Lights! Camera! Pillage!: Viking Films

An accessible, recent reassessment of Viking scholarship is *The Oxford Illustrated History of the Vikings*, ed. Peter Sawyer (Oxford: Oxford University Press, 1997). Other works well worth reading include: Johannes Brøndsted, *The Vikings*, trans. K. Skov (Harmondsworth, Middlesex: Penguin, 1960); P.H. Sawyer, *The Age of the Vikings* (London, 1962); Gwyn Jones, *A History of the Vikings* (Oxford, 1968); Peter Foote and David M. Wilson, *The Viking Achievement: The Society and Culture of Early Medieval Scandinavia* (London: E. Arnold, 1970); *The Vikings*, ed. R.T. Farrell (London: Phillimore, 1982); P.H. Sawyer, *Kings and Vikings: Scandinavia and Europe*, A.D. *700–1100* (London and New York: Methuen, 1982); Judith Jesch, *Women in the Viking Age* (Woodbridge, Suffolk: Boydell, 1991); Else Roesdahl, *The Vikings*, trans. S.M. Margeson and K. Williams, 2nd ed. (Harmondsworth, Middlesex: Penguin, 1991); John Marsden, *The Fury of the Northmen: Saints, Shrines and Sea-Raiders in the Viking Age*, A.D. *793–878* (New York: St. Martin's Press, 1993); and Henry Loyn, *The Vikings in Britain* (Oxford: Blackwell, 1994).

The two most authoritative, and recent, biographies on Alfred the Great are: Alfred P. Smyth, *King Alfred the Great* (Oxford: Oxford University Press, 1995), and Richard Abels, *Alfred the Great: War, Kingship and Culture in Anglo-Saxon England* (London and New York: Longman, 1998). I used the following sources on Alfred: *The Anglo-Saxon Chronicle*, ed. D. Whitelock (New Brunswick, NJ: Rutgers University Press, 1961); and *Alfred the Great*, trans. S. Keynes and M. Lapidge (Harmondsworth, Middlesex: Penguin, 1983).

Valuable insights into Viking movies were gained by consulting Tony Thomas, *The Films of Kirk Douglas* (Secaucus, NJ: Citadel Press, 1972); Derek Elley, *The Epic Film: Myth and History*

(London: Routledge, 1984); Allan Hunter, *Tony Curtis: The Man and his Movies* (New York: St. Martin's Press, 1985); Gary A. Smith, *Epic Films: Casts, Credits and Commentary on Over 250 Historical Spectacle Movies* (Jefferson, NC: McFarland, 1991).

God (and the Studio) Wills It!: Crusade Films

Standard textbooks on the history of the medieval crusades include: Jonathan Riley-Smith, *The Crusades: A Short History* (New Haven: Yale University Press, 1987); Hans Eberhard Mayer, *The Crusades*, 2nd ed., trans. John Gillingham (Oxford: Oxford University Press, 1988); Jean Richard, *The Crusades, c. 1071–c.1291*, trans. Jean Birrell (Cambridge: Cambridge University Press, 1999); Thomas F. Madden, *A Concise History of the Crusades* (Lanham, MD: Rowman and Littlefield, 1999); *The Oxford History of the Crusades*, ed. Jonathan Riley-Smith (Oxford: Oxford University Press, 1999); and *The Crusades: The Essential Readings*, ed. Thomas F. Madden (Oxford: Blackwell, 2002). The formerly revered, three-volume work by Steven Runciman, *A History of the Crusades* (Cambridge: Cambridge University Press, 1951–1954) is now outdated. Good collections of primary sources about the crusades are to be had in: James A. Brundage, *The Crusades: A Documentary Survey* (Milwaukee, WI: Marquette University Press, 1962); *Chronicles of the Crusades: Eye-Witness Accounts of the Wars between Christianity and Islam*, ed. Elizabeth Hallam (New York: Welcome Rain, 2000); and *Arab Historians of the Crusades*, trans. Francesco Gabrieli and E.J. Costello (Berkeley: University of California Press, 1969). For a history of the crusades from the Arab point of view, readers should consult: Carole Hillenbrand, *The Crusades: Islamic Perspectives* (New York: Routledge, 1999), which is much more reliable than the popular book by Amin Maalouf, *The Crusades through Arab Eyes* (New York: Schocken Books, 1984). An adequate history of the Teutonic Knights can be found in Desmond Seward, *The Monks of War: The Military Religious Orders* (Harmondsworth, Middlesex: Viking Penguin, 1972), and a revisionist history of Alexander Nevsky is to be had in John Fennell, *The Crisis of Medieval Russia, 1200–1304* (London and New York: Longman, 1983). On the Cid and 11th-century Spain under Alfonso VI, see: Ramón Menéndez Pidal, *The Cid and His Spain*, trans. H. Sunderland (London: Frank Cass, 1934); José Fradejas Lebrero, *El Cid* (Ceuta: Instituto Nacional de Enseñanza Media, 1962); Richard Fletcher, *The Quest for El Cid* (New York: Knopf, 1990); and Bernard F. Reilly, *The Kingdom of León-Castilla under King Alfonso VI, 1065–1109* (Princeton: Princeton University Press, 1988). There are two useful collections of documentary sources on the Cid: *Christians and Moors in Spain*, eds. Colin Smith, Charles Melville, and Ahmad 'Ubaydli, 3 vols. (Warminster, UK: Aris and Phillips, 1988–92); and *The World of El Cid: Chronicles of the Spanish Reconquest*, trans. Simon Barton and Richard Fletcher (Manchester: Manchester University Press, 2000). Debate concerning the dating of the *Poema de Mio Cid* is summed up in: Derek W. Lomax, "The Date of the 'Poema de Mio Cid'" in *"Mio Cid" Studies*, ed. A.D. Deyermond (London: Támesis Books, 1977); and Colin Smith, *The Making of the Poema de Mio Cid* (Cambridge: Cambridge University Press, 1983). Readers should also consult María Eugenia Lacarra, *El Poema de Mio Cid: Realidad Histórica e Ideología* (Madrid: J. Porrúa Turanzas, 1980).

My interview with Charlton Heston was conducted at his home in Beverly Hills on October 18, 1999. Other personal memoirs that proved useful for this chapter include Cecil B. DeMille, *The Autobiography of Cecil B. DeMille*, ed. Donald Hayne (New York: Garland, 1959); Sergei M. Eisenstein, *Notes of a Film Director* (New York: Dover, 1970); Sergei M. Eisenstein, *Immoral Memories: An Autobiography*, trans. Herbert Marshall (Boston: Houghton Mifflin, 1983); Charlton Heston, *The Actor's Life: Journals, 1956–1976*, ed. H. Alpert (New York: E. P. Dutton, 1978); and Charlton Heston, *In the Arena: An Autobiography* (New York: Simon and Schuster, 1995). Selections of Eisenstein's other writings on the cinema include: Sergei M. Eisenstein, *S. M. Eisenstein: Selected Works*, eds. and trans. Richard Taylor and William Powell, 3 vols. (London: British Film Institute, 1988–96); and *The Eisenstein Reader*, eds. and trans. Richard Taylor and William Powell (London: British Film Institute, 1998).

Among the numerous biographies and filmographies of Eisenstein, readers should consult: Ion Barna, *Eisenstein* (Bloomington, IN: Indiana University Press, 1973); Norman Swallow,

Eisenstein: A Documentary Portrait (London: Dutton, 1976); Marie Seton, *Sergei M. Eisenstein: A Biography* (London: Dobson, 1978); Jay Leyda and Zina Voynow, *Eisenstein at Work* (New York: Pantheon Books, 1982); James Goodwin, *Eisenstein, Cinema, and History* (Urbana, IL: University of Illinois Press, 1993); David Bordwell, *The Cinema of Eisenstein* (Cambridge, MA: Harvard University Press, 1993); and Ronald Bergan, *Eisenstein: A Life in Conflict* (Woodstock, NY: Overlook Press, 1997). Two important essay collections that have recently appeared about Eisenstein are: *Eisenstein Rediscovered*, eds. Ian Christie and Richard Taylor (London and New York: Routledge, 1993), and *Eisenstein at 100: A Reconsideration*, eds. Al LaValley and Barry P. Scherr (New Brunswick, N.J.: Rutgers University Press, 2001), with an essay by Scherr, "*Alexander Nevsky*: Film without a Hero." A good explanation of Eisenstein's theoretical ideas, based on his original lectures, is Vladimir B. Nizhny, *Lessons with Eisenstein*, trans. and eds. Ivor Montague and Jay Leyda (New York: Hill and Wang, 1962). Also useful are general works on the Soviet and East European film industry: Michael Jon Stoil, *Cinema Beyond the Danube: The Camera and Politics* (Metuchen, NJ: Scarecrow Press, 1974); Jay Leyda, *Kino: A History of the Russian and Soviet Film*, 3rd ed. (Princeton: Princeton University Press, 1983); and R. Taylor, *Film Propaganda: Soviet Russia and Nazi Germany*, 2nd rev. ed. (London and New York: I.B. Tauris, 1998). A comparable work for the Spanish film industry is Peter Besas, *Behind the Spanish Lens: Spanish Cinema under Fascism and Democracy* (Denver, CO: Arden Press, 1985). The film script of *Alexander Nevsky* is available in Sergei M. Eisenstein, *Classic Film Scripts: October and Alexander Nevsky*, ed. Jay Leyda and trans. D. Matias (London: Lorrimer, 1984). Franz Hoellering's review of *Alexander Nevsky* is reprinted in *American Film Criticism: From the Beginnings to Citizen Kane*, eds. Stanley Kauffmann and Bruce Henstell (Westport, CT: Greenwood, 1979). For the life and work of Leni Riefenstahl, see: Glenn B. Infield, *Leni Riefenstahl: The Fallen Film Goddess* (New York: Crowell, 1976); David B. Hinton, *The Films of Leni Riefenstahl* (Metuchen, NJ: Scarecrow Press, 1978); and Renata Berg-Pan, *Leni Riefenstahl* (Boston: Twayne, 1980). Readers may also want to consult the English translation of Riefenstahl's memoirs: Leni Riefenstahl, *Sieve of Time: The Memoirs of Leni Riefenstahl* (London: Quartet Books, 1992).

Commentaries on epic films such as *The Crusades* and *El Cid* are to be found in: Tony Thomas, *The Great Adventure Films* (Secaucus, NJ: Citadel Press, 1976); Jeffrey Richards, *Swordsmen of the Screen: From Douglas Fairbanks to Michael York* (London: Routledge, 1977); Mike Munn, *The Stories Behind the Scenes of the Great Film Epics* (Watford, UK: Illustrated Publications, 1982); Steve Neale, "Masculinity as Spectacle: Reflections on Men and Mainstream Cinema," *Screen* 24 (1983): 2–16; Derek Elley, *The Epic Film: Myth and History* (London: Routledge, 1984); Baird Searles, *EPIC! History on the Big Screen* (New York: Harry N. Abrams, 1990); Gary A. Smith, *Epic Films: Casts, Credits and Commentary on over 250 Historical Spectacle Movies* (Jefferson, NC: McFarland, 1991); Leon Hunt, "What are Big Boys Made of? *Spartacus, El Cid* and the Male Epic," in *You Tarzan: Masculinity, Movies and Men*, eds. P. Kirkham and J. Thumim (New York: St. Martin's Press, 1993); and P. Lucanio, *With Fire and Sword: Italian Spectacles on American Screens, 1958–1968* (Metuchen, NJ: Scarecrow Press, 1994). Other useful insights into *El Cid* can be gleaned from: Alexander Paal, William Schneider and James Poling, *The Making of El Cid* (Madrid: The Campeador Press, 1962); Jeff Rovin, *The Films of Charlton Heston* (Secaucus, NJ: Citadel Press, 1977); and J. Basinger, *Anthony Mann* (Boston: Twayne, 1979).

The political background on Egypt, Nasser, and the Suez Crisis around the time of the making of *Saladin* is available in: *Egypt and Nasser: Volume 1: 1952–56*, ed. Dan Hofstadter (New York: Facts on File, 1973); Nissim Rejwan, *Nasserist Ideology: Its Exponents and Critics* (New York: Wiley, 1974); Donald Neff, *Warriors at Suez: Eisenhower Takes America into the Middle East* (New York: Linden, 1981); *Suez 1956: The Crisis and its Consequences*, eds. W.M. Roger Louis and Roger Owen (Oxford: Clarendon Press, 1989); *The Suez–Sinai Crisis: 1956 Retrospective and Reappraisal*, eds. Selwyn Ilan Troen and Moshe Shemesh (London: Frank Cass, 1990); and Peter Woodward, *Nasser* (London and New York: Longman, 1992). The standard accounts of the Great Famine and the Great Terror in the Soviet Union under Stalin are by Robert Conquest, *The Harvest of Sorrow: Soviet Collectivization and the Terror-Famine* (New York: Oxford University Press, 1986), and *The Great Terror: A Reassessment* (New York: Oxford University Press, 1990); in addition, see Paul

Johnson, *Modern Times: The World from the Twenties to the Eighties* (New York: Harper and Row, 1983). On the Spanish Civil War and the career of Francisco Franco, two good works in English are: Burnett Bolloten, *The Spanish Civil War: Revolution and Counterrevolution* (Chapel Hill, NC: University of North Carolina Press, 1991); and Paul Preston, *Franco: A Biography* (New York: Basic Books, 1994). The modern political context of *El Cid* can also be studied in light of the career and historiography of the film's advisor, Menéndez Pidal. See: María Eugenia Lacarra, "La Utilización del Cid de Menéndez Pidal en la Ideología Militar Franquista," *Ideologies and Literature* 3 (1980): 95–127; and Steven Hess, *Ramón Menéndez Pidal* (Boston: Twayne, 1982).

Splendid in Spandex: Robin Hood Films

An indispensable collection of articles on the literary, historical, and cinematic aspects of Robin Hood is *Robin Hood: An Anthology of Scholarship and Criticism*, ed. Stephen Knight (Woodbridge, Suffolk: D.S. Brewer, 1999). See also Stephen Knight's *Robin Hood: A Complete Study of the English Outlaw* (Oxford: Blackwell, 1994), and "A Garland of Robin Hood Films," *Film and History* 29 (1999):34–44. Another important study of the Robin Hood ballads and games is Jeffrey L. Singman, *Robin Hood: The Shaping of the Legend* (Wesport, CT: Greenwood, 1998). An excellent survey of Robin Hood films is Scott Allen Nollen, *Robin Hood: A Cinematic History of the English Outlaw and his Scottish Counterparts* (Jefferson, NC: McFarland, 1999); but see also David Turner, *Robin of the Movies* (Kingswinford, UK: Yeoman, 1989). Other essential reading, especially on the historical issues associated with Robin Hood's legend, are James C. Holt, *Robin Hood*, 2nd rev. ed. (London: Thames and Hudson, 1989); Maurice Keen, *The Outlaws of Medieval Legend*, rev. ed. (London and New York: Routledge, 1987); and John Bellamy, *Robin Hood: An Historical Enquiry* (London: Croom Helm, 1985). A sensationalist treatment of Robin Hood history is Graham Phillips and Martin Keatman, *Robin Hood: The Man Behind the Myth* (London: O'Mara, 1995). Two articles on real-life medieval criminal bands analogous to Robin Hood's are E.L.G. Stones, "The Folvilles of Ashby-Folville, Leicestershire, and their Associates in Crime, 1326–1347," *Transactions of the Royal Historical Society*, 5th ser. 7 (1957):117–136; and John Bellamy, "The Coterel Gang: An Anatomy of a Band of Fourteenth-Century Criminals," *English Historical Review* 79 (1964):698–717. Printed texts of the original Robin Hood ballads and garlands are available in R.B. Dobson and John Taylor, *Rymes of Robyn Hood: An Introduction to the English Outlaw*, rev. ed. (Stroud: Sutton, Gloucestershire, 1997). Dobson and Taylor's lengthy introduction considerably updates their original essay, "The Medieval Origins of the Robin Hood Legend: A Reassessment," *Northern History* 7 (1972):1–30.

There are plenty of other publications on the subject, but I include only the most useful. Robin Hood movies are discussed in the following film surveys: Tony Thomas, *The Great Adventure Films* (Secaucus, NJ: Citadel, 1976); James Robert Parish and Don E. Stanke, *The Swashbucklers*, ed. T. Allen Taylor (New Rochelle, NY: Arlington House, 1976); Jeffrey Richards, *Swordsmen of the Screen: From Douglas Fairbanks to Michael York* (London: Routledge, 1977); Rudy Behlmer, *America's Favorite Movies: Behind the Scenes* (New York: F. Ungar, 1982); Jerry Vermilye, *The Films of the Thirties* (Secaucus, NJ: Citadel Press, 1982). There are also a number of biographies of movie stars and directors that discuss their Robin Hood films: Ralph Hancock and Letitia Fairbanks, *Douglas Fairbanks: The Fourth Musketeer* (New York: Holt, 1953); Tony Thomas, Rudy Behlmer, and Clifford McCarty, *The Films of Errol Flynn* (New York: Citadel Press, 1969); Peter Valenti, *Errol Flynn: A Bio-Bibliography* (Westport, CT: Greenwood, 1984); Tony Thomas, *Errol Flynn: The Spy Who Never Was* (New York: Carol, 1990); Tony Thomas, *The Films of Olivia de Havilland* (Secaucus, NJ: Citadel Press, 1983); Sidney Rosenzweig, *Casablanca and Other Major Films of Michael Curtiz* (Ann Arbor, MI: UMI Research Press, 1982); R. Kinnard and R.J. Vitone, *The American Films of Michael Curtiz* (Metuchen, NJ: Scarecrow Press, 1986); James C. Robertson, *The Casablanca Man: The Cinema of Michael Curtiz* (London and New York: Routledge, 1993); Robert Sellers, *The Films of Sean Connery* (New York: St. Martin's Press, 1991); Andrew Yule, *Sean Connery: From 007 to Hollywood Icon* (New York: D. I. Fine, 1992); Alexander Walker, *Audrey: Her Real Story* (New York: St. Martin's Press, 1995); Barry Paris, *Audrey Hepburn* (New York: Putnam, 1996); Neil Sinyard, *The Films of Richard*

Lester (Totowa, NJ: Barnes and Noble, 1985); Todd Keith, *Kevin Costner: The Unauthorized Biography* (London: Ikonprint, 1991); Adrian Wright, *Kevin Costner: A Life on Film* (London: Robert Hale, 1992). Useful works on specific films include Garth Pearce, *Robin Hood: Prince of Thieves. The Official Movie Book* (New York: Mallard, 1991); Ina Rae Hark, "The Visual Politics of *The Adventures of Robin Hood*," *Journal of Popular Film* 5 (1993): 3–17; and Verna Huiskamp, "Historical Approach: The Political Implications of *The Adventures of Robin Hood*," in *An Introduction to Film Criticism: Major Critical Approaches to Narrative Film*, eds. Tim Bywater and Thomas Sobchack (New York: Longman, 1989). Printed screenplays of *The Adventures of Robin Hood* and *Robin and Marian* are available in: *The Adventures of Robin Hood*, ed. Rudy Behlmer (Madison, WI: The University of Wisconsin Press, 1979); and James Goldman, *Robin and Marian* (New York: Bantam, 1976).

Welcome to the Apocalypse: Black Death Films

The most recent textbooks available on the Black Death include: John Aberth, *From the Brink of the Apocalypse: Confronting Famine, War, Plague, and Death in the Later Middle Ages* (New York: Routledge, 2000); Norman F. Cantor, *In the Wake of the Plague: The Black Death and the World it Made* (New York: Free Press, 2001); Samuel K. Cohn, Jr., *The Black Death Transformed: Disease and Culture in Early Renaissance Europe* (London and Oxford: Arnold and Oxford University Press, 2002). But some older works are still worth consulting: Philip Ziegler, *The Black Death* (New York: Harper and Row, 1971); *The Black Death: A Turning Point in History?*, ed. William M. Bowsky (New York: Holt, Rinehart and Winston, 1971); Jean Noël Biraben, *Les Hommes et la Peste en France et dans les Pays Européens et Méditerranéens*. 2 vols. (Paris: Mouton, 1975–6); William H. McNeill, *Plagues and Peoples* (Garden City, NY: Anchor, 1976); Michael W. Dols, *The Black Death in the Middle East* (Princeton, NJ: Princeton University Press, 1977); *The Black Death: The Impact of the Fourteenth-Century Plague*, ed. Daniel William (Binghamton, NY: Center for Medieval and Early Renaissance Studies, 1982); Robert S. Gottfried, *The Black Death: Natural and Human Disaster in Medieval Europe* (New York: Free Press, 1983); and David Herlihy, *The Black Death and the Transformation of the West*, ed. Samuel K. Cohn, Jr. (Cambridge, MA: Harvard University Press, 1997). Good source books on the Black Death are: John Aberth, *The Black Death: The Great Mortality of 1348* (New York: Bedford/St. Martin's, forthcoming); and *The Black Death*, trans. and ed. Rosemary Horrox (Manchester: Manchester University Press, 1994). Two revered, but now demonstrated to be fundamentally flawed, analyses of European society during the time of the Black Death are: Johan Huizinga, *The Waning of the Middle Ages: A Study of the Forms of Life, Thought and Art in France and the Netherlands in the Dawn of the Renaissance*, trans. F. Hopman (London: E. Arnold, 1924); and James Westfall Thompson, "The Aftermath of the Black Death and the Aftermath of the Great War," *American Journal of Sociology* 26 (1920–1):565–572.

There are two major autobiographical works by Ingmar Bergman that have been translated into English: Ingmar Bergman, *The Magic Lantern: An Autobiography*, trans. Joan Tate (New York: Viking, 1988); and Ingmar Bergman, *Images: My Life in Film*, trans. Marianne Ruuth (New York: Arcade, 1994), which focuses on Bergman's career as a film director. In addition, there is a collection of other writings by Bergman in *Ingmar Bergman: An Artist's Journey. On Stage, on Screen, in Print*, ed. Roger W. Oliver (New York: Arcade, 1995). Also worth consulting are recorded interviews with Bergman: *Bergman on Bergman: Interviews with Ingmar Bergman*, eds. Stig Björkman, Torsten Manns, and Jonas Sima, and trans. Paul Britten Austin (New York: Simon and Schuster, 1973); and *Talking with Ingmar Bergman*, ed. G. William Jones (Dallas, TX: SMU Press, 1983).

There are, of course, many filmographies and biographies on Bergman, but among the most useful are: Jörn Donner, *The Personal Vision of Ingmar Bergman* (Bloomington, IN: Indiana University Press, 1964); Birgitta Steene, *Ingmar Bergman* (New York: Twayne, 1968); Arthur Gibson, *The Silence of God: Creative Response to the Films of Ingmar Bergman* (New York: Harper and Row, 1969); Robin Wood, *Ingmar Bergman* (New York: Praeger, 1969); Vernon Young, *Cinema Borealis: Ingmar Bergman and the Swedish Ethos* (New York: D. Lewis, 1971); Philip Mosley, *Ingmar Bergman: The Cinema as Mistress* (London and Boston: Marion Boyars, 1981); Peter Cowie, *Ingmar*

Bergman: A Critical Biography (New York: Scribner, 1982); Charles B. Ketcham, *The Influence of Existentialism on Ingmar Bergman: An Analysis of the Theological Ideas Shaping a Film-maker's Art* (Lewiston, NY: Edwin Mellen, 1986); Frank Gado, *The Passion of Ingmar Bergman* (Durham, NC: Duke University Press, 1986); Robert E. Lauder, *God, Death, Art and Love: The Philosophical Vision of Ingmar Bergman* (New York: Paulist Press, 1989); Hubert I. Cohen, *Ingmar Bergman: The Art of Confession* (New York: Twayne, 1993); Egil Törnqvist, *Between Stage and Screen: Ingmar Bergman Directs* (Amsterdam: Amsterdam University Press, 1995); and Marc Gervais, *Ingmar Bergman: Magician and Prophet* (Montreal: McGill-Queen's University Press, 1999). Works specifically devoted to *The Seventh Seal* include: *Focus on The Seventh Seal*, ed. Birgitta Steene (Englewood Cliffs, NJ: Prentice Hall, 1972); and Peter Cowie, "Milieu and Texture in *The Seventh Seal*," in *The Classic Cinema: Essays in Criticism*, ed. S.J. Solomon (New York: Harcourt, Brace, Jovanovich, 1973). I have used the official screenplay for all dialogue and stage direction quoted from *The Seventh Seal* in this chapter; it is available in Ingmar Bergman, *Four Screenplays*, trans. Lars Malmstrom and David Kushner (New York: Simon and Schuster, 1960). Bergman's one-act play, *Wood Painting*, which served as the genesis for *The Seventh Seal*, is printed in an English translation in *Theatre in the Twentieth Century: The Tulane Drama Review*, ed. Robert W. Corrigan (New York: Grove Press, 1963).

By contrast, there is not much in print about *The Navigator* and *Book of Days*, but two articles that I have found useful are: Michael Wilmington, "Firestorm and Dry Ice: The Cinema of Vincent Ward," *Film Comment* 20 (1993):51–54; and Joan Driscoll Lynch, "Book of Days: An Anthology of Monkwork," *Millennium Film Journal* 23–24 (1990–1):38–47.

Movies and the Maid: Joan of Arc Films

The best general textbook on Joan of Arc is Régine Pernoud and Marie-Veronique Clin, *Joan of Arc: Her Story*, trans. Jeremy duQuesnay Adams (New York: St. Martin's Press, 1999). Other works on Joan of Arc worth consulting include: Edward Lucie-Smith, *Joan of Arc* (London: Allen Lane, 1976); Frances Gies, *Joan of Arc: The Legend and the Reality* (New York: Harper & Row, 1981); and Karen Sullivan, *The Interrogation of Joan of Arc* (Minneapolis: University of Minnesota Press, 1999). The works by Marina Warner, *Joan of Arc: The Image of Female Heroism* (New York: Knopf, 1981); and Anne Llewellyn Barstow, *Joan of Arc: Heretic, Mystic, Shaman* (Lewiston, NY: Edward Mellen, 1986) are too skewed by feminist jargon and theory to be really useful. Mary Gordon's popular biography, *Joan of Arc* (New York: Lipper/Viking, 2000) says nothing new about the historical Joan, but it does include a good discussion of Joan's legacy in literature and on film. I have quoted from the following English translations of the transcripts of Joan's condemnation and rehabilitation trials: *The Trial of Joan of Arc: Being the Verbatim Report of the Proceedings from the Orleans Manuscript*, ed. W.S. Scott (London: Folio Society, 1956); Régine Pernoud, *Joan of Arc by Herself and Her Witnesses*, trans. Edward Hyams (New York: Stein and Day, 1966); Régine Pernoud, *The Retrial of Joan of Arc*, trans. J.M. Cohen (New York: Harcourt, Brace, 1955), and reprinted in *Joan of Arc: Fact, Legend, and Literature*, eds. Wilfred T. Jewkes and Jerome B. Landfield (New York: Harcourt, Brace and World, 1964).

An important collection of articles on all aspects of Joan of Arc studies is *Fresh Verdicts on Joan of Arc*, eds. Bonnie Wheeler and Charles T. Wood (New York: Garland, 1996), which includes Kevin Harty's survey of Joan of Arc films, "Jeanne au Cinéma". For additional surveys of the Joan of Arc film genre, see: Robin Blaetz, "Strategies of Containment: Joan of Arc in Film" (Ph.D. diss., New York: New York University, 1989); Gerda Lerner, "Joan of Arc: Three Films," in *Past Imperfect: History According to the Movies*, eds. Ted Mico, John Miller-Monzon, and David Rubel (New York: Henry Holt, 1995); Carina Yervasi, "The Faces of Joan: Cinematic Representations of Joan of Arc," *Film and History* 29 (1999):8–19; and Kathryn Norberg, "Joan on the Screen: Burned Again?" *AHA Perspectives*, 38/2 (February 2000):1, 8–9. An exhaustive bibliography on Joan of Arc is Nadia Margolis, *Joan of Arc in History, Literature, and Film* (New York: Garland, 1990).

The following filmographies and biographies of Carl Theodor Dreyer contain extensive discussions of *La Passion de Jeanne d'Arc*: Ebbe Neergaard, *Carl Dreyer: A Film Director's Work*, trans.

Marianne Helweg (London: British Film Industries, 1950); Kirk Bond, "The World of Carl Dreyer," *Film Quarterly* 19/1 (1965):26–38; Tom Milne, *The Cinema of Carl Dreyer* (New York: A. S. Barnes, 1971); Mark Nash, *Dreyer* (London: British Film Institute, 1977); and David Bordwell, *The Films of Carl Theodor Dreyer* (Berkeley: University of California Press, 1981). Other works specifically devoted to the *Passion* include: Ken Kelman, "Film as Poetry," *Film Culture* 29 (1963):22–7; David Bordwell, *Filmguide to La Passion de Jeanne d'Arc* (Bloomington, IN: Indiana University Press, 1973); Roger Manvell, "Psychological Intensity in *The Passion of Joan of Arc*," in *The Classic Cinema: Essays in Criticism*, ed. S.J. Solomon (New York: Harcout, Brace, Jovanovich, 1973); Tony Pipolo, "Metaphorical Structures in *La Passion de Jeanne d'Arc*," *Millennium Film Journal* 19 (1987–8): 52–84; and Charles O'Brien, "Rethinking National Cinema: Dreyer's *La Passion de Jeanne d'Arc* and the Academic Aesthetic," *Cinema Journal* 35 (1996):3–30. An English translation of the screenplay for the *Passion* is available in Carl Theodor Dreyer, *Four Screenplays* (Bloomington, IN: Indiana University Press, 1970). Dreyer's own writings on abstraction and the *Passion* are reprinted in: Carl Theodor Dreyer, "Thoughts on My Craft," in *Film: A Montage of Theories*, ed. Richard Dyer MacCann (New York: E. P. Dutton, 1966); and Carl Theodor Dreyer, *Dreyer in Double Reflection*, ed. Donald Skoller (New York: E. P. Dutton, 1973). Hélène Falconetti's memoirs of her mother are in *Falconetti* (Paris: Editions du Cerf, 1987).

Useful works relating to other Joan of Arc films include: Cecil B. DeMille, *The Autobiography of Cecil B. DeMille*, ed. Donald Hayne (New York: Garland, 1985); Kevin J. Harty, "The Nazis, Joan of Arc, and Medievalism Gone Awry: Gustav Ucicky's 1935 Film *Das Mädchen Johanna*," in *Rationality and the Liberal Spirit: A Festschrift Honoring Ira Lee Morgan* (Shreveport, LA: Centenary College, 1997); Ingrid Bergman and Alan Burgess, *Ingrid Bergman: My Story* (New York: Delacort Press, 1980); Laurence Leamer, *As Time Goes By: The Life of Ingrid Bergman* (New York: Harper and Row, 1986); Donald Spoto, *Notorious: The Life of Ingrid Bergman* (New York: HarperCollins, 1997); Gerald Pratley, *The Cinema of Otto Preminger* (London and New York: A. S. Barnes, 1971); Willi Frischauer, *Behind the Scenes of Otto Preminger: An Unauthorised Biography* (New York: Morrow, 1973); Otto Preminger, *Preminger: An Autobiography* (Garden City, N.Y.: Doubleday, 1977).

Afterword

Aside from my interview with Mr. Heston, insights about the making of *The War Lord* may also be obtained in the following works: Charlton Heston, *The Actor's Life: Journals, 1956–1976*, ed. H. Alpert (New York: E.P. Dutton, 1978); Charlton Heston, *In the Arena: An Autobiography* (New York: Simon and Schuster, 1995); and Erwin Kim, *Franklin J. Schaffner* (Metuchen, N.J.: Scarecrow Press, 1985). I also benefitted from a conversation with Jeremy duQuesnay Adams at Southern Methodist University, who organized the AHA forum at which Heston appeared in Chicago in 1991. For historical background on the setting of the *The War Lord*, see David Nicholas, *Medieval Flanders* (London and New York: Longman, 1992).

Braveheart has received a lot of attention from film scholars in recent years. Two articles that are especially useful are: Colin McArthur, "Braveheart and the Scottish Aesthetic Dementia," in *Screening the Past: Film and the Representation of History*, ed. Tony Barta (Westport, CT: Praeger, 1998); and Sid Ray, "Hunks, History and Homophobia: Masculinity Politics in Braveheart and Edward II," *Film and History*, 29 (1999):22–31. John Boswell's interpretation of medieval attitudes toward homosexuals in *Christianity, Social Tolerance, and Homosexuality: Gay People in Western Europe from the Beginning of the Christian Era to the Fourteenth Century* (Chicago: University of Chicago Press, 1980), is contested by Vern Bullough and James Brundage in their contributions to *Sexual Practices and the Medieval Church*, eds. Vern L. Bullough and James A. Brundage (Buffalo, N.Y.: Prometheus Books, 1982). The homosexual relationship between Edward II and Piers Gaveston is exhaustively analyzed and confirmed by J.S. Hamilton in *Piers Gaveston, Earl of Cornwall, 1307–1312: Politics and Patronage in the Reign of Edward II* (Detroit, MI.: Wayne State University Press, 1988). Pierre Chaplais' attempt to "heterosexualize" their relationship in *Piers Gaveston: Edward II's Adoptive Brother* (Oxford: Clarendon Press, 1994), has not found general support in the academic community.

INDEX